The Lord's Radio

The Lord's Radio

*Gospel Music Broadcasting
and the Making of
Evangelical Culture, 1920–1960*

MARK WARD SR.

McFarland & Company, Inc., Publishers
Jefferson, North Carolina

LIBRARY OF CONGRESS CATALOGUING-IN-PUBLICATION DATA

Names: Ward, Mark, 1958– author.
Title: The Lord's radio : gospel music broadcasting and the making of evangelical culture, 1920–1960 / Mark Ward Sr.
Description: Jefferson, North Carolina : McFarland & Company, 2017. | Includes bibliographical references and index.
Identifiers: LCCN 2017028613 | ISBN 9781476667348 (softcover : acid free paper) ∞
Subjects: LCSH: Gospel music—United States—20th century—History and criticism. | Gospel musicians—United States. | Radio in religion—United States—History—20th century. | Religious broadcasting—Christianity—History—20th century. | Evangelistic work—United States—History—20th century.
Classification: LCC ML3187 .W37 2017 | DDC 269/.260973—dc23
LC record available at https://lccn.loc.gov/2017028613

BRITISH LIBRARY CATALOGUING DATA ARE AVAILABLE

ISBN (print) 978-1-4766-6734-8
ISBN (ebook) 978-1-4766-2889-9

© 2017 Mark Ward Sr. All rights reserved

No part of this book may be reproduced or transmitted in any form or by any means, electronic or mechanical, including photocopying or recording, or by any information storage and retrieval system, without permission in writing from the publisher.

Front cover image of Washington, D.C., Sunday afternoon radio program, 1943, Esther Bubley, photographer (Library of Congress); on the air microphone © 2017 Graffizone/iStock

Printed in the United States of America

McFarland & Company, Inc., Publishers
  Box 611, Jefferson, North Carolina 28640
  www.mcfarlandpub.com

To Donna

Table of Contents

Acknowledgments	viii
Preface	1
Introduction	6
One—The Twenties: Prophets and Pioneers	15
Two—The Thirties: Preachers and Programs	57
Three—The Forties: Crusades and Conventions	103
Four—The Fifties: Words and Music	184
Five—Other Notable Songwriters	219
Epilogue	256
Chapter Notes	263
Bibliography	273
General Index	283
Song Index	292

Acknowledgments

LIKE A FINE WINE, A MANUSCRIPT can improve with age. Better to let it sit, let some time pass by, that the author might mature, deepen, be more fully steeped in the story he would tell. So it was with the present work, for which the bulk of initial research and drafting was done in 2003. Passion for telling the story carried me far. Yet more seasoning was required, more study on the historical context, more research on evangelical popular culture, more training in ethnographic and academic writing. Not to mention time out to earn a Ph.D., start a second career in academia, and build a research program on evangelical culture and media. But after a dozen years I felt ready to take the manuscript down from the shelf, dust it off, and finish the story.

More than that, I felt an urgency. Many scholars have written about the rise of fundamentalism between the Gilded Age and the Roaring Twenties, and many have written about the rise of the Christian Right in the seventies and eighties. But other than a few works—Joel Carpenter's *Revive Us Again*, George Marsden's *Reforming Fundamentalism*, and Molly Worthen's *Apostles of Reason*—little has been written about the crucial midcentury period of American evangelicalism, and none at all about its popular culture. Yet today's mass movement, now grown into a transdenominational community of faith with which 1 in 4 American adults identifies, is not comprehensible without its midcentury antedecents.

As Marsden has noted, scholars whose research agendas are influenced by their personal experiences of Christianity may discern connections that others miss. Thus, along with Marsden, church historians such as Mark Noll, Nathan Hatch, and Harry Stout have approached historical problems of American Christianity in fresh ways that have contributed new insights and been praised by colleagues. Similarly, the sociology and ethnography of American Christianity has been advanced by numerous mainstream scholars, such as Robert Wuthnow and Christian Smith, with active religious commitments. Just so, the present book makes new connections between media and religion that are informed by my own personal experiences.

Acknowledgments

As a college student I "trusted Christ" in the 1970s, in time to experience the rise of the Christian Right. The midcentury evangelical popular music described in this volume was still widely sung in churches. As a new convert who had studied music and could play and sing, the genre's infectious spirit greatly appealed to me. In the 1980s, I began a career in "parachurch" ministries that served the evangelical movement through publishing, broadcasting, and music. Along the way, I became familiar with a broad informal network of organizations whose history of interconnections dated to the midcentury period; in fact, I met or heard in person many figures described in this book, or their successors. My viewpoint, then, bridges two eras. A generation from now this perspective will disappear. And so my urgency to write.

The initial drafting of the book is a serendipitous story. In 2003, I lived and worked in South Carolina, where I later went on to earn a doctorate at Clemson University. At the time I directed an agency that, among other things, provided production and syndication services for the radio programs of Bob Jones University. Then, too, my prior experience with the genre included creative services for Word of Life Fellowship, a major producer of evangelical programming during radio's golden age, plus a commission from the National Religious Broadcasters association to write an official history that was published in book form as *Air of Salvation: The Story of Christian Broadcasting*. So I would occasionally spend an afternoon on the Bob Jones University campus trolling the library stacks for obscure volumes by evangelical figures from the past. Indeed, the story behind the present volume begins the day I stopped at the music library and noticed a table piled high with old songbooks and a "Please Take" sign. Pawing over the table, I found vintage songbooks, about to be thrown away, from Charles Fuller's *Old Fashioned Revival Hour*, Percy Crawford's *Young People's Church of the Air* and Pinebrook camps, plus other radio ministries and popular evangelical songwriters of the radio days. These were the very people I had written about in *Air of Salvation*. As it turned out, an elderly benefactor of the university, Martha Stone, had passed away and given the music library her old songbooks. The staff, however, had little interest in storing "outdated" music that today's students would likely never need. Yet, as their loss became my gain, the germ of an idea occurred to me: What about drawing on primary materials such as these to write a history of midcentury evangelical popular culture using its media and music as a focus?

As I began drafting a manuscript, things started falling into place. Two seminal books on the history of broadcasting that had been out of print were both republished in newly updated editions just before I began writing. Then, as I wrote the first section of the book on Paul Rader, that same month his longtime staff pianist, Merrill Dunlop, passed away—and seven volumes of oral history tapes, recorded with Dunlop more than twenty years earlier by the Billy Graham Center Archives of Wheaton, Illinois, were transcribed and made available in his honor via the Internet. Through this I learned of other interview transcripts very recently posted online, including oral histories recorded with men who had since passed on: Jack Wyrtzen, Torrey Johnson, and key associates of Paul Rader and Percy Crawford. Further, the Archives had just posted "online exhibits" about Rader and Crawford that included troves of ephemera. In a similar vein, I enjoyed unexpected access to oral history interviews about Al Smith, who spent his last years in Greenville, South Carolina, and often used the recording facilities of Bob Jones University. A student there, Robert Sims, assisted Smith in this work. For his senior thesis Sims produced a posthumous documentary of Smith's career featuring interviews with his wife Nancy Smith; his longtime Singspiration editor, John W. Peterson, who became a gospel songwriting legend (and passed away in 2006); and former Smith associates Harry Bollback, Brian Donley, and Frank Garlock. Generously, on hearing of my own project Sims allowed me the use of his materials for my book.

Then as I began the next section on Wendell Loveless, I learned that the Bob Jones library had just installed a new online search program that enabled me to locate several obscure volumes written by Loveless and several others in my study. Next, as I undertook the section on Homer Rodeheaver, I discovered a new biography had been published by Bob Jones University Press, written by retired faculty member Bert Wilhoit, who had once been Rodeheaver's staff pianist at his School of Sacred Music in Winona Lake. Similar happenstances mounted during the writing of the manuscript. Perry Straw, the final executor of Paul Rader's original Chicago Gospel Tabernacle, sent me primary material. So did Dean Crawford, son of Percy Crawford. Then a chance phone call led me to a rare, out-of-print biography of Percy Crawford sent to me by James Autry, then manager of the Crawford Broadcasting Corporation station in Portland, Oregon. And back in South Carolina, a visit to the old record closet of the Bob Jones campus radio station turned up a shelf of LP music albums from the *Old Fashioned Revival Hour, Haven of Rest* and *Back to the Bible*, all in their original jackets with complete liner notes. Finally, as my 2003 draft neared completion I was unexpectedly invited to Chicago by Paul Butler, then at the Moody Broadcasting Network (and now a freelance radio producer), to tape an interview on the life of Paul Rader for his Northern Illinois University master's thesis in documetary filmmaking. During the visit I also spent many fruitful hours in the Moody Bible Institute archives room to fill some holes in several sections of the manuscript. There I consulted files on the many men in my story, from Wendell Loveless to George Beverly Shea, who had once served at Moody. To all those mentioned above, explicitly or by implication, I am grateful.

The past dozen years have produced a second list of people to thank:

my professors at Spring Arbor University, where I earned a master's degree in communication, and at Clemson University, where I completed the Ph.D. in rhetorical and communication studies; my colleagues at the University of Houston–Victoria (UHV), including my dean, Jeffrey R. Di Leo, and chair, Andrew P. Baerg, who have encouraged my research in religious communication and media; Lou Ellen Callarman and Kristen Kelly, of the Victoria College/UHV Library, who obtained many obscure volumes for me through interlibrary loans so that I might recheck quotations and document my research according to academic standards; and my wider circle of colleagues in the Religious Communication Association who provide me a scholarly "home" to exchange ideas and resources. Most of all, I am grateful for my wife Donna. At a season of life when many people look to be settled, we have twice relocated, splitting our years since 2003 between finishing graduate school and building a new career. Through it all, she has entered into the adventure with a whole heart and, as so often needed, much valued wisdom.

Preface

In 1938 when Albert Brumley published his classic gospel song "Turn Your Radio On," he exhorted believers to dim the lights and "listen to the Master's radio." If they would but "listen to the music in the air" then they, too, could "get in touch with God." In other gospel songs of the day, the telephone was often a metaphor for prayer; in Brumley's lyrics, the radio was a metaphor for spiritual awakening and awareness, of tuning in to the wavelength of the divine. Today Brumley's tune is regarded as only a novelty song, relic of quaint and bygone era, a time that may have a few passing similarities to our own day but in the end somehow eludes us. After all, broadcasting and mass communication have been a fact of modern life for nearly a hundred years. Who today would even understand, much less be inspired by, "the Master's radio" as a symbol for spiritual rebirth and vitality?

Yet in the early days of radio—which began November 2, 1920, when Pittsburgh's KDKA launched the nation's first regular broadcast service with its coverage of the Harding-Cox presidential election—there was a palpable excitement about this miraculous new medium. Today we find this hard to grasp, for we are now the fourth and fifth generations of Americans to grow up in a mass media society. To us the marvel of television is an old story and even the Internet and social media have quickly been taken in stride. But in that now-distant America of the twenties and thirties, people witnessed a revolutionary transformation of their society right before their very eyes. In an instant, literally with the turn of a dial, the modern world of instant mass communication was born.

Evangelicals were also caught up in the excitement. William Ward Ayer, later the founding president of National Religious Broadcasters, never forgot the day in 1922 when he first listened to the radio. Knocking on doors as a young Baptist pastor in Valparaiso, Indiana, he was invited by a neighbor to come inside and hear the man's newly built crystal set. Joining the man in the back room of the house, Ayer donned a set of earphones and then adjusted the receiver. After some squeals and screeches, he was astounded to hear music coming all the way from Chicago, fifty miles away! It was a miracle! Yet Ayer was even more astounded when, in later years as pastor of New York City's Calvary Baptist Church, he would preach by radio to an estimated weekly audience of more than a quarter-million listeners.[1]

Today, more than 20 percent of all radio stations in the United States—some 3,400 outlets in total—air religious teaching, talk, or music formats.[2] Evangelical radio networks boast hundreds of stations, while many radio preachers and talk shows are syndicated nationwide on up to 2,000 outlets.[3] Deregulation of radio ownership rules sparked massive consolidation of the industry and birthed evangelical radio conglomerates that today dominate the genre.[4] Meanwhile, more than a dozen evangelical television networks are carried by mainstream satellite and cable services with a potential reach of 100 million households.[5] The top televangelists attract weekly audiences of up to 7 million viewers[6] and each year collectively raise more than $1 billion.[7] In fact, American evangelical popular culture now sustains a "Christotainment"[8] industry with annual revenues approaching $5 billion.[9] One in every seven books purchased in America is a religious book.[10] Christian and Gospel music artists sell more than 10 million albums each year and regularly put songs on the *Billboard* Top 100 singles chart.[11] Religious films are backed by major Hollywood studios.[12] Altogether, one in five U.S. adults consumes religious mass media on a daily basis. More people are exposed to these media each month than attend church.[13] In turn, this evangelical popular culture has a profound impact on American civic discourse. Numerous studies have noted how Americans increasingly get their news from partisan sources[14] and warned that American society is being split into "media enclaves."[15]

Seen in this light, an understanding of evangelical popular culture matters. Stories about the rise of this culture often begin with the Jesus Movement of the 1960s and emergence of the Contemporary Christian Music industry in the 1970s.[16] But the making of evangelical popular culture goes back further, to a time when "suddenly, evangelicals were—even across traditional denominational boundaries—referencing the same celebrities, listening to the same music, purchasing the same books, using the same catchphrases."[17] Though elements of a shared evangelical culture emerged in the late nineteenth century with the advent of mass-circulation printing, "believers consumed this text in their myriad private settings.... [M]issing was a means to socially integrate these masses into a broadly coherent culture—missing, that is, until radio."[18] For the medium provided, in the words of an early broadcaster, "a vast ethereal cathedral, the dimensions of which are unknown" but exist "anywhere where the receiving sets are in operation [so that] one may find a pew and thoroughly enjoy the services."[19] Soon, evangelicalism "was less a matter of denominations than a mass cultural movement ... [and] subculture serviced as much by books, radio ... and freelance evangelists as by [standard] churches."[20]

During the golden age of radio, evangelical listeners across the country formed what media theorists call an "interpretive community"[21] or a mass audience bound together by their shared interpretation of religious radio. In the early days when few could boast any experience in the new medium, preachers stuck with what worked for them in the past. This turned out to be a boon as radio preachers literally adapted the familiar format of the tent crusade—opening song, musical program, testimonies, punchy sermon, closing invitation hymn—to the airwaves. For their part, listeners were initiated into a shared evangelical popular culture as they engaged in familiar media rituals. Charles Fuller and his *Old Fashioned Revival Hour* (OFRH), for example, drew 20 million weekly listeners who ritually tuned in each Sunday night over the Mutual Radio Network for an opening theme song ("Give the winds a mighty voice! Jesus saves, Jesus saves!"), musical program (featuring professional OFRH musicians), testimony letters from listeners (read by Mrs. Fuller), a short folksy sermon, and closing hymn.

The one area of innovation in evangelical popular culture during radio's golden age was music. In part, this innovation was practical. Where Gilded Age evangelists such as Dwight L. Moody and Billy Sunday drew crowds to their citywide crusades because they were literally the only show in town, radio evangelists such as Fuller and his peers realized that inferior quality would drive away audiences who could now access the finest music even in the remotest reaches of the country.[22] Yet at the same time, those heady days of radio and the wonder at helping unprecedented millions "get in touch with God" also inspired new forms of religious music. For these reasons, the music popularized on radio from the twenties through the fifties provide a fruitful avenue to explore the rise of evangelical popular culture in this pivotal generation.

Of course, the genre of late-nineteenth-century revivalist hymns—by the likes of Fanny Crosby, Ira Sankey, Philip Bliss, and Daniel Towner—were carried by radio to more people than ever before. But a new generation of evangelical songwriters and musicians emerged with a sound all their own. Men like Wendell Loveless, Homer Rodeheaver, Phil Kerr, Charles Weigel, and Al Smith wrote and published collections of "radio songs." And the great radio preachers of the day—Charles Fuller, Percy Crawford, Paul Myer, Theodore Epp, and more—showcased this new music on network radio through such popular groups as the Old Fashioned Revival Hour Quartet, Haven of Rest Quartet, and Back to the Bible Quartet. Meanwhile, out in the rural heartland of the South and Midwest, local radio stations were airing "gospel" music programs that provided an early start for groups such as the Stamps Quartet, the Blackwood Brothers and The Statesmen, who set the standards of the genre.

This flowering of midcentury evangelical music began in the twenties with the dawn of radio and lasted through the fifties. By the sixties and seventies, the Jesus Movement and the genre of Contemporary Christian Music had taken hold. Meanwhile, the sheer wonderment of listening to "the music in the air" had become but a memory. Today, this heritage of "radio songs," whose sweet melodies and lush harmonies echoed the radio orchestras of the day, has largely become lost in the church. The classic revival hymns of Crosby and her contemporaries are rightfully prized and preserved by the church—and have the added virtue of being in the public domain, their copyrights having expired many years ago. On the other hand, churches that prefer contemporary worship styles have long since adopted the music to match. And so the evangelical music of midcentury, of the "radio days," has fallen between the cracks.

The difference between revivalist songs and radio songs is in "the sharps and flats." The classic hymns of the nineteenth-century revival era are intended for congregational singing and therefore feature "square" melodies and harmonies. For that reason, these hymns are beloved for their straightforward power and singability. By contrast, the music of the radio days—think of songs such as "Only One Life" by Merrill Dunlop (1937), "Now I Belong to Jesus" by Norman Clayton (1943), and "I Believe in Miracles" (1956) by John W. Peterson—featured beautiful chromatic or "sliding" melodies around which the genre's luscious, close harmonies were built. Such songs were intended not only for churches but to be heard—by people who were accustomed through mass media to music of high quality—on radio programs and at Bible conferences and large public rallies.

Such outreaches excited evangelicals who, after the Scopes "Monkey Trial" of 1925, were dismissed by mainstream society and excluded from mainline Protestant denominations that increasingly hewed to a more "modernist" or liberal theology. The advent of radio, however, offered a means to bypass denominational power structures, take the evangelical message directly to the masses, and regain a measure of legitimacy in the public eye. And as evangelicals severed their former denominational ties, they established webs of independent churches, associations, Bible colleges, seminaries, publishing houses, and mission boards. Because of this independent spirit, they readily adopted the new medium of radio and soon built an impressive programming infrastructure.

This infrastructure of evangelical network radio broadcasters and the fan culture they generated are key to understanding the rise of evangelical popular culture. Yet this important chapter in American religious life has seldom been told. This book chronicles the media and the music that evangelical listeners heard during the "radio days" and explores the decisive impact of radio on the evangelical spirit of the times. The present volume is therefore divided into four parts that correspond to the four decades of the period.

"The Twenties: Prophets and Pioneers" (Chapter One) tells the stories of those in the 1920s who first utilized the new medium of radio, spreading their message and music through the early radio stations of the day. "The Thirties: Preachers and Programs" (Chapter Two) follows those who, in the 1930s when the emphasis of evangelical broadcasting shifted to the network level, founded national radio ministries that popularized evangelical music as never before. "The Forties: Crusades and Conventions" (Chapter Three) highlights those who were leaders in the mass rallies and stadium crusades that, mobilized by radio, characterized evangelism and animated evangelical music during the decade. "The Fifties: Words and Music" (Chapter Four) presents some of the era's major songwriters who, by the 1950s when radio stations—due to the emergence of television—switched to the music formats known today, could make independent careers in the music industry. The concluding chapter, "Other Notable Songwriters" (Chapter Five), summarizes the stories of important evangelical songwriters who were active during the golden age of radio. Each chapter begins with a section that describes key developments in radio during the decade and their impacts on the presentation of the evangelical message and its music. Finally, an epilogue outlines how radio and evangelical broadcasting have fared in the decades after their golden age and up to the present day.

In telling the rise of evangelical popular culture during the first half of the twentieth century, it is appropriate to set that story within the context of radio. Radio was the spark that animated the evangelical movement of that era, providing an outlet to disseminate its cultural products—including its new musical forms—and popularize these products with the evangelical public. Even today, evangelical radio and evangelical music are inseparable.[23] But back then, when broadcasts were live and featured a variety format of preaching and music—far different than the prerecorded preaching and talk programs on religious radio today—the link between music and radio was even closer. To understand the making of evangelical popular culture, one must understand the medium and the music of gospel radio.

Introduction

THE 1920S THROUGH THE 1950S were pivotal decades for American evangelicalism. The "first wave" of the movement, which gathered force beginning in the 1870s, pitted orthodox "fundamentalists" against theologically liberal "modernists" over higher criticism of the Bible and control of the mainline Protestant denominations. The battle reached its heighth in the twenties when fundamentalists ultimately lost the denominational battles and incurred public scorn after the 1925 Scopes "Monkey Trial," one of the first news events broadcast nationwide via radio. In defending a Tennessee law that barred the teaching of evolution in public schools, fundamentalist hero William Jennings Bryan was himself baited into a disastrous attempt at defending the Bible against modern science. "It would be difficult," observes George Marsden, "to overestimate the impact of the 'the Monkey Trial' at Dayton, Tennessee, in transforming fundamentalism."[1] At a stroke, notes Alan Brinkey, "It transformed the popular image of the movement."[2] Though fundamentalist leaders were highly educated and the movement had primarily been active in the North and in urban areas, the public concluded that fundamentalism must be obscurantist, southern, and rural. "The fallout from the trial destroyed the cohesiveness and political strength of fundamentalism" as its public activism "quickly fell apart" and "the effort to purge the [mainline] denominations also failed completely."[3] Many predicted the final demise of fundamentalism in American life. What they did not realize, however, was the degree to which evangelical sensibilities were woven into the fabric of American life and the vibrant web of fundamentalist institutions able to sustain the movement.

From the Puritan colonization of the New World, Protestantism took a different course than in the Old World, emphasizing personal religious experience over institutional loyalties. America's First Great Awakening broke out in the 1730s and '40s, launching American churches on a fateful trajectory. "No one knows," writes Mark Noll, "where gradual change would have taken the American churches, for they were not destined to continue unimpeded" once the movement "revived experiential piety" with a focus on individual spirituality.[4] In frontier revivalism, observes Harry Stout, "For the first time in American society, a rhetoric appeared whose object was to persuade or communicate on a large, impersonal level, detached from any one church or community," a development that "created new concepts of authority and order by leaving existing institutional channels behind and creating alternative settings based solely on the consent of the audience."[5] American Christianity became, as Nathan Hatch puts it, democratized.[6] By the 1790s, when the success of the American Revolution was followed by the stunning events of the French Revolution, citizens of new United States of America were swept up by apocalyptic thoughts of a coming new age. A Second Great Awakening erupted in the 1790s and lasted through the 1840s. Because these years coincided with the founding decades of the new republic, there developed, as Noll has shown, a "compound of evangelical Protestant religion, republican political ideology, and commonsense moral reasoning" that "defined the boundaries for a vast quantity of American thought, while also providing an ethical framework, a moral compass, and a vocabulary of suasion for much of the nation's public life."[7]

By the nineteenth century, writes George Marsden, American evangelicals adapted the rationalism and empiricism of the European Enlightenment to suit their own needs.[8] First, they deemed the Bible a storehouse of facts; by "scientifically" arranging and classifying those facts, divine patterns could be observed and universal spiritual laws derived. As a complement to this view, evangelical theologians formulated the doctrine of "inerrancy" or the idea that, since God cannot err, the Bible has no errors. Second, they took from Scottish Common Sense Realism the conviction that all human beings are naturally endowed with sufficient reason to read the Bible, observe for themselves the "plain" meaning of the text, and discern its "self-evident" truths without interpretation by ecclesiastical authorities. Following the Civil War, these twin beliefs came under increasing attack. The old notion of science as simple observation and classification, which undergirded evangelicals' approach to biblical truth, was challenged by "modern" Darwinian science. And the rise of "higher criticism," or the application of critical academic scholarship to biblical texts, challenged the view that biblical truths were self-evident through a plain or "literal" reading of the scriptures. Popular evangelical reaction to these threats coalesced around Dwight L. Moody, a Chicago-based evangelist who in the 1870s and '80s pioneered modern organizational methods for mass evangelism through citywide crusades. He readily cooperated with the "penny press," a product of the late-nineteenth-century technological "revolution in cheap print"[9] and perhaps the first true form of mass communication. Moody realized that publicity would fill his pews, while editors discovered that puffing the evangelist's crusades into major stories would generate excitement and sell newspapers. As Bruce Evensen recounts, "Revival became a mass media campaign" where "religion would be played out in the nation's press as civic spectacle, commodifying belief and making Moody ... the star of the show." In this way, "the historical intersection of mass media and popular religion comes into view, and with it a glimpse of modern America."[10]

Moody was a pivotal figure for another reason, notes Ernest Sandeen.[11] As a lay evangelist more interested in winning souls than debating doctrine, Moody used his celebrity to mediate between different evangelical traditions and gain their cooperation in a common cause. In particular, he was friendly to advocates of "dispensational premillennialism." This apocalyptic theology, which holds that a secret "rapture" of believers into heaven will trigger seven years of "Great Tribulation" after which Christ will defeat Satan at the climactic battle of Armageddon and reign on earth for a thousand years, was developed by British lay teacher John Nelson Darby. Between 1862 and 1877, Darby traveled widely in the United States and Canada and his teaching eventually gained increasing numbers of adherents among American evangelicals. In turn, these dispensationalists not only infused the evangelical movement with their fervor to win souls before the apocalypse; they also organized informal networks of Bible conferences and journals that brought evangelicals together across traditional denominational lines. Such interconnections were further strengthened, as Virginia Brereton has documented, by a wave of independent Bible Institutes founded in the late nineteenth and early twentieth centuries to train lay workers and missionaries.[12] Interdenominational ties spread at the popular level through the 1909 publication and wide use of the dispensationalist *Scofield Reference Bible*. Meanwhile, at the professional level, an array of evangelical theologians contributed articles on doctrinal orthodoxy to a 12-volume anthology entitled *The Fundamentals*. Published between 1910 and 1915, three million copies were distributed free of charge to clergy worldwide. Perhaps just as important, the movement became popularly known in the twenties as "fundamentalism" and adherents proudly adopted a shared transdenominational identity as "fundamentalists."

This, then, is the milieu in which the story of gospel music broadcasting begins. In Chapter One, the personalities whose stories are told—Paul Rader, Wendell Loveless, James Vaughn, Homer Rodeheaver—are buoyed by the highwater mark of "first wave" fundamentalism during the twenties. They are expansive and optimistic in their fervor to defeat "modernist" foes and convert the lost. By contrast, the personalities—Charles Fuller, Percy Crawford, Paul Myers, Theodore Epp, Virgil Stamps—in Chapter Two inhabit the wilderness into which fundamentalism was cast after its ecclesiastical and public disgrace the previous decade. They are concerned with arresting the nation's cultural and moral decline by bringing America "Back to the Bible"

(Epp), launching an "Old Fashioned Revival" (Fuller), and winning the next generation through the "Young People's Church of the Air" (Crawford). Bereft of institutional support from traditional denominations, they exercised entrepreneurial skill to appropriate the tools of mass communication and create alternative institutions and fan cultures. They put their hopes in what Quentin Schultze called the "mythos of the electronic church," a technological utopianism in which the mere broadcasting of the gospel could, like a "magic bullet," convert the world in a single generation.[13]

In Chapter Three, the personalities covered—Jack Wyrtzen, Torrey Johnson, Billy Graham, Al Smith, the Blackwood Brothers, The Statesmen—lived in a different world. They came of age after the fundamentalist-modernist controversies of the twenties and instead grew up with radio and mass culture. They were ready to launch a "second wave" of fundamentalism but struggled with the form it should take. Because mass communication gave them the ability to engage mainstream mass culture, this new generation of evangelicals became disenchanted with the militant separatism that their fundamentalist fathers preached in the twenties. By the late 1940s, they began to coalesce around a new identity as "evangelicals" committed to engaging with, rather than withdrawing from, American society. And so the outlines of American evangelicalism, as it is known today, came into view. The songwriters whose stories are told in Chapter Five—John W. Peterson, Stuart Hamblen, Ira Stanphill, Mosie Lister, Bill and Gloria Gaither—sought to carve out a place for their music in popular mass culture.

The ensuing decades of the sixties to the present do not figure in this book. Yet the "third wave" of American fundamentalism that arose in the late twentieth century—and that continues today—can only be understood in terms of what went before. The willingness of "second wave" midcentury evangelicals to forsake cultural separatism and pursue cultural engagement laid the foundation for "third wave" evangelicals to overcome their traditional antipathy to political activism and organize the Christian Right in the 1970s and '80s. "The evangelical strategy of involvement with the larger culture in the third quarter of the twentieth century," notes Randall Balmer, "prepared evangelicals for fuller [political] engagement beginning in the mid-seventies."[14] Meanwhile, the decision of midcentury evangelical broadcasters and songwriters to participate in popular mass culture prefigured the rise of the Contemporary Christian Music industry and, more generally, the commodification and consumerism of evangelical popular culture today. The full arc of these stories, however, spans nearly a century.

Not far beneath the surface of these stories, however, is the white male character of midcentury evangelical mass culture. The structural racism of this culture bubbles to the surface, for example, in evangelist Gerald B. Winrod's introduction to a popular 1936 gospel songbook: "Heathenism has only a few dull notes, such as the thud of the tom-tom. Unbelievers favor jazz, which is composed of a series of conflicting sounds and discordant notes. Christianity alone reaches to the depths of the human soul. Only believers really have anything to sing about."[15] Gendering was also integral to the movement. Women are seen in the following pages only as supportive wives and occasionally as song lyricists and arrangers. Betty DeBerg and Margaret Bendroth have shown how preservation of traditional gender norms was a central concern of fundamentalists from the start.[16] And as the twentieth century progressed, even the "radio program titles of the 1930s through the 1960s ... openly encouraged binary modes of thought (us/them, saved/lost, truth/error, biblical/unbiblical, light/darkness) that privileged 'masculine' values of militancy, expansion, and conquest."[17] Then, too, the embrace of radio as a technological solution to the problem of mass evangelism fostered what Steven Katz called an "ethic of expediency" that privileges masculine values of speed, power, and efficiency.[18] These aspects of American evangelicalism continue to the present day. Sunday mornings remain the most segregated time in America as white evangelical Protestants and black Christians remain separate communities.[19] At the same time, numerous ethnographic studies confirm that gendering is central to the lived experience of contemporary evangelicals.[20]

Though this book presents a history of evangelical popular culture during the "radio days" of the twenties through the fifties, it is written in the form of a *historical ethnography*. The word "ethnography" literally means to "write the culture." Thus, the work of the ethnographer is to observe a culture and describe it as nearly as possible on its own terms and in members' own words. The challenge of historical ethnography is to comprehend and describe a past culture that can no longer be observed in real time by analyzing artifacts it has left behind. Fortunately, the "radio generation" of American evangelicals left a wealth of primary material on which I have drawn. Most major figures presented in these pages published autobiographies or were subjects of biographies written by family members or close associates with access to interviews and organizational records. And during the 1970s through the 1990s, the Billy Graham Center Archives recorded oral history interviews with many golden-age radio evangelists and key associates. These have since been transcribed, along with many other documents and ephemera, and made available to researchers via the Internet. Recordings of vintage radio programs are also accessible online, not only from various archives but from the organizations themselves. An astonishing number of golden-age evangelical radio broadcasts remain in wide syndication and most have published their own official histories.

The musical culture of the "radio days" in American evangelicalism also yields rich troves of artifacts. The popular evangelical songs of the era, both words and music, uniquely convey the spirit of the times. And to my knowledge, this book is the first to tap three resources never before used in other works on the period. First, the best-known evangelical radio programs and songwriters published songbooks, often titled "Radio Songs" and including information about the broadcasts and personalities printed in the flyleaves. The same is true of printed sheet music from the period. Second, liner notes on LP record albums issued by the era's popular radio quartets frequently contain detailed information about the musicians and the radio programs on which they were featured. Thus, research for this book draws on my own extensive personal collection of songbooks from the Young People's Church of the Air and its Pinebrook camps, the Old Fashioned Revival Hour, Youth for Christ, the Singspiration *Favorites* series, and "radio song" collections from individual composers such as Wendell Loveless, Homer Rodeheaver, and Charles Weigle. Moreover, my collection includes LP recordings issued in the fifties and sixties by the Old Fashioned Revival Hour Quartet, Haven of Rest of Quartet, and Back to the Bible musical team. Supplementing these artifacts is a third source perhaps unique to the evangelical popular culture of the era. Books of "song stories," the often-dramatic tales behind the composing of the day's favorite songs, were immensely popular. Many such anthologies were published and their authors frequently interviewed songwriters firsthand to gather information.

Finally, this volume draws on a wealth of secondary sources. Church historians over the past generation have given increasing attention to the growth of the fundamentalist movement during the late nineteenth and early twentieth centuries and its "reawakening"[21] in the decades of the thirties through the fifties. Especially since the emergence of the Christian Right as a potent political force in the 1980s, historians and sociologists of American religion have shown a growing interest in the history of evangelicalism in order explain its persistence in American life. This books makes an original contribution to that effort by presenting an historical ethnography of midcentury evangelical popular culture through the lens of its radio and music.

To carry out the ethnographic emphasis of this book, and to convey the spirit of the times by describing midcentury evangelical popular culture on its own terms and in its own words, I have chosen not to employ dry "historical writing" but to give the text a strongly narrative quality. In other words, what follows is a series of stories that, as the text goes along, add up to a larger story which gives readers an overall sense of what midcentury evangelical popular culture was about. Toward that end, the book takes a decade-by-decade approach. In each chapter I narrate the stories of key figures who not only reflected and shaped each decade, but whose individual stories also advance the larger story of evangelical popular culture. Such narrative writing, however, presents a challenge. In every section, about every personality, maintaining narrative flow meant piecing together each individual story from numerous sources that were frequently unclear about dates and sequences of events, were sometimes conflicting in details, and were often written for inspirational, devotional, or public relations purposes rather than historical accuracy. Many times I was compelled to consult a half dozen or more sources, even for a single event, and ultimately had to be satisfied with checking and cross-checking dates and details to the best of my ability. Nevertheless, true guesswork was the exception rather than the rule. The result is a book that, I am confident, is as nearly true to the ascertainable facts as is reasonably possible for a volume of this type, and that presents a picture which is faithful to the sense and the spirit of midcentury evangelical popular culture and of the generation that turned the lights down low and listened to the Master's radio.

Garth Rosell, whose father Mervin was a prominent midcentury itinerant evangelist, observes that "Most of the events and [evangelical] personalities of the Forties and Fifties are now forgotten."[22] Why, then, should they matter today? Postwar evangelicals, buoyed by an optimism that Christ could transform American culture, publicly disavowed fundamentalist separatism and announced their determination to engage the mainstream as "salt and light" against the decay and darkness they perceived around them. Yet within a short time, a more serious problem proved to be "the almost invisible dangers lurking within the evangelical movement itself." As Rosell explains,

> [E]vangelical leaders were genuinely committed to the task of reclaiming the culture for Christ, [but] their tendency to build a wide range of parachurch organizations that they could immediately control rather than infiltrating and seeking to transform the older and sometimes moribund institutions that were outside of their control seemed to lead future generations of evangelicals in quite a different direction from that which the first [postwar] generation of leaders intended to travel.[23]

Despite the energies and resources at their command, midcentury evangelicals refrained from "reentering and reenergizing the mainline denominations, the ecumenical organizations, the universities," and other social institutions. Instead, they "seemed content to operate mainly and sometimes exclusively within their own subculture ... [of] new organizations [that] seemed to be remarkably successful."[24] Randall Balmer takes up the same theme in describing four great turning points in the history of American evangelicalism. Two turning points, in the eighteenth and nineteenth centuries respectively, were theological; the other two, both in the twentieth century, were tactical. In the third turning point, "The construction of the evangelical culture after the Scopes trial of 1925 and through the middle decades of the twentieth century provided evangelicals with their own ... insular world, a refuge from the depradations of the larger culture ... at the price of almost total segregation from the outside world." Yet paradoxically, this laid the groundwork for a fourth turning point as "the maturation of those institutions associated with the evangelical subculture by the Seventies provided the platform for evangelical reengagement with the broader society ... [through] right-wing political conservatism."[25]

The present work is a story of the subculture that midcentury evangelicals created and that became the foundation for the evangelical "parallel universe"[26] of today. American society would now be much different if midcentury evangelicals had followed their announced intention to put separatist tendencies behind them and joined mainstream institutions. What "might have been" can never be known. Yet by telling the story of that generation's emergent mass culture in a way that evokes the spirit of their times, this book gives a glimpse into why the siren song of a comfortable cultural separatism ultimately proved so irresistible. Though what "began with such promise in the Thirties, Forties, and Fifties was all too quickly overrun," suggests Rosell, "there is still much to learn."[27] Indeed, the proliferation of media in our day is breaking up audiences into smaller and smaller fragments that have less and less interaction.[28] In such a media universe, secular and religious narratives are becoming mutually unintelligible. Public discourse often amounts to little more than talking past one another, a worrisome prospect since "the conflict between these spheres is very real" and "the issues raised by the tension between faith and reason ... impacts us all."[29] If the best intentions of past generations who had far less media at their disposal were unrealized, we who have far more media to contend with at least have their example.

ONE

The Twenties
Prophets and Pioneers

IT WAS UNDERSTANDABLE. The senior minister, tired after the busy Christmas season, had taken the night off. So Lewis B. Whittemore found himself in charge of the weekly vespers service that first Sunday evening after New Year 1921.[1] His call to Pittsburgh's landmark Calvary Episcopal Church was an honor and his seminary training served him well. The senior minister had confidence that he would keep the service as normal as possible. What made Whittemore nervous, however, were the two radio engineers who were setting up some strange-looking equipment in the church chapel. Even now they were placing a large, ungainly microphone on top of the pulpit from which he would be presiding. This was certainly not a situation his seminary professors had ever covered.

Yet the senior minister had told Whittemore not to worry. Radio was probably just a passing fad. The management of KDKA only wanted to score a marketing coup by being the first station in America to broadcast a religious service by radio. And since KDKA was owned by Westinghouse, they figured the hype might sell more of the company's store-bought radio sets at a time when most receivers were homemade. Just two months earlier the station had created a national sensation when it signed on the air, though fewer than a thousand radio sets were in operation to hear it. Yet on November 2, 1920, KDKA launched the nation's first regularly scheduled commercial broadcast service—becoming America's first true radio station—by airing live returns of the presidential election. And though Warren Harding won in a landslide, the newspapers said radio was the real revolution.

Yet as Whittemore saw the mass of tubes and wires being set up in the chapel, he had his doubts. The radio hookup would never work. How could it? The station was a full ten miles from the church! Nevertheless, since one of the men in the church choir was a Westinghouse engineer, the senior minister felt he had to allow the attempt. Of course, he didn't have to be there—and that's where Whittemore came in.

The two KDKA engineers, one Catholic and the other Jewish, signaled that they were ready to begin. If only their apparatus didn't make too much noise, perhaps everything would be all right. But just to make sure, Whittemore ordered the two engineers to put on choir robes—and then hoped for the best. After all, the service was supposed to be as normal as possible. Once the service started and Whittemore could focus on the job at hand, the big microphone on the pulpit, and even the two engineers dressed in choir robes, weren't such a distraction. Even the radio equipment was quiet enough. The congregation took it all in stride and afterward KDKA said the hookup worked just fine. In fact, response was so favorable the station wanted to make the Calvary vespers service a regular Sunday night program. Of course, for that first broadcast—January 2, 1921—Whittemore was only filling in. Naturally, the senior minister would be resuming the pulpit in the future. After all, even if KDKA could be heard across the counry, the Sunday services should still be as normal as possible.

The Prehistory of Radio

For that first religious broadcast, radio was so new that even the engineers wore choir robes. Yet like most technologies, radio had a long "prehistory" before the right combination of circumstances allowed it to burst upon the national consciousness at the dawn of the twentieth century.[2] The idea of sending messages by electricity was, in fact, suggested as early as the thirteenth century by the English philosopher Roger Bacon. But the best place to begin the story of radio is with the invention of the electric telegraph in 1835 by Samuel F.B. Morse.[3] Securing a patent for his telegraph in 1840, Morse obtained an appropriation of thirty thousand dollars from the U.S. Congress in 1843 to build a demonstration line between Washington and Baltimore. For his first official telegraph message sent May 24, 1844, Morse chose a quotation from Numbers 23:23, "What hath God wrought!" The full passage is a blessing from God, confirming that his people would cross over into the land he had promised them.

> God is not a man, that he should lie; neither the son of man, that he should repent: hath he said, and shall he not do it? or hath he spoken, and shall he not make it good? Behold, I have received commandment to bless: and he hath blessed; and I cannot reverse it.... God brought them out of Egypt.... [A]ccording to this time it shall be said of Jacob and of Israel, What hath God wrought!

Perhaps as important as Morse's successful demonstration of telegraphy was Congress' decision three years later to sell the line back to its inventor. That precedent, of renouncing government ownership of telecommunications, remains the standard today. European countries in the 1850s opted for government control. Now a century and half later, the American practice of privately-owned, single-faith radio and television stations still remains almost unique in a world where most national governments directly own and operate the means of broadcast communication.

Though the telegraph provided instant communication on land, it stopped at the water's edge—until American businessman Cyrus Field organized the laying of the first successful transatlantic cable in 1866.[4] Even so, messages could still only be sent from one fixed point to another. What about transmitting messages to a moving point, such as a ship at sea? Telegraph wires were also prone to breakage and difficult to string over great distances and rugged terrains. For those reasons, nineteenth century inventors raced to devise a practical system for "wireless" telegraphy. The laws of physics allow three possible methods: conduction, induction, and radiation. Those who tried *conduction* would need to transmit impulses through a medium capable of conducting electricity, such as salt water or earth. By contrast, *induction* would involve a system of inducing electrical current to "jump" across the gap from one nearby circuit to another. In the end, however, neither method proved workable over anything but very short distances. Numerous inventors also explored the use of *radiation* as a method for wireless telegraphy. The existence of radio waves was first predicted in 1864 by Scottish physicist James Clerk Maxwell. During the 1880s and '90s several inventors contributed advancements toward a system by which electromagnetic signals, radiating outward into space from a transmission point, could be detected by a distant receiver.

One of these men, the German scientist Heinrich Hertz, was later recognized for his pioneering work when the basic unit of measurement for radio frequencies was named in his honor. But the man who put it all together—ironically, not to understand *how* radio worked but rather to profit by *making* it work—was the Italian entrepreneur Guglielmo Marconi.[5] By pulling together and refining the different developments of earlier inventors, he constructed the first successful wireless radiotelegraph in 1895. Four years later Marconi sent a radio signal across the English Channel. And in a famous 1901 experiment he transmitted the letter in "S" in Morse code, two thousand miles across the Atlantic from Cornwall, England, to Cape Cod. Just as important, Marconi's Wireless Telegraph Company raised significant capital and attracted the brightest managers and technicians to the new business. Marconi himself was awarded the Nobel Prize for physics in 1909 and, a year later, his corporation posted its first profits. It seemed that the future of radio, as a means of wireless telegraph messaging, was assured.

At the turn of the century, the notion of *broadcasting*—or sending regularly scheduled programming to a mass audience—was completely unknown or undreamed of. Radio was only an improved kind of telegraph, a better way of sending messages from one point to another. The first important wireless experimenter in the United States was actually a Canadian, Reginald Fessenden, who worked for the U.S. Weather Bureau in Pittsburgh. He noted that the use of electrical impulses to transmit voice communications had been patented in 1876 by Alexander Graham Bell. (Evangelist Dwight L. Moody and songleader Ira Sankey may be due credit for the first religious "transmission" when in 1876 they transmitted an evangelistic program via telephone.[6]) Bell's American Telephone and Telegraph Company had been successfully offering wired telephone service to the public since 1878. Fessenden believed that Marconi's wireless technology could be improved to carry voice transmissions. If that were true, Fessenden's brainchild would be a huge advance in telegraphy. Compared to human speech, the telegraph was slow and could not convey emotion or word emphasis. Wireless voice communication would eliminate the need for trained Morse code operators and permit two-way communication. In 1901 Fessenden demonstrated that wireless voice communication was possible and a year later formed the National Electric Signaling Company to seek investors, finance his research, and pay for a new kind of transmitter that took three years to design and build.

By 1906 Fessenden was ready. A summer cottage in Brant Rock, Massachusetts, was converted into an experimental wireless station. To drum up publicity he sent Morse code telegraph messages to ships along the East Coast that on Christmas Eve he would transmit something they had never heard before—voices and music sent by wireless. On that night in 1906, telegraph operators on ships hundreds of miles out to sea donned their earphones and heard a person speaking, a woman singing, the reciting of a poem, and then Fessenden himself playing the violin, reading verses from the Bible, and wishing his listeners a Merry Christmas. Fessenden also arranged for New York City reporters to hear the transmission so that the next day's papers carried stories of astonished shipboard radio operators claiming to hear angel voices from heaven. Fessenden's transmission on Christmas Eve 1906 is recognized today as the first true broadcast—though he was only attempting to interest the maritime world in adopting his new form of wireless radiotelegraph. In that he was less successful, as a financial panic in 1907 wiped out his company and led to lawsuits that ultimately cost Fessenden control over his patents.

Ironically, the same fate also awaited the man who has become known as the "father of radio." Lee de Forest earned a Ph.D. from Yale with an 1899 dissertation on wireless telegraphy. Like Fessenden, he sought to develop a wireless voice communication system that could beat Marconi. So in 1906, improving on a Marconi patent, he invented the triode vacuum tube, or "Audion," which amplified wireless signals so they could be heard over long distances—thus making modern radio possible. He set up the De Forest

Wireless Telephone Company and, to gain attention, offered occasional classical music broadcasts in 1907, transmitted a phonograph record concert from the Eiffel Tower in 1908, and in 1910 (for an audience of less than fifty people) broadcast two Enrico Caruso operas from the Metropolitan Opera House in New York. But in a bitter dispute, De Forest's company was dissolved by its backers. When the inventor established a second corporation, lawsuits and charges of stock fraud led to bankruptcy in 1911. Nevertheless, his Audion tube became the basis for development (in 1918 by Edwin Armstrong, later the inventor of FM radio) of the superheterodyne receiver that allowed radio sets to be tuned to a desired frequency without drifting. Refinements to De Forest's Audion tube also made possible the first transcontinental telephone line in 1915.

Three years before the *Titanic*, in 1909, the sinking of the *Republic* made worldwide headlines. Even more remarkable, however, was the fact that after the liner collided with another vessel, everyone aboard was rescued because the telegraph operator stayed at his post and radioed a call for help. Congress took note and passed the nation's first radio law, the Wireless Ship Act of 1910, requiring most oceangoing ships to install and use a radio. When the 1912 *Titanic* disaster occurred, however, it was discovered that loopholes in the radio law contributed to the loss of life. The Radio Act of 1912 plugged the loopholes and, for the first time, required that all operators and stations obtain licenses from the government.

The decade of the 1910s witnessed an ongoing series of "patent wars" as powerful corporations vied to control and monopolize wireless communications. When America entered the First World War in 1917, the War Department was forced to authorize "patent pools" and indemnify companies against infringement lawsuits, just to get the radio equipment it needed. Even before the war—especially since the foreign-owned Marconi Corporation controlled ninety percent of ship-to-shore commercial communications in America— some were calling for a government takeover of the emerging radio business. For reasons of national security, the Navy Department seized all privately owned radio stations for the duration of the war. After the conflict ended in November 1918, legislation was introduced in Congress to make government ownership of radio permanent. But that year's Republican sweep of the congressional elections put an end to the effort and in 1919 President Wilson ordered the Navy to return all stations to their owners by the following year.

Slowly, the idea of using radio for "broadcasting" began to develop. By 1912 more than a thousand amateur radio hobbyists had receivers and, by 1915, their own magazine and national membership association. That same year Doc Herold, a local engineering professor, made daily broadcasts from the San Francisco Exposition to receivers he set up in hotel lobbies. Several colleges and universities around the nation were constructing experimental stations, offering occasional broadcasts of weather reports. And a young manager at the American Marconi company, David Sarnoff—who would later become one of the most powerful men in broadcasting—wrote a 1916 memo to his general manager suggesting that radio could be marketed as a kind of "music box." When the world war was over in 1918, thousands of young men came home from the Army who had been trained as radio operators and engineers.

It was only a matter of time until someone would begin operating a radio broadcast station according to a regular schedule of programming intended for public reception. That someone was Frank Conrad, assistant chief engineer at Westinghouse who as early as 1916 obtained a license for an amateur experimental station. Broadcasting from the garage of his East Pittsburgh home, Conrad delighted fellow ham operators when on October 17, 1919, he put a phonograph up to his microphone. When requests poured in for more music, he began airing two hours of songs each Wednesday and Sunday rather than deal with individual song requests. In the summer of 1920 a local department store placed ads in the *Pittsburgh Press* for ten-dollar amateur wireless sets and cited Conrad's broadcasts as an inducement. A Westinghouse vice president saw the ad and suggested the company sponsor its own radio station to create a market for its factory-built receivers. An application was filed with the Department of Commerce, then responsible for radio licensing, and a license for KDKA granted on October 27. The first broadcast, on election night, November 2, originated from a small, hastily built shack on the roof of the Westinghouse manufacturing plant in East Pittsburgh. Signing on the air at six and continuing until noon the following day, the KDKA announcers were fed election returns via telephone courtesy of the *Pittsburgh Post*.

Radio in the Twenties

From that beginning, radio grew at an explosive rate. It was simply in the right place at the right time.[7] More than two hundred stations were licensed by the end of 1921, and about one in every five hundred American homes had a receiver. The next year, the first broadcasts of a heavyweight championship fight (the winner was Jack Dempsey) and of a World Series (between the New York Yankees and New York Giants) were each heard by more than half a million listeners and prompted thousands of consumers to buy radio sets. By the end of 1924, two and half million sets were in use; a year later, one in every six homes had a radio. Then in 1926 sales boomed again when models were introduced that could run on household current rather than bulky (and leaky) batteries, and that looked like furniture rather than lab equipment.

Early stations were often owned by radio set manufacturers, such as Westinghouse, and by newspapers hedging their bets against a potential competitor in the news business. In the ensuing years, however, it became apparent that radio could not be run successfully as a sideline business. Various schemes were tried to find a financial basis for broadcasting. One idea was a subscription service, similar to cable and satellite TV today. Another was a pay-per-program arrangement by which listeners purchased "season tickets" to broadcasts of concerts and other events. Voluntary contributions from listeners were solicited, but without success. One entrepreneur sold radio sets capable of receiving faxes and sent customers a small daily "newspaper" each morning. In Britain, broadcasting was (and is) financed by a sales tax on receiver purchases. The ultimate answer, which seems obvious today but was not so clear in the twenties, was advertising. The first radio commercial was aired August 28, 1922, when a New York real estate firm offered to pay for a program on WEAF if the station would broadcast an announcement about condominiums the company had for sale. After paying WEAF one hundred dollars for five days of announcements, the firm reaped sales of several thousand dollars—and commercial radio was born.

Broadcasters also experimented with radio networking or "chain broadcasting." The 1922 World Series broadcast was one early attempt that linked two stations in New York and Schenectady. A 1923 hookup between New York, Washington, and St. Louis carried a speech by President Warren Harding to an unprecedented audience of more than a million people. When Harding died of illness a year later, a network of seven stations was quickly assembled so that America could hear its new president, Calvin Coolidge, address Congress. Also that year, chain broadcasts were aired from the 1924 Democratic and Republican conventions. After Coolidge was reelected, two dozen radio stations carried his 1925 inaugural address by transcontinental hookup to more than thirty million listeners. By 1926, however, further growth in radio was limited by two factors. First, the powerful American Telephone and Telegraph Company had a monopoly on the long-distance telephone lines needed for radio networking. And it claimed that stations must pay fees to "hire" these lines, as well as a "toll" when they were used to carry paid advertising. The stalemate was broken when an arbitrator found in favor of the broadcasters and a settlement with AT&T was reached in 1926. Soon afterward, the National Broadcasting Corporation established the country's first regular radio network with a coast-to-coast debut broadcast, over 19 stations, of the 1927 Rose Bowl. A few months later the rival Columbia Broadcasting System was organized with an initial chain of sixteen stations.

The second and most pressing problem was the simple fact that radio was choking on its own growth. In the absence of regulation, stations could—and did—change their frequencies, signal strengths and direction, and hours of operation at will. The many Americans who had invested in still-expensive radio sets often could not receive a clear signal. The outcry was heard in Washington and in 1927 Congress responded by creating the Federal Radio Commission to bring order out of the chaos. The FRC was authorized to issue licenses, allocate frequencies, and limit power. Almost immediately, the new agency took action. The airwaves were public property and government must ensure they would be used for the public interest, which "is of superior importance to that of the broadcaster." Thus the Commission believed "it is better that there should be a few less broadcasters than that the listening public should suffer from undue interference."

Early Religious Broadcasters

The FRC was true to its word. Within months, one out of every five radio stations in America—about 150 of the 732 outlets on the air in 1927—relinquished their licenses. Stations were now required to use professional equipment and hire licensed professional operators, so that the cost and complexity of broadcasting were beyond the reach of amateurs. Among the more than sixty stations owned by religious organizations, by 1933 about half went off the air. Purchasing professional equipment and hiring licensed operators simply wasn't worth it for churches that operated their transmitters for only a few hours each Sunday.[8]

Yet in the small town of Boone, Iowa, one church pastor decided to make a go of radio.[9] The venture started in 1926 when the folks at Crary Hardware Store, who liked to tinker with every new gadget, had built themselves a ten-watt transmitter and even gone to the trouble of getting a license. Now that new government regulations were coming, they wanted to sell their "station" for one hundred fifty-five dollars. Nobody in Boone was interested. Even the town paper turned it down, figuring a radio station might cut into subscriptions. Then someone at Crary's suggested, "There's a man in west Boone who likes to preach. Maybe he'll take it." That man was J. Charles Crawford, a Congregational preacher from Kansas whom God had called to Boone in 1891. Since then he had established a church, along with the "Boone Biblical College, Christian Boarding School & Boys Home."

But when Crawford agreed to buy the radio station, his daughter Lois disapproved. "I was opposed. I didn't like radio," she later wrote. "One of our high school students had invited me to listen on his homemade receiver. He handed me earphones and I heard a scratchy squeal, and fled as soon as possible!" Nevertheless, the purchase of the equipment went through on May 13, 1926. "When it was delivered," she recalled, "it could have fit into an old-fashioned clothes basket: a carbon microphone, some wire, a makeshift antenna. The most impressive item was a large shiny copper coil, which looked as if it had gotten its roundness from being wrapped around a number-ten fruit can." Even worse, "Papa" Crawford wanted to broadcast from three to four on Sunday afternoons, just when Lois was teaching Sunday School at the village across the river. "We loved the children, and we loved to tell them about Jesus," she pointed out, "and we loved the long walk, the fresh air and the scenery." To add to her disapproval, Papa selected the basement of the church—a gloomy, dark place—for the broadcasts. But he insisted and on January 25, 1927, KFGQ made its first broadcast from the hardware store. Lois listened on the radio from the college. "Was that singing," she asked Papa later, "or was it a kettle banging against the wall?"

Yet if the ten-watt signal didn't go far, word was getting around. A former student sent four thousand dollars in government bonds to buy parts and make repairs. And Verne Schaeffer, one of the boys at the boarding school, offered to ride a bicycle over to Ames—a round trip of nearly thirty miles—to get help from the engineer at WOI, the radio station at Iowa State University. The man not only drew up the wiring diagrams but even gave some spare parts he didn't need. When the station generator needed a new motor, Papa took one from an old broom-making machine. When the radio tubes needed a battery to work, they got one out of an old Dodge. And if the antenna needed to be high in the air, why buy a tower when they could string the wire from the church steeple to the top of the Boys Home? By April 3, 1927, KFGQ was ready to go on the air. The first live broadcast from the church was scheduled for one hour, starting at 2:30 p.m. "One hour of broadcasting! We must pray much about that hour," Papa exclaimed. Then he turned to Lois and informed her, "You are to announce."

Lois reluctantly agreed; the first broadcast began with musical numbers from the church orchestra and a vocal solo, followed by Papa's prayer of dedication. "With his hands, one on my head," Lois recalled, "and one on [a co-worker], he jumped as he led the congregation in shouting 'Hallelujah!' It was a precious hour." Then some weeks later, Papa felt the Lord giving him assurance that someone listening to the broadcast would be converted that day—and sure enough, it happened! In fact, their first new convert lived in the village across the river and had never been to Lois's Sunday school.

But there was one more thing the station needed. The law was the law, and so Papa had to hire a student from Iowa State University, one who had a First Class Radio License, to operate the station. It was outrageous, Lois thought, to pay him five whole dollars just for one hour of work each Sunday. Often the boy could barely keep the transmitter operating for the entire hour. If the equipment failed, Papa would sternly command, "Stop talking! Bow your heads and pray until you are given the signal!" Charles Crawford "could stop preaching in the middle of a sentence and pick up exactly where he left off," his daughter explained, but "the musicians couldn't do quite that well."

At last Lois had had enough of such foolishness. "If that pink-cheeked boy can get a First Class License," she declared, "I can!" And so she got all the books about radio that she could find at the library. She even *bought* a book. "I found the best way for me to learn radio law," she noted, "was to pace across the room, knock my head against the wall, turn around, pace back, and knock my head again. The knocks kept me awake." After studying for weeks and weeks, she drove all the way to Chicago for her exam. It took her two tries, but she passed the test. "Papa came to Chicago that day," Lois remembered. "He shed tears of joy, kissed me, and gave me some butterscotch candy from home." Later somebody told her she was one of the first woman in the United States to earn a First Class Radio Operators License. But by then, she and Papa had more important things on their minds. When people said KFGQ's tiny transmitter was too weak to ever be heard outside of town, Papa simply replied, "There are plenty of sinners in Boone!"

Technical mastery of radio was one thing, but what to actually *say* on the radio was entirely another matter. When preachers of the early twenties thought about mass evangelism, their models were the great crusades of men like Dwight L. Moody and Billy Sunday. These methods had been honed and perfected by more than forty years of practice. As early as the 1870s Moody had advertised his citywide crusades in mass-circulation daily newspapers, which in turn built Moody into a celebrity evangelist as a means of boosting their own circulation—and in the process generating unprecedented crowds. In comparison to these proven methods, what was radio? Indeed, would evangelism by radio even work? In an auditorium, the dynamics of a large crowd exerted a powerful pull on undecided listeners. And when crusade audiences heard the Word of God, they were being confronted *in person* by His annointed messenger. Could that same annointing be present in a crackling, disembodied voice on a radio receiver? As one preacher put it at the time, "Can unction be transmitted?"

That preacher was R.R. Brown, a young Christian and Missionary Alliance pastor who in 1923 headed the new Omaha Gospel Tabernacle.[10] That year the city had gotten its first radio station and was looking for a local minister to solemnize its first Sunday on the air—April 8, 1923—with a sermon. Brown had been in Omaha less than a year and, though the last pastor to be asked, was the first to accept. When that Sunday came, Brown went down early to the radio station. And though the staff at WOAW (later WOW) tried to show him how to use the microphone, the idea of preaching alone in a studio was simply too foreign a concept for him to grasp. So he imagined the holes in the microphone to be his audience and preached to the holes in the microphone! And not trusting the radio to carry his voice, he shouted his sermon to make sure it would be heard.

After the message, Brown thanked the station staff and turned to go home. He still needed to get ready for the Sunday service later that morning at Omaha Gospel Tabernacle. But as he stepped out the station door, someone was waiting for him. The man was obviously excited, huffing and puffing, red-faced and out of breath. Then as he gasped out his story, it was Brown's turn to be excited. The man had heard the broadcast, been converted—and then bolted out of his home, running all the way across town to tell Brown. "Hallelujah!" shouted the surprised pastor. "Unction *can* be transmitted!" Later that broadcast of April 8, 1923, would be seen as the first nondenominational religious service carried by radio. Encouraged by the response, Brown accepted an offer to become the regular radio pastor of WOAW. In those days when few radio stations existed in the American heartland, his weekly messages could be heard for hundreds of miles across the prairies. Soon letters began arriving, many from families who couldn't get to church when their rural roads were impassable, and from congregations without pastors who met around the radio for their Sunday morning sermons. Brown started to see that his *Radio Chapel Service* provided ministry opportunities that were unique to the properties of the new medium. Unlike crusade preachers who came for a series of meetings and then left town, radio preachers could build a continuing bond with their listeners. And though the radio preacher was not physically present, audiences perceived the messages as one-on-one conversations, fostering an intimacy of communication not possible in a crowded auditorium. Then too, radio offered the chance to preach every week to more people, in more places, than any crusade evangelist could hope to reach in a lifetime.

In time, Brown strove to become more than just a voice on the radio but to challenge his listeners to pray for and contribute to the needs of others. He even invited listeners to write in and receive a "World Radio Congregation" membership card, mobilizing them to give toward foreign missions and disaster relief. Within two years of his first broadcast Brown was preaching each week to more than one hundred thousand listeners, and within ten years his *Radio Chapel Service* enjoyed a weekly national audience of more than half a million. Brown himself became known as the "Billy Sunday of the Air," but he never did stop shouting at the microphone.

By the late 1920s preachers were starting to "tune in" to what worked on radio. Some leading evangelists, including Billy Sunday, could not or would not adapt their speaking styles to the new medium. But others did. Bob Jones, Sr., whose name as an evangelist was second only to Sunday's, quickly saw the potential of radio.[11] His Pittsburgh Crusade of 1925 was carried nationwide over KDKA, the first religious broadcast to originate from a crusade and first to be remotely controlled from a station. Two years later, Jones adapted his method once more by launching a regular program over a regional network, in which he spoke informally to listeners rather than preached at them. The format proved so effective that within a decade he was carried by more than one hundred fifty stations. Jones continued recording programs for the next thirty-five years and, even today, his *Word of Truth* broadcast is heard on stations across the country.

The first preacher to purchase airtime on a national radio network was Donald Grey Barnhouse.[12] A veteran of the world war, he had learned about radio while serving in the Army Signal Corps. So when he accepted the call to Philadelphia's Tenth Presbyterian Church, Barnhouse stipulated that broadcast equipment be installed in the pulpit. Beginning in 1927 with a local program, Barnhouse ended his first year on the air with a net balance of eleven cents. Yet with faith in God and in the new medium of radio, in 1928 he signed a contract for forty thousand dollars with the CBS network for a year of weekly broadcasts. Within a few years, his program was heard on more than a hundred stations across America.

Other men who would also be among the leading radio preachers of their generation began their broadcast careers in the 1920s, including Paul Rader, Charles Fuller, and Walter Maier. Indeed, the emergence of national networks to carry religious programs was seen as a God-sent opportunity. Why? At that very same time, the new federal regulations were making it too costly and complex for most churches and religious groups to operate stations of their own. There were a few notable exceptions such as Moody Bible Institute's WMBI (founded 1926) in Chicago, Maier's home station KFUO (1924) in St. Louis, and KFSG (1924) of Los Angeles, operated by evangelist Aimee Semple MacPherson's Church of the Four Square Gospel. (WMBI and KFUO remain on the air today, while KFSG was sold in 2003.) But the notion of "Christian-owned" local radio stations would not become a reality until after the Second World War and the concept of religious radio networks not until the sixties. Nevertheless, even as God seemingly closed the door in the twenties on local radio *ownership* as the principal vehicle for religious broadcasting, the faithful saw him opening an even better door. By launching a *program* rather than a station, preachers were spared the expense of operating a broadcast facility and instead could simply purchase time on a network that afforded immediate access to regional and national audiences.

In those days before the invention of long-play records (much less magnetic tape), it was not possible to pre-record sermons for later broadcast. Radio programs were aired live and music played a vital part in the variety format that was to become common for paid religious broadcasts of the period. And because music was so important in capturing an audience, many of the pioneers in religious radio, men who often were do-it-all entrepreneurs, simply added songwriting and composing to their list of varied talents.

Paul Rader and WJBT

On a warm July day in 1938, Paul Rader lay awake in his bed at the Los Angeles Hospital.[13] He heard a door close in the room next door and asked, "Who just came in? I know somebody just came in." His wife Pauline and daughters Willamine and Harriet had taken an adjoining suite where they could keep a vigil on the famed evangelist. "Well," replied Pauline, "it's Merrill and Lenore." Rader called back, "Oh, have them come in, I want to see them."[14]

Merrill Dunlop had been staff pianist during the heyday of the great Chicago Gospel Tabernacle, where every week Rader had preached to crowds of five thousand and more—as well as to multiplied thousands by radio. Now Dunlop and his wife Lenore had flown out from Chicago to visit his old boss, who had fallen ill some weeks earlier on the way home from a preaching tour of England. To Dunlop, who remembered the evangelist as a powerfully built "man's man" of two hundred fifty pounds, the sight of his mentor and friend was a shock. Rader now weighed less than a hundred pounds and clearly had not long to live.

Dunlop went over to stand at the left side of Rader's bed while his wife stood at the right.

"Merrill and Lenore," said the evangelist quietly, "I want you to sing for me." So the two sang a new Homer Rodeheaver song, then a couple of favorites from the old days at the Tabernacle. And though Rader was now thin and drawn, his smile was as big and bright as Dunlop remembered. Then suddenly, Rader's eyes flashed and the Dunlops stopped their singing. "Say, who's dying here, anyway?" the evangelist exclaimed in a loud voice that surprised his visitors. In his excitement he tried to sit up, but had to lean back. Years later, Dunlop recalled the moment.

> [H]e reached down and took a hold of my hand.... He said, "Merrill, there's no more death in me this moment than there is in you." ... I thought, "Boy, there must be something wrong up here in his mind." ... [He] kept on holding my hand. "There is no more death in me this moment than there is in you." And then he smiled and he said, "I died twenty-five years ago." ... [W]e knew just exactly what he meant. It was twenty-five years ago that he had met the Lord in a very special way.[15]

It was actually in 1911 that Rader had found himself walking at night down New York's Times Square. A sparkplug of a man, it was easy to imagine he had once been a prospector, bronco buster, boxer, and football player. It was harder to envision him as a former minister—especially given the restless and discontented spirit within his soul. Born August 26, 1879, in Denver, Colorado, Rader was the son of a Methodist Episcopal preacher. Not only had his father Daniel been a minister but so had his grandfather and great-grandfather. As a boy Rader would often accompany his father on preaching tours and sing hymns before the services. Once when the youngster went to a packed Dwight L. Moody crusade but was turned away, a kindly old man helped him get in the back door—a man who turned out to be the great evangelist himself. By his teens, Rader even began a preaching ministry of his own in the small communities of Wyoming.

But as a student at the University of Denver and then the University of Colorado, Rader began to doubt the gospel and experience a spiritual crisis. He transferred to Central College in Fayetteville, Missouri. Then, when his father received a pastorate in St. Paul, Minnesota, Rader came along and landed a job as athletic director of Hamline University. A year later he was hired as football coach at the College of Puget Sound in Tacoma, Washington. There he met and married his wife Mary and the couple remained in Tacoma until 1905. The following year, though he had left his father's God, Rader nonetheless secured ordination in the Congregational Church and accepted a pastorate of his own in Boston. Soon he moved again to a second church in Portland, Maine. But by 1908, after two churches in as many years, he had found no satisfaction in the ministry. That's when he moved to New York to enter business and manage public relations for an oil company.

For the next three years Rader drifted, fighting the Lord, going his own way—until one night he found himself on the streets of Times Square. Looking up at the brilliant lights of Times Square, Rader's attention was drawn to one of the well-known electric signs of the day. The sign was an advertisement for a silk company and at first only the white paw of a kitten was visible. Then as the entire kitten was outlined in electric bulbs, a red thread appeared. The kitten would paw at the thread, which got larger and larger until the kitten was completely ensnared. "That's Paul Rader up there," said the former minister, "he's all tangled up. I've got to get right with God."[16] Rader rented a nearby room, locked himself inside, took a Bible, and spent the next three days on his face before God. He emerged a changed man, one who had truly died to self. As Rader told the story, on the third day he placed his Bible on the floor and then stood upon it to signify his commitment to stand on God's Word. Soon he was preaching on New York street corners, proclaiming the gospel to all who would hear. In time, he heard about a new Christian movement based in New York, one that disdained hierarchy and emphasized an active faith. It was aggressive, determined, and had a vision as big as the world. They called it the Christian and Missionary Alliance and, within a year, Rader had rejoined the ministry as an associate at the Alliance Tabernacle in Pittsburgh.

In those days the CMA was not a denomination but a movement to support missions and evangelism. So in 1915 Rader accepted a call to pastor the famous Moody Church in Chicago. Soon the services were packed to overflowing, so that property was purchased—a whole city block—and a huge wooden tabernacle erected. "Paul Rader wanted to make the meetings as unlike a church meeting as possible," explained Andrew Wyzenbeek, who played flute in the Moody Church band. "That's why he started a beautiful band and orchestra and a big choir. And we used to play a band concert a half hour or even an hour before church started.... I had friends of mine that came in from Hammond, Indiana, on the train. [People] came from a hundred miles around."[17]

In 1919 when CMA founder A.B. Simpson passed away, Rader was chosen to lead the growing movement as international president. He urged the group to organize regional units for supporting nondenominational "tabernaclism" and envisioned great evangelistic campaigns that might continue daily for months at a time. Rader himself was in great demand as a revival speaker. In cities and towns across America—and in addition to his pastorate at Moody Church—he preached in temporary tabernacles seating audiences of up to three thousand people, seeing hundreds of people come to salvation in Christ. In this spirit, Rader left the Moody Church in 1921 to build a gospel tabernacle in New York City, site of CMA headquarters and then the leading city in the world. He envisioned the new tabernalce as a permanent center for evangelism and Christian events in the region and, within several months, property was acquired and the steel structure erected. A disagreement arose over the plans and finances, however, and the tabernacle was never finished—leaving Rader with nothing but the steel.

A group of Christians in Chicago had invited Rader back to the city to conduct meetings. So the evangelist accepted and, in 1922, had his steel shipped to the Windy City and erected on a suitable lot at the corner of Barry and Halsted. As Dunlop later recalled,

> Paul Rader just intended it to be a big summer campaign ... [with] concrete blocks as the roof ... [and] big sheets of white canvas which they attached to the sides.... That was the beginning of the Chicago Gospel Tabernacle. And that big summertime, the crowds just came there, just surged through that building and filled it up night after night. And Paul Rader had his big set-up of the band and choir. And when the fall days came along, he had planned to take the tabernacle down. There was such a hue and cry to keep it going that he decided to brick it in.[18]

As well known as Rader was for building "the Tab," which opened June 18, 1922, he ultimately became better known to history for a work that began two weeks before—June 3, 1922. And that was when the great tabernacle evangelist launched into something entirely new—what would later be recognized as the first ongoing radio ministry. The broadcast was over WBU, among the first radio stations in Chicago—and built by the city's flamboyant and publicity-seeking mayor, William Hale Thompson. When Rader arrived at City Hall for the broadcast, bringing with him a brass quartet, the group was quickly ushered to the roof of the building. There in the open air, the men were led to a small booth slapped together with unfinished pinboards. It looked like a sentry box with a hole cut in one of the sides. "You just get ready and point your instruments at the hole there in the side of the box," a technician told the puzzled musicians, "and when I say play, you play."[19] At his cue, suddenly an old telephone receiver was shoved through the opening. The quartet struck up a lively chorus. Then Rader took the "microphone." In 1922, a station such as WBU could be heard nationwide. And within days, public response surpassed anything Rader expected. But characteristically, he soon sized up the possibilities. One of the young musicians on that first broadcast, Clarence Jones (who in 1931 founded HCJB in Quito, Ecuador, the world's first missionary radio station) never forgot how the fiery preacher showed "a ready comprehension and acceptance of radio as a means of getting the Gospel to the unchurched masses.... [He] perceived that here was a twentieth century miracle method to preach the first century message to a wider audience than could ever crowd the biggest tabernacle, so he went all out for radio."[20]

During those days of 1921–22 when Rader was first building a tabernacle in New York, then Chicago, and would soon be expanding into radio, he wrote one of his best-remembered songs.[21] The idea came to him one day while he and his four-year-old daughter Harriet were crossing one of Chicago's busiest boulevards. The girl held his hand, gaily smiling and talking and seemingly oblivious to the traffic around them. "Aren't you afraid to cross the street, Harriet?" the evangelist asked. "No, not when *you're* with me," she replied. "Why should I be afraid?" Reminded that all Christians need the same childlike faith in their Heavenly Father, Rader returned home and, finding staff musician Lance Latham, dictated to him the words and music of "Only Believe." Ever the promoter, gifted and brilliant, songwriting was among the many talents of the multifaceted evangelist. The song, inspired by his daughter's innocent trust, expressed the utter faith which characterized Rader's entire ministry: "All things are possible, only believe!"

Rader began regular broadcasts in 1925 over WHT, a separate station built by Thompson and housed in modern studios at the famous Wrigley Building. At first Rader broadcast from the station, but soon he engaged the telephone company to run wires out to the Chicago Gospel Tabernacle. For a while, however, the organist would have to play in the WHT studios and listen on earphones to keep up with the service and even to accompany the soloists—a situation only remedied when a large pipe organ was installed at the Tab. When the Columbia Broadcasting System built a flagship station, WBBM, in Chicago, then Rader switched to the higher-powered network facility. But characteristically, he would not settle for half measures. Learning WBBM was idle on Sundays, the evangelist bought fourteen hours of time, the entire broadcast day. He called his broadcast ministry the *National Radio Chapel,* "conducting its services every Sunday in a vast ethereal cathedral" with "pews" located wherever a radio set could be heard. To set the right tone, Rader had a sign posted on the wall of the Tabernacle radio studio: "Broadcasting without Prayer is only Entertainment."[22]

Rader saw the Tabernacle not as a church, however, but as an evangelistic center without membership. Therefore, so as not to compete with local churches, Sunday morning services were not conducted. But for the radio that still left a three o'clock afternoon service and then the evening service at seven. Afterward Rader stayed around to broadcast two popular evening programs, *March of the Ages* and *The Back Home Hour.* "He went on the radio when it was a brand new thing. In fact, his musical program was desirable on the radio," recalled Wyzenbeek, a member of the Tabernacle band. He himself was assigned the task each night to oversee the radio studio, under the supervision of radio director and chief announcer Floyd Johnson. "So I got the microphones in the proper place and so forth," recounted Wyzenbeek. "We had the old carbon microphone. We used to hit it with a pencil before we started to speak to jar the carbon granules loose. I [saw] some wonderful things in these meetings and especially in that radio studio."[23]

For *March of the Ages,* Rader might declare, "Well, fellows, tonight it's going to be the fall of Jericho," and that was all the idea he would give his staff as the men scrambled for hymns and songs that fit the theme and narration for the night.[24] By contrast, *The Back Home Hour* (so named because Sunday night Tab attenders could listen when they arrived back home) was a well-prepared musical program put together by the staff, followed by a brief message from Rader and an invitation to convert to Christ. The rest of the broadcast schedule was filled in with such programs as a missions hour, women's Bible class hour, guest preacher hour, an hour for shut-ins, an hour for listeners to call in song requests, and even *Radio Rangers* and *Aerial Girls*. A boys and girls program, the *Shepherd Hour,* was aired as part of the youth work of Chicago Gospel Tabernacle. Directed by Lance Latham and Clarence Jones, the two men developed a "Tabernacle Scouts" club that later became today's AWANA youth ministry.

It was common through the twenties and thirties for the federal government to mandate that different stations must split their hours and share the same frequency. So when Rader took the entire day on Sunday over WBBM he was required to use his own call letters. After asking listeners to phone in suggestions, the moniker WJBT was selected for "Where Jesus Blesses Thousands," which also became the slogan for Chicago Gospel Tabernacle. Later, Rader bought time on the weekdays—seven thirty to eight thirty, Monday thru Friday—to air *The Breakfast Brigade* over WBBM. The theme song cheerily promised, "We'll be sugar in your coffee and honey on your bread. We'll be any kind of sweetness to get you out of bed. We'll be telling you a story and singing you a song, and we'll be fellowshipping with you all day long!"[25] During the 1930 season the program was even aired over the CBS network.

At the height of the Rader ministry, the radio broadcasts generated up to ten thousand letters a week. Chicago Gospel Tabernacle employed a staff of fifteen secretaries, eighteen musicians, an office manager, business manager, Sunday school administrators, even staffs for a cafeteria that operated on Sundays, as well as the Paul Rader Pantry food bank for the needy. In 1932 alone, the Tabernacle distributed a quarter of a million pieces of literature to radio listeners.[26] That year's culminating Christmas musical pageant drew a total attendance of forty thousand people to the Tab.[27] But the driving force behind it all was Paul Rader. One listener in those days of the twenties was a young Torrey Johnson, who as an adult went on to start the *Songs in the Night* broadcast still heard today, and founded Youth for Christ in the 1940s. As a boy, he later recalled, "we had little crystal sets, and we improvised with little Quick Oats boxes and wired them up and had a little crystal. And that was a great thing, to put on an earphone and hear the voice of Paul Rader."[28] It was a voice that Johnson never forgot.

> [H]e was a big, two-fisted man, and he had very great masculinity. He was a great storyteller. He often started his sermons with some kind of a story, and you didn't know where he was going, but he was sneaking in through the back door.... [H]e held you spellbound.... And he rarely was on the platform very much before it was time to preach. He had a room down below that he came from where he had been quiet and meditating and praying, so that he was what you would call spiritually red-hot when he got to the platform.... [W]hen he gave the invitation to receive Christ, there was a continual stream of people coming. And later on the air, multitudes were converted to Christ by listening on the air.[29]

Dunlop, who joined the Tabernacle staff in 1925, was converted as a twelve-year-old boy at the Moody Church when Rader was its pastor. Though he heard the evangelist preach countless times over the years, he never tired of hearing Rader's "great, wonderful resonant voice, beautiful voice" and his "tremendous gift of using illustrations. Oh, I mean he could tell a story! Put you on the edge of your seat, listening to that story. And then he would apply that story to the Gospel." Yet Dunlop was always cognizant that "one of the great aspects of his preaching was his love for souls, his love for people. He just exuded love and compassion for people, and he had a great missionary passion."[30] Despite the great success of his platform style, however, Rader was among the first to understand that radio called for a different kind of presentation. Rather than shout into the microphone, he imagined himself sitting with listeners in their living rooms or breakfast tables. And so he spoke in a warm, intimate manner, as in a one-on-one conversation. As a *Chicago Tribine* radio critic put it, Rader was an effective radio speaker because he projected an informal, pleasant, humorous, and friendly style.[31]

Music was also a key component in Rader's evangelistic and radio ministries. Johnson remembered how, listening to broadcasts of Tabernacle services as a child, he was impressed that Rader "surrounded himself with an excellent group of musicians, and they had a great musical program, and always surprises, always testimonies, always challenges, always people from near and far, [before] he would preach."[32] Sundays at the Chicago Gospel Tabernacle would begin at two o'clock with Sunday school. The afternoon service followed from three to five, and visitors could have supper at the cafeteria before a band concert at six thirty. "During that time," Dunlop recalls, "people were pouring into the auditorium to get there for the evening service. And the evening service started at seven and the big Tabernacle choir would come in and take their places there and we would have a big musical program."[33] Coming to the Tab for Sunday afternoon services and concerts became a favorite pastime, like going to ballgames were for other people. The band was directed by Richard J. Oliver, who formerly directed the Salvation Army Band. His son, Richard W., was staff pianist until replaced in 1925 by Merrill Dunlop. Lance Latham sat at the organ while Clarence Jones played the trombone and his brother Howard the cornet. The Tabernacle brass quartet of Howard Jones and James Neilson at cornet, plus Clarence Jones and Richard J. Oliver at trombone, became famous throughout the Chicago area. Neither was the Tab idle on weekdays, as Rader would invite guest preachers to come for a week of nightly meetings. So the music staff was on hand every night, Sunday through Friday, as the crowds continued to come all through the week. As Dunlop exclaimed, "We had a big musical program. So it was an every night deal at Chicago Gospel Tabernacle!"

Rader's own contributions to the music program are well illustrated by the story of his 1928 song, "I've Found the Way." The manner in he wrote the song is typical, not only of how he composed music, but of the man himself. During an evangelistic campaign that year in Toronto, Rader and his team stayed at a city hotel. The main dining room was featuring a new orchestra that advertised "the sweetest music this side of heaven." Curious, Rader and Dunlop went to hear for themselves as they took their dinner one night. "Merrill, that's a good orchestra and I'm sure it will go places," Rader allowed. "But you know, they may say they are playing the 'sweetest music this side of heaven,' but I disagree with them. For I feel that there is nothing sweeter this side of heaven than a song that tells people about Jesus and His love. Merrill, I feel a song coming on, one that will beat anything we've heard tonight. Goodnight, Merrill. See you in the morning!" Early the next morning Dunlop received a call from his boss: "Merrill, I've got to see you before breakfast. Meet me in a half hour at the piano in the big dining room where we were last night and bring some manuscript paper with you." The two men met at the appointed time and, as Dunlop sat down at the piano, Rader sang the melody and words he had devised during the night. "I've found the way through the blood past the veil," Rader intoned on the chorus, "There by his pow'r over sin I prevail." Dunlop followed along on the piano and soon had the new song scored and ready to use—most likely at Rader's revival service that night.[34]

As might be guessed, Rader had an independent and entrepreneurial spirit—and knew where he wanted to go. "I think probably a part of his difficulty," observed Torrey Johnson, "was [that] he was too far ahead of the people, and they couldn't quite either catch up or keep up with him."[35] (Characteristically, Rader once preached a sermon, "Who Put the Ad in Advertising?" in which he proclaimed that God "is the leading advertiser. He has written His ads in every rock."[36]) Rader departed the Moody Church in 1921 after six years as its pastor, in part because the church leadership was not prepared to keep pace with his burgeoning plans for evangelism—and because the executive committee was already concerned he spent too much time on outside endeavors. That same year Rader's plan to build a steel tabernacle in New York City fell through due to disagreements about its direction. And in 1924 he stepped down as president of the Christian and Missionary Alliance, again amid feelings within the CMA governing board that Rader was too independent.

Yet his work continued to expand, and not only at the Chicago Gospel Tabernacle. The year 1926 alone saw the purchase of a summer camp and conference center in Michigan called Lake Harbor (later renamed Maranatha), three months in Los Angeles filling in for Aimee Semple McPherson at her Angelus Temple, and the founding of a new missionary society Rader dubbed the Christian World Wide Couriers. The latter work often took Rader away from Chicago to conduct large missions conferences, recruit workers, and raise funds. Indeed, he is credited with being the first to broadcast appeals for "faith promise" pledges over the radio. During his years at the Tabernacle, Rader twice toured the world (1929 and 1931) and conducted major evangelistic campaigns in Philadelphia (1923 and 1926); Ocean Grove, New Jersey (1925); Belfast, Ireland (1930); and Los Angeles (1932). He assisted in starting gospel tabernacles in Toronto, Los Angeles, Minneapolis, Toronto, and Asbury Park, New Jersey.

Then in 1932, during the low point of the Depression, the old pattern reasserted itself. Rader's aspirations ran ahead of his resources. Large crowds were still coming to Tabernacle six nights a week, but giving was down because no one had money to give. Rader's largest financial backer was the president of a national insurance company, and the company went out of business. The last straw was an accumulated debt of forty thousand dollars to WBBM for radio airtime, so that the Tabernacle property had to be placed into receivership. To prevent the work from being closed, Rader in 1933 resigned his pastorate and personally assumed the debt, though it would mean his own bankruptcy. He asked Clarence Erickson, a pastor from Indianapolis who had been speaking weeknights at the Tabernacle, to take over. "One of the first things we did," Dunlop remembers, "was to go around and screw out all the big, high-wattage electric bulbs all over the Tabernacle and put in the smaller ones."[37] They also canceled the WJBT radio broadcasts, switching to a more modest schedule on a smaller station. As for Rader, he remained in Chicago and in 1933 held tent services at the city's Century of Progress World's Fair. In 1934 he was called to the Fort Wayne Gospel Tabernacle, where he pastored for two years and broadcast over the radio. And by 1937 he left Indiana, made a home in Los Angeles, and embarked on a lengthy preaching tour of England. It would be his last.

By May of 1938, Rader had fallen ill and booked passage home on the *Queen Mary*. Fearing a heart condition and thus afraid to fly, he instead took the long train ride from New York to Los Angeles. For weeks, confined to his home on Barnum Boulevard, he grew increasingly worse. His ministry ceased and, by July, the evangelist was moved to Los Angeles Hospital. The diagnosis was carcinoma. That's when Merrill Dunlop came to visit, as it turned out, just two or three days before Rader died. In one of their final conversations Rader confided to his old friend,

> You know, Merrill, it's a strange thing. Last night [in a dream] I felt as though I was suspended over a great chasm, a huge chasm. I began to be lowered just little by little over that chasm. Oh, it took so long! I was hours going down. And I didn't know where the bottom would be. All of a sudden I sensed that I had reached the lowest point. I began to ascend just about as slowly. It took hours and I came to the top. Then it was daylight [and] I was back again. This happened another time. I went through that experience twice. Merrill, I said to the Lord, "Quit kidding me, Lord. Take me over! I want to go."[38]

A day or two later Rader quietly lapsed into a coma. He died July 19, 1938. At the memorial service, held at the Hollywood Presbyterian Church, Dunlop was asked to share a remembrance of the man who led him to Christ. And he told the story of how Rader had actually died, to himself, more than twenty-five years earlier when he saw that tangled-up kitten in the lights of Times Square.

Over the course of his long evangelistic career, Rader converted thousands of men and women to Christ. Among them was Charles Fuller, who became the greatest radio preacher of his generation. And Rader was a seminal influence on men who would later go on to establish great works—including Oswald Smith, Clarence Jones, Lance Latham, Torrey Johnson, and a young student named Percy Crawford who was studying at Wheaton College near Chicago. In the end, however, the ministry of Paul Rader was effective not only because of his dynamic speaking, stiring music, or inventive methods. Johnson, who came to know Rader in later years, credits the evangelist for imparting to him and others "a vision for the world—and he had a heart that was big enough for the world.... He was very daring. He was a great promoter. He had a great deal of imagination. He probably was a little bit ahead of his time ... [so] that he pioneered a great deal of what other people did later on.... [Rader] was a pioneer in taking missions out of the nineteenth century and putting it into the twentieth century."[39]

Even more important than Rader's personal qualities were the way, Clarence Jones believed, "he showed us by example to depend entirely upon the Holy Spirit for the unction of heaven upon the Word."[40] As Rader himself expressed it in 1921 with the words of his best known song, he relied upon the "The Old-Time Power."

Wendell Loveless and WMBI

The Illinois Products Exposition of 1925 was being held again in Chicago that October and radio station WGES had planned to draw attention to its own exhibit by staging a live broadcast. The program director had put together what promised to be a good program. But then a violent storm struck the city and the musicians he had engaged didn't show up. What was he supposed to do now? It was only a few minutes to go before the broadcast was scheduled to air. Nearby, however, two students from the Moody Bible Institute were playing their cornets and handing out tracts from an exhibit booth the school had set up for the exposition. So the WGES program director sprinted over to the exhibit and asked, "May we borrow your two young musicians?" The students were excited about the opportunity and gladly agreed. The musical program they presented that October day was the Moody Bible Institute's first radio broadcast. Soon afterward WGES repaid the favor by giving the school, at no charge, an hour of programming each Sunday. Response was so great that, within a few months, the school was broadcasting two hours of music and lectures six evenings a week.[41]

But what about a radio station of its own? The possibility was discussed as early as 1921. Yet James Gray, president of Moody Bible Institute, was unsure and could not bring himself to support the idea. Was radio of God or the devil? Most of what you heard on the radio, he observed, was worldly music and entertainment that appealed to the flesh. And with the "Roaring Twenties" in full swing, the nation's moral fiber was already under serious attack. Was mass media a captive of the enemy? Was it a tool that Christians should embrace? By early 1925, however, designated gifts started arriving at Moody from donors who urged the construction of a radio station. The board of trustees reevaluated the matter and, this time, approved the project. Later that year Gray hired a recent Yale engineering graduate, Henry Crowell (whose father, H. P. Crowell, chaired the board of trustees), to be assistant to the president in charge of radio development. And even as the Institute was broadcasting nightly over WGES, Crowell began installing a five-hundred-watt Western Electric transmitter on the Moody campus.

Though the station was ready to sign on the air in March 1926, its license from U.S. Department of Commerce had not yet been approved. Determined to operate within the law at a time when many broadcasters simply ignored any regulations, school officials made an arrangement with local station WENR. Six days a week, Moody Bible Institute would broadcast an hour of programming from its own studios and have it aired over WENR. James Gray was still skeptical but, as president, agreed to deliver the first radio message from the new studios. Two hours of airtime were secured for the inaugural broadcast, from eight to ten o'clock on the night of March 3, 1926. After the program, Gray left the radio studios and walked across campus to his office in Building 153. And almost at the very moment he entered, the telephone rang. It was from Florida. Gray was astonished. The caller had heard his radio message from Chicago. In the following days, as calls and letters kept coming, Gray was converted from skeptic to enthusiast. When someone from North Dakota wrote and asked, "Is radio of God or the devil?" Gray replied without hesitation, "We think it is of God."

At last the station license was approved and the call letters WMBI chosen. Moody Bible Insitute could now broadcast over its own transmitter, with the initial broadcast set for Wednesday, July 28, 1926. As the date approached, Henry Crowell was glad he had gotten his Yale degree. The school had been raising funds for months and the opening of the station was a big event. School officials, students, and alumni were all eagerly awaiting the occasion. Crowell was determined that, from an engineering standpoint at least, they would not be disappointed. As that first WMBI program signed on the air, July 28, 1926, everything seemed to be going great. The equipment was all working properly. So Crowell relaxed a bit and allowed himself a smile. The months of sweat and hard work were paying off. As he turned back to his work, however, someone was trying to get his attention. Something was going horribly wrong! People were tuning in their radios but the signal was having trouble getting through. Crowell frantically checked over his equipment, hoping to find the problem. What was going on? Though nothing turned up wrong, it didn't take long to discover the real problem. Another radio station, WKBA, had been licensed to the same wavelength and was broadcasting its own inaugural program on the very same day as WMBI. Crowell was understandably dismayed. Yet he knew, in those days before government regulation, it was an all-too-common occurrence.

The two stations, WMBI and WKBA, were able to work out a satisfactory division of airtime. Then in just a matter of months, an even larger challenge loomed. Regulations were needed to bring order from the chaos that was radio. But with the creation of the Federal Radio Commission in 1927, all licenses were to be reviewed. Under the new Radio Act stations could only remain on their current frequencies for sixty days while hearings were held in Washington. The game was now being played by a different set of rules. On the advice of Henry Crowell, WMBI took swift action. The day after the legislation was passed to create the Commission, President Gray sent a letter to every person on the Institute mailing list. A postcard was enclosed and, in response to his appeal, nearly fifty thousand cards were sent to the radio commission in support of a new license for WMBI. Crowell himself traveled to the hearings in Washington to personally plead the station's case.

> Would it not be possible to allocate a small number of wave channels to be used jointly by educational and religious stations? This channel [could] be suitably located, not at the remote ends of the present band, but where they would be of service to the average listener with their present receiving sets. I think it will be found that such Institutes are fairly well scattered throughout the country and that each, with its limited schedule of hours would have small difficulty in agreeing to a division of time. Thus it would be possible to relinquish many present wave channels now devoted to this type of service and greatly consolidate the number of stations into a few channels. This would result in the releasing of many channels now used for such a service for the use of commercial stations.[42]

The arguments presented by the Yale-educated engineer proved persuasive, and on April 22 the agency granted WMBI a special permit to continue broadcasting beyond the sixty-day limit. As the commission considered the application of WMBI for a renewed license, Crowell even hoped for approval to boost WMBI's power. Instead the agency wired him back, "Power increase absolutely out of question and cut in power may be necessary. Please consider this situation carefully before making final conclusion." Crowell knew what the commission was driving at. Signal interference was a concern shared by all. But the FRC's solution, as the telegram seemed to insist, was that WMBI reduce its broacast hours to a minimum level and share time on the same frequency with several other stations. As soon as the agency's telegram was received Crowell headed again to Washington, this time with an attorney for the Institute and the chairman of the board of trustees. The five-member commission cordially welcomed the three visitors for a private meeting and showed sincere interest in WMBI. Later, after deliberation the FRC unanimously agreed the station was "operating in the interests of public convenience, interest, and necessity." A planned consolidation with another station was waived and tentative approval for a new wavelength assignment granted. The action was confirmed on May 23 when WMBI was assigned a frequency of 1140 kilocycles, which it had to share with only one other station. The station could thus proceed with a power increase and, in January 1928, a five-thousand-watt transmitter was erected on property purchased in suburban Addison, Illinois. Appropriately, the cornerstone of the radio tower bore the inscription, "Dedicated wholly to the service of our Lord and Savior Jesus Christ." The stone was also inscribed with two scripture references, 2 Timothy 2:19 and Isaiah 55:11, that testified to the surety of God's foundation and the effectiveness of His Word.

During 1928, however, new legislation was enacted that aimed to equalize the number of radio stations allowed in different regions of the country. Chicago, a major urban area, was way over the limit allowed under the new law. For a time it appeared that WMBI's plight was "extremely serious," but ultimately the station was only reassigned to 1180 kilocycles and compelled to share time with two other stations. More irksome was WMBI's new classification as a "limited time" facility that prevented any evening broadcasts until very late. When Moody appealed in 1929 for a new frequency assignment, however, the station faced an unexpected roadblock when another religious station in Chicago was disqualified from seeking a new wavelength. Moreover, the Federal Radio Commission went on record as suggesting that all religious stations should be classified as "propaganda outlets" that benefitted only a small segment of the public. The FRC was even threatening religious stations with limited hours and exile to the remote end of the AM radio band. Yet WMBI was prepared to make a strong case. At an FRC hearing in Washington several witness testified to the value of WMBI, followed by a forty-minute presentation from James Gray. The Moody station, he pointed out, was operated as a nondenominational, educational radio outlet with programs that appealed to both religious and non-religious listeners. Strong propaganda and direct financial appeals were avoided. Slanderous statements attacking other religious viewpoints were prohibited. Guest speakers were chosen with care and strictly warned against careless comments. As a result, no formal complaint had ever been lodged against WMBI. By 1930 Henry Crowell had made a total of ten trips to Washington since WMBI went on the air. And though that year the station lost its case for a new wavelength, Crowell won an important victory. Commision members expressed their appreciation for the professional organization and presentation of Moody's case. In 1931 the commissioners unanimously stated their belief that WMBI was operating in the public interest. And the agency assured Crowell that WMBI was safe as long as its license was not directly challenged by another station—and if it continued to play by the rules.

Though the opening of WMBI was attended by difficulty, the Institute already had on staff a man whose talents would ultimately ensure the new radio station not only succeeded but in time would become a worldwide outreach. That man was Wendell Loveless.[43] Born February 2, 1892, Loveless became interested in music during his boyhood school days in the Chicago surburb of Wheaton, Illinois. At first he studied piano and organ, but his gifts were not limited to the keyboard. After graduating from high school in 1911—and spending three years as a salesman for the Waterloo Skirt and Garment Company—in 1914 a friend heard Loveless sing and suggested he audition for further training. That year he was admitted to study voice at the Lyceum Art Conservatory in Chicago. Quitting his sales job, he traveled across the country with a Conservatory concert company on the Chatauqua and Lyceum circuits. During the pre-radio days of the nineteenth and early twentieth centuries, the Chatauqua and Lyceum movements flourished as a means of bringing arts and culture to ordinary people. Named after a lake in upstate New York where the movement began, Chatauqua meetings invited people to country retreats where they could hear a week of lectures, plays, and concerts. By contrast, lyceums were meeting halls built in cities by non-profit associations for the purpose of offering cultural events to the community. As a member of the Conservatory troupe Loveless sang in a quartet, played the piano, and did impersonations.

After three years on the road, Loveless's artistic career was interrupted in 1917 by the First World War. He enlisted in the Marine Corps, was selected for officer training and, after being commissioned a lieutenant, spent the war as a drill instructor. When the conflict ended in 1918 Loveless returned to civilian life as sales and advertising manager for a Chicago auto parts manufacturer. He married in 1920, in time had three sons, and joined the army of commuters who rode the train each day from Wheaton to Chicago and back. By 1924, he had achieved the good life. Loveless had traveled the country, sung before appreciative crowds, married an attractive woman, and settled down into an executive position with a large and growing company. Though he had grown up in a churchgoing home and even served for a time as church choir director, he had shown no interest in spiritual things. Yet at thirty-two, he had reached the age when men often begin to ask questions. As Loveless recalled,

> Neither Mrs. Loveless nor I was saved at the time of our marriage in 1920. While we were "members of the church" in good standing, our real interests were in the things of the world.... One day, during that year [1924], while playing with our two-year-old son [Robert], the Holy Spirit suddenly spoke to my heart, and this thought came

to mind: "I am not living a very good life before my boy. I must set him a better example." That was the first definite thought I had given to spiritual things.[44]

Robert Loveless remembered later from hearing his father's testimony, "[I was] playing on the living room floor" and "it was this sight one evening when I was two years old that stunned him into spiritual consciousness." From that moment his father was disturbed by the questions, "Where will I lead my boy? What do I have in myself to give him?"[45] Wendell Loveless felt suddenly driven to read the New Testament at almost every opportunity. His wife feared, he recounted, "lest I was becoming a bit daft." But after several weeks of Bible study, he later recalled, "there flashed through my mind this glorious thought, 'Why, Christ has died, was buried, and has arisen from the dead, that He might pay the penalty for my sins. Now all I have to do, in order to obtain eternal life, is to receive Him as my Savior' ... I cannot express in words the joy and peace which flooded my soul as that realization took possession of me."[46] Shortly after his 1925 conversion Loveless took what he believed was a crucial step by going forward at a revival meeting to publicly confess to Christ. Within a year his wife Velma also was converted, so that their home became "one in the Lord."

Over the next year Loveless continued his daily commute by train to Chicago. Now as a "born-again" Christian he was drawn to other believers with whom he could spend his commute and talk about spiritual things. Soon he became acquainted with fellow commuters who worked at the Moody Bible Institute in Chicago. About a year after Loveless's conversion his friends told him about an opening in the school's Extension Department. Since the position involved representing the Institute to the public, God could put his background in sales and advertising to good use. Thus in January 1926 Loveless joined the Moody extension office. Two months later, however, the school found itself with a brand new radio station and studio—and a quandary over who would run it. "Radio was in its pioneer stages everywhere," Robert Loveless explained, and

> There were no experienced radio executives around. So the Moody administration looked at its own staff and asked, "Who among us has the combination of talents and experience which might prove useful in running a radio station?" When they began to think along this line, the name of Wendell P. Loveless came to the fore. Of course, he had no radio experience. But then, who had? He had experience in personnel management as well as artistic performance.... So they said, "Let's let Wendell give it a try!"[47]

Wendell Loveless, doubting he could have a future in radio, twice refused the post. But after being drafted to participate in WMBI's inaugural broadcast, the audience response changed his mind and he agreed to serve as manager and program director. Instead of the large staff he had supervised in the business world, at WMBI it was just two people—Loveless and his secretary. In the months that followed the first broadcast of March 3, 1926, he was not only director but also announcer, pianist, vocalist, and speaker. Somehow by 1927 he managed each week to fill thirty-two hours of programming. Often Merrill Dunlop, staff pianist at the Chicago Gospel Tabernacle and a Moody graduate, would come and help. Nevertheless, "In the early days Loveless was a one man radio station.... He would announce the musical number, rush to the piano on which he played, then resume his place at the microphone, announce the next song, and begin to sing. During the course of a program the listener might hear five different voices—yet each was Loveless."[48]

Not only did WMBI broadcast school chapel services, special meetings, and conferences. Loveless also developed an array of popular weekly programs such as *Radio School of the Bible*, *Family Altar League*, and the *KYB Club* (for Know Your Bible), plus music from staff, student, and guest artists. By 1930, enrollment in the *Radio School of the Bible* topped 1,900 students. That year a new *Morning Glory Club* children's program attracted more than two thousand members within a few weeks of signing on the air. Eight-year-old Robert Loveless, pressed into service with his younger brothers David and Wendell Jr., as cast members, remembered how the *Morning Glory Club* was broadcast from the WMBI transmitter facility in Addison. "One morning on the show," he later recalled, "to simulate going on a car trip, we backed up the old Model T Ford to the open studio window and cranked 'er up! Those were surely days of rude experimentation."[49] Yet in 1930 the station received more than twenty thousand letters from listeners. Volunteers from seventy-one local churches participated in various broadcasts. Five foreign language programs were aired on a regular basis and eighteen more on an occasional schedule. And when WMBI held its first radio rally that year, more than four thousand listeners showed up for the meeting. More important to Loveless, fifty people stood to their feet and gave testimony of how they had come to Christ by hearing the gospel over the radio.

Loveless himself sang in an Announcers Trio that became highly popular throughout Chicago and the upper Midwest, and even made some records on the Victor label. Personal appearances by Loveless, the trio, and other WMBI radio personalities soon numbered in the hundreds. It was during the late twenties, a time of small staffs, lean budgets and tremendous creativity, that Loveless began to write songs. At first he wrote songs out of necessity, just to fill airtime and because there was not enough other people to do it. But soon he discovered that he was composing music "simply because I could not help it. The Lord has given me eternal life as a free gift of his grace, and I love to sing about the Lord Jesus and His wondrous grace to me. I live to get other people singing about Him too."[50] As he saw it, songwriting is "a perfectly normal means of expressing the joy and the blessedness of the knowing the Lord Jesus Christ as the One Who saves and keeps and abolutely satisfies every longing of this old heart of mine."[51] One of his earliest efforts from 1928, "Precious Hiding Place" with words by Avis Christiansen, proved in his lifetime to be among his most popular. The soft and lyrical chorus encourages believers to trust in the promise that Christ provides a "precious hiding place in the shelter of His love" where there is "not a doubt or fear since my Lord is near."

In the years that followed, the outreach and influence of WMBI continued to grow. When the Moody Bible Institute constructed a high-rise educational building on its campus in 1938, the station took two floors and moved into state-of-the-art studios. By 1940 the *KYB Club* boasted more than 17,500 members and *Radio School of the Bible* served 11,500 students. In 1941 the station was assigned its own full-time frequency, as some eighty staff members produced more than 250 programs per week—of which 25 or 30 featured Loveless as an announcer, narrator, tenor soloist, or piano accompanist (sometimes all in the same program). An FM station, WDLM (named for the school's founder, Dwight Lyman Moody) also went on the air in 1943, two years after the government allowed FM stations to be licensed. And some of WMBI's programs, including *Miracles and Melodies, Moody Presents* and *Stories of Great Christians*, were recorded and distributed to stations across the country. The influence of WMBI and Loveless is seen in the many evangelical songbooks, published in the forties and fifties, which bear photographs of vocalists standing before a WMBI microphone. The music of WMBI was regarded as a standard for evangelical popular music of the period. Then too, most people heard the new songs for the first time on radio and aspired to sound like the duets, trios, and quartets they heard on WMBI. In 1946, at the height of his ministry, Loveless wrote a textbook, *Manual of Gospel Broadcasting*, which was widely used at Bible colleges and training schools. In its more than three hundred pages the volume covered principles of radio programming, script writing, announcing, production, and promotion. In a chapter on "Presenting the Musical Message," Loveless explained the relationship between music and broadcasting through a series of practical pointers:

1. The gospel broadcaster should choose the musical talent with great care. It must be remembered that some musicians who are very acceptable for public performance before a visible audience, are not desirable for radio....
2. Musical talent should be selected by means of auditions. These auditions should be conducted in the radio studio, using a microphone ... [and judged] as they come through the amplifier....
3. Resonant voices, especially those of the lower register, are usually

the most desirable. Listeners generally seem to prefer male voices. Some sopranos are very good for radio, but these are the exceptions rather than the rule.... When women are used ... they should be used in combinations, such as duets, trios, [mixed] quartettes, and ensemble groups.
4. It is not necessary to have a large vocal group for the average program broadcast from a radio studio....
9. [E]xtreme care should be taken to use the best taste possible at the same time being sure that there is a sparkle, and brightness in the musical presentation. Do not mistake the funereal type of music for spirituality, nor the dull, drab execution of a hymn for high-level piety....
13. Choose instrument combinations for broadcasting with great care. Some combinations are far better for broadcasting than others. Some instruments, like some voices, are better for radio than others....
16. It is not "good radio" to use too much of any one song or musical during one program. While a [church congregation] should sing the entire hymn or gospel song ... the broadcaster must not expect his radio audience to be agreeable to that sort of thing....
19. In presenting gospel songs and music on the air, further variety must be sought along two lines: (a) the selection of songs of varied style, key, and tempo: and (b) so placing the song in the program format so that variety shall be preserved throughout the broadcast....[52]

These instructions offer some explanation of why certain kinds of evangelical popular music emerged during the golden age of radio. For example, male quartets were especially favored by audiences because their sound was a good fit for radio. Women's trios were also well liked but female soloists were less common. The high register of soprano voices could sound shrill and produce distortion on the radio—especially, as Loveless noted, if they sang with too much vibrato or tended to "punch" high notes. Furthermore, a new type of song became popular during the radio days. Called "choruses," these were simply short refrains without accompanying verses. Choruses proved to be a great fit for radio; they provided catchy tunes and lyrics that mass audiences could enjoy and remember, added variety to the musical portion of a program, and saved precious extra seconds of radio time. Choruses also were popular in the Christian camping and youth rally movements that emerged in the thirties and forties. Though some criticized Loveless's choruses as being too "jazzy," he explained that his songs relied not on jazz idioms but on rhythm. "Don't be afraid of rhythm—[though] sinful when used for wrong purposes," he said. "The value of the music is to convey the message of the words. I believe in meeting the young people's needs."[53]

> No [one] believes that gospel choruses should supplant the fine hymns of the church, but ... regardless of [one's] personal prejudices one way or another, the gospel chorus can perform a real service if rightly used. A chorus that is attractive and Scriptural has the value of brief expression of eternal truth in a way quickly learned by a large group—and thus forms a rallying point for the greatest number of people.[54]

One of the most enduring examples of a radio chorus, "Every Day with Jesus," was composed by Loveless in 1936. Yet in composing more than a hundred gospel songs and choruses (mostly written during his daily commute by train to work or while driving to Bible conferences) Loveless showed, as his contemporary Al Smith pointed out, that "his style is varied—from the lilting 'Every Day with Jesus' to the assuring hush of 'Precious Hiding Place.'" For that reason Smith could say, "Rare indeed, is the young people's meeting, Sunday school sing, singspiration, or radio broadcast that does not frequently include a Loveless song or chorus in its program."[55] The musical literature of the period also suggests that Wendell Loveless created a genre unique to himself, one not heard before or since. Others have written hymns and gospel songs, but Loveless stands alone in writing gospel *marches*. These include "Assurance March" (1931) and "Service March" (1937), "V is for Victory" (1942), and the "King's College Victory March" (1939) for the school founded by radio evangelist Percy Crawford. Even the theme song—which is still heard today—that he wrote for the *Children's Bible Hour*, entitled "Boys and Girls for Jesus" (1944), has a martial air. The most enduring example that has come down to the church today, written in 1940 as war clouds gathered over Europe, is the stirring song, "I Have Christ in My Heart."

Though songs by Wendell Loveless were ubiquitous in his generation, virtually none have come into common use in hymnbooks today. In his day, Loveless was not only a noted songwriter and radio personality but a popular conference speaker and Christian author. He spoke frequently at the day's top Bible conferences: Winona Lake, Gull Lake, Cedar Lake, Ben Lippen, America's Keswick, Percy Crawford's Pinebrook, and Jack Wyrtzen's Word of Life camps. (Loveless was known for being able, given his radio experience, to condense a ninety-minute sermon into fourteen minutes.) His devotional books released in the forties included *Sunrise Meditations, New Sunrise Meditations, Plain Talks on Romans, Plain Talks on Practical Truths, Little Talks on Great Words,* and *Christ and the Believer.*

In 1947, after twenty-one years at WMBI, Loveless left the station to devote more time to Bible teaching and conference ministry. He accepted the call to pastor the Wheaton (Illinois) Evangelical Free Church in 1952, then five years later was named pastor of Florida's Boca Raton Bible Conference and Church. In 1961 he returned to religious broadcasting as a director of radio station KAIM in Honolulu, Hawaii. Deciding to live his remaining years in the islands, in 1966 he accepted a call as associate pastor of the First Chinese Church of Christ, where he served for more than fifteen years. As for WMBI and Moody Bible Institute, the school ended its first foray in FM broadcasting in 1952 when the new band simply had not yet caught on. By 1958, however, the Institute became one of the early pioneers among religious broadcasters in multiple station ownership; that year WCRF in Cleveland, Ohio, signed on the air. In 1960, Moody Radio grew into one of the first Christian networks when WDLM of East Moline, Illinois, began operation. The school also reentered FM radio when WMBI added an FM signal to its AM output. With six stations added on the East and West Coasts during the seventies, the foundation of today's extensive Moody Broadcasting Network was in place.

When Loveless passed away on October 3, 1987, at the age of ninety-five, it was the final chapter in one of the pioneer stories from radio's golden age. Forty-five years earlier, however, Loveless had already written a poignant valedictory. Composed in 1942, the song "Goodbye" went on to close many radio broadcasts over the years. After affirming the biblical promises that "God is watching o'er you" and "His mercy goes before you," the closing chorus simply intones, "So goodbye, may God bless you."

James Vaughn and WOAN

When James Vaughn passed away in 1941 the undertaker was curious about one thing.[56] Why were there callouses the size of quarters on each of Vaughn's knees? The funeral home asked the family about it and they replied that Vaughn was a man of prayer. He had spent many an hour on his knees, talking with God in a life that spanned the tumultuous years between the Civil War and the Second World War. In between, he had almost singlehandedly given birth to gospel music as it is known today.

Only the week before Vaughn was born—on December 14, 1864, in Giles County, Tennessee—General Sherman had completed his March to the Sea, setting Atlanta afire and bringing devastation and ruin across the Southern heartland. Nineteen years later, however, Vaughn began his musical training at a school founded by two men who had been soldiers on opposite sides of the conflict. Ephraim Ruebush was a Union soldier who, toward the end of the war, rescued a young Confederate prisoner of war from a Union camp. Aldine Kieffer was a talented musician and, in time, he and Ruebush became brothers-in-law and business partners. In New Market, Virginia, the two men founded a company to publish sacred songbooks. At the time, Southern sacred music was customarily written in a four-note "Sacred Harp" system. Ruebush and Kieffer instead used a seven-note system based on a type of notation called "shaped notes" in which various shapes each stood for different musical intervals. The shaped-note system gave to Southern sacred folk music a new kind of harmony and sound. In 1874 the "Ruebush Kieffer Normal School" of music was established and Vaughn enrolled as student in 1883. Later Vaughn married, moved to Texas, then returned to Tennesse and embarked upon a career as a school teacher and principal. Yet music continued to pull at him. In 1900 he privately published a book of gospel songs. Then two years later he made the difficult decision to give up the security of his education career and go full-time into the music publishing business.

Headquartered in Lawrenceburg, Tennessee, the James D. Vaughn Publishing Company struggled in its early years. But in 1910 Vaughn had an idea. He was planning that year to print a special new songbook for male quartets. Why not have the company organize its own quartet, pay them a salary, and send them out to promote the books? And that is how the nation's first professional male gospel quartet hit the road. The group initially consisted of Vaughn's brother Charles, George Sebren, Joe Allen, and Ira Foust. Songbook sales doubled that year to sixty thousand copies and had nearly tripled by 1912. The growth enabled Vaughn to establish his own school of music in 1911 and an influential monthly journal, the *Vaughn Family Visitor*, in 1912. Branch offices of the Vaughn company were opened in Arkansas, Mississippi, South Carolina, and Texas. Vaughn Phonograph Records followed in 1921 and cut its first record—featuring on the flip side an original song, "Look for Me," by V.O. Stamps—a full year before the first country music record was produced. Though sacred music recordings had been made before by Homer Rodeheaver and others, the Vaughn recording was the first to feature a gospel quartet.

Despite the impressive growth, Vaughn knew his songbook and record sales were primarily limited to Southern audiences. The *Vaughn Family Visitor* was advertised as "the leading music journal of the South" and Vaugh Phonograph products as the "first and only Southern records to be placed on the market." A devout man of God, Vaughn had a deep desire to share his music as widely as possible. As the nation entered the decade of the Roaring Twenties, when standards of music and morality would undergo rapid change, he wanted to provide a wholesome, enjoyable, and "godly" alternative.

In 1922 Vaughn ran into Fred Green, a Lawrence County friend and neighbor who had been a signals officer during the First World War. As they struck up a conversation in the town park one day, Green explained that during the war he had been trained in "a new form of communications, actually, called radio. It works like a telephone but there are no wires involved."[57] He told Vaughn how radio could carry voices and music, and then exclaimed, "Radio is going to be the biggest thing that's happened to this country. Everybody will have a radio set." At the time, not many people who lived in places like Lawrence County had radio sets. Vaughn himself had never heard one. In fact, not a single viable radio station existed in 1922 in the entire state of Tennessee. But as the two men sat on the park bench that day, Vaughn through his *pince-nez* glasses looked his friend straight in the eye and asked, "Fred, could you build me a radio station?" Green described the parts and equipment he would need and Vaughn suggested they go to his office to settle the deal. "We will build a radio station," Vaughn declared as he got out his checkbook, "and broadcast this gospel music all over the country!" That same year, 1922, Vaughn was contemplating the future in a different way when he collaborated with staff lyricist James Rowe (composer of "Love Lifted Me," "Sweeter as the Days Go By," and "I Would Be Like Jesus,") to write the music for a song he entitled "God Holds the Future in His Hands." Perhaps the new radio venture was on their minds when the duo wrote, "On Him depend, He is your Friend; He holds the future in His hands."

Within a few months Fred Green had completed his assignment. A federal license was applied for and granted on November 21, 1922. Vaughn chose the call letters WOAN which stood for "Watch Our Annual Normal," a reference to the company's yearly music school. The antenna consisted at first of eight copper wires strung horizontally between two windmills. In 1923, WOAN was the only functioning radio station in Tennessee and, in those days when the airwaves were uncluttered, its 150-watt signal reached into neighboring states as well.[58] When a power increase to 500 watts was granted in 1925, Vaughn began to receive mail from as far away as New York, Pennsylvania, Minnesota, Illinois, South Dakota, Texas, and Oklahoma. WOAN had its own twelve-piece orchestra whose director had previously led the famous Barnum & Bailey circus band. The Vaughn Publishing Company now had sixteen professional quartets traveling across the country to sell its songbooks. Music schools (lasting three weeks for a tuition of ten dollars) were conducted from Florida to New Mexico. And in 1924 the Vaughn Quartet made a record for the Edison Company in New York.

During the decade of the 1920s the WOAN nighttime broadcast was its most popular—and due to the special properties of AM radio, it reached the farthest distance. Vaughn used the program to showcase not only quartets but also trios, duets, soloists, choruses, and the WOAN orchestra. Listener reponse was so great that the Western Union telegram office in Lawrenceburg remained open each night until the station signed off the air. WOAN and other early radio stations, such as WREC in Memphis and WSM in Nashville, popularized gospel music to national audiences. The Depression forced Vaughn to sell WOAN in 1929, but in the thirties the Vaughn Quartet purchased airtime twice a week on WSM and continued to enjoy a large audience. One devoted fan was a young James Blackwood who, because his Mississippi sharecropping parents did not own a radio set, walked a mile to a neighboring farm to hear the broadcast each Wednesday night and Thursday morning.

Vaughn and his company successfuly rode out the Depression. Attendance at the 1939 music schools broke all previous records. And alumni of the schools were now making an impact in Christian work. Before the thirties, the idea of making a career in a full-time gospel singing group was unknown, and so most people who attended the Vaughn schools studied to improve their usefulness in church or evangelistic ministry. Vaughn himself had provided tuition, lodging, meals, and even salaries for many students who would later be influential in their service for the Lord. He could never turn away a person who had talent or was in need. "They'll pay me some time," he would say.

A gifted songwriter himself, Vaughn composed more than five hundred hymns and gospel songs including "All Glory to Jesus," "I Dreamed I Searched Heaven for You," "If I Could Hear My Mother Pray Again," "I Need the Prayer," "Just One Way to the Gate," and "My Loved Ones Are Waiting for Me." His own favorite hymn was "Amazing Grace" which he often requested to be played at the gospel "singing conventions" that are a tradition across the South. When Vaughn made his own final journey on February 9, 1941, more than seven thousand people crowded into the Nazarene Tabernacle of Lawrenceburg for his memorial service. The preacher was the Rev. J.M. Allen who, fittingly, had been a member of the first professional Vaughn quartet in 1910 before going on to become a noted preacher in Georgia. "Thousands of students left his school prepared for Christian work and living through his love of humanity," Allen said of Vaughn, "He never turned them away, whether they had money to pay him or not. Many of his students went on to preach and sing the gospel. Truly his influence for good was far-reaching. He lived his religion every day."[59]

Homer Rodeheaver and KDKA

Of all the men who began their ministries working the "sawdust trail," none adapted more readily or successfully to the new age of mass communication than Homer Rodeheaver.[60] His early career reached the very top of last, best days of the old crusade evangelism. And when the opportunities presented by radio and the new mass media society came along he turned into a phenomenon, the first man in evangelical popular music to became a true media celebrity. As songleader for Billy Sunday, the greatest evangelist of his generation, Rodeheaver's name was already well known. But in contrast to his old boss who could not adapt to the new conditions, Rodeheaver thrived as never before. Not only was he the first man to broadcast a gospel song program on the radio in the early days of KDKA, he went on to host network programs carried by both NBC and CBS,[61] and to become a seminal figure in evangelical music publishing and recording, music education, and Bible conference ministry. As his own published collection of *Rodeheaver's Radio Songs* stated at the time, "He has introduced, popularized, and made phonograph records of more gospel songs than any other person."[62]

"Rody," as he was known to all, was born in 1880 about as far from cities and celebrities as it is possible to get—on a small farm in Simcoe Hollow, two miles over the southern Ohio hills from the post office at Union Furnace, and about forty miles from the West Virginia state line. His mother died when Rodeheaver was eight and his father, who owned a sawmill, thought the best thing he could do for his three sons—Yumbert, Joseph, and Homer—was put them to work. So in addition to his schooling, Rodeheaver would take the family's old blind mule to haul logs for the mill and drive a spike team in the coal mines. As boys are wont to do, however, the brothers found time for fun. Yumbert played the organ and liked to direct amateur plays; Homer, with his pleasing contralto voice, enjoyed singing and acting. The brothers also organized a band as Homer taught himself to play bass drum and cornet. Rodeheaver had an ear for music and for good harmony. Though he occasionally sang the mountain music popular in rural Tennessee, he liked best the spirituals that the local black boys his age would sing. "I much preferred the negro spirituals to the hill-billy songs. The hill-billy songs are mostly all melody, seldom even two part[s] and lack harmony, while the negro spiritual has rhythm, melody, and harmony. The spiritual stands in vivid contrast to the hill-billy ballad in that while the ballad tells a story of varied import, the spiritual has, as the name indicates, a definite religious purpose."[63]

In time, his two older brothers went on to college. At the urging of his brother Joe, young Homer finished high school at age sixteen and enrolled that year in Ohio Wesleyan University. Over the next years Rodeheaver would pay for his education by working for six months in the coal mines, sawmills and logging camps, and then going to school for the other six months of the year. His first college activity was to join the school band, playing the cornet but secretly wanting to try the slide trombone. When a classmate who had a trombone ran out of money and offered to sell the instrument for seven dollars, Rodeheaver bought it with some borrowed cash from his brothers. In later years that trombone was almost as famous as Rodeheaver. It was the very same trombone he carried with him to the Spanish-American War and the First World War, and on his worldwide Billy Sunday campaigns and network radio appearances.

Rodeheaver entered Ohio Wesleyan with the intention of becoming a lawyer. But his gift for "yelling" ultimately steered the young man into music evangelism. Early in his college career Rodeheaver was chosen as the school's yell leader—akin to a cheerleader today—because of his dynamic personality and ability to hold a crowd. When the evangelist R.A. Walton came to town for a two-week campaign he needed a songleader and inquired on campus about possible candidates. He was advised to speak with that young yell leader, Homer Rodeheaver—who took the songleading job and discovered he was as good at it. When the meetings were done Rodeheaver thought nothing more of it. But two years later the famed evangelist W.E. Biederwolf required the services of a temporary songleader. Rodeheaver was recommended, hired for two weeks—and stayed five years. Many years later, in 1923-24, the two men would be reunited for a worldwide tour with campaigns in Japan, Korea, and the Congo.

However, it was on a hot summer day in 1908 in Winfield, Kansas, that Billy Sunday first witnessed the almost magical way that Rodeheaver could rouse a crowd into full-throated song. That day he was leading a "community sing" at a Chatauqua meeting—not even a religious gathering—when Rodeheaver coaxed the perspiring crowd into such singing as Sunday himself had never heard before from an audience. From that moment, Sunday determined that Rody was the man he needed. A year later Rodeheaver joined the Sunday organization and, in the twenty years of their association, led an estimated seventy million people in song. When in 1917 the United States entered the First World War, he left Sunday for a time to entertain the troops in France as a Young Men's Christian Association (YMCA) representative. His sunny disposition and "talking" trombone (the same trombone he played in Cuba as a member of Fourth Tennessee Regiment Band during the Spanish-American War of 1898) became known to nearly every soldier.

After the armistice in 1918 he rejoined Billy Sunday and their crowds were larger than ever. Rodeheaver's evangelistic work afforded not only national notoriety and useful contacts, but also time in between campaigns to develop new avenues for music ministry. From his earliest days with Billy Sunday, he began to issue gospel songbooks for use in their campaigns. This soon grew into the founding in 1911 of the Rodeheaver Publishing Company with offices in Chicago. His motivation was not primarily to publish his own works but to bring good Christian music to the public. Throughout his career, Rodeheaver was less known as a song composer than as a songleader, radio personality, and publisher. Yet in the year that Rodeheaver founded his company, he published a song of his own that later became particularly associated with his ministry. The song, "Somebody Cares," was a favorite because it captured Rody's bright, optmistic view of life. "Somebody knows when your heart aches," the song begins, yet "Somebody knows when the shadows need chasing away...."

Phonograph records followed in the late 1910s, as Rodeheaver made some of the first commercial recordings of sacred and gospel music ever produced. Committed to using every possible means of disseminating the gospel in song, Rodeheaver was quick to embrace the new technology. The first records were a quarter of an inch thick and made for the old hand-cranked Edison phonograph. In later years he recorded 78s and LPs for the Victor, Columbia, and Decca labels. Among the songs composed by Rodeheaver himself, one of the best known releases, "You Must Open the Door," was issued by Decca Records in 1934. As the refrain reminds listeners, "When Jesus comes in He will save you from sin, but you must open the door."

Another outlet for Rodeheaver's growing ministry was provided through the annual Bible Conference in Winona Lake, Indiana. The idea for the conference originated with the Chatauqua movement of the late nineteenth century. To promote arts and culture for ordinary people, Chatauqua meetings would offer a week of lectures, concerts, and plays. Many sessions were held outdoors or in tents and other specially built structures. In 1894 a Presbyterian minister wanted to found a "religious Chatauqua" and purchased property at Winona Lake in northern Indiana. The meetings grew in popularity, drawing families from the surrounding areas and from nearby Chicago. Billy Sunday and his wife Nell built a home in Winona Lake in 1910, and Rodeheaver—who never married—purchased a house in 1912. He became active in the Bible Conference and, in 1925, established there a School of Sacred Music held each August. In the years to come, the school would be a mecca for the close fraternity of popular evangelical songwriters and composers of the day. Luminaries such as Benton and Alfred Ackley, Virgil and Blanche Brock, Merrill Dunlop, Harry Dixon Loes, George Bennard, and others served regularly as faculty. Many evangelists also came to the conferences to find singers, pianists, choir directors, and songleaders for their ministries. The two-week sessions, supervised by Rodeheaver himself, emphasized practical training and offered instruction in voice, organ and piano, instrumental music, choral conducting and songleading, hymn accompaniment and improvisation, and platform speech and decorum. Because the school was intended to equip students for lay ministry in churches, Rodeheaver invited local pastors and preachers to address a general forum on their music concerns. Another highlight was the afternoon platform hour when vocal soloists, women's trios, and men's quartets performed before the entire school and were critiqued by Rodeheaver.

The story behind one of Rodeheaver's most-requested songs illustrates the dynamism and excitement of the Winona Lake Bible Conference during its heyday.[64] One evening in the late thirties, the large Billy Sunday Tabernacle auditorium was crowded to capacity to hear evangelist Mel Trotter describe his recent crusade in the British Isles. But when Trotter noticed how many young people were in the audience, he decided instead to relate his own testimony—how he had been an alcoholic father who caused the death of his infant child, and at the brink of suicide was converted at Chicago's famed Pacific Garden Mission. Later that night at his home, Rainbow Point, Rodeheaver discussed the story with his friend Harry Rimmer who also was speaking at the Conference that week. Rimmer likened the story to that of Lazarus, who was dead but "then Jesus came and that changed everything." Another guest then exclaimed, "Why doesn't somebody write a song about that?" Unable to forget the suggestion, Rodeheaver was in his company's Philadelphia office the next week when in walked Oswald Smith, the Toronto preacher and songwriter. Smith happened to be speaking in Philadelphia and, on hearing the Trotter story from Rodeheaver, agreed to write the words for "Then Jesus Came." Before the day was over Smith had composed the lyrics, and immediately a melody came to Rodeheaver. That night in an evangelistic meeting Rody sang of a blind man who "sat alone beside the highway begging" until hearing the good news that "when Jesus comes the tears are wiped away."

In the early twenties—*Rodeheaver's Radio Songs* only puts the time as "the early days of Station KDKA"—Rodeheaver aired the first program of gospel songs ever heard on radio.[65] Whether this was a one-time broadcast or a regular program, the record does not state. But it began an association with radio that was to last for the rest of Rodeheaver's career. During the later twenties and thirties he would make literally hundreds of radio appearances on all the important stations in every major city of America, and would himself host a "community sing" program carried by the NBC and CBS networks. One of the songs that might have been featured on his first KDKA broadcasts is "Good Night and Good Morning." Rodeheaver composed the music in 1922—about the time of those "early days" at KDKA—and it became one of his most famous and best loved songs. Written by Lizzie DeArmond, who several months earlier had lost her daughter to a sudden illness, the words of hope came one night as she looked despairingly into the starry sky: "We'll say 'good-night' here but 'good-morning' up there."[66]

As the renown of both Rodeheaver and Sunday grew during the twenties, it affected each man differently. Rodeheaver moved easily into the world of radio, recordings, and publishing that were now opening up as America became a mass media society. All three media—broadcast, phonograph, and print—were interrelated as each reinforced the growth of the others. Rodeheaver could see that vision and seized upon it, but Sunday was finding it increasingly difficult to understand the changes. For one thing, radio and movies were competing for people's increasingly scarce leisure time. By the twenties, crowds at the Sunday campaigns were starting to diminish and invitations to hold meetings in major cities were not forthcoming. Characteristically, Sunday continued to preach as he always had. Yet now, even the roughest rural farmer could sit at home and hear the best radio speakers and presenters of the day. Sunday's style was not what people were growing accustomed to hearing on the radio. His manner of preaching did not translate well into the new medium and he did not attempt to alter it—as did other evangelists, such as Paul Rader and Bob Jones, when they began broadcast ministries.

In the early thirties, Sunday was approached by Hollywood about putting his message on film. Some advised him to leave the road and launch a radio ministry, and a New York station with listenership in the millions offered him a weekly time slot. Rodeheaver pled with his mentor to accept the movie offer and start a national radio program as a means to reach new audiences and build his base of support. Sunday emphatically rejected the motion picture proposal but agreed that radio could revolutionize evangelism and had "scarcely scratched the surface of its usefulness."[67] He made a 1934 appearance on the *Haven of Rest* radio program and a few others, attracting mail from New York and Boston to Virginia and Tennessee. But in the end he could not leave his beloved sawdust trail.

The coming of the new mass media society, and the mass audiences it afforded, also changed the way that an organization must be led and managed. A large staff was needed to do advance work for the campaigns but Sunday took no interest in this aspect of the ministry. Morale among the staff suffered and even Rodeheaver himself was disheartened when his boss would prance on the platform and appear fidgety and distracted during the song service. Then, too, as audiences grew in size and sophistication, Sunday was increasingly uncomfortable in "working the crowds" before and after meetings. Yet at the same time, he complained more and more vociferously in public about the "stinginess" of offerings. His altar calls became confused so that listeners sometimes did not know if the invitation was for the converted or unconverted. Sunday never wavered in his doctrine and later learned his lesson about the enticements of fame. But the independent style that served him in his earlier "sawdust" days was becoming out of place in the America of the radio age. In the mid-1920s he suffered a breakdown; his wife Nell, who directed the staff, began to experience ulcers. Rodeheaver expressed his concerns but, when things did not change, in 1929 he reluctantly decided to leave the Sunday organization. Six years later Billy Sunday died of a heart attack; Rodeheaver sang at his memorial service in Chicago's Moody Church.

By then, Rodeheaver was at the height of his fame and influence. He lamented what had been lost with the advent of mass communication: "We appreciate the radio, but must admit that it has taken from the young and old much of the initiative and desire for [music] participation.... Why learn the piano or violin when by simply turning a little knob you can bring into the home the masterpieces of music?"[68] But rather than indulge in nostalgia, he moved forward. By the thirties he was a staple on network radio. The School of Sacred Music was attracting some of the finest voice teachers in the world to serve as faculty. His records were selling well and his publishing concern had bought out two other companies—in the process becoming known as the Rodeheaver Hall-Mack Company with offices in Chicago and Philadelphia. In 1941 Rodeheaver moved the company headquarters to Winona Lake and purchased the Westminster Hotel to serve as its offices. The influence of the Rodeheaver Hall-Mack Company was profound, for the list of writers whose careers were introduced and songs popularized through its publishing efforts is a "who's who" of popular evangelical songwriters and composers.

In the 1960s, the Rodeheaver Hall-Mack Company was acquired by Word Music. The heyday of the Winona Lake Bible Conference passed into history and the School of Sacred Music ultimately ended in the sixties. By then the exciting days of which Rodeheaver had played such a part were only a memory. He himself had passed away December 18, 1955, at the age of seventy-five. Sadly, his beloved trombone had gone before him, stolen in 1952 and never recovered. After that, friends could see that Rody's performances were never quite the same. Yet his legacy endures. Rodeheaver is remembered for his music and for the bright, cheery attitude he always displayed. (Decades later, George Beverly Shea recalled his "huge smiles" and that Rodeheaver "seemed eternally happy to me."[69]) Sometimes he was criticized for including "light" songs in his meetings and crusades. "Brighten the Corner Where You Are" was one of his favorites and, presaging a music philosophy that many evangelists carried over into radio, he later recalled,

> We used many other [choruses in the Sunday crusades] ... but none were universally popular as "Brighten the Corner Where You Are." It was not written for a devotional song, and we were criticized for introducing a song of this kind into a religious service; but those who criticized never [k]new the real pupose back of it. It was never intended for a Sunday morning service nor for a devotional meeting—its purpose was to bridge that gap between the popular song of the day and the great hymns and gospel songs, and to give men [sic] a simple, easy, lilting melody which they could learn the first time they heard it, and which they could whistle and sing wherever they might be.[70]

Undaunted by criticism of his "light" approach to life, Rodeheaver chose the rainbow as his emblem. He named his Winona Lake home Rainbow Point, his custom music label Rainbow Records, his Music School auditorium the Rainbow Room, and a Florida home for boys founded in the 1940s as Rainbow Ranch. The symbol was even incorporated into the logo of his publishing company. Why? In his early campaigning days, at the Billy Sunday Philadelphia Crusade of 1915, he introduced to a simple chorus—also written by Lizzie DeArmond, who lived in nearby Swarthmore—whose refrain Rodeheaver never forgot and by which he lived his life: "Every cloud will wear a rainbow if your heart keeps right!"

Two

The Thirties
Preachers and Programs

WALTER MAIER ALREADY HAD FIVE YEARS of broadcasting experience when in 1929 he walked into the New York offices of the Columbia Broadcasting System.[1] Excited about what he called "the miracle of radio," he believed the time was right for a nationwide program dedicated to "preaching an authentic Christianity." Network radio offered a national outreach that his own small Missouri station, tucked away in a makeshift studio on the grounds of his seminary campus, could never hope to match. With radio, everything seemed possible—except that CBS was now asking him to do the seemingly *impossible*. Network executives were willing to sell him airtime for a half-hour weekly program, but at a cost of two hundred thousand dollars for one season. That was a staggering, unimaginable sum of money. Could Maier take such an incredible leap of faith? CBS respected his experience and sincerity, but doubted whether thirty minutes of preaching and church music would attract an audience. Was he foolish, reckless, or even vain, to think he could succeed?

Yet Maier recalled his first experience with radio. It was in 1922 at the annual youth league convention of his denomination, the Lutheran Church Missouri Synod (LCMS). By age twenty-nine he had recently graduated from Concordia Seminary, been ordained, earned a masters degree in Old Testament and Semitics from Harvard, and then elected national leader of the LCMS youth league. His keynote address was carried by the local radio station in Louisville, Kentucky, site of that year's convention. Soon afterward, Maier accepted a professorship at Concordia. But his turn for scholarship was coupled with a burning burning desire to reach lost souls. The Louisville radio broadcast was still on his mind when in 1924 he met a young St. Louis engineer who was also interested in the new medium. So the two men proposed to the seminary president that, if he would agree to have a radio station on campus, Maier would raise the funds. Since he was still editor of the LCMS youth league magazine, one of the largest evangelical journals in the nation, Maier could appeal to his readers for help. Within a few months the goal was met, and by December 1924 KFUO was on the air. Though the call letters were assigned by the government, Maier triumphantly declared that the new radio station would "Keep Forward Upward Onward!"

The next years were busy ones. Maier's Hebrew class was said to be the largest in America. He was in great demand as a conference speaker, even as he continued to edit the youth journal and study toward a Harvard doctorate. Yet he was always at the microphone for his two weekly radio programs on KFUO. For most men this would have been enough. But Maier's vision reached far beyond the walls of his seminary. The potential outreach of network radio was enormous. But two hundred thousand dollars? After the news of October 29, 1929, the nation was in a financial panic. They called it "Black Tuesday," the Great Stock Market Crash that ushered in what economists were calling a "depression." How could Maier obtain two hundred thousand dollars? Yet he believed that God was still in control of the economy. If God had moved on the hearts of the CBS executives to offer Maier a half-hour of network radio time, then he would also supply the financial need. So Maier signed the CBS contract. The Lutheran Laymen's League, the national organization of LCMS laity, agreed to sponsor the broadcast. A fundraising campaign brought in nearly one hundred thousand dollars, only half the total needed for the year but enough to get the program started. Maier took it as a sign to proceed, trusting God to build a listening audience sufficient to support the broadcast with its contributions.

On a chilly Thursday night, October 2, 1930, listeners across the country tuned in *The Lutheran Hour* for the first time on the CBS radio network. Since the KFUO studio at Concordia Seminary was too small, Maier arranged to broadcast from WHK in Cleveland. He planned a brief opening announcement, then ten minutes of classical church music by the Cleveland Bach Chorus, concluding with a nineteen-minute sermon from the Word of God. When the engineer gave Maier his cue, he quickly warmed to his message. Boldly declaring that *The Lutheran Hour* was dedicated "to the fundamental conviction that there is a God," he addressed himself to a nation that was struggling desperately for answers in the depths of its greatest Depression. "In the crises of life and the pivotal hours of existence," Maier told his audience,

> only the Christian—having God and, with Him, the assurance that no one can successfully prevail against him—is able to carry the pressing burden of sickness, death, financial reverses, family troubles, misfortunes of innumerable kinds and degrees, and yet to bear all this with the undaunted faith and Christian confidence that alone make life worth living and death worth dying.[2]

In just eight weeks, more letters were pouring in to *The Lutheran Hour* than to *Amos 'n' Andy*. By the end of the season CBS estimated Maier was reaching a national weekly audience of more than five million listeners—a stunning outreach for a small denomination whose total membership was less than two million. Contributions averaged two thousand dollars a week, enough to sustain the broadcast. Skeptics were incredulous. But letters from listeners of all denominations praised *The Lutheran Hour* for its clear message and emphasis on traditional Christian beliefs. Maier's "vigorous reassertion of classic Christianity," as he put it, had struck a responsive chord. Thus did Walter Maier became the first "big name" preacher on network radio. At the height of his ministry *The Lutheran Hour* was heard in thirty-six languages on more than twelve hundred stations with an estimated potential worldwide audience of nearly seven hundred million listeners.

Radio in the Thirties

If radio's golden age lasted until the advent of television, the luster of that age shone brightest in the thirties.[3] Popular offerings included "general variety" programs (the first such broadcast debuted in October 1929 with Rudy Vallee as host and Fleischmann Yeast as sponsor) and "semivariety" that combined talk and entertainment (Ed Sullivan, who went on the air in 1931, was among the earliest). As for music, Depression-era listeners generally preferred light music built around popular bands and singers, including a young Bing Crosby who made his first radio appearance in 1931. "Comedy variety" programs also drew large audiences. Jack Benny, George Burns and Gracie Allen, Eddie Cantor, and Ed Wynn all got their starts in the early thirties. "Situation comedy," in which regular characters encountered various predicaments each week, was introduced in 1929 with *Amos 'n' Andy* starring Freeman Gosden and Charles Correll. Western drama came to the airwaves in 1930 with *Death Valley Days*, while a year later *Sherlock Holmes* aired as the first crime drama. *Little Orphan Annie*, based on a newspaper comic strip, in 1931 began the genre of children's adventure serials. And daytime soap operas gained wide popularity when *The Romance of Helen Trent* debuted in 1933. Broadcast news came of age in 1932 with radio coverage of the sensational kidnapping of the baby of Charles Lindbergh, the famed aviator. When the listening public eagerly snatched up the latest radio news bulletins—even when these interrupted their favorite entertainment programs—the networks learned that their ability to transmit breaking news instantly was a powerful programming tool and a decided advantage over newspapers. The 1935 trial of suspected kidnapper Bruno Hauptmann was perhaps the nation's first "media circus." And the eyewitness radio report of the 1937 *Hindenburg* disaster remains one of the most powerful news accounts ever recorded.

Radio programming in its golden age was unlike the niche formats known today in which stations air the same content—Top 40, rock, country, oldies—all day long. Instead, radio was more like television is today, as people had their favorite weekly programs or simply tuned in to hear "what was on." And as the thirties progressed a lot was on, indeed. Popular music programs ranged from *Your Hit Parade* and *National Barn Dance* to the immensely popular *Major Bowes and His Original Amateur Hour*. Soaps ran the gamut from *Back Stage Wife* to *The Guiding Light*. Children of the thirties thrilled to the adventures of *Tom Mix, Captain Midnight, Terry and the Pirates, Dick Tracy, Buck Rogers, The Lone Ranger, The Green Hornet,* and *Jack Armstrong—The All-American Boy*. For crime drama, *The Shadow* and *Gangbusters* set the standard. "Serious" anthology dramas also had a following with programs such as *Lux Radio Theater, Columbia Workshop,* and *Mercury Theater of the Air* (creators of the famous 1938 "War of the Worlds" broadcast starring Orson Welles). On the lighter side, comedy with the likes of *Fibber McGee and Molly*, Edgar Bergen and Charlie McCarthy, Fred Allen, Bob Hope, and Jimmy Durante delighted thirties audiences.

The thirties witnessed other important developments in radio. Congress established the Federal Communications Commission in 1934 as a permanent agency, replacing the old Federal Radio Commission which needed to be reauthorized each year. In 1935 inventor Edwin Armstrong first demonstrated FM radio and then built the first FM station in 1938, though FM would not become important until the 1970s. And a new type of phonograph record, introduced in 1933, spun at 33 rpm with fifteen minutes of sound on disks up to sixteen inches in diameter. While these "long-play" records did not reach the consumers until the early fifties and radio networks did not allow prerecorded or "transcribed" programs until the late 1940s, the disks provided local stations with better music and improved programming flexibility. Yet perhaps the greatest technical innovation in radio during the thirties was the smallest and least expensive. In 1933 the Emerson Radio Company introduced the tabletop radio. By the end of the decade such models sold for less than ten dollars, had captured eighty percent of the market, and prompted many households to buy more than one set. In 1935, radios with easy-to-read dials and antennas for improved reception came on the market. By the late thirties, portable battery-operated radios and car radios were widely available. Radio ownership doubled between 1930 and 1938, and in 1941 sets could be found in more than eighty percent of American homes.

Seen in this context of proliferating radio programming choices, the accomplishment of Walter Maier was all the more outstanding. How did he, and the other great radio preachers of the day, attract mass audiences? These evangelists, of course, would credit the power of the Word of God. Yet even though far more religious programming is available today on radio (and television) than was ever heard in the thirties and forties, audience share is not nearly as high. Why? Today's proliferation of channels and stations has "fragmented" (to use the industry term) the audience. Special interest or "niche" programming has been "ghettoized" so that popular evangelical fare is largely confined to evangelical outlets that primarily attract committed evangelical listeners and viewers. In the days of Walter Maier and his contemporaries—indeed, until the growth of cable television in 1980s—national programming was only available on three major networks. This guaranteed access to a potentially large audience but also dictated the manner in which programs such as *The Old Fashioned Revival Hour* and *Young People's Church of the Air* were presented to the public. Today, popular evangelical radio and TV programs are geared to the expectations of evangelical audiences. But in the golden age of radio, preachers were compelled to use formats that appealed to all listeners. As such, music played a significant role in the success of these ministries. "Radio gospel broadcasts require an entirely new technique," declared gospel songwriter Phil Kerr in a 1939 essay. "Methods of conducting evangelistic campaigns which were entirely successful in generations past may possibly be entirely valueless in this modern radio age."[4] He then went on to explain that

> musical features were a tremendous attraction in the days of old-fashioned revival campaigns.... But in this modern radio age the humblest home in the remotest region of America is constantly filled with the highest-grade music and entertainment.... If the religious program is inferior to the secular program on an adjacent wavelength, what is to prevent the listener from seeking the better program?[5]

Since most Americans do not want to go to church, Kerr advised, neither do they want to hear a church radio service. Because "the average dialer will refuse to listen to any radio program which is even slightly religious," he continued, successful broadcast ministries were those that could "catch [the listener] off guard, suddenly capture his interest, and *hold* his interest long enough to give him the gospel message."[6] Effective evangelical radio programs would "begin with a musical selection, perhaps instrumental, which is beautiful enough and interesting enough to attract his attention," Kerr pointed out. Next up was "a vocal selection, of the very best talent available, and well-rehearsed." Spoken introductions to songs should be short or omitted, and "rarely are more than two stanzas required."[7] Then, having gotten the listener's attention,

> Make a bid for his further interest by telling a story, leading up to a spiritual climax. Then, before he gets the idea that you're *preaching*, suddenly present another musical feature, this time perhaps a more serious number.... [Next] offer a brief message, short and directly to the point, keeping in mind the thought that you are speaking to *one person*.... Speak in a conversational tone, giving him to understand that you have great respect for his intelligence. By doing so, you'll have a much greater

chance of holding his attention than by treating him as a worthless, unintelligent reprobate who needs to be *shouted at* and *preached at!*[8]

The best gospel radio broadcasts of the day would then conclude, Kerr noted, with "possibly a brief prayer [and] another musical number; then perhaps an announcement of the church which is sponsoring the program, and an invitation to listen to the next broadcast."[9] There in a nutshell were the ingredients of popular evangelical radio: an attention-getting musical opening, relevent storytelling, a conversational message that speaks directly to each listener, and a brief musical close. It was the format followed by Walter Maier, Charles Fuller, Percy Crawford, Theodore Epp, Paul Myers and the best-rated gospel radio ministries of the era. Compelling Christian music was a vital component, broadly popularized by singing groups—such as the Old Fashioned Revival Hour Quartet, Back to the Bible Quartet, and Haven of Rest Quartet—that became nearly as famous and eagerly followed as the preachers themselves. "If the powerful medium of radio can be used to exploit coffee and toothpaste and automobiles and tobacco and breakfast food," Kerr pleaded, "then certainly Christian soul-winners should awaken to the tremendous opportunity of using radio to attract men and women to the gospel of Jesus Christ!"[10] During the thirties, preachers used the medium of network radio to do just that.

Charles Fuller and the Old-Fashioned Revival Hour

As a boy, Charles Fuller wasn't much interested in spiritual things. He was interested in gopher tails. When his father Henry Fuller sold the family's Los Angeles furniture store in 1893 to start an orange grove near Redlands, he decreed that his three sons must do their share of the work. Because six-year-old Charles was the youngest, he was given the job of setting gopher traps. And for each gopher tail he brought home, his father would pay him a dime.[11]

Henry and Helen Fuller were devout Methodists. Each day they gathered their sons for family devotions as father read the scriptures and mother played an old pump organ while the boys would sing. But Charles was more interested in hunting rabbits, playing pranks, sleeping under the orange groves—and in gopher tails. Once he saved his dimes to buy a watch and another time to buy a shotgun of his own. And when he was in high school he used his gopher money to buy a telegraph set from a mail-order catalog. Charles taught himself Morse code and even strung telegraph wires throughout the Fuller ranch house so he could send messages to his brothers. He ran a wire out to the mailbox so the postman could ring a buzzer when mail arrived. And after school he practiced sending real messages from the nearby Southern Pacific railway station where the manager was glad to oblige. As a senior in high school Charles even set up the first wireless telegraph in Redlands. One day that summer he picked up a news flash that a congressman had caught a three hundred-pound bass off Catalina Island. His father didn't believe it, but the next day's *Los Angeles Times* confirmed the report. "Well, I'll be jiggered," his father laughed.

Henry Fuller was intensely interested in foreign missions, an interest kindled through the work of A.B. Simpson, founder of the Christian and Missionary Alliance. In 1902 his "Fuller's Fancy Oranges" were selling so well that he decided to take a trip around the world, bringing along his second son Leslie who was planning to enter the ministry. Afterward, his dispatches to the local Redlands newspaper were printed as a book, *A Californian Circling the Globe*. Impressed by his father's firsthand descriptions of foreign missions, the now-teenage Charles began to feel he too might someday be a missionary. In 1906, however, Fuller entered Pomona College and was soon engrossed in varsity football, track, and debate. His major was chemistry—a useful skill for an orange grower—and his professors' views of evolution contradicted the faith of his parents. By his senior year Fuller was both football captain and class president, graduating in 1910 with *cum laude* honors—and having forgotten about being a missionary.

Fuller's high school sweetheart, Grace Payton, had likewise drifted from her parents' Baptist faith and accepted Unitarianism while attending the University of Chicago. But before she could finish her studies, her father died and Grace, an only child, returned home to be with her mother. During those trying days a friend of her mother who was an evangelical Christian would frequently visit. One day she quoted to Grace the words of Jesus: "No man cometh unto the Father but by me" (John 14:6). In that moment Grace was converted and, as she recounted later, "I instantly became a new creature in Christ."[12]

After Charles and Grace were married in 1911, the Fullers set up house in Redlands. Charles went to work for his father as a day laborer and also supplemented his income by selling fertilizers. A year later the couple saved enough money to buy a ten-acre orange grove of their own. Everything was looking up and financial security seemed assured, until a cold north wind blew into Redlands in January 1913. Temperatures plunged to thirteen degrees, not only wiping out the year's crop but killing the trees themselves. The Fullers lost everything. But an orange packing house in Placentia was looking for a manager and hired Fuller at one hundred dollars a month. Within a few days the twenty-seven-year-old Fuller had so impressed his employers that they raised his salary to one hundred fifty dollars. Fuller even partnered with another man to form a profitable trucking company. And within the year, he had attained an important position in the community as an elder of the Placentia Presbyterian Church.

Yet it was Grace Fuller who manifested the most interest in spiritual matters. She wanted to attend church regularly, while her husband at times preferred to stay home and read the Sunday paper. When she began attending a Thursday night Bible study in Anaheim, Charles would drive her there and then go to a movie. And while he enjoyed playing cards at a local club, she felt a conviction against joining him. It would take another tragic loss—not of an orange grove, but of their first child—to begin Fuller's turn toward God. During his wife's pregnancy, toxemia set in and the child was stillborn. Grace herself contracted tuberculosis and became an invalid for the next three and a half years. To escape the stifling summer heat she would often go with her mother to one of the lodges at Big Bear Lake in the San Bernardino Mountains. For Fuller these were lonesome months. Work at the packing house occupied him from Monday to Saturday. But on Sundays after church he had little to do. Then one Saturday—July 29, 1916—he read in the local newspaper that Paul Rader would be preaching the next day at the Church of the Open Door in Los Angeles. Not only was Rader a famous evangelist, but he was a former athlete like Fuller. So the young packing-house manager from Placentia decided to go and hear this "new Elijah."

Rader's text that Sunday morning was taken from Ephesians 1:18, "The eyes of your understanding being enlightened; that ye may know what is the hope of his calling, and what the riches of the glory of his inheritance in the saints." His message, entitled "Out of the Cave," implored listeners to forsake their blindness, convert to Christ and, guided by the indwelling of the Holy Spirit, emerge into the light and claim the blessings God desired to give them. Fuller realized he was still blind, living in a cave. Trembling and coming under a powerful conviction, he bowed his head on the pew in front of him. He did not respond to the preacher's invitation at the close of the service. Instead Fuller drove out to Franklin Park in nearby Hollywood and parked his car under a eucalyptus tree. There he knelt on the floor of the back seat of the car and, after converting to Christ, remained in prayer until it was time to return for the afternoon service.

The change in Fuller was immediate and dramatic. Excited to share his newfound faith with others, he started teaching a new Sunday school class at his church in Placentia—at eight in the morning, *before* the normal Sunday school program began. At times, he and Grace would leave after class and drive to Los Angeles for services at the Church of the Open Door to hear the preaching of Reuben Torrey, a longtime associate of the late Dwight L. Moody. Often during the week the couple would read and study Christian books together. In time, Fuller became restless about his work at the packing house which he began to see "as just a continuous whirlygig and year-round race to get a cent a box more for the growers' fruit, and when it was all said and done, not much was accomplished for eternity."[13]

In the spring of 1919 he felt a growing conviction that he should give his life to Christian service. But how could he resign his position? He and Grace had just put down five thousand dollars to buy a twenty-acre orange grove. How would he make the payments? "Oh, Lord, I will walk in your path," he prayed one April morning at the packing house. "I will even try to preach. I will resign my position and trust you to supply our needs as I prepare for the ministry."[14] Feeling at peace, a few days later he notified his employers of his decision. That summer, his small orange grove did not yield enough fruit to make the yearly payment. But an oil well had recently been discovered north of town and an oil company offered Fuller twenty thousand dollars for rights to drill on their property. The company never did drill, but the money was Charles Fuller's to keep; it cleared the way for him to enroll in the Bible Institute of Los Angeles that fall.

During his two years at "Biola," Fuller remained an elder of the Placentia Presbyterian Church and in 1920 was asked to teach the adult Sunday school class. By the next spring, about the time Fuller graduated from the Bible Institute, his Placentia Bible Class had outgrown the 125-seat sanctuary of the church and decided to meet in a nearby community clubhouse. The group even voted to support an independent missionary. These actions disturbed some of the elders who felt the class was becoming too separate from the church. When a new pastor was called to the church in 1923, he addressed the situation by suggesting a new adult Sunday school class be organized that would meet at the church. Fuller did not know of the decision until it was announced and he was told that his class was no longer part of the church. Unsure of what to do, Fuller submitted the matter to a vote of the Placentia Bible Class. Some decided to return to the official Sunday school but most voted to continue. Fuller accepted the vote and resigned his eldership. By now, his vision was reaching beyond his hometown. In 1924 the Placentia Bible Class started advertising in the *Fullerton Tribune*. In the spring of 1925 a youth crusade sponsored by the class resulted in more than forty conversions. Thus the group now faced the need to organize a children's Sunday school alongside its own meetings. In April the Placentia Bible Class voted to form Calvary Church. Having resigned from the Presbyterian church, Fuller obtained ordination from the Baptist Bible Union and in May accepted the call to Calvary.

Fuller's orange grove was now producing enough income so that he could serve as Calvary's pastor without salary. But he believed this also freed him to undertake other evangelistic endeavors that were close to his heart. Soon he was in demand as a conference and crusade speaker. In 1926 he became a field representative for Biola and, a year later, a member of its board of trustees. Among these new outreaches was radio, the medium in which Fuller had been so interested as a boy. On March 10, 1922, Biola went on the air with KJS, a 750-watt facility believed to be the first exclusively religious station in America. Some trustees were wary of the venture, afraid it would draw funds away from other projects, encourage some churchgoers to stay home on Sundays, and did not permit converts to be followed up in person. Besides, should Christians use an instrument associated with worldly entertainments—or even use the airwaves at all, since Satan was "the prince of the power of the air" (Ephesians 2:2)? Yet when conversion testimonies started arriving from KJS listeners as far away as Mexico and Hawaii, skeptics warmed to the new outreach. Fuller himself began his radio career in 1924 when he broadcast Bible lessons two mornings a week over KJS (renamed KTBI in 1925).

Elevated to chairman of the Biola board of trustees in the fall of 1928, Fuller now traveled frequently to visit supporters and recruit new faculty and administrators. In February 1929 he accepted an invitation to speak at a Defenders of the Christian Faith Conference in Indianapolis where he would share the platform with Paul Rader, now a well-known radio evangelist. During the meeting and without advance notice, Fuller was asked to substitute for the regular speaker on a local gospel radio program. He took as his text Mark 4:35–41, the story of how Jesus calmed the raging sea. His four points—Great Peril, Great Plea, Great Peace, Great Personage—were necessarily straightforward and direct, given the lack of time for preparation. So Fuller and the regular program speaker were surprised at the large volume of letters and calls received in response to what had been a very simple message. The Indianapolis conference continued through the week, after which Fuller stopped briefly in Philadelphia to preach two Sunday services. On the train home to California, however, he suddenly awoke in his Pullman berth—later he put the date at Monday, February 11, 1929—with the overwhelming impression that God wanted him to begin a regular preaching ministry on the radio at the earliest opportunity. He wrestled for a time that night with the decision but at last said yes to God, then turned over in his berth and slept peacefully until morning.

Fuller's opportunity soon presented itself when the *Santa Ana Register* newspaper built a new radio station, KREG, that was dedicated to culturally uplifting programming. Religious programs were part of this mission and the station offered Fuller a one-hour time slot each Sunday at eight to broadcast his evening service. A radio fund was established at Calvary Church to pay for the airtime, at the rate of one hundred eighty dollars. On February 23, 1930, the inaugural broadcast prominently featured music—a vocal solo by the wife of renowned gospel songwriter Robert Harkness, plus a marimba solo by Leland Green—and a sermon by Fuller on "The Greatest Peril of the Hour." After two months, response to the program encouraged Fuller to contract for an additional hour of airtime. Following the Calvary evening service, he would continue for a second hour with a program of special music by the young people of the church. For this *Happy Hour* broadcast he also had a telephone installed in the pulpit so that in between musical numbers he could answer Bible questions from listeners—which poured in faster than he could handle. But the weak signal of KREG greatly limited its reach. To solve the problem, Fuller in September 1930 switched to KGER, a thousand-watt station in Long Beach. Further, he contracted to air both the Sunday morning and evening services at Calvary Church. Responses came from Idaho, Washington, and Iowa. By the next year Fuller was emboldened to also begin the *Calvary Church Radio Bible Class* each Thursday morning from eight to nine. When the Depression forced Biola in 1931 to close its radio station, Fuller tried to make up the loss by launching *The Pilgrim's Hour*. The half-hour weekly program was carried by the seven stations of the Columbia Broadcasting System's Pacific Coast Network, from San Diego to Seattle, until lack of response (due to an undesirable time slot) forced cancellation two months later.

Though the excitement of the radio broadcasts helped fill the pews at Calvary Church, Fuller's commitments were pulling his time—and his heart—away from a strictly local pastoral ministry. As he developed a radio following in Long Beach, the church in Placentia was gravitating toward its youth director who felt a clear call to service in a local church. Thus Fuller relinquished his pulpit in March 1933. Calvary Church called its youth director to be pastor and, voting "to put the church program on a basis of strict economy," canceled the radio broadcasts. "Charles Fuller's constant urge to extend his ministry," as his son Daniel later wrote, "had finally made it impossible for him to work from a church as his base of operations."[15]

Throughout the twenties, Fuller had prospered through California land speculation. Ultimately he built the family an oceanfront vacation home in Newport Beach and bought a cabin on Bluff Lake in the San Bernardino Mountains. But as the Depression worsened in the first years of the thirties, some of Fuller's speculations went sour. Worse, in the summer of 1930 the Fuller's five-year-old son Daniel came down with whooping cough and bronchitis, serious infectious diseases in those days before antibiotics. The trials mounted until, the very day in January 1932 that Fuller sat in a lawyer's office to avert the loss of his home, he received word that his son was near death. His first reaction was, "Oh Lord, I have tried to serve you, but if you take our little boy I'm through!" But as he drove back to Placentia his heart changed and he surrendered to whatever God might bring. "Yes, Lord, Thy ways are always best. I yield to Thee and want Thy will done."[16] By the time Fuller reached home, Daniel had no discernible pulse and the doctor ordered an ambulance to rush him to a hospital in Los Angeles. Charles and Grace implored God to intervene, even as they both told the Lord that he might take their son if that was his will. However, the Fullers felt God answered their prayers when the mucus plug blocking Daniel's bronchial tubes dissolved of itself and he revived.

Later that year, 1932, Fuller decided to cut his losses, liquidate his properties, and cash in his wife's inheritance to pay off their debts. Now at least the slate would be clean and the couple could start over. It proved just as well that Fuller should be rid of these entanglements; when he decided in March 1933 to pick up the Calvary Church radio contracts and continue them on his own, a worse time to launch an independent ministry could not be imagined. On March 6—the day after his final sermon at Calvary—President Franklin Roosevelt closed all of the nation's banks to prevent a financial panic. Then on March 11 a powerful earthquake struck Long Beach, killing 115 people and causing forty million dollars in damage. The next day as U.S. Marines patrolled the streets to prevent looting, Fuller had to argue with a sergeant before being allowed to enter the KGER studio for his first independent Sunday broadcast. During the program Fuller felt a powerful aftershock rock the floor beneath him. He looked out the studio window to see the radio tower swaying dangerously back and forth. For weeks afterward he received letters from worried listeners who heard him cry "Look out!" over the live microphone.

Two months later, in May 1933, Fuller recruited a board of directors and incorporated the Gospel Broadcasting Association; its first fundraising letter went out in September. Then in November, a Saturday evening program called the *Sunday School Hour* was added over KFI in Los Angeles, a fifty thousand-watt station that could be heard in eleven western states and Canada. The new broadcast was intended to help Sunday school teachers prepare for their lessons the following day and encourage all listeners to teach the Word and win souls. Within a month, listeners were responding—and sending donations—from as far away as New York, Pennsylvania, and the South. Thus Fuller was now broadcasting four times a week including the three KGER programs, *Radio Bible Class* on Thursday nights and preaching broadcasts each Sunday morning and evening.

In March 1934 the Sunday night program was switched to KNX in Hollywood, which at fifty thousand watts was ten times more powerful than KGER. Then in October, Fuller rented the Women's Club House in Hollywood and invited listeners to attend the broadcast every Sunday night that month for an "old-fashioned revival hour." When only fifty people showed up in the thousand-seat auditorium, Fuller pleaded for volunteers to sing in the choir. But while the turnout was disappointing, radio audiences reported having the impression of listening to a packed house. And that was the first "Old Fashioned Revival Hour," though at the time Fuller used the name *Radio Revival Hour*. The Thursday *Radio Bible Class* was also switched to KNX and a Tuesday edition added, prompting Fuller in 1936 to cancel the *Sunday School Hour*. That year, however, KNX was acquired by CBS which had a policy of not selling airtime for paid religious programs. As an alternative, Fuller bought time on seven independent stations that would actually provide better coverage than KNX. To be able to buy the best time slots available, he used a new technology called "electrical transcriptions" to prerecord his programs and send the long-play disks to the radio programs. Within a few months, transcription disks were being sent to more than a dozen stations—at the time, the greatest use that anyone was making of the new long-play technology. The decision to use independent stations also boosted listenership. By 1936 the airwaves were filled with stations. Most people, rather than trying to pick up faraway stations, were now more interested in tuning to local stations of their own. However, buying time not on one station but on a dozen outlets significantly increased Fuller's costs. Mobilizing his new listeners to sustain the broadcasts would be important—and would require something new. Fuller needed a corps of faithful supporters at each station location. Since commercial air transportation was now becoming widely available he could fly—to Seattle, Portland, Boise, Salt Lake City, Albuquerque—for public meetings and return to Los Angeles in time for his live Sunday morning broadcast on KGER.

Though the two original networks, NBC and CBS, refused to sell airtime for paid religious programs, a third network debuted in 1934 that needed the money and was willing to deal with Fuller. Beginning in January 1937 he therefore secured time for the *Radio Revival Hour* on fourteen outlets—from San Francisco to Chicago—of the new Mutual Broadcasting System. For the first two months, response encouraged Fuller to consider extending his network to the East Coast. By spring, however, donations were down and the possibility had to be weighed of cutting back his coverage to California only. Fuller stuck with it, though, trusting in God to maintain his current network. Yet by summer's end a new crisis emerged. A tobacco company had told Mutual it wanted the *Radio Revival Hour's* prime Sunday evening one-hour time slot. And they were willing to sign a contract to buy time on *all* of Mutual's affiliates, coast to coast, starting in October. Unless Fuller was willing to do the same, he would be canceled. Fuller's radio agent fully expected to concede defeat. How could the ministry afford to jump from the sixteen stations it was currently on, to ninety or more? The cost of airtime would jump from $1,441 a week to $4,500. "Do you think you can make it, Charlie," the agent asked. "No," Fuller replied, "but God can."[17] In the end, he cut a deal to relinquish his time slot if Mutual would sell him an earlier Sunday spot and allow him to expand nationwide on a gradual basis. Mutual agreed and, as it turned out, the earlier slot actually worked out even better for Fuller. The old spot of 7:30 Pacific time would have been 10:30 on the East Coast, but the new six o'clock slot would only be nine in East. For the first broadcast under the new contract, October 3, 1937, Fuller renamed his program the *Old Fashioned Revival Hour*. He increased his outreach to thirty stations, going "coast-to-coast" for the first time by securing time on a Mutual outlet in Boston. Six weeks later, the *Old Fashioned Revival Hour* was being heard on eighty-eight stations to an estimated weekly audience of ten million listeners.

For that first nationwide broadcast of the *Old Fashioned Revival Hour*, Fuller chose as his opening theme music the rousing hymn, "Jesus Saves." To him, the phrases "Spread the tidings all around," "Tell to sinners far and wide," and especially "Give the winds a mighty voice," captured what gospel radio ministry was all about. In addition to an attention-getting opening theme, Fuller knew he needed better and more varied music for a successful network broadcast. Out of that desire came the Old Fashioned Revival Hour Quartet and its pianist, Rudy Atwood, who all went on to longtime recording careers.[18] Yet the group actually had its roots (as did Fuller himself) in the ministry of Paul Rader. After Rader founded the Chicago Gospel Tabernacle, a counterpart work in Los Angeles named the Paul Rader Tabernacle was begun under Josiah Hogg, who in turn brought Atwood and the quartet onto his staff. Then in 1933 Hogg founded the Country Church of Hollywood, gaining local fame through an unusual radio broadcast (actually begun during Hogg's days with Rader in Chicago) aired each morning at eight. Hogg would portray the fictional "Parson Hopkins" while Atwood and the quartet would play the parts of Tennessee bumpkins on the way to "go to meetin.'" After the sketch, the broadcast would shift to the service itself, featuring music and then a message.

In their days with the Country Church of Hollywood, the four men were known as the Goose Creek Quartet. When Fuller asked them and Atwood to join his staff, they became simply the Old Fashioned Revival Hour Quartet. The original members were Bill MacDougall, first tenor; John Knox, second tenor; Al Harlan, baritone; and Arthur Jaissle, bass. For many years the group maintained a dual ministry with both the Country Church and the *Old Fashioned Revival Hour*. The quartet made numerous recordings for the Victor, Christian Faith, and Word labels—some of which have been reissued on compact disc and are sold today. They were featured on the broadcast until February 1958 when the network reduced all programs to thirty minutes. Jaissle remained with the quartet throughout its existence and later became an executive with an evangelical book publisher. The final group, which made most of quartet's recordings, also included first tenor John Lundberg, who later headed the music department of Westmont College; second tenor Jack Coleman, who went on to be director of a music company; and baritone Kenneth Brown, who entered business. Rudy Atwood, who released numerous solo albums on the Christian Faith label, continued with the *Old Fashioned Revival Hour* even after Fuller's passing in 1968. An ordained minister, he later served as youth director for a Baptist church in California.

Throughout 1937, Fuller gradually increased his network to 108 stations. Then came word from Mutual that he must expand to all 128 network outlets in order to hold his time slot. By then, to build up and secure his base of support, Fuller and his team decided to occasionally do broadcasts from other cities. Now that they were "live" on a network, the *Old Fashioned Revival Hour* could originate from anywhere—and during the 1937–38 season the program was broadcast from packed auditoriums in Des Moines, Chicago, and Detroit. To keep his prime-time spot, Fuller believed the music on the program needed to be further upgraded. In 1938 he asked Leland Green to join the permanent staff and assemble an Old Fashioned Revival Hour Choir made up of professional-quality, dedicated singers who would be paid a small salary for each Sunday broadcast.

Green had been converted under Fuller's ministry in 1921 and been part of his original broadcasts over KJS in 1925. The following year, when Fuller spoke at a missions conference in Arizona, Green came along to provide the music by singing and playing different instruments. While playing the invitation song at a campfire meeting, he himself surrendered his musical gifts to God. Working his way through college as a janitor—and spurning offers of big fees to play in dance bands—he eventually earned a doctorate and became music director for the Pasadena public school system. Since the first coast-to-coast Fuller broadcast in 1937, Green had been a regular on the *Old Fashioned Revival Hour* to sing solos and play the vibraharp. After joining the staff, the choral music of the program quickly set the standard in evangelical popular music. With the choir and the quartet, plus Rudy Atwood at the piano and George Broadbent (and later Anne Ortlund) on the organ, the broadcast now had a top-notch musical team. Like Atwood, Green too remained with the ministry for the next thirty years until after Fuller's death. Looking back in later years, Fuller noted that

> music has played a large part in the ministry of the broadcast.... Trained singers were assembled to sing the praises of the Lord and these added a whole new dimension to the expanding ministry of the broadcast as it went around the world. Letters by the hundred tell of hearts gladdened and comforted as friends listen to the music ... [and how it] softened their hearts in preparation for the Gospel message.[19]

During the late thirties and early forties, Mutual continued to add affiliates. Thus Fuller was continually compelled to add more stations to keep his time slot, and to maintain a full schedule of radio rallies in major cities across the country. By 1939 the *Old Fashioned Revival* was heard on 152 stations, more than any other broadcast in America. A year later, as funds allowed Fuller to record transcription disks and add independent outlets to his network, the station count reached 256. By 1942, with the country at war and many listeners looking for spiritual sustenance, the count nearly doubled again to 456 stations. In 1943, Fuller's peak year on the Mutual network, the Gospel Broadcasting Association spent a total of $1,566,130 (about $21.5 million in 2015 dollars) to purchase airtime, fully fifty percent more than the next-largest (secular) program. When asked about his success, however, Fuller refused to take the credit. "I'm not interested in figures," he replied. "I'm interested in souls. Some say I reach twenty million people. I don't know. All I know is that I preach the greatest message in the world. There may be greater orators, but nobody can preach a greater message because I preach from the world's greatest Book. It is the old Gospel, the simple Gospel that pulls."[20]

Along with "Jesus Saves," a second song came to be associated with the *Old Fashioned Revival Hour*. After a series of meetings in 1941 at the famed Boston Garden, the Fullers had dinner with their close friends, the Whitwells. In years past Cutler Whitwell had been a top Standard Oil executive but had resigned his position to preach the gospel. During the twenties he had served as dean of men at Biola, while his wife broadcast a children's program over KTBI. Whitwell had been holding meetings in New England and was glad for the chance to renew fellowship with his old friend. He mentioned how the song "Heavenly Sunlight" had been a particular blessing in his services. Then he and his wife sang the chorus for the Fullers. "I want that song for the *Old Fashioned Revival Hour!*" Charles Fuller declared. But before Whitwell could send him the music, Fuller could not get the song out of his mind and kept singing it to himself—except that, unsure of the words, he substituted "heavenly sunshine" for the correct lyrics. The next Sunday morning Fuller decided at the last moment to try the song on his KGER program, *The Pilgrim's Hour*—itself now carried on 135 Mutual stations. Only it was Fuller's version of the song that came across the airwaves that day, and ever after became a theme song for his ministry: "Heavenly sunshine, heavenly sunshine! Hallelujah! Jesus is mine!"[21]

After 1944 when Mutual restricted all religious programs to half-hour slots on Sunday mornings only, Fuller switched the *Old Fashioned Revival Hour* again to independent stations and moved the broadcast to the cavernous Long Beach Municipal Auditorium. The facility could seat three thousand five hundred people and had been used by the Fuller team to host the Sunday morning *Pilgrim's Hour* on KGER. The latter program remained on Mutual another three years as Fuller hoped the network would change its policy, but that did not happen and in 1947 he canceled the broadcast. A fourth radio network, the American Broadcasting Company, was formed in 1945 when government antitrust actions forced NBC to divest one of the two networks it owned. At first ABC followed the other three networks in disallowing (or in Mutual's case, severely limiting) paid religious programs. But by 1950, with advertisers starting to shift their dollars to television, ABC offered to sell Fuller a one-hour Sunday evening time slot on its two hundred eighty radio stations. *The Old Fashioned Revival Hour* enjoyed some of its best years on ABC. In the fall of 1950 Fuller even attempted a half-hour television program called *The Old Fashioned Meeting*. The broadcast was carried nationwide on twenty-five ABC stations and response was encouraging. But the hot lights and heavy makeup required for TV in that day were for Fuller a "nightmare" that utterly sapped the energy of himself and his staff. And despite good viewer response, the high cost of television production could never be met through donations.

Deciding that God had not called him to be a televangelist, Fuller continued to attract radio audiences in the millions. After the ABC network decided in 1957 to limit all its radio programs to no more than a half-hour, Fuller—who was then seventy years old—reluctantly ceased broadcasting the *Old Fashioned Revival Hour* live from the Long Beach Municipal Auditorium and moved to the studios of ABC. The final live broadcast was aired January 12, 1958. Six years later, in 1963, ABC made the decision to eliminate nearly all of its religious programming and drop the *Old Fashioned Revival Hour*. Fuller continued on independent stations until, in June 1967, he was diagnosed with congestive heart failure. David Hubbard, then president of Fuller Seminary—which Charles Fuller had founded in 1947—took over the broadcast. The program continued into the 1980s under the name *The Joyful Sound*, a reference to the lyrics of the original theme song, "Jesus Saves." Fuller passed away March 18, 1968. Among the last things his son Daniel remembered him saying was, "As I look back on my life, how glad I am that I spent it preaching the Gospel. I'm so glad I gave my life over to the Lord to become a preacher that day I knelt in the packing house in Placentia."[22] In the end, it was estimated that two million souls had come to Christ through Fuller's radio preaching. (One 1952 convert, the teenage Jerry Falwell, became a pioneer in television ministry with the 1956 debut of his *Old Time Gospel Hour* telecast, named in honor of his mentor's radio program.)

A memorial service was held at Lake Avenue Church in Los Angeles. Then a funeral procession of nearly one hundred cars made its way to Forest Lawn Cemetery—where Paul Rader, under whose preaching Fuller was converted, had been buried almost exactly thirty years earlier. At the end of the day Rudy Atwood, Fuller's pianist since his original coast-to-coast broadcast in 1937, came home and sat at the piano. After a moment of reflection he began to play a song that had been heard many times over the years on the *Old Fashioned Revival Hour*. Now as his fingers moved silently over the keys, Atwood whispered the title chorus: "He the pearly gates will open…"

Percy Crawford and the Young People's Church of the Air

With the birth of her third son, Margaret Crawford decided the family should move to Vancouver.[23] The small Canadian town of Minnedosa where they lived, in the province of Manitoba, was a community of only nine hundred people. Her boys could only hope to be farmers someday or go to work in the sash factory or grist mill. But in the city of Vancouver, the bustling seaside port of British Columbia, the Crawfords could dream of bigger things. Thus, shortly after their son Percy was born on October 20, 1902, Margaret and her husband Thomas, along with their older sons Willowbee and Alphaeus, left for Vancouver. There Thomas plied his trade as a blacksmith while Margaret opened a small grocery store and soda fountain on the outskirts of Chinatown.

The Crawfords struggled and even Percy, by the age of seven, sold newspapers to help the family. In time his father demanded that Percy quit school to help his mother operate the grocery store. Thomas Crawford was of Irish descent, quiet and emotionally distant, a hard and unsympathetic man who demanded obedience and backed it up with a raging temper. He himself never attended church. But if his sons ever missed a Sunday then he would beat them with a rawhide whip. For their part, the boys were embittered by their father's hypocrisy and all vowed to grow up and have nothing to do with religion. "I wonder if there really is a God," Percy would think. Then in frustration at his father's demands, the boy would tell himself, "Oh, if only I knew what field to enter, I would begin now and work with all my strength to be successful."[24]

Over the years his father's cruelty grew to the point that Margaret asked her husband to leave. Thomas Crawford did so, forever. Percy, who had long nursed a hatred of his father, now felt he had at last been set free. He gave up selling newspapers, quit working at the store, and took a job as a delivery truck driver for $23.50 per week. When he thought about leaving home, however, his mother begged him to stay. In the end, Percy offered to pay her ten dollars a week for room and board—but on the condition that he would only attend church if and when he pleased. With a good job and a good salary, Percy Crawford now answered only to himself. He took up smoking and frequented the pool halls and dance halls that he had always been warned against. Vancouver, the city where his mother had dreamed of a better life for her boys, now became the place of Percy's youthful dreams for fun and excitement. Some nights he stayed out so late that, to keep from waking his mother, Percy had to climb up the wooden pole outside the back porch and squeeze through his second-story bedroom window.

When he was nineteen Percy determined to be on his own and moved to Portland, Oregon. There he enrolled in high school and finished the four-year program in two years. After a brief time back in Vancouver with his mother and brothers, he again grew restless. This time, with a suitcase in one hand and a red blanket in the other, he boarded a boat for Los Angeles. Perhaps there he would finally find a place that was big enough for his dreams. Indeed, as the boat approached the great California metropolis on that Thursday afternoon, September 19, 1923, its skyline glinted in the sun. His reverie was interrupted, however, when he overheard someone exclaim, "Oh, it's beautiful!" Two young women, who were standing next to Percy at the rail of the boat, could not help but express their admiration as the Los Angeles skyline came into view. Crawford too was fascinated by the unimaginable size of it all, unlike anything he had ever seen. In their excitement, the three young people struck up a conversation until the boat docked and Crawford bid the two women farewell.[25]

"So this is L.A.," he thought. "Maybe here I'll find enough excitement to keep me happy." Several hours later, however, finding that excitement seemed less important than finding some dinner and a place to stay. Tired after carrying his suitcase all around town, Crawford stopped at a diner for a sandwich and then headed down Broadway in search of lodgings.

"Well, hello again, Percy!"

Much to his surprise, he turned and saw the two women from the boat. "Oh, hi girls," he replied.

"Haven't you found a place to stay yet?" the taller of the two women asked.

"Why, no, I haven't. Any suggestions?"

"Sure," the taller girl responded. "Why not try the Bible Institute? They have dormitory space that's not being used now, since school doesn't begin for a couple of weeks yet. They rent rooms pretty cheap."

"The Bible Institute, huh?"

"Yes, it's right down on Fifth Street. You'll see a big sign on the roof saying, 'Jesus Saves.' You can't miss it." And with that, Crawford thanked the women and hurried off in search of the big sign, "Jesus Saves."

The Bible Institute of Los Angeles was a long walk from Broadway. But when he arrived with his suitcase and red blanket, even before he could catch his breath, the dormitory clerk asked Crawford, "Son, are you a Christian?" Afraid to lose his lodgings and telling himself that he was certainly no "heathen," Crawford answered in the affirmative. He got his room, but the clerk's question continued to haunt him that evening. To escape his nagging conscience he went to a dance that night—then a party on Friday night, and took a date to the Cinderella Roof Dance Hall on Saturday. But each night, despite all the big city excitement that he could possibly crave, he came home feeling strangely empty.

The next day, September 23, was Sunday. Crawford felt he had to keep up the pretense of being a Christian in order to stay in the Bible Institute dormitory. So for the first time in a great while, he went to church. More than that, Crawford felt a sudden conviction that God really did exist and could provide the fulfillment he sought. Besides, going to church was convenient. The Church of the Open Door was located in the same huge building as the Bible Institute of Los Angeles. To Crawford's astonishment, the church auditorium that Sunday morning was filled with more than four thousand worshipers. He sat in the back, near the door, but was surprised by the lively singing and soon joined in. Then the speaker was introduced, the famed Irish evangelist Willie Nicholson whose revival campaigns had won thousands of converts in his homeland and around the world.

"[He] preached on heaven and hell and sin," Crawford later recalled, "and told me Christ was the One I needed. He seemed to pick me out of that great congregation and speak directly to me. God knew I was at the crisis, the crossroads, and that I was either going one hundred percent for the devil or for Jesus Christ."[26] In the churches Crawford attended as a boy, he was accustomed to hearing "a nice, sweet, soothing voice [with] poetry and book reviews" that put him pleasantly to sleep. Now he was confronted with a fiery Irish preacher who thundered, "The wages of sin is death" and "All have sinned and come short of the glory of God." But Nicholson also declared that God had provided a way of salvation. "But as many as received him, to them gave he power to become the sons of God," the evangelist quoted the scriptures. "Behold, the Lamb of God that taketh away the sin of the world." At the close of the service, Nicholson invited those who wished to become Christians to raise their hands. In response, Crawford put up his hand for a moment but then took it down. When Nicholson asked those who had raised their hands to come forward and kneel at the front of the auditorium for prayer, Crawford determined not to go. Then he felt a touch upon his shoulder. It was the man seated in the pew behind him, a converted Jew who had seen Crawford raise his hand. "Come on, boy," said the man softly, "I'll walk up with you." This, Crawford knew, was the turning point of his life. After a moment's hesitation he got up from the pew, walked down the aisle with the Jewish man at his side, then knelt at the altar to pray and be converted. There in the same church where Charles Fuller had heard the gospel seven years earlier, "something happened" to Percy Crawford that determined the course for the rest of his life. Years later, the same wonder of how "Something Happened" was captured in a chorus that became a favorite on his broadcasts: "Something happened when he saved me, happened in my heart..."

When Crawford knelt at the altar that day to become a Christian, he also made God a promise. That promise was to "go one hundred percent for Christ" and, for him, he knew that meant becoming a preacher. For the moment, though, Crawford needed a job and found work as the night janitor in a large office building located near the Bible Institute. During the day he earned extra money as a part-time carpenter's helper for a Hollywood contracting firm. Most of all, however, he "had a longing to reach others for Christ, but thought I was not qualified." Unbelievably to those who knew him later, Crawford confessed that "when I started to do personal [evangelism] work I thought I would never be able to succeed. I was timid and backward and unable to open my mouth before people, but gradually, after many attempts and many apparent failures, the art was acquired."[27] The first soul he won to Christ was a strapping young Swede who joined Crawford's work crew one day. That morning it started to rain and so the two men sat in Crawford's old, broken-down Ford to pass the time and wait out the downpour.

> As we sat there I thought, "Here is my chance to 'fish' for this fellow." We talked about everything under the sun but religion, until finally, very hesitantly, I handed him a Gospel of John; then I read to him from it. I pointed out that God saw our lost condition in sin, and that God had provided a Sin-Bearer. I asked him if he would recognize these two facts, and that big Swede put out his hand, grasped mine, and said, "Yes." My, what a joy![28]

Though Crawford diligently memorized verses of scripture during his long nights of sweeping and waxing floors, the young janitor soon realized he would need formal Bible training to become a preacher. So a few days after his conversion, he applied for enrollment at the Bible Institute of Los Angeles. Over the next two years—years that coincided with the founding of the school's radio station, KJS, and the early broadcast ministry of Charles Fuller—he earned his certificate. One of his instructors, Reuben A. Torrey who also pastored the Church of the Open Door, exerted a special influence on the young "Biola" student. Torrey fired his pupil with a zeal that soon saw Crawford on street corners around Los Angeles, playing his cornet until a large enough crowd gathered to begin preaching. Crawford even served as pastor of a small church that met outdoors in a Los Angeles park. To the end of his days, Crawford credited Torrey with shaping his views on evangelism. He acknowledged the debt by naming his second son, Richard Torrey Crawford, after his old mentor.

Graduating from Biola in the spring of 1925, Crawford and some other students bought an old Dodge and organized a summer evangelistic team that traveled north through California, Oregon, Washington, and up to Vancouver—where Margaret Crawford was thrilled to see her son for the first time profess Christ. That fall, Crawford felt the need for more education and enrolled at the University of California at Los Angeles. There he began to sense that God had given him a special gift for leadership and organization. Repelled by the fraternity life on the UCLA campus, he organized an alternative—a *Christian* fraternity named Alpha Gamma Omega Christian Fellowship. Reflecting on his newfound leadership skills, he thought to himself, "I used to be shy and awkward and withdrawn. I'm not like that anymore. Christ has not only changed my life, He has changed my personality."[29] Two years later Crawford obtained his UCLA degree but knew that seminary training was important. Someday, he believed, "the majority of our population in America will be college graduates, and an uneducated preacher will be laughed out of the pulpit."[30] Yet to enter a seminary he would first need a Bible college degree, so in 1927 he moved to Chicago and transferred to Wheaton College. By his senior year in 1929 he was president of the Debate Union and a popular student whose yearbook picture caption read, "A little nonsense now and then is relished by the wisest men."[31]

In Chicago, Crawford found another role model for his future ministry. A Wheaton classmate, Torrey Johnson who later patterned his own Youth for Christ organization after Crawford's work, said that "there's no doubt about it, Percy could not have escaped being greatly influenced by Paul Rader." The ministries of Rader's Chicago Gospel Tabernacle were the talk of the city, Johnson noted, so that "nobody could have been at Wheaton College, student or faculty, that wasn't influenced ... in some way by Paul Rader."[32] Crawford certainly reflected the zeal of Rader as the young Wheaton College student began a practice he would follow the rest of his life. Gathering four other men, his team traveled to meetings across the Midwest as Crawford preached and the quartet sang and gave testimonies. In the summer of 1929 the team toured the country. Perhaps they sang a brief but haunting chorus, "Into My Heart," then recently written and published in Chicago, that became one of the most requested songs on Crawford's later radio broadcasts: "Come in today, come in to stay; come into my heart, Lord Jesus."

Many souls were won during Crawford's days in Chicago. So it was little wonder that, when he moved in 1929 to Philadelphia and entered Westminster Seminary, he was soon out preaching the gospel to all who would hear. Finding a vacant Presbyterian church on Washington Square, he rigged a diving-board platform—complete with lectern, microphone, and overhead speakers—that turned the entire city of Philadelphia into his "congregation." In 1930 while Crawford was still a seminary student, the work for which he became world-famous started to take shape. Even by today's standards, the rapid growth of his outreach seems breathtaking. Crawford was especially burdened for teenagers, for he remembered his own rebellion at that age. So that year, 1930, he launched a series of Saturday night evangelistic youth rallies at Philadelphia's Barnes Memorial Church on Seventh and Spruce Streets. Within months, similar youth rallies were being held up and down the East Coast.

By 1931, the *Young People's Church of the Air* (YPCA) debuted on Philadelphia's WIP at a cost of sixty dollars for each weekly hour of airtime. The Sunday afternoon broadcasts were soon attended by hundreds of young people, while a loyal listenership quickly developed to financially support the program. After Crawford graduated in 1931 from Westminster Seminary and could devote his full time to gospel work, he incorporated the YPCA ministry in 1932. Soon after the Mutual radio network was formed in 1934—and was willing, unlike NBC and CBS, to sell airtime for religious programs—Crawford could be heard coast-to-coast. His was the first religious broadcast to be heard nationwide over the Mutual system of some four hundred stations in every state of the union.

In 1933, Crawford established the Pinebrook Bible Camp for teens and adults in the Pocono Mountains of Pennsylvania. The facility was joined later by Shadowbrook camp for boys and Mountainbrook for girls. Crawford was amazed that "there were no outstanding summer Bible conferences in America" and thought, "It's funny that nobody ever started a camp where Christians could go for a vacation without hearing cursing and choking to death on cigarette smoke and the smell of liquor."[33] So as he had done with his original Alpha Gamma Omega fraternity, Crawford decided to launch his own alternative.

When in February 1933 Crawford announced on the *Young People's Church of the Air* broadcast that he was looking for a summer Bible conference property, calls and letters poured into the ministry. One listener—a lumberman from Stroudsburg, Pennsylvania—got in touch with the president of the local Chamber of Commerce, who in turn invited Crawford to look at some Pocono real estate. The four properties he saw on his first visit were not quite right. But the fifth property that he inspected on a follow-up visit had everything the ministry needed—twenty-six scenic acres, a body of water, an existing inn to house guests, highway access, proximity to major cities, and a below-market price. Crawford had only sixty dollars in ministry funds to put toward a camp property. But with donations from supporters and radio listeners, he raised the down payment of five thousand dollars needed by March 1, 1933. The remaining sixteen thousand dollars was also duly raised and paid on time. All he had to do now was open America's first evangelistic camping center by June.

A rough hotel named the Pinebrook Inn was already on the property—though it was best known not for its lodgings but for the bar in the basement.

Crawford decided to keep the name but dismantle the bar. Then with lumber donated by the listener who first suggested Stroudsburg, volunteers from local churches constructed a tabernacle. By June, Pinebrook Bible Conference was hosting visitors for twelve dollars per week, including a two-dollar registration fee and ten dollars for room and board. That first summer some twelve hundred campers aged fourteen and older poured onto the property—followed by sixteen hundred in 1934, twenty-two hundred in 1935, and more than three thousand in 1936.

Fueled by the radio broadcast and the camps, music publishing also became a major endeavor with nearly a dozen songbooks dedicated to Pinebrook and the *Young People's Church of the Air*. A magazine, *Youth Today*, was founded, plus a Pinebrook Bookstore in Philadelphia and Pinebrook Book-of-the-Month Club. By the end of the decade, in 1938, Crawford opened the doors of The King's College to its first class of students. Tuition was fifity dollars a semester, plus three hundred dollars per year for room and board. Fittingly, the campus that Crawford purchased in Belmar, New Jersey, had once been headquarters of the American Marconi Company. The school's fight song, "King's College Victory March" composed by Wendell Loveless, perfectly captured the dynamism of the entire ministry: "On to victory we'll upward, onward go! On to victory, God will His grace bestow!"

And so from a diving board in Washington Square, Crawford in a few short years almost singlehandedly developed a model for evangelistic youth ministry that is still practiced today—exciting youth events and dynamic youth camps, all connected by its own subculture of music, magazines, and media. Yet Crawford himself was the motive force. For he left such a vivid impression on those who heard him—though he seldom spoke for more than fifteen minutes—that even today many testify to his unique power in the pulpit. To Bill Drury, a member of Crawford's staff, it seemed that the evangelist's pointer finger "was about eighteen inches long. And he would point that finger at you like a shotgun. And he would go around the audience very quickly. 'You, you, right there, yeah, you, you, you, and you and you and you. You're outside the family of God and you're going to a sinner's hell.'" Crawford always called himself an evangelist and not a revivalist, said Drury, because "he was not there to revive people. I never was in a meeting, I don't care how small it was, that somebody didn't get up" to be converted.[34] Billy Graham, a frequent speaker at Pinebrook, was in awe of Crawford the first time he was on the camp program: "I remember how excited I was and how afraid I was, and how nervous I was to stand and preach in front of Percy Crawford, and how encouraging he was all week long."[35] He later called Crawford his "spiritual father" and said his own entry into citywide evangelism was motivated by Crawford urging him to "launch out into the deep" (Luke 5:4).[36]

A reviewer for the *Allentown Beacon* of Pennsylvania said of Crawford's on-air preaching that the evangelist was "direct and to the point. He doesn't hold with a lot of learned adjectives. *That* is what makes him appeal to kids. Crawford ... looks at no one but you. Folks get all red in the face and look out of the corner of their eyes to make sure no one else can see their embarassment.... He deals with faults that are common to all people, everyone. You can't get perturbed at him because deep down you know it is true."[37] Jack Wyrtzen, whose own Word of Life youth ministry was inspired by Crawford, observed that "when he'd get up there, the Spirit of God would come upon him and the quartet would sing 'It was for you the Savior died,' and boy, people would respond all over the place."[38]

Because Wyrtzen was an evangelist himself, he saw in Crawford "something I don't think his kids ever saw, maybe not even his wife. He just had a gift for evangelism [so] that when he got going in the pulpit, he came alive. I look back and I've heard a lot of evangelists. I even heard Gypsy Smith a couple of times. I don't know of anybody that I felt had the power of God come on like Percy Crawford when he got up to speak." In Wyrtzen's opinion, "I think he could have gotten up there and said, 'Mary had a little lamb,' and the quartet would have sung 'It Was for You,' and the people would have accepted the Lord."[39] So powerfully moved was Wyrtzen by his mentor's preaching that he adopted Crawford's trademark invitation song as the closing theme of his own broadcasts. In all of Crawford's years, observed his son Dean, the evangelist was never without a quartet to accompany him on his travels. Even in recording a fortieth anniversary album the group chose "It Was for You" as its closing song.[40]

Looking back on those years, son Donald Crawford affirmed that music played a vital role in his father's ministry: "Though not much of a musician himself, [he] recognized the power and influence of gospel music." To provide the necessary leadership in that aspect of the work, Dean explained, "at the right time, the Lord he loved led him to Ruth Duvall, a young, talented, sensitive musician and pianist who soon became his wife and spiritual partner for life."[41] The two met when a seminary classmate of Crawford's offered to get him a date for the school dinner. Ruth was fifteen and excited about going to a dinner with a college student, but nearly backed out when she learned her date was twenty-nine years old. Yet at the end of the evening, Crawford knew he had fallen in love and Ruth thought her date—though a bit old—was the nicest man she had ever met. Having lost her father in a tragic accident when she was three, Ruth found in Percy Crawford a man whom she could obviously look up to. More dates were soon planned. Then at a family hymn sing in the Duvall home, Crawford learned that Ruth was an accomplished pianist and talented singer. So he organized a quartet out of Ruth's church, First Methodist of Collingswood, New Jersey. She played the piano and her brother, R. Fenton Duvall, was one of the singers. For the rest of

Crawford's career, the quartet formed the basis of his services. Through various personnel changes over the years, the quartet would always accompany the evangelist on his almost nightly schedule of meetings, covering tens of thousands of miles each year.

In time, Ruth and Percy were married in a ceremony held at Pinebrook on September 18, 1933, nearly ten years to the day after Crawford was converted. Over the next three decades Ruth ministered as a pianist and organist, songwriter and arranger, and vocalist. She trained a total of seven quartets, led many choral groups including The King's Singers, and conducted orchestras for radio and television programs. During the years her husband preached, Ruth Crawford compiled fourteen songbooks, many of them inspired by the camping and radio ministries: *Pinebrook Victory Songs, Pinebrook Choruses, Pinebrook Praises, Pinebrook Melodies, New Pinebrook Songs, Mountainbrook Melodies, Young People's Church of the Air Hymnbook,* and *Radio Requests I & II.* Her son Dan Crawford described how his mother's song arrangements and keyboard accompaniment created a distinctive sound as she directed the musical programs of both the YPCA radio broadcasts and Pinebrook camp services. The relationship between Percy and Ruth, he observed, was "contrasting and symbiotic ... [as the] melodious, flowing, warm feeling ... of music that Ruth composed complemented perfectly Percy's hard-driving, staccato preaching style."[42] Through it all—directing music for the broadcasts, for Pinebrook and King's College, and compiling songbooks and hymnals—Ruth Crawford raised five children. Four of these were sons—Donald (born 1937), Richard (nicknamed Dick, 1939), Dan (1941), and Dean (1944). Inevitably, they formed a quartet. As "The Four D's" the youngsters "started out, right in the beginning, the four boys singing," noted Ruth. Then in 1949 a fifth "D" was added when Donna Lee was born. "When she was able," her mother recalled, "she would sit there and wave her hands and lead the boys while they sang."[43]

The atmosphere of music that surrounded the Crawford ministries was vividly remembered more than forty years later by Perry Straw, who as a boy was a camper at Pinebrook. The daily schedule consisted of two meetings in the morning and one in the evening, with the afternoon set aside for recreation. Speakers were selected for their ability to reach youth but were strictly enjoined by Crawford not to go more than thirty minutes. Altogether, Straw recalled, the camp was

> a fantastic place for me as a kid.... Ruth Crawford, when she'd sit down at that piano, tickled those ivories.... [There would be] some trumpet trios and maybe some sax and maybe a quartet or a small ensemble. That was a tremendous thing, the music input with the message, you know. The Crawfords were the best at it.... [T]he music and the message seemed to be equal, about as much preaching as there was music.[44]

The *Young People's Church of the Air* was just as dynamic. Using a precisely timed variety format, a typical broadcast might include a rousing opening, then Ruth at the piano accompanying the quartet, followed by a dramatic guest testimony, a brass trio, some opening remarks from Crawford and then a vocal ensemble, followed by the message and an evangelistic invitation. Drama and skits were also frequently employed. The reviewer from the *Allentown Beacon* marveled at the high quality and attractiveness of the broadcasts: "The old and beautiful gospel hymns pour from the lips of young singers with more sincerity and belief than any of our wise and pious elderlies can assume." Audiences could only smile, he wrote, at a show without the "stuffiness that develops from most [broadcast] religious presentations. The typical off-key trios that turn gospel songs into heart-rending wails are finally performed with the beautiful harmony they deserve." Even more compelling, the reviewer continued, was the vibrant faith displayed by the young singers who exemplified "the real American youth, relieved of the psychological wraps of toughness [that] modern environments have garbed them in. The young people do not perform with over-sentimental expression; in [them is] the good, clean expression of the young. To them, their program is one of the finer experiences of their lives. Yet it is religion." The Crawford program proved, he concluded, "one thing beyond all others—that young people can have religious tendencies without being termed 'ickies' or 'sissies' by their friends."[45] That spirit is captured in another Wendell Loveless song, a favorite both at Pinebrook and on the air: "V is for victory! Sing it out, 'tis a glorious word!"

The man at the center of all this activity, Percy Crawford, was unstoppable. He earned a bachelor of theology degree from Westminster in 1931 and a masters degree in history from the University of Pennsylvania in 1932, and was awarded a doctor of divinity degree by Bob Jones University in 1940. "Running the race was important both spiritually," son Donald Crawford remembered, "and physically too. There were sports of all kinds ... whether football, basketball, baseball, soccer, and even tennis. The love of sports and physical activity was an essential part of the family."[46] Characteristically, Bill Drury recalled, "You'd be going to a meeting with Percy, and Percy would have his New Testament on the steering wheel. He was a fast driver.... But he would be reading his New Testament while he was driving sixty, sixty-five miles an hour." When Crawford was struck by a particular Bible verse, Drury added, he would exclaim, "Bill look at that, look at that! I don't know that I saw this before. Look, look and see what John says here." To which Drury would silently offer a quick prayer to God and then reply, "Percy, the road!"[47] Jack Wyrtzen, who often spoke at Pinebrook, marveled how Crawford was out "seven nights a week out with the quartet and working all the day long on radio mail and running a Christian bookstore in Philadelphia.... He was a tireless worker. And he used to say to me, 'How'd you learn to delegate?'"[48] One story Wyrtzen tells of his mentor is when Crawford tried to cook supper the first camping season at Pinebrook. "It was burnt spaghetti!" Wyrtzen chuckled.[49]

Crawford was also widely known for his colorful dress, often walking around Pinebrook in a pink shirt and green pants or perhaps a favorite pair of orange pants plus a blue sports shirt. It was not that Crawford craved attention. As his biographer Bob Bahr explained, "Everything he did was done for one of two reasons. Either it was a necessity, like eating or sleeping, or it would help win souls to Christ.... The reason for the wild colors was that he just didn't have time to worry over what [color] went over what—nor did he care about it."[50] With the irrepressible Crawford at the helm, the ministry not only expanded throughout the thirties but accelerated as it entered the 1940s. The *Young People's Church of the Air* was more popular than ever, heard on some six hundred stations, including the four hundred fifty affiliates of the Mutual network. Crawford's rallies filled arenas and stadiums as never before, and in 1945 he addressed seventy thousand people who filled Chicago's Soldier Field for what then the largest gospel youth rally in history.[51] Pinebrook was going strong and expanded to more than five hundred acres. And when the government commandeered the King's College campus in New Jersey for wartime military purposes, the school acquired an even larger facility in Delaware. (In 1955 the college found its permanent home in Briarcliff Manor, New York.)

The Crawfords were also a major force in gospel music. Songs introduced on the *Young People's Church of the Air* and printed in the YPCA and Pinebrook songbooks sparked the careers of many new songwriters. One of these was a young John W. Peterson whose 1948 song, "It Took A Miracle," debuted on the Crawford broadcast and became an immediate hit that launched his own career. In those days it was common practice for music publishers to buy songs outright from composers and copyright them under the publishers' names. Peterson was paid forty dollars—a fee that he himself named—for "It Took A Miracle," from which he requested that Crawford retain four dollars as a tithe to the ministry. "I would have gladly *given* him the material," Peterson remarked, "for the chance to be heard on his broadcast." Though he received no royalties, he knew that because of *Young People's Church of the Air* his song's popularity "was instantly established. I was astounded and delighted. For once my fantasy came true."[52] Similarly, Dan Crawford later recalled,

> Over the years, Percy and Ruth cultivated a new breed of composers who wrote lively choruses that expressed the joyful Christian life and conveyed the simple story of what Christ has done for us. But many of the songs had a more inspirational and moving quality, appropriate for solos or duets.... A few of the main contributors to

the [YPCA] chorus books ... either launched their careers or established themselves through working with ... the YPCA.[53]

On October 9, 1949, Crawford was again a pioneer by broadcasting the nation's first coast-to-coast evangelistic television program. On that Sunday evening, from ten thirty to eleven, *Youth on the March* was aired over the ABC network from its Philadelphia affiliate, WFIL-TV. The technology to link up multiple stations in a network had only recently been developed so that the initial broadcast was carried by "most" of ABC's eleven affiliates. By the end of its first year, however, the program was aired by twenty-two stations and enjoyed an estimated audience of fifteen million viewers.[54] This was quite a feat when, in 1950, less than four million U.S. households owned a TV set.[55] Dubbed "A Twentieth Century Crusade," the *Youth on the March* theme song ("On to victory, we'll upward, onward go!") began with the male chorus and then featured a voiceover from the announcer:

> Down through the ages our nation was founded by young men with a vision. This vision was based upon a sincere reverence of both God and country. Such a voice today is Percy Crawford whom God has raised up to challenge the youth of the twentieth century to preserve that foundation and to build upon it for a greater tomorrow. It's "Youth on the March" with words of eternal life for our nation in a critical hour![56]

The history-making first telecast followed the opening theme with an upbeat gospel quartet song, "These Are They," followed by a fully orchestrated musical montage, "It Is Wonderful," featuring a female soloist, male chorus, ladies trio, and combined chorus. After the musical segment, a weightlifter hoisted his one-hundred-sixty-five-pound adult son for the cameras and then gave a brief testimony, followed by the King's College Trumpet Trio with "Onward Christian Soldiers." Viewers were urged to write the broadcast and then Crawford invited everyone to a sing-along of "Every Day with Jesus." Crawford's sons came next, appearing as The Four D's with an upbeat presentation of the old spiritual, "Do, Lord." The telecast turned serious as the YPCA quartet sang "Rock of Ages," followed by a seven-and-half-minute evangelistic message by Percy Crawford from Matthew 19:16. In the final two minutes of the telecast Crawford gave an invitation for viewers to convert to Christ as the male chorus sang "It Was for You." Then the announcer closed by asking those who had watched the program to write "Percy Crawford, Post Office Box 1, Philadelphia, Pennsylvania."[57]

Television critics responded positively to the program's high production quality and evident sincerity. "Undoubtedly the most inspiring television show to date," gushed one reviewer in 1949, the first year of network television in the United States. "The program is 'pure' television with the visual effects arising entirely from the personalities and the participants.... It is simple in design but packed with visual impact that serves its purpose fully.... There is more quality programming this one evening than all the other six days combined." From the *Pittsburgh Sunday Sun-Telegraph* came the observation in 1952 that *Youth on the March* was "among the most wonderful developments at this stage of the American experience ... [which has] confounded those who sit in the seats of the TV mighty ... [by] starting out as incidental presentations and making the top on their merits." Noting that television was characterized by a "habitual resort to banality," the paper believed TV moguls had "overlooked the fine character of our people" and it had taken the Crawford programs "to prove this point." *Christian Life* magazine declared in 1950 that the "fast-paced" broadcast was "probably one of the best musically arranged Christian programs on the air today—AM, FM, or television. In format it compares favorably with similar variety-type television programs ... [as] seen in bags of fan mail, the unusual high [audience] rating, and the compliments which have come from television experts."[58] Ruth Crawford, however, had a somewhat different memory of the first 1949 telecast. Seven months pregnant with her fifth child, she recalled that according to the television standards of the day "I just played behind the organ. They didn't show anything but my face!"[59]

Nevertheless, costs for airtime and production of between five thousand and twenty thousand dollars per week (even though most musicians and singers were students from King's College) were heavy to bear. In characteristic Crawford style, *Youth on the March* became the flagship for an array of related outreaches (and revenue streams). Youth on the March Fishing Clubs for children and teens, and a *Youth on the March* magazine, were launched. Churches in areas without television service were invited to sponsor weekly showings of the broadcast on film. Even a separate film unit, The King's Productions, was established. And Ruth Crawford had her own *Pinebrook Praises* daily radio program on four hundred Mutual stations. The TV broadcasts directed campers to Pinebrook ("A $50 Vacation for Only $15!") and students to King's College. For information viewers need only write to "Percy Crawford, P.O. Box 1, Philadelphia 5, Penna."

By 1953, however, the high costs of *Youth on the March* and the demands of other projects compelled Crawford to depart the ABC network and instead purchase airtime on independent stations around the country. This continued through 1956—after a respectable run of seven seasons—when *Youth on the March* became chiefly a local broadcast, and then ceased altogether in 1958. At the same time, by the mid-1950s the *Young People's Church of the Air* declined to less than three hundred stations—though still a large number, especially as the golden age of radio was coming to a close. In 1953-54 the Crawfords conducted a successful world tour with the YPCA vocalists and founded The King's Korean Mission. Ever with a keen eye for anticipating the next trend, in the late fifties—as the focus of religious radio was shifting from network programs to locally-owned religious stations—Crawford began to purchase FM outlets and assemble his own network, the Crawford Broadcasting Corporation which he organized in 1958. Over the next two years he purchased stations in Chicago; Detroit; Des Moines; Buffalo; Miami; Portland, Oregon; and Lancaster, Pennsylvania. Then in 1959 he acquired Philadelphia's WPCA-TV, becoming the first evangelical ministry to own a television station, which went on the air in 1960.[60]

Having pioneered youth ministry and youth camping, and then gospel radio and television, Crawford was poised again to lead the next wave as Christians began to take ownership for themselves of the means of broadcasting. What might have happened next, however, will never be known. In November 1960, the front cover of *King's Life* magazine issued the following article:

> On October 29, Dr. Percy Crawford was driving to a Youth for Christ rally in Lancaster, Pennsylvania. Stopping at a restaurant on the New Jersey Turnpike he suffered a heart attack as he entered the building. He was rushed to St. Francis Hospital in Trenton. He was placed in an oxygen tent and showed improvement the following day. Monday evening [October 31] Dr. Crawford suffered a second attack and was called home to be with the Lord. The valiant warrior for Christ who had said that he would rather burn out for the Lord than live a long life had finished his course and was received into the presence of his Savior whom he served with untiring effort.[61]

Crawford was fifty-eight. The previous year, 1959, he had suffered a heart attack and decided to take Ruth on a Caribbean cruise to relax. Upon their return, however, he continued his grueling schedule. On that twenty-ninth day of October 1960, as he and Ruth drove to the Lancaster rally, Crawford slowed down when he saw a white-and-orange Howard Johnson's. "Say, Ruth," he commented, "Last week when I was coming up from Philly I left my topcoat at that Howard Johnson's. How about running across and getting it for me." His wife agreed, but in a few minutes returned empty-handed. "They have a topcoat there, Percy," she explained, "but you'll have to go and identify it. They won't give it to me." Crawford grumbled at the waste of time, but got out of the car and strode determinedly across the highway. He disappeared into the restaurant, but even after several minutes he had not come out. Then someone rushed out of the glass doors of the Howard Johnson's and motioned excitedly for Ruth to come inside. Her husband had been stricken with another heart attack.[62] Two days later, on the morning that Percy Crawford passed away, his voice was heard on the prerecorded *Pinebrook Praises* program: "I'd like to recognize my mother's birthday today, living in Philadelphia out on Stenton Avenue. Eighty-five years old. That's pretty good, isn't it, eighty-five? Well, bless your heart! I don't think I'll hit sixty-five." Margaret Crawford was listening; she had outlived all three of her sons. "Oh, my Percy," she sobbed.[63] Two months later, in answer to her prayers, she too passed away in the hope of being reunited with her son in heaven. Sunday, November 6, a memorial service was held in Philadelphia's town hall. Billy Graham spoke to 2,500 mourners who jammed the auditorium, while hundreds more listened outside over hastily erected speakers. At the close of the service, as Crawford had wished, an invitation was given. Some twenty people came forward to be converted. Afterward, Percy Crawford was buried at Pinebrook, at the lawn in front of the dining room.

Though the rallies and camps and clubs, and the radio and TV broadcasts are no more (King's College, however, moved to New York City in 1999 and continues today from offices near Wall Street[64]), Crawford was correct in his assessment that station ownership would be the next step in evangelical mass media. Though WPCA-TV could not survive without his leadership and was sold, a young Pat Robertson was inspired by Crawford's venture to start a television station of his own.[65] Meanwhile, Crawford Broadcasting Corporation has grown to a network of more than twenty stations in major markets nationwide. For her part, Ruth Crawford continued her *Pinebrook Praises* radio program until about 1965 and traveled with her son Donald in an evangelistic ministry until about 1967. In 1966 she was remarried to Dr. Robert Porter, a chiropractor. Through it all, she kept writing music and published the songbooks *Sing My Heart* (1962), *Hearts in Harmony* (1978), and *Singing and Making Melodies* (1983). With her sister Esther Eden, for several years Ruth produced a brief daily radio program entitled *Bible Women Speak Today*. She passed away October 28, 1986.[66] In an interview a few years before her death she exclaimed, "I'll never get over the opportunity the Lord gave me."[67] As her body was laid to rest in her beloved Pocono Mountains, in a final act of devotion the quartet sang one of her favorite songs, "Near to the Heart of God," that she had arranged for the broadcasts, "There is a place of quiet rest, near to the heart of God...."

On an April day in 1989, the quartet gathered again for a reunion—appropriately, in a recording studio. Forty years earlier, in 1949, they had sung as the Telecasters Quartet on the nation's first coast-to-coast gospel television program, *Youth on the March*. Before that, they had been heard on the radio with the *Young People's Church of the Air*. Now as they gathered around the studio microphones, like they had so many years ago, they opened the session with a familiar old song, "I Was There When It Happened." The four men—Steven Musto, Bob Straton, Samuel Seymour, and Donald Crawford—could each say they had been there when it happened. "A special, wonderful ministry, different than anything before," is how they described it. "We were there when so much of it happened. We were there when it was salvation time for so many. We were there, and we sang as 'It Was for You' laid claim to the lives of thousands. No two people had a more unique, effective, and universal ministry for their times than Percy and Ruth Crawford. God raised them up to do something special, and they did."[68]

Theodore Epp and Back to the Bible

Soon after the Norse Gospel Trio moved from Kansas to Tulsa, the group received an invitation to sing at a small town in the Oklahoma panhandle.[69] Roads were poor in the mid-1930s so that driving to the church in Goltry, a distance of more than three hundred miles from Tulsa, would take all day. But in those days of the Great Depression, Oklahoma had been hit especially hard. If the trio could be a blessing, they were glad to come. The Norse Gospel Trio consisted of three brothers who had started in radio over KFBI in Abilene, Kansas. Now they were broadcasting over KVOO in Tulsa, a powerful clear-channel station that reached half a dozen states. A fourth brother, the youngest and still living at home in Kansas, had just arrived to spend the summer traveling with the group as soloist and songleader. Together the four climbed into the car and started the long drive to Goltry.

Years later, the youngest brother still vividly remembered that trip. "When we arrived for the service," he recalled, "the church was so packed that there was no way to get in through the doors. Finally the pastor led us around to the back, and we climbed through a window to get to the platform." After the service, the four singers spent some time to visit and encourage the pastor. "[He] was not rich in worldly goods," the brother observed. "The parsonage, as I recall, was scantily furnished and gave mute testimony to financial struggle. But my brothers and I were impressed by the man's dedication to the Lord and by his keen interest in radio broadcasting. Subsequently he found his own outstanding ministry in the medium, for the pastor's name was Theodore Epp—the same Theodore Epp who is known to millions as founder and director of the Back to the Bible broadcast ministry."[70] The young songleader's name was John W. Peterson, who himself went on to become a famed gospel songwriter.

Born 1907 in Oraibi, Arizona, the son of missionaries to the Hopi Indians, Theodore Epp was converted to Christ at the age of twenty and soon afterward answered God's call to preach.[71] He attended the Bible Institute of Los Angeles and Hesston College in Kansas, then graduated in 1932 from Southwestern Baptist Theological Seminary of Forth Worth, Texas, and accepted the call to pastor a small Mennonite church in Goltry, Oklahoma. There he could minister among the hard-pressed farmers of the panhandle and, as his parents had done, among the many Native Americans who lived in the region. And more important to his future in radio, it was in Oklahoma that he met an evangelist who had a profound impact on Epp's life and career.

Originally, T. Myron Webb had studied for the medical profession. So in 1930 he had begun to broadcast health lectures over a Texas radio station. Though a Christian believer who had a burden for souls, he resisted the growing conviction that God wanted him in the ministry. "I'll minister to the physical needs of people," he told the Lord. "Someone else can minister to their spiritual needs."[72] Yet in time, Webb surrendered his life to enter evangelism. But how? Judging by the response, his radio health lectures had reached a wide audience and benefited many listeners. If radio could be effective to promote good health, he reasoned, it could have an even greater impact in proclaiming the gospel. On June 26, 1930, over a radio station in Amarillo, Texas—not far from Goltry, Oklahoma—Webb signed on the air with his first gospel broadcast. By 1934, he moved to Enid, Oklahoma, and began conducting a Sunday afternoon Bible class that aired live over the radio. Drawn by the broadcasts, several hundred people were coming to Webb's classes. Later the group even added its own Wednesday prayer meeting. Originating from KCRC in Enid, Webb called his radio program *Back to the Bible*. Though that broadcast is not considered the first *Back to the Bible* program as listeners know it today, Webb planted a seed that would someday lead Theodore Epp into a worldwide gospel radio ministry.

After hearing Webb on the radio, in 1934 Epp was introduced to the well-known evangelist. Their association sparked in Epp a vision for radio and in November 1934 he broadcast his first radio sermon on Webb's weekly program. Two years later he resigned his pastorate in Goltry to join Webb full-time. Epp learned much about radio ministry while serving with Webb, even as his burden for broadcasting deepened into a definite calling from God. In time, Webb moved his program to KVOO in Tulsa—the same powerful station that had been the home base of the Norse Gospel Trio—and renamed the broadcast *Bible Fellowship Hour*. About that same time, in 1938, Epp went to visit his parents in Nebraska. Upon learning there was not a single daily gospel radio program in the entire state, he felt God moving on his heart to do something about it. When Epp told his mentor that he was planning to leave the Southwest and launch a radio ministry of his own in Nebraska, Webb was supportive. He even suggested to his young protégé, "Since we're changing our name, you can use our old name, *Back to the Bible*, if you like."[73] That is how *Back to the Bible* was started. As for Webb, in 1945 he was appointed director and speaker of the *Light and Life Hour*, the worldwide radio ministry of the Free Methodist denomination. In its own right, the *Light and Life Hour* and its radio choir did much to introduce popular evangelical music in its weekly broadcasts and numerous recordings. The program originated from Seattle Pacific College which became Webb's base of operations until his retirement in 1964.

All that was in the future, however, when Theodore Epp moved to

Lincoln, Nebraska, in 1939 in hopes of somehow launching a gospel radio ministry. He began by making an appointment with the manager of KFAB, a ten thousand-watt station heard throughout the Great Plains. "To be quite frank," Epp later recalled of that visit, "I was very much afraid." Nevertheless he boldly declared to the manager, "We note that you have everything on your broadcasts that people want except something from the heart. We have that and would like the opportunity of presenting it to the people."[74] Impressed by Epp's sincerity and his argument for a gospel broadcast, the manager expressed a willingness to consider airing the new *Back to the Bible* program. Epp had asked to purchase a half-hour daily time slot on KFAB, but a few days later the manager came back with a counter-proposal. Time was available on a sister station that was also owned by KFAB. It was only fifteen minutes a day and the KFOR signal was only two hundred fifty watts. But Epp could have it for $4.50 per program. Would he like to sign a contract? Epp agreed, signed the contract, and on May 1, 1939, the first *Back to the Bible* broadcast went out over the air.

Two years later Epp added a second station, WNAX in Yankton, South Dakota. Later in 1941, time was also purchased on KMA in Shenandoah, Iowa, and KVOD in Denver. Five more stations were added to the *Back to the Bible* network in 1942, and in 1943 an international outreach was begun when HCJB—the missionary station founded by Paul Rader's former staff trombonist, Clarence Jones—picked up the program. From there, the work of *Back to the Bible* grew rapidly. The broadcast ministry was incorporated under the name Good News Broadcasting Association, and in time many other outreaches were begun. By the time of its twentieth anniversary in 1959, the program was carried by more than two hundred stations that covered ninety percent of the globe. Letter volume had climbed to one hundred thousand a month, readership of the *Good News Broadcaster* magazine topped half a million, and up to five million pieces of literature were being distributed annually.[75] Epp retired from the radio program in 1984, the fiftieth anniversary of his first broadcast with Myron Webb and forty-five years after founding *Back to the Bible*. In his lifetime the program came to be heard on more than six hundred stations. Epp published seventy books and two periodicals, *Good News Broadcaster* (later *Confident Living*) and *Young Ambassador* (later *Teen Quest*); and founded a correspondence school and Back to the Bible Missionary Agency. He continued to serve the ministry and was in demand as a conference speaker until his death in 1985.

From its earliest years, *Back to the Bible* featured music as a key ingredient of the broadcast—as each program opened with the rousing gospel hymn, "I Love to Tell the Story," as its theme song. Heard regularly on the broadcast were the Back to the Bible choir, male chorus, soloists and, most popular of all, the Back to the Bible Quartet. These groups made many recordings on the Victor and Zondervan labels during the heyday of the forties through the mid-sixties. "Music is vital to the radio ministry," reads a liner note from a recording of the period, "because it is chosen with a spiritual message and clothed in musical settings to best convey this message. Evidence that music is a ministry is the steady flow of letters from those experiencing deep spiritual results through these songs." The music of *Back to the Bible* also tended, as the liner note explained, towards "simplicity and meaning."[76] Unlike some other radio ministries of the day, *Back to the Bible* was not associated with any particular style of music and presented a large and pleasing variety—from older hymns to newer songs, and gospel quartet numbers to Negro spirituals. Neither did Back to the Bible attempt to enter the songbook and music publishing business. Only one tune, "Nothing Is Impossible," copyrighted in 1966 by the Good News Broadcasting Association has come down into hymnbooks today.

Though the Back to the Bible Quartet set the standard in its day (and survived in various forms through the end of the century) its membership changed frequently. Photographs of the quartet on record albums of the period show changing personnel and the names of the men are not given. Neither was the quartet featured on recordings of its own as albums offered selections from all of the *Back to the Bible* vocal ensembles. Not until the late 1960s, when evangelical radio programs no longer presented musical variety formats or maintained large music staffs, did the Back to the Bible Quartet become a featured group with its own recordings and consistent membership. Their singing was featured in the opening segments of *Back to the Bible* through the mid–nineties but then taken off the air. As the ministry admitted when it announced the decision to listeners, *any* music on an evangelical radio program today will please some people and turn away others. Ironically then, with audiences split between traditional and contemporary styles, the only solution was *no* music.[77]

Paul Myers and the Haven of Rest

"Ahoy there, shipmates! Eight bells, and all's well!"

So began, with the sounds of the waterfront and the clanging of eight bells, each new daily broadcast of the *Haven of Rest*. In the same way, on a real waterfront in 1934, began a new day for the program's founder and speaker, Paul Myers.[78] He was known to listeners simply as "First Mate Bob." Why only first mate? Because Jesus was his Captain.

Myers was well acquainted with sorrow.[79] His first wife had died soon after the birth of their daughter. He remarried in 1920 and a second daughter was born. Within a year, however, both his children had come down with severe cases of whooping cough, then a very serious disease. Yet Myers was too caught up in a successful Hollywood career to care much about problems at home. In those days of silent films he led a movie orchestra called the "Happy-Go-Luckies" that worked for Hal Roach Studios, producers of the Keystone Cops and, later, L'il Rascals serials. He was a popular man on the Hollywood scene, drinking and going to parties, seeing other women, and staying away from home for weeks or months at a time. Night after night Thelma Myers was left alone with two gravely sick little girls. Then through her mother, Thelma heard about a woman evangelist, Aimee Semple McPherson, who had recently built a meeting center in Los Angeles and was broadcasting over her own radio station, KFSG. Thelma decided to attend one of the meetings at the Angelus Temple. At the close of the service, July 24, 1924, she answered the altar call and converted to Christ. For the next ten years Thelma prayed for her husband. The few times he was home, she would plead with him to convert to Christ. She clung to the scripture, "Believe on the Lord Jesus Christ and thou shalt be saved, and thy house" (Acts 16:31). Later, two more children were born, another daughter and then a son. She took them to church, taught them to pray, and in time all four of the children came to Christ.

When her son was five years old he became desperately ill with a fever of 105 degrees. But Paul Myers, who by then had become a radio personality and director of two California stations, had been gone for months. Then one night Thelma felt a powerful urge to pray. Kneeling at her son's bedside she prayed, earnestly and fervently, far into the night. She did not know where her husband was. Nor did she did know he had become a shell of a man, wandering aimlessly in a drunken haze beside the waterfront in San Diego. He was tired and sick, sick in body and soul. "Oh, God," he groaned, "Oh, God." Yet his small voice was lost in the stillness of the night, a stillness broken only by the harbor noises and the lapping of the water against the wharf. Myers looked down at the dark, oily water. Memories of his childhood flashed into his mind, of his mother teaching him about the love of Jesus, of kneeling before the family altar to pray. Scenes of his wife and children, of their sad and pleading faces, bore down upon him. Waves of awful self-condemnation tormented him. Suddenly, the thought occurred to Myers that nobody knew where he was, and possibly no more than a handful of people even cared. He had lost his job and probably his family as well. What if he jumped in the bay and made an end of it all? No, that wasn't the answer. But what? He fumbled for his bottle, found it empty, and tossed it in the water.

Then Myers heard a new sound coming faintly across the harbor, the sound of a ship's bell. Two bells, then four, six, and eight. It was four o'clock in the morning. He had been walking all night in a drunken stupor. And still the rise and fall of the water continued its monotonous rhythm. "Like me," he thought to himself, as he recalled a Bible verse from his childhood: "But the wicked are like the troubled sea when it cannot rest" (Isaiah 57:20). Though the dawn had begun to break, the harbor was still foggy and cold. The cardboard in his shoes, where the soles had worn out, no longer protected his feet from the chill. His suit coat was badly worn and, though Myers pulled it tightly around him, afforded little protection from the cold. Then, suddenly, he felt strangely warmed. By some trick of his memory it seemed he could almost feel his dear mother's hand upon his head. "Jesus loves you, Paul," his mother seemed to tell him as she had done so often in his childhood. "Remember that no matter where you are, no matter what you do, Jesus does love you." Verses of hymns she had once taught him now came to his mind. He tried to mouth the words. But for more than a year his voice, once so well known on the radio, had been nothing but a husky whisper. Then Myers heard it again, the clanging of the ship's bells coming across the water. Two, four ... this time it was ten bells. Eight o'clock in the morning. Suddenly it occurred to him that today was Sunday. People would soon be gathering for church and he wanted to go too. Perhaps it wasn't too late. Maybe he could find someone to pray for him, to bring him peace.

Myers pointed his feet toward downtown. He spent his last pennies on a meager breakfast, then found a gas station washroom to clean himself up as best he could. At the nearest church he went inside and slipped into the pews with a sense of eager anticipation. All around him worshipers were happily chatting as they gathered before the morning service. But no one spoke to Myers, not even the minister. The service was cold and formal and Jesus was not mentioned. Myers felt completely let down. Weak from lack of food and rest, Myers staggered back to his cheap hotel room. Behind a week's rent, he was afraid they wouldn't let him in. But he made it to his room and tried to find the words to express his grief. All that came out were desolate sobs of "Oh, God." Then his gaze fell upon a Gideon Bible. He had ignored it before, but now the book seemed to offer a slim ray of hope.

Hands trembling, heart pounding, Myers picked up the Bible and opened its pages. But the lines blurred in his teary, bloodshot eyes. So he placed the book on a chair, knelt down before it, and simply poured out his heart to the Lord. "Oh, God," he cried out, "I'm a terrible sinner. I'm lost. I believe You can help me. Please. Please God, save me. Oh, Jesus, I need you so much." And then—February 15, 1934—Paul Myers was converted. His load was lifted and a new peace suffused his soul. "But would my wife take me back?" Myers asked himself. Afraid she would not take a phone call, instead he sent a brief telegram: "Thank Him for a direct answer." She would know what it meant. And so he hitchhiked home to Los Angeles.

When Thelma Myers saw her husband at the door, she was startled by the appearance of a man who had so recently been broken and derelict. Tears filled her eyes and she was speechless. "Thelma, it's me, I've come home," Paul told her, now crying himself. "But this time it's different. I've found Christ." They embraced and were reunited "in Christ." After a few days Myers shared with his wife a promise he had made. "Honey, I'm going into full-time service for the Lord. I don't know where or how. But I made Him that promise down in San Diego when He came into my heart. And I know He'll open up a door somehow, somewhere." Myers was not a preacher and had no formal Bible training. But in a moment the answered dawned on him. "We can start a radio program!" With his radio experience, this was something Myers knew how to do. Immediately, ideas for the program's format began to formulate in his mind. He would use a quartet, pipe organ, vibraharp, and some poetry—a successful combination in his previous commercial broadcasting. And given the experience of his conversion, the selection of "Haven of Rest"[80] as both the program title and theme song was a natural.

> I've anchored my soul in the haven of rest,
> I'll sail the wide seas no more;
> The tempest may sweep o'er the wild stormy deep,
> In Jesus I'm safe evermore

But where would Myer find the talent needed for his new broadcast? The official history of the Haven of Rest ministry tells the story.

> Starting out in blind faith, and having to walk much of the time because there was no money for car fare, he came in contact with Kenny Nelson. Kenny had been singing in a Gospel Quartet and was looking for a field of service. Then someone suggested looking at the Southern California Bible College at that time located in Pasadena. There he found Ernie Payne, bass, and Bob Bowman, baritone. As they talked, he mentioned the need of an organist and at that moment Lorin Whitney came walking up the hill. Ernie and Bob said, "He plays the organ very well." So, after talking with Lorin, the Lord had put together the talent for the program. David Kleinsasser joined them as the lead tenor of the quartet.[81]

With the format decided and talent lined up, Myers now needed to secure the airtime. Having worked before with KMPC in Los Angeles, he spoke with the station manager about his idea for a new program. The manager knew that Myers had written, produced, and announced radio programs that had once been heard across the Southwest and so he agreed to carry the new broadcast. Thus in March 1934—just one month after Myer's conversion—*Haven of Rest* was on the air bringing "words of life on the wings of melody." Now the same clang of the bells that had once awakened Myers to a new life was calling multiplied thousands to hear the gospel. After a few months, Myers switched to the more-powerful KFI—where *Haven of Rest* soon set a record of receiving 2,800 letters in a single day, more than any other program on the station at that time. Soon the broadcast was picked up three days a week by the West Coast affiliates of the NBC Blue Network and also once a week nationwide on the Red Network. Later, the same arrangement was carried over to the Mutual network.

In the early years Myers could often be seen walking or hitching a ride to the studio. For travel to recording sessions, concerts and church meetings, all six men—Myers, the quartet, and the organist—would often pile into Kenny Nelson's 1932 coupe with its rumble seat and running boards. From these humble beginnings grew what would become a worldwide ministry— and one that also helped start other ministries, including the Far East Broadcasting Company missionary radio outreach and the World Vision relief agency. Myers as "First Mate Bob" stayed at the helm until his retirement in 1971 and death in 1973. The broadcast continues today under the name of *Haven*, while the quartet transformed into a contemporary group and recorded albums through about 2003.

Through its heyday, the Haven of Rest Quartet enjoyed relative stability in its membership.[82] Baritone and soloist Bob Bowman was known as "Second Mate Bobbie" and filled in for Myers when he was sick. Bowman left for the Philippines in 1946 when, having been so impressed by the effectiveness of radio, he founded the Far East Broadcasting Company as a missionary endeavor. His replacement, Leonard Fox, remained with quartet for the next twenty years. Kenny Nelson sang first tenor for thirty-two years and Ernie Payne the bass for forty-two years. The lead tenor/soloist position changed a couple of times until Charley Turner joined the quartet and stayed through the late fifties. He was replaced by Herman Hosier, who remained until 1970. At the Wurlizter organ was Lorin Whitney, who accompanied group through 1958, and then Dean McNichols took over until his retirement in 1984. The Haven of Rest Quartet made numerous albums for the Christian Faith and Word labels, and the group frequently accompanied Myers on nationwide evangelistic tours. As a liner note from the period attests, "Many hundreds of persons have been won to the Lord through the personal testimony and singing of these men. They have held services in churches, auditoriums, factories, baseball stadiums, railroad shops, hospitals, military and naval bases, to name a few places open to this unique ministry."[83]

The four men also served in their local churches as choir directors, songleaders, and other roles. In addition to singing in the quartet, each man had a full-time staff position with the Haven of Rest ministry—Nelson as chief accountant, Hosier in tape editing, Fox in shipping and music arranging, Payne as music coordinator and librarian, and McNichols in tape duplication. Yet despite all these activities, at the time their albums were recorded the group had an astounding repertoire of more than seven hundred songs. Not surprisingly, the Haven of Rest Quartet performed and recorded a wide variety of songs, and so no particular songs became associated with the group. But music with a nautical theme was always a favorite and featured on many recordings—including "Shine on Me," "Jesus Savior Pilot Me," "Crossing the Bar," "I Will Pilot Thee," and a popular radio song of 1944, "In Times Like These."

V.O. Stamps and the Stamps Quartet

Making a gold record is a feat that, like plane rides or even space flights, people today seldom remark upon. In today's mass culture, music albums sell in the tens and hundreds of thousands as a matter of course; indeed, they would not be produced in the first place if such sales were not already guaranteed. Yet in all the history of music, the million mark in sales was not broken until 1899 by sheet music sales of Scott Joplin's "Maple Leaf Rag."[84] Even now, for a Christian or Gospel music recording to sell more than a million units, and also be ranked as a hit on the same level as secular songs, is an accomplishment. Yet Virgil Oliver Stamps and the Stamps Quartet did both in 1927 when they were the first gospel quartet to work for a major recording company and the first to sell a million records.[85]

Today the phrase "Stamps-Baxter music" is generic term that describes a unique style of gospel singing. Behind the phrase, however, are two real people, V.O. Stamps and J.R. Baxter. If James Vaughn can be credited with inventing the professional quartet and using radio to introduce "gospel music" to America, then to Stamps goes the credit for using radio and records to bring the music into mass popularity.

Stamps's career was marked by innovation and adaptability. His father, W.O. Stamps, worked variously as a lumberman, merchant, and state legislator. Even the place of his birth—Upshur County, Texas, on September 18, 1892—was located in the northeastern corner of the state near the borders of Louisiana, Arkansas, and Oklahoma. His inner drive manifested itself in Stamps's early teens when, upon attending the Upshur County Singing Convention, he instantly gained a love of quartet singing that defined the rest of his life. At the age of fifteen, in 1907, he enrolled in one of the singing schools then common throughout the South. Four years later while still in his teens, Stamps was teaching singing schools while working at the family store in Ore City, Texas. In 1914 Stamps not only composed his first song, "Man Behind the Plow," but even sold it for ten cents a copy. Even today, few songwriters sell their first compositions. In the case of V.O. Stamps, he was so encouraged by his initial success that—not surprisingly—he stopped teaching singing schools, quit the family store, and went to work for a music company.

His early music career brought a series of moves—from Texas to Atlanta in 1917 to work for another music company, and then in 1918 to Lawrenceburg, Tennessee, and the headquarters of the famous James D. Vaughn Publishing Company. A year later Stamps and his brother Frank were sent to open a Vaughn branch office in Jacksonville, Texas, midway between Dallas, Texarkana, and Shreveport, Louisiana. Virgil ran the office while Frank managed the traveling Vaughn quartets that were based in Texas. In time, Stamps developed an ambition to launch a music company of his own. He saved his money and, apparently, sold songbooks for the rival A.J. Showalter Music Company on the side to earn extra cash. After this discovery seemed to be confirmed by the Vaughn office in Tennessee, Stamps in 1924 finalized the split by forming his own V.O. Stamps Music Publishing Company in Jacksonville and releasing his first songbook. Frank Stamps joined the business not as a partner but as quartet manager, and soon the first Stamps Quartet—consisting of Frank and former Vaughn singers J.E. Hamilton, Lee Myers, and J.E. Wheeler—was on the road.

Within two years, however, the V.O. Stamps Music Publishing Company was on the verge of bankruptcy. Even the quartet disbanded after going through several personnel changes and drumming up little interest. Then in 1926, Stamps met Baxter. J.R. "Pap" Baxter Jr., born in 1887, made his early career with the Showalter company in DeKalb, Georgia. In joining Stamps, the promoter without peer, Baxter provided what the renamed Stamps-Baxter Music and Printing Company desperately needed. Not only did Baxter put up a forty-nine percent stake in the business, he brought a trained knowledge of music theory and harmony. Unlike some earlier releases, Stamps-Baxter songs became highly singable with easy lead-ins and no tricky meters or difficult jumps in the voice parts. Yet the company developed a unique and infectious "Stamps-Baxter" style that offered straightforward verses, followed by choruses that typically featured a strong lead or bass solo with the other three parts rhythmically echoing the words on the afterbeat.

Joining the Stamps-Baxter partnership was another key figure in the later success of the company. Baxter's wife Clarice was a part owner in the business and, like her husband, a well-trained musician. Born in 1898 and raised in DeKalb County, Georgia, she developed a lifelong love of sacred music while attending singing schools near her home. After her marriage in 1918 she gave up her position as a teacher to join her husband in his work with the Showalter company. For four decades she was an important influence on the printing operation of the Stamps-Baxter company and on its annual School of Music. When her husband died in 1960, Clarice Baxter became company president and the first woman to hold such a position in the gospel music industry.

With J. R. Baxter in the fold, songbook sales soon took off and the company was restored to financial health. As such, the enterprise was well positioned to ride the crest of a new wave in American society. The year 1927 was perhaps the year that American mass culture came into its own: the advent of national radio networks, the first "talking" motion picture, the thrilling transatlantic flight of Charles Lindbergh, the famous "long count" boxing victory of Gene Tunney over Jack Dempsey, and a Babe Ruth slugest that set a new record of sixty homers during the 1927 season.

The Stamps Quartet also reorganized that year with Frank Stamps singing bass, Odis Echols at baritone, and brothers Roy and Palmer Wheeler at lead and tenor, respectively. And for the first time ever with a gospel quartet, the group hired a pianist who did not double as a singer. Brock Speer brought a syncopated style of play inspired, he later said, by hearing a circus drummer and asking himself, "I wonder if I could do that on the piano." On stage the men always dressed sharply in matching suits and often in tuxedos. Officially named the All-Star Quartet (for the company was now putting other Stamps quartets on the road), the group adopted as its theme song a 1925 composition by M.L. Yandell and Otis Deaton, "Give the World a Smile," and reworked it in the Stamps-Baxter style. Audiences were captivated by the number and, to loud and enthusiastic applause, requested encore after encore.

By the late 1920s, with numerous professional quartets—sponsored by the Stamps, Vaughn, Showalter, and other companies—on the road, singing conventions in the South took on a new dimension. Drawn by the opportunity to sell a high volume of songbooks, several professional groups would show up for the events. The custom of the day was for all the quartets to sit on the stage together and, in a friendly competition, each take their turn to sing. The Frank Stamps quartet, however, so took the public by storm that an impressed talent scout from the Victor Talking Machine Company (later RCA Victor) offered the group a recording contract. The first recording session took place October 20, 1927, at the Victor studios in Atlanta. Because the 78 rpm records of the day could only feature one song per side, the Victor representative wanted the quartet to sing his two favorite hymns, "Bringing in the Sheaves" and "Rescue the Perishing." Stamps and his group then cut the recording, plus a second one that featured "Love Leads the Way" and its upbeat and catchy theme song, "Give the World a Smile," which urged believers to "Give the world a smile each day, helping someone on life's way."

Within months, on the popularity of "Give the World a Smile," the record sold more than a million copies. Soon quartets nationwide picked up the song to open their own performances. In 1928 the Stamps-Baxter Company moved its main office to Dallas and opened up a branch in Chattanooga, Tennesse—close to its chief rival, the James D. Vaughn Company. The Frank Stamps All-Star Quartet continued to produce more Victor records, now featuring songs newly published by the Stamps-Baxter Company. Even Virgil Stamps, a strong bass singer who had his own quartet in the Dallas area, cut two records in 1929 and 1930 for the locally-based Brunswick label. In 1934 the company brought its songbook printing operations in-house and constructed its own printing plant, at the time the largest printing concern in the world devoted to gospel music. But Virgil Stamps, always the promoter ready to anticipate the next big trend, was soon aiming to parlay his recording and publishing success into an even higher level of exposure. In the thirties that meant radio.

Stamps's first venture into radio began in 1936 when he reorganized his own V.O. Stamps Quartet and broadcast twice a week over KRLD in Dallas, a fifty-thousand-watt station that covered Texas and beyond. Eager to enlarge his coverage, he used the then-new technolgy of electrical transcription to record 33 rpm long-play discs and sent them to such stations as WOAI in San Antonio, WSM in Nashville, and even XENT and XERL in Mexico. Response was so encouraging—"Give the World a Smile" was as big a hit on radio as it has been on records—that Stamps made a deal with XERL, one of the most interesting stations in the history of radio. Boasting an incredible half a million watts of power, the facility was built by John "Doc" Brinkley to evade U.S. regulations and promote a goat-gland medicine he had developed on his North Carolina farm. Brinkley set up his studio in Del Rio, Texas, but located the transmitter just across the Mexican border and pointed the signal back toward Texas. Though the station only penetrated fifty miles into Mexico, because of the propagation properties of AM radio its nighttime signal could be heard all across North America. Stamps made an agreement with XERL to furnish the station with a bulk supply of Stamps Quartet transcription discs that would be played continuously each night from nine to midnight and then again the next morning starting as early as four o'clock. James Blackwood, whose Blackwood Brothers quartet was then in the Stamps organization, remembered being in the Dallas office one morning in the thirties when several trucks backed up to the loading platform. At the time, the company was selling *V.O. Stamps Quartet Radio Favorites* and "most of the mail was orders for that songbook," Blackwood recalled. "They had orders that day from twenty-one states, all Canadian provinces, and even some islands in the Pacific Ocean."[86]

Success in radio led the way in 1938 for the V.O. Stamps Quartet to secure a contract with Columbia Records, a major label. At its first studio session the group recorded several songs including, of course, "Give the World a Smile." Meanwhile the Frank Stamps Quartet—which had made the company's first breakthrough recording with Victor in 1927—sang on radio in Greenville, South Carolina, and then in 1938 moved its base to Hot Springs, Arkansas, and station KTHS. A year later the group relocated again when it was hired to sing on powerful KVOO in Tulsa. Radio in the thirties also energized another venture, the annual Stamps-Baxter School of Music begun when the company was founded in 1924. Young people nationwide, especially those in rural areas, were hearing the Stamps Quartet on radio and eager to attend the school. Two who enrolled in the thirties were James Blackwood from Mississippi and a young Glen Payne from Texas who later went on to fame as lead singer for the Cathedrals Quartet. Every June for many years, well into the fifties, the last session of the annual Stamps-Baxter School of Music was an "all-night singing" at the Dallas Sportatorium broadcast over KRLD. The 1939 event, for example, ran from 8 p.m. to 7 a.m. and was aired for eight straight hours. During its heyday the convention was also heard nationwide over the CBS network which broadcast a half hour of the event.

At the height of his career in 1940, on August 19 Stamps unexpectedly passed away at the age of forty-seven. That year he was supervising more than a dozen quartets that, from their respective home bases, were all singing on the radio and maintaining full schedules of appearances. Stamps himself was editor of the influential monthly *Gospel Music News* and president of the Texas State Singers Association. Upon Stamps's death his brother Frank returned to Dallas to assist in the main office, while J.R. Baxter became president of the company. The two men, however, were unable to duplicate the chemistry that had existed between the original partners and Frank Stamps left in 1946 to form his own Stamps Quartet Music Company. For many years afterward, the split resulted in a bewildering array of "Stamps Quartets" traveling across the country. In time, Baxter prospered most in the publishing area and Frank Stamps in the quartets. Stamps sold his company in 1964 to J.D. Sumner, who carried on the Stamps Quartet name until his death in 1998—fully seventy-one years after the group recorded its original million-selling record. To the general public Virgil Oliver Stamps is best remembered for writing in 1937 the tune to "When the Saints Go Marching In." But in the world of gospel singing he is credited with giving the music a distinct style and bringing it to national prominence. He understood before his contemporaries how radio, recording, personal appearances, and publishing were all interrelated and self-reinforcing in a mass media society. Though less known as a songwriter, Stamps regularly contributed to his company's songbooks. In one of his efforts, from 1922, he expressed "My Prayer."

> O Father, hear me as I pray to Thee,
> I know that I am far from purity;
> But Jesus died that sinful men might live,
> So in His Name I ask Thee to forgive.

When news of Stamps's sudden passing reached the gospel music world, all were saddened by the loss but grateful for his ministry. Homer Rodeheaver expressed these sentiments when, in a telegram referring to Stamps's powerful bass voice, he wrote, "We are thinking of the great rejoicing over in Heaven because of the many souls won to Christ through his music. They will probably let all the rest of the bass singers in the heavenly choir take a vacation, at least for a little while, and just put Virgil O. Stamps in their place!"[87]

Three

The Forties
Crusades and Conventions

WHEN CHARLES FULLER READ the editorial in the *Christian Century*, the leading journal of liberal Protestantism, he knew who they were talking about. The magazine thundered in 1943 about "irresponsible exhorters, freelance evangelists, and independent peddlers of spiritual nostrums who have no more 'church' behind them than a microphone with which to send forth their appeals and a post office box in which to receive their proceeds."[1] Leaders of the nation's mainline denominations were not taking the fundamentalist resurgence on the radio lying down. They saw Fuller and other gospel radio preachers as a "network religious radio program racket, capitalized by independent superfundamentalist revivalists" and complained that the situation "will not be eliminated until Mutual"—the network of Fuller, Maier, Crawford, Myers, Epp, and others—"goes the whole way and bans paid religious programs altogether, as other networks have done."[2]

And Fuller knew his foes were winning. NBC had refused to sell airtime for paid religious programs since 1928, and CBS since 1931.[3] Though the networks cited concerns about the allegedly inferior quality of independent religious programs, their policies were—with the constant urging of the Federal (later National) Council of Churches—prompted by a desire to avoid controversy over issues of sectarianism and on-air fundraising. Their concerns about the misuse of religion on the radio seemed validated by the politicized, antisemitic preaching of a Roman Catholic priest, Father Charles Coughlin. After railing against the United States' entry into World War II as a "British-Jewish-Roosevelt conspiracy" and amassing a network audience of forty million listeners, in 1942 the Vatican at last took the extraordinary step of forcing him off the air. To avert criticism, NBC and CBS hit upon a solution that, to them, seemed "made in heaven." Religious programs were a public service, they declared. Such programs were only to be broadcast on a "sustaining" basis with airtime donated at no charge by the networks. To be fair, NBC and

CBS granted the time to the representative organizations of the Protestant, Catholic, and Jewish faiths. In turn the Federal Council, acting for the Protestant denominations, would allocate airtime among its member churches. As an NBC advertisement in a radio program guide magazine of the period explained,

> [B]roadcasting of religious programs is a vital public service. First principle is that time devoted to religion is donated. The reason is obvious. To sell time would give an advantage to the religious organization with the most funds available for such use. In general, NBC relies for religious programs on the central or national agencies of the great religious faiths.... [N]o speaker ever attacks another faith, nor seeks to change the religious convictions of listeners...."[4]

Ironically, Fuller mused, the NBC and CBS policy had the *opposite* effect of ensuring that only the largest and wealthiest religious groups—those represented by the Federal Council—would receive any airtime. Fundamentalist churches and ministries were locked out because they were not members of the Council. Only the Mutual network, founded in 1934 and in need of funds to compete with its older rivals, would sell time for religious programs. By 1943 these broadcasts accounted for one-fourth of Mutual's gross income, bringing the network revenues of $3.3 million a year. Yet Fuller knew that Mutual was wavering. The network was more established now, was sensitive to the criticisms of the Federal Council about being beholden to religious fundamentalists—and more to the point, was losing money on any prime Sunday evening slots adjacent to religious programs. Advertisers complained that any broadcasts which followed Fuller or Maier or Crawford would find only religiously-inclined people tuned in.

The Federal Council of Churches had mounted a frontal assault, signing more than fifty radio stations to "ironclad contracts obliging them to use the Federal Council-approved programs and no other" and vowing to enroll every station in America. "The Council was working very hard to keep gospel broadcasters off the air," recalled Chicago preacher Torrey Johnson. "In our area, the Chicago Council of Churches would decide who would be on the air and who wouldn't be on the air, and they had a strong bias. And they would put the liberals on, and the others were omitted."[5] Recently, an influential new organization called the Institute for Education by Radio had emerged as a pressure group in the campaign to have Mutual change its policy on paid religious programs. As Fuller wrote to supporters in a July 1942 newsletter,

> There is now organized opposition to all Fundamental radio programs in the United States, and this organization is bringing pressure to bear on the radio stations, asking them to refuse time to all religious programs which are not approved by a committee (though these programs are paying for their time). They plan later to have time given free of charge to approved religious programs, and the *Old Fashioned*

Revival Hour would not be on that approved list! Why? Because the hour is Fundamental and too evangelistic in its teaching.⁶

The threat was serious. By mid-decade, the three major networks controlled the programming of ninety-five percent of the nation's radio stations. Local outlets needed popular network offerings to survive—and because the networks knew it, they imposed one-sided contracts on local affiliates. Network dominance was so great that, by the early 1940s, the FCC had begun antitrust investigations. If Mutual succumbed to the pressure and joined NBC and CBS in refusing to sell airtime for paid religious programs, then Fuller knew the gospel could literally be taken off the air.

It was twenty years earlier, 1922, that William Ward Ayer had first listened to radio on a neighbor's homemade crystal set while he was a young pastor in Valparaiso, Indiana. Now twenty years later he was preaching by radio each week to a quarter of a million people throughout the largest city in America. He had been converted at a Billy Sunday meeting in 1916 and attended the Bible Institute founded in Chicago by the great evangelist Dwight L. Moody. Yet in 1942, as pastor of New York's famed Calvary Baptist Church, Ayer could reach more people in one day by radio than Sunday or Moody could in a year. Each week his sermons were carried by radio station WHN and its fifty thousand watts of power to a potential audience of twenty-two million. Not only had hundreds of people come to Christ through the radio outreach, but the broadcasts had strengthened the ministry of the church. Attendance at Calvary Baptist had risen from four hundred to more than sixteen hundred people. More than five thousand had walked the aisle and were converted. And the church was publishing a widely read periodical, *The Calvary Pulpit*, that expanded the Gospel ministry to thousands more each month.

Like Fuller, Ayer too was dismayed by the mounting "liberal" assault on paid religious programs. They not only wanted all of the donated airtime to themselves but were now trying to eliminate all other religious programs—even those that, like Fuller and Ayer, paid their own way. If people were blessed by the broadcasts and willing to support them, why shouldn't the preachers be allowed to purchase airtime? Liberal preachers such as S. Parkes Cadman and Harry Emerson Fosdick, who had been featured on NBC's *National Radio Pulpit* since 1928, had received millions of dollars worth of free airtime. Yet their programs were only listened to by small audiences and certainly were not popular enough to survive on their own. *There won't be a single evangelical, Biblical broadcast of the Gospel on the air in America if something isn't done immediately*, Ayer thought to himself. To alert his friends and listeners, he rushed into print with a lengthy article, "Will Americans Be Allowed to Broadcast the Gospel?"⁷ in *The Calvary Pulpit*. Response was encouraging but without an organized effort it wouldn't be enough. The Federal Council of Churches represented less than forty percent of Protestantism but it was the only group speaking for the historic Protestant movement.

However, Ayer was not the only preacher worried about the freedom to broadcast the gospel. Other evangelicals from around the country had seen the need to organize and present a united front. When a group of leading fundamentalist pastors and ministers wanted to organize a national conference, Ayer invited the planning committee to meet in the offices of Calvary Baptist Church. One of the men involved in the effort was J. Elwin Wright. Wright had been vitally concerned for many years about the need for united action. From his New England base, he had been active in evangelistic campaigns, literature crusades, radio broadcasts, musical tours, and in 1929 had organized an annual Bible conference in Rumney, New Hampshire. In time the meetings coalesced into the New England Fellowship and its summer conferences became an informal meeting ground for leaders from across the country. Men such as Walter Maier, Charles Fuller, and Donald Barnhouse were often booked for NEF events, and Wright gained both valuable contacts and a growing reputation.

The talk in Rumney was often about the need for an organized evangelical voice on the national level, and in 1941 the NEF board of directors authorized its president to work toward that end. Since Wright owned a bookstore and real estate business to provide his needs, he was in a position devote his time to the project—even if the New England Fellowship couldn't always pay its founder and president a full salary. Wright's first stop was Chicago where an invited group of evangelical leaders, including Fuller and Ayer, met October 27-28, 1941, on the campus of Moody Bible Institute. The men called for a conference to be held the next April in St. Louis for the purpose of organizing a national cooperative association. Wright was named to head a "temporary committee for united action" which met at Ayer's church in New York, and soon Wright was headed across the country to recruit delegates for the April meeting.

The efforts of Wright and Ayer and the planning committee culminated on April 7, 1942, when more than one hundred fifty evangelical leaders arrived at the Hotel Coronado in St. Louis for the organizing conference. Among those present was Harold Ockenga, pastor of the famed Park Street Church in Boston. Recently he had met with NBC executives at its Boston affiliate, WBZ, and sadly reported, "We shall have absolutely no opportunity of sharing equally in the broadcast facilities of that great network" unless the evangelical movement could organize on a national basis. In his keynote address to the conference, Ockenga decried the sad fact that,

> Evangelical Christianity has suffered nothing but a series of defeats for decades. The programs of few major denominations today are controlled by evangelicals.

Evangelical testimony has sometimes been reduced to the witness of individual churches.... Evangelicals have been so frozen out ... [as] one by one, various forces have discredited or attacked them, or even forced them out of positions of leadership, until today many of them are on the defensive or even the decline. The hour calls for a united front for evangelical action.[8]

The irony, Ockenga continued, was that evangelicals "are a very large minority, perhaps a majority, in America," but are "discriminated against because of the folly of our divided condition." To keep the gospel on the air, he believed, "this millstone of rugged independency which has held back innumerable movements before, in which individual leaders must be the whole hog or none, must be utterly repudiated by every one of us."[9] Then William Ward Ayer, who was respected as one of the most prominent of the fundamentalist leaders, lent his voice to the call for a united front. "Millions of evangelical Christians, if they had a common voice and a common meeting place," he declared, "would exercise under God an influence that would save American democracy." Radio could play an important part, he believed, but "if religious radio is relegated to sustaining time only, it will be reduced to the minimum and spread over such a wide variety of religious ideas as to spoil its effectiveness."[10] The conference moved to establish a National Association of Evangelicals for United Action, electing Ockenga as temporary president and Ayer to serve on the executive committee, and voted to call a constitutional convention in Chicago for the spring of 1943. Even before then, in August 1942, a twice-monthly newspaper, *United Evangelical Action*, was rolling off the presses. If the freedom to broadcast the gospel was under threat, they were ready to fairly join the battle.[11]

A month after the organizing conference, J. Elwin Wright found himself on the Columbus campus of Ohio State University. As representative of the month-old National Association of Evangelicals, he was hoping for the chance to address the annual conference of the Institute for Education by Radio. In 1941 the group had established a committee to study religious radio and now in May 1942 its recommendations would be voted upon. Because IER was composed of academics, it was the kind of "expert" organization the networks heeded. So it was important, Wright believed, for broadcasters of the gospel to be represented. When Wright had made his reservations for the IER conference, he hoped for the best. Yet until he arrived in Columbus he would have no idea whether the Institute would take him seriously or not. To his relief, he was invited to address the Institute session on religious programs. Sustaining time would continue no matter what action was taken on paid broadcasts, so Wright spoke to that issue first. To achieve "a fair division of time between representatives of the principal faiths," he argued, "we believe there should be *four* rather than three faiths taken into consideration." In addition to the Catholic and Jewish faiths, Wright went on,

> We have two great divisions of the church, probably of approximately equal numerical strength. The first is represented by the Federal Council of Churches of Christ in America. This includes the so-called liberal or modernist groups. The second is the evangelical or conservative group which, up to the present time, has been without cohesion and consequently without representation. The National Association of Evangelicals for United Action seems likely to become the representative of this group of between fifteen and twenty million church members.[12]

After urging that NAE be a "fourth force" in the allocation of sustaining time, Wright then focused his remarks on the issue of paid time. On this issue, the IER task group had recommended that all religious broadcasts be addressed to "a cross section of the public … [and] not to members of any one faith," that paid programs be eliminated and only sustaining time broadcasts allowed, and that on-air fundraising prohibited. While Wright could "heartily agree … [that] religious programs should not attack the beliefs of members of other faiths," he explained that the first IER recommendation would so dilute religious content that programs "will cease to have the power to bring conviction of spiritual need." NAE would find this unacceptable, he told the audience, for "we believe that this is a matter of eternal life or death, whether men accept Jesus Christ as Deity and the only Savior of mankind. Believing this, we would be lacking in sincerity … if we failed to do all in our power to win men to faith by the preaching of His Gospel." In fairness, he added that evangelicals would equally defend the rights of Catholics and Jews "to be just as positive in their programs as we wish to be in ours."[13]

Elimination of paid religious programs, Wright went on, had been done at NBC and CBS with the practical effect of "almost entirely exclud[ing] … doctrinally conservative groups." Even if NAE were treated as a "fourth force" in distribution of sustaining time, he pointed out, "The broadcasting companies are not likely to be willing to contribute the amount of time which the presentation of religion deserves and requires. We believe that groups financially able to carry a broadcast should be permitted to buy time." If a broadcaster pays for time, Wright urged, "it is only reasonable that opportunity be given to the listeners to share in the expense." Audiences tune in gospel programs—voluntarily—for spiritual benefit and may rightly be asked to share the expense through free-will donations in the same way that churches invite worshipers to contribute. "There is undoubtedly a good deal of racketeering going on in connection with religious broadcasts," Wright admitted to the IER session, but "[such] racketeering is almost wholly confined to a certain type of program which is undesirable from every standpoint." Evangelicals are "desirous of giving full cooperation in curbing such programs," he said, perhaps by requiring broadcasters to obtain certification according to standards set by NAE or their respective church councils. But he candidly suggested the proposed ban against on-air fundraising was aimed "not only against racketeering broadcasters but [also against] others which provide no reasonable ground for complaint." In the end, the Institute of Education by Radio rejected Wright's argument and endorsed a ban on solicitations. But he was encouraged as the conference agreed NAE should have a fair allotment of sustaining time, that some paid-time slots should be preserved, and that evangelicals had a right to broadcast their convictions "without dilution." Since IER was a private organization its guidelines were not binding on stations and networks, but carried the force of "expert" consensus. In his report to the NAE executive committee, Wright declared these gains showed "the vast amount of constructive work which may be accomplished" now that evangelicals "are in a position to speak through a central organization."[14]

Wright had arrived on May 3, 1942, for the opening of the IER conference. One year later to the very day, he joined more than a thousand delegates in Chicago for the constitutional convention of the National Association of Evangelicals for United Action. By the time delegates left Chicago they had approved an ambitious agenda for missions, evangelism, education, military chaplain recruitment, and government relations. Wright was commissioned to lead the new staff, as well as raise the money. With the country now at war, there was a great need for united action in areas ranging from missionary travel to ministerial draft deferments. Yet the issue that had first galvanized the movement, the threat to gospel broadcasting, had grown more urgent. It was no longer a matter of simply voicing evangelical arguments for academics who had never heard them before. Now it was a matter of exercising real leverage and doing real battle. NAE was being pulled in many different and important directions. Could the association muster the concentrated effort needed at this crucial juncture for religious broadcasters?[15]

Then in the fall of 1943 the worst-case scenario happened. The Mutual network announced that, although paid religious programs would still be accepted, beginning in 1944 they could last no more than half an hour and would only be aired on Sunday mornings. Furthermore, no on-air solicitation of funds would be permitted. For Charles Fuller, Walter Maier, and others who broadcast one-hour programs in prime Sunday afternoon and evening time slots, the decision could be a death knell—as it proved to be for some lesser-known radio preachers. Fuller responded by putting his *Old Fashioned Revival Hour* into syndication on independent stations, while keeping his *Pilgrim's Hour* broadcast on Mutual under the new restrictions in hopes the network might later change its mind. But for Mutual the new policy seemed to offer the best of both worlds. The network could not completely forego the revenues brought in by paid religious programs. And in restricting these broadcasts to Sunday mornings, Mutual could still take the preachers' money while opening up prime-time slots that enabled the network to better compete with NBC and CBS.

Evangelicals across the country, however, were utterly dismayed by the Mutual decision. The announcement sparked a spontaneous nationwide protest from the evangelical community. Reaction was intense and immediate. Some groups held mass meetings, mounted publicity campaigns, or threatened legal action. James DeForest Murch, the dynamic young radio preacher of *The Christian's Hour*, was also incensed. An accomplished writer, he rushed into print with articles and editorials condemning the Federal Council of Churches for its policy and the Mutual network for its action. But as he thought about such tactics, he became uneasy. Murch believed those in positions of authority with the government and radio industry wanted to be fair-minded and public-spirited. From their viewpoint, their policies were a rational response to a thorny issue. To impugn them in public as "enemies of religion" would only alienate them. Filing lawsuits or pushing congressional legislation were all-or-nothing propositions in which gospel broadcasters were as likely to lose as to win. Better to work with the networks in a constructive way, Murch thought, to earn their respect and show how gospel broadcasters could satisfy their concerns if paid programs were reinstated.

But how? To be credible, the effort would need the support of the National Association of Evangelicals. Through his involvement with the NAE radio committee, Murch knew the association would do whatever it could to help. Yet with NAE occupied by so many other vital wartime concerns, how could a sustained and effective campaign be mounted to lobby the networks and counter the powerful Federal Council of Churches? Murch was thinking the matter over without much success, when the telephone rang. To his surprise, on the other end of the line was Eugene Bertermann, business manager for Walter Maier and *The Lutheran Hour*. He had read Murch's articles and asked if he and Maier could meet with Murch in Cincinnati later that month. Murch agreed and hung up. When the three men met at Cincinnati's Gibson Hotel, the discussion lasted the entire day. In time, they agreed to approach the National Association of Evangelicals and request, as Murch said, that NAE sponsor a "move for the organization of all evangelical broadcasters into an effective pressure group which could deal officially with all the broader and deeper problems involved."[16]

Radio was a large and complex industry, now under wartime rules that made things even more complicated. Religious broadcasters could not afford to assign others to fight their battles for them. So Murch was heartened when NAE agreed to hold a meeting of gospel broadcasters in conjunction with its second annual convention slated for April 1944 in Columbus—the same city where, two years earlier, J. Elwin Wright had won their first victory at the Institute for Education by Radio. Some one hundred fifty broadcasters turned out on April 7, 1944, for the two-day radio session of the NAE convention.

The enormity of the challenge they faced was daunting, now that all three radio networks had restricted paid religious programs. But once the meeting was gaveled to order, the broadcasters got quickly down to business. First item was the selection of a temporary president to lead the meeting. As a member of the NAE executive committee, Ayer was a logical choice. In starting the meeting, he set an urgent tone. Sports, politics, and news had unlimited freedom, he pointed out, while religious broadcasting was continually being put under restriction. "We must maintain our freedom of speech in America," Ayer believed, "whether it be in the pulpit, or on the street corner, or over the radio."[17]

Dale Crowley, Sr., of Washington, D.C., speaker for *The Right Start for the Day*, was named secretary to record the session. Discussion went back and forth, but soon the consensus was clear. When pastor Vincent Brushwyler of Muscatine, Iowa, stepped forward and moved that "we form a national association of Gospel broadcasters, to be affiliated with the National Association of Evangelicals," the response was a resounding "Aye!"[18] A statement of faith was adopted and a new name approved, National Religious Broadcasters, suggested by Crowley. The new association would need a constitution and bylaws, and Murch agreed to chair a drafting committee. The panel would submit its draft at a constitutional convention to be held at Chicago in September. The task of developing a code of ethics, one that would promote high standards and reassure the industry and public that evangelical broadcasters could use the airwaves responsibly, was assigned to a committee headed by Ayer. In doing so, Ayer enlisted the help of Rosel Hyde, general counsel of the FCC and later its chairman.

The constitutional convention was called for September 21, 1944, at Chicago's Moody Memorial Church. The new NRB constitution was presented to the delegates, with the code of ethics developed by Ayer's committee incorporated into the document. The code was written in two parts with a section for producers of radio programs and another for station owners and operators. It covered issues of sponsorship, character, production, cooperation, advertising, financial accountability, regulatory compliance, and responsibility to uphold the gospel, the family, and the nation. The association would endeavor to "establish and maintain high standards with respect to the end that such programs may be constantly developed and improved, and that their public interest and usefulness may be enhanced."[19] By acclamation the new constitution was approved. Ayer was confirmed as president, a board of directors was created, and a select group of leading broadcasters were appointed to an executive committee. Two months later, on December 18, 1944, NRB was awarded its charter of incorporation. Religious broadcasting, which had once been a primary concern of NAE, now shifted to broadcasters themselves. The one-time parent organization would remain a supportive observer, but for better or worse broadcasters were now on their own in the fight to keep the gospel on the airwaves.

Today's evangelicals take "Christian radio" for granted. Yet when NRB was formed in 1944, evangelicals in the United States were largely gone from network radio. In the years after World War II, however, the slow but patient work of persuading the networks to accept paid religious programs eventually bore fruit. In 1949 the ABC network (which had been formed four years earlier when antitrust regulations forced NBC to sell one of two networks it owned) became the first to reverse its policy. Over the decade of the fifties—and aided by a 1956 endorsement from the influential *Broadcasting* trade journal—the other networks followed suit. In the complex area of religion, media executives ultimately came around to the conclusions that the easiest way of ensuring fair treatment was to neutrally sell airtime to all legitimate comers. In 1960 the FCC ruled that stations could count paid religious programs, and not just sustaining broadcasts, toward their public service requirements. With stations able to sell time they had once donated, paid religious programming boomed. Sustaining programs, which accounted for forty-seven percent of religious broadcasts in 1959, fell to just eight percent twenty years later.[20] In 1978 the National Council of Churches bowed to reality, reversed its policy, and declared that all religious groups should have the opportunity to buy airtime.

In time, the victory of evangelical broadcasters had consequences they could not have foreseen. When the system of sustaining religious broadcasts ultimately unravelled, liberal groups that had depended on the system had nothing to fall back upon; to this day, they are not a factor in broadcasting. By contrast, evangelicals who had to pay for airtime and independently create their own productions, thereby established an infrastructure that carried them into the next phase of broadcasting. By the time evangelical broadcasters convinced the networks to allow paid religious programs, radio was no longer a national network medium—but television was. Charles Fuller and Walter Maier never made it on TV, but others who followed them did. And in radio, the expertise that evangelicals gained in producing their own programs was instrumental in allowing them to be major players in what radio was starting by the late 1940s to become. Since the twenties, government regulation put the cost of station ownership and operation outside the reach of most churches and religious groups. Thus, in the thirties and forties religious programs enjoyed their greatest outreach on national network radio. Now in the late 1940s with the advent of television, the door of network radio was starting to shut. By contrast, in the aftermath of World War II the demand for more local radio stations exploded. Evangelicals, with a wealth of religious programming available to them, were ready to start owning some of those stations—and give birth to "Christian radio" as it is known today.

The first locally owned religious radio station licensed on a commercial basis was launched in 1946 by a man who loved to sing.[21] One night, David Hofer and his quartet were singing at an evangelicalistic rally in Dinuba, California. Yet once the group finished its musical program and then listened to the evening's message, Hofer sensed that God was aiming the preacher's altar call at *him*. Every gospel rally was special, of course. But Hofer and the quartet had been to evangelistic meetings before. Why had God chosen this night, this place, to move upon his heart? It was true that the Youth for Christ evangelist, Paul Pietsch, was preaching with great power and conviction. That was part of it, Hofer knew, but not all. As he stood on the platform, he felt a growing assurance that God had brought him here, to this town, for an appointment. Dinuba was just a tiny dot on the California map, about thirty miles east of Fresno. It was like many small towns, scattered across the vastness of San Joaquin Valley, where the quartet had sung before. But as the warm night air of the valley hung over the hall, mixed with the faint piney scent of the Sierra Mountains beyond, Hofer became certain that here was the place God had called him.

Dinuba did not look like anyplace special when Hofer had driven up from Los Angeles that day. Like Hofer, the men in the quartet were all students at the Bible Institute of Los Angeles. Their thoughts were about getting to the rally, staying on pitch, and returning home to their studies. It was 1945, the war in Europe and Asia was just about over, and young men were looking ahead now to getting an education and exploring the new world that lay beyond. The Youth for Christ rally promised to be exciting, but Dinuba just happened to be a place to have a meeting. Yet as Paul Pietsch wrapped up his message and issued a challenge, he told a story that got Hofer's attention. In the valley was a group of business leaders who were praying for a revival. They had called prayer meetings across the San Joaquin Valley and had petitioned God for a Christian radio voice that could be heard throughout the region. Was anyone in the audience willing, Pietsch asked, to be that voice? Would anyone take the challenge to begin a radio station in the San Joaquin Valley, perhaps right here in Dinuba? With the war nearly over, the government freeze on new radio stations was being lifted and the number of new licenses was going to boom. Why couldn't any of those new stations be owned by Christians for the purpose of providing air time for gospel broadcasters? In a moment, Hofer came under the conviction that God was prompting him to be that voice in the valley. He looked at the friends standing with him on the platform, but especially at his brother Egon who sang beside him in the quartet. When his brother caught the glance he nodded. Together they slipped quietly to the front, to pray together and commit themselves to the task.

Less than a year later Hofer was praying again. This time he was thanking

God. His FCC license had finally arrived and a new evangelical radio station, KRDU, would soon be on the air from Dinuba. Whether Hofer would receive a license was no sure thing. Would the FCC even approve an avowedly religious station as serving the public interest? Not since the early days of radio, before government regulations had driven up the cost and complexity of operation, had evangelicals owned the means of broadcasting in any significant numbers. Yet the idea of operating KRDU as a *commercial* radio station was something new. Would it work? The weeks counted down quickly, almost too quickly, as the KRDU launch date approached. To generate income Hofer sought out producers of "time tested Gospel programs" and found they were very receptive to purchasing time on a station owned and operated by evangelical Christians. They had been buying slots on independent mainstream stations for years but had no control over the programming that came before and after their broadcasts. A gospel program might be preceded by a soap opera and followed by a variety show. And stations across the country were changing their formats with dizzying speed, often without warning.

With the controversy over paid versus sustaining time, evangelicals often had to plead for crumbs or wrangle with abrupt changes in station policies. So the idea of a "Christian" radio station that sold time exclusively to religious broadcasters was intriguing. Radio preachers liked the idea, Hofer found, that they could reach two audiences. Now they could attract not only listeners who tuned in for their specific *program*, but also those drawn by the *station* and its sacred atmosphere. From the first, KRDU prospered. And by 1950 more than ten commercially licensed religious radio stations were on the air—and their numbers grew steadily each year throughout the ensuing decade.

Radio in the Forties

The 1940s were a momentous decade in broadcasting.[22] Even before the United States entered the Second World War on December 8, 1941, several landmark developments had occurred. NBC began regular television programming in April 1939, launching the service with its coverage of President Franklin Roosevelt's speech to open the New York World's Fair. In February 1941 the FCC approved standards for commercial television and for the manufacture of TV sets. The agency that year also authorized commercial FM radio operations, as well as issued an important rulemaking to limit the monopoly power of the radio networks. For the first time the FCC claimed regulatory authority not only over individual station licensees but, in effect, over the *structure* of the broadcast industry. Because the new rules would compel NBC to divest itself of either its Red or Blue network, the company brought suit. The case, *NBC v. United States*, went to the Supreme Court as the FCC was upheld in a landmark 1943 decision. NBC sold its less-popular Blue Network to Edward Noble, the millionaire maker of Life Savers candies, and in 1945 it became the American Broadcasting Corporation.

When war broke out, amateur radio stations were closed for national security reasons, as they had been in World War I. To conserve war materials, the FCC in 1942 placed a freeze on licensing and construction of new radio stations, while production of radio sets was also ended. TV licensing and set manufacture were also frozen. President Roosevelt established an Office of War Information as broadcasters voluntarily censored themselves in following the agency's guidelines. After the war's end in 1945 the FCC not only had to deal with a huge backlog of AM radio station license applications, but to sort through the implications of FM and TV which had been on hold since 1941. Both FM and TV used the same spectrum, so the agency opted to promote television at the expense of assigning FM radio (which it viewed as duplicating AM) a less desirable spot on the dial. In so doing, the FCC rejected calls by CBS to continue the TV freeze until standards for color television could be decided. Instead the agency backed the NBC position that audiences wanted "TV now" with black-and-white sets. By 1949, the development of coaxial cable made it possible for television stations to be networked for the first time.

Meanwhile, hundreds of licenses for new AM radio stations were granted. Demand for more stations in more communities had been pent up for fifteen years, first by the Depression and then the war. Now the number of radio outlets grew exponentially and Christians were able to enter station ownership for the first time in a generation. In that final decade in which radio remained king, the medium was enormously helped by wartime tax laws that encouraged companies to plow their excess profits into advertising, ensuring that network radio would remain well-funded. Most of the big stars from the thirties remained popular. Thrillers gained new urgency due to the war, and quiz shows and audience participation programs were popular. Variety shows continued to draw big audiences as Ed Sullivan, Arthur Godfrey, and Perry Como all debuted during the decade. Enduring comedies that got their start in the 1940s included *The Great Gildersleeve*, *The Life of Riley*, and *Ozzie and Harriet*. As always, music remained the staple of radio programming with the networks devoting a third of their hours to such big band favorites as Glenn Miller, Benny Goodman, and Harry James. At the local level, the 1948 introduction of long-play "microgroove" records—which revolved at 33 rpm and contained up to twenty-five minutes of music per side—were a boon to stations. To play radio singles, 45 rpm records were also developed. And though 33 rpm transcription discs had been around since the thirties, the vinyl-based microgroove system made it possible for LP records to be sold to the public.

For evangelical radio broadcasters the 1940s were also an eventful decade, and not only for the battle over paid religious programs and the advent of locally-owned commercial Christian stations. The network broadcasts of Charles Fuller, Walter Maier, Percy Crawford, Paul Myers and others were at their height. An evangelical popular culture now fully emerged as these national broadcasts generated a new "industry" of books, recordings, camps and conferences, giving rise to a common religious vocabulary and shared experience among American evangelicals. Through the tools of mass communication Christians were now hearing the same preachers, listening to the same songs, buying the same books. One aspect of this development, the Youth for Christ movement, became so pronounced that an historian of the period has called it "a national fad." All across America, evangelicals were expressing their faith by gathering together in massive rallies—mostly connected somehow with radio—and were filling arenas and stadiums by the tens of thousands. In turn, these mass rallies gave rise to music that emphasized triumphal affirmation of the Christian faith. While the rousing revival hymns of the late nineteenth century proved a good fit for congregational singing in these large rallies, a new genre of simple choruses—easy to sing without hymnals or song sheets—were also widely used. A stadium filled with thousands of people was not a place for quiet introspection or complicated singing. For evangelicals of the day, anything seemed possible.

Jack Wyrtzen and Word of Life

Jack Wyrtzen was standing in front of his home on Forest Parkway in Woodhaven, New Jersey.[23] His friend Al Kunz had come to visit and the two men were discussing an idea Wyrtzen had. He was going to hold large youth rallies each Saturday night at Times Square and broadcast them live over one of New York City's most powerful radio stations—at a cost of $3,500 for thirteen weeks. Kunz urged caution. It was less than a year since Wyrtzen had quit the insurance business to enter full-time evangelism. In a good week his offerings might be thirty dollars. He had not yet completed his Bible school training. And his small radio program had just been canceled because the station—which had charged him nothing for the air time—had gone bankrupt. But Jack Wyrtzen believed the answer to adversity was not to step backward but to try something even bigger and better. As he thought of Times Square, of the legions of lost youth who gathered there each Saturday night at the clubs and dance halls, his heart was broken. God wanted him to reclaim the city for Christ. He was sure of it.

To understand why Wyrtzen was so sure is to understand the spirit of the times. By the start of the forties radio had been around for a generation. In cities such as New York the new mass culture meant an accelerated pace of life. An emerging generation of young evangelicals was being molded by mass media and the dynamism of the evangelical message and music they heard on the radio. Wyrtzen and his contemporaries had not known the sawdust trail of Billy Sunday. Indeed, Wyrtzen himself was only four years old when, in 1917, the great evangelist campaigned in New York City. The formative years of Wyrtzen's generation had coincided with the growth of radio. For many evangelicals who came of age in the thirties, national broadcasts such as Percy Crawford's *Young People's Church of the Air* and Charles Fuller's *Old Fashioned Revival Hour* were the shared experience of their Christianity. They had seen the power of mass media and now they were ready to take the next step. Radio could be a tool not only to proclaim the gospel but, they believed, to mobilize new legions of believers for action in the cause of Christ. Today, mass culture is taken for granted as a normal aspect of life. But in 1941 when Jack Wyrtzen was planning to conquer Times Square for Christ, the possibilities for harnessing the tools of mass culture to create a youth movement that would sweep across America were new and exciting. After all, as Wyrtzen saw it, so many miraculous and unimaginable things had already happened in the nine years since he become a "new creature" in Christ.

The train of events leading to his conversion began in 1931 when he met an old friend. Jack Wyrtzen had not seen George Schilling in years, not since they had played in the Boy Scout band together as kids. But on that day in 1931 when the two men ran into each other, George said, "How'd you like to join the United States Army Band?" It was a reserve unit, explained Schilling, the 101st Cavalry Band out of Brooklyn, New York. "It's only Monday nights and they'll give you a horse. It's a lot of fun, and they'll pay you for doing it!"[24] Jack was eighteen, pretty sharp on the trombone, and even had his own twelve-piece dance band. He liked the idea of playing on horseback in a smart military uniform and agreed to sign up. That summer, for its annual Guard training the band was posted for two weeks at Pine Camp (present-day Fort Drum) in upstate New York. George Schilling soon proved his reputation as the wildest guy in the band. One night he came back so drunk that he vowed to Jack and the dozen men in their tent that he was going to spit in the colonel's eye. It was about four in the morning and, to avoid trouble, the men appeased him by going over to the officers quarters and letting him spit on the colonel's tent. But George was still mad, as well as cockeyed drunk. So he climbed up the flagpole and refused to come down. Jack and his buddies just threw up their hands and went back to bed.

Despite his reckless and uncontrolled lifestyle, Schilling was an accomplished musician. He had played at a West Point prep school, the New York Military Academy. There he met a chaplain who urged Schilling at every opportunity to convert to Christ. At the chaplain's suggestion he agreed to attend a special watch-night service, January 1, 1932, at New York's famous Calvary Baptist Church. Harry Rimmer, a leading anti-evolutionist, would be the guest speaker. The Calvary pastor, Will Houghton who would later become president of Moody Bible Institute, would also bring a message. That night Schilling was converted and, at the next Monday drill, told all thirty-five members of the Cavalry Band what had happened. They were stunned. Yet in the weeks that followed Schilling came to the weekly drill nights with Bibles and Gospels of John to give to the men. Everyone refused the literature, including Wytzen. "George, you're the last man I'd ever expect to see with a Bible," Jack scoffed. But to be polite he finally accepted a Gospel of John, stuffed it in his pocket, and forgot about it.

That night on the way home, standing at the train platform Wyrtzen remembered the booklet in his pocket. He took it out and read the title, "Gospel of Saint John." For some reason, the "saint business" really made him angry. *Boy, what a sissy, what a Holy Joe I would be to carry a Gospel of* SAINT *John*, he thought. So he promptly tore the booklet to pieces and threw it off the platform. The next Monday night Schilling asked, "How are you getting along with that Gospel of John I gave you last week?" Wyrtzen didn't remember at first, then it came to him: "Oh, you mean that little booklet with Saint John on the cover?" "Yes," replied Schilling, "have you read it?" Then Jack reared back and laughed, "Read it? George, I threw it away before I even got home!" But Schilling was unperturbed and quietly replied, "You did? Here's another one."[25] That's how it went for the next six months. With his insurance job during the day and then leading his own dance band at night, Wyrtzen felt he was too busy for God. Each time George gave him a Gospel of *Saint John*, Jack threw it away. Someday he was going to be a famous bandleader like Guy Lombardo. Already his group was getting enough fancy gigs—yacht clubs, hotels, fraternity dances—for Jack to drop out of high school. Perhaps he might also be a big insurance executive someday, with a big office in Manhattan.

Another man, Ray Studley, was also witnessing Christ to Jack during their daily subway rides into town. But to Wyrtzen this was all "Billy Sunday stuff." His father, foreman at a glass factory and a Unitarian, had always warned his son against this kind of fanaticism. When Jack was four and learned "Jesus Loves Me" one morning in Sunday school, he never forgot the song because it was so *unusual* to him. When Jack was eleven, his father even refused to let his son take a free carpentry class at the Hanson Place YMCA in Brooklyn. "They'll try to convert you and all that nonsense!" his father feared. In time his father relented—and in fact, the carpentry teacher read the Bible to the boys and tried to convert them to Christ. Though Jack was outwardly uninterested, he later believed the teacher had planted a seed. Even as a boy, when others told dirty jokes or used bad language, Jack was uncomfortable. He dreamed of living a clean life and having a girlfriend who might help him straighten up—until he discovered that all the girls he dated struggled with the same problems he did. So if he drank and smoked and cursed, he told himself, it was only to be acceptable. Besides, if his gang went to the beer joints, pool halls and dances during the week, they still went to church on Sunday. Jack himself had been a Unitarian, then a Methodist (until he lost a fist fight after church), a Presbyterian (to find a better crowd), and a Baptist (to join the Boy Scout troop). And when he began dating the pretty Margaret Smith who went to a Reformed church, Jack became Reformed—but not converted.

The months passed by and, when it was summer again and time for the Cavalry Band's yearly National Guard camp in upstate New York, Jack was interested to see whether George Schilling's newfound faith had held up. *Oh, he'll forget about his religion in this man's army,* Jack thought. He remembered how, the summer before, George had done every sin a soldier could commit. But as taps were sounded and the lights went out, Schilling took a flashlight from his bag, sat up on the edge of his cot, and quietly read the Bible and prayed. The other men swore at him, cursed him, one even threw a shoe. Yet day after day Schilling never answered the catcalls, and night after night he read his Bible. After two weeks, Jack could see that the change in his friend was real. So when he returned home from Guard camp that fall, Jack started reading the Gospel of John that George had given him. The Cavalry Band had resumed its weekly drills and, since the men were often invited to give concerts at local events, Jack gladly obliged when George asked him to play a trombone solo at a church in Brooklyn. It was October 1932. Unknown to Jack, the meeting was an evangelistic service and George was getting his friend to go the only way he knew how. Nearly sixty years later Wyrtzen vividly recalled the events of that night.

> I played *At Dawning*, I think. I didn't know any hymns. And then I guess they had some testimonies and ... [to me] that was rather strange. Then they introduced this [evangelist] and he preached on hell, the lake of fire, judgement. I mean, he was all over the book of Revelation and then they gave an invitation. And that was the first time I'd ever seen anything like this. And I said, "These are a bunch of nuts, this is what my father must has been talking about, Billy Sunday stuff." So while they were all praying, I packed my trombone and slipped out the back door.[26]

Yet when he got home that night Wyrtzen could not sleep. At last he dropped to his knees and stammered, "God, all this that I've been fighting against is the truth!"[27] He could never remember exactly what he prayed that night, but the sermon had triggered a memory Jack had forgotten until then.

Lost forever, lost forever, lost forever. As Jack bowed his head, the phrase kept ringing in his mind. He recalled when he was sixteen and just starting his dance band, how he would sometimes go to the Woodhaven Baptist Church. The "liberal" pastor had died and a new preacher, just out of Bible school, was zealous to convert everyone—and therefore quickly forced to leave. Before then, however, Pastor Sheldon one day visited the Wyrtzens when Jack happend to be home by himself. "What will happen if I don't believe?" asked the teenager, rather arrogantly. "You'll be lost forever," was the pastor's reply, "and you'll go to hell." Angrily Jack retorted, "Look, my family doesn't believe any of that," and then nearly threw the young preacher out the door.[28] But now in October 1932, the seeds planted by the YMCA carpentry teacher, the Baptist pastor, and his friend George Schilling were ready to be harvested. "I know that I passed from death unto life, from the power of Satan unto God," Wyrtzen later testified of that night he prayed beside his bed. "My eyes were opened and forgiveness of sins became my portion. That night Jesus became real to me."[29]

When George called at seven the next morning, to speak with Jack before he left for work, Wyrtzen was ready to turn the tables on his friend.[30]

"I want to apologize for that preacher last night," George said over the phone. "That was an awfully heavy dose, first time hearing all about the lake of fire and judgment."

"George," replied Jack, "it's just what I needed."

On the other end of the line, Jack could hear that his friend was clearly puzzled. "What do you mean?" Schilling asked.

"I got saved when I got home!"

"You got what?!" Schilling nearly dropped the phone out of his hand.

Jack told George Schilling and Ray Studley about his conversion but nobody else—especially not his girlfriend, Marge Smith. How could he? Jack might lose her, so he decided to play it cool. Her family was rich and sophisticated. Marge had even been engaged once to a man who was an opera singer. Yet as the weeks went by Marge began to notice that Jack was uncomfortable at the movies they saw together. And she was shocked when Jack said he preferred that girls not smoke. She decided his "Christian" friends, George and Ray, were to blame. They were always hanging around Jack, the three of them looking so strange. George and Ray had to go! Marge Smith was the adopted daughter of a leading Brooklyn surgeon. Though her parents had a Christian background, social obligations took most of their attention. They overlooked the late hours their daughter kept and did not voice objections to her lifestyle or friends. Yet Mrs. Smith was uneasy about Marge taking up with a dance band leader. So when she chanced to hear Percy Crawford's *Young People's Church of the Air* one Sunday, it got her attention. The young people on the program talked in a personal way about Jesus Christ. Mrs. Smith had never heard young people talk like that before. It was very interesting. "Why don't you kids get home early and listen to this program?"[31] Mrs. Smith would say to Jack and Marge. The broadcast was from five to six, but somehow the two of them always found ways to miss the show. Sometimes, though, their timing was off and Jack would bring Marge home just as Percy Crawford was closing the broadcast with an invitation for listeners to convert to Christ. Then they would laugh and mock the testimonies and make fun of the preacher. Yet Marge would feel uneasy at hearing the invitations. Even so, after an emergency appendectomy brought her to the point of death, her fears were in time forgotten and life went on as before.

Months went by and then summer came. It was July 1933 and, though Jack had been converted since October, still no one knew about it but George and Ray. All the while, however, Mrs. Smith continued listening regularly to the *Young People's Church of the Air*. Then she heard something that piqued her interest. Percy Crawford was starting a new Christian camp for young people called Pinebrook. What's more, it was in the Poconos, a favorite vacation spot for the Smith family. So she decided Pinebrook might be just what her daughter needed. "We're going on a vacation," Mrs. Smith announced to her surprised daughter.[32] When Marge learned they were going to the Poconos, however, she was delighted. They must be going to the Pocono Manor, she thought, an exclusive hotel. So she packed fifteen evening gowns. And when her mother said they were taking the family's brand new car—and that Marge could drive—her happiness was complete.

On the day of the trip they got as far as Stroudsburg, the town nearest Pinebrook, when Mrs. Smith asked her daughter to pull over and stop the car. "I have something to tell you," she said. "Marge, we're not going to the Pocono Manor. We're going over to Pinebrook Bible Camp." Marge brought the car to a complete stop. "Is that the man you listen to on the radio each Sunday—the *Young People's Church of the Air*? Percy Crawford? Forget it," she declared. "Count me out. You'll never get me to a place like that!" And with that, Marge turned the car around and headed back toward home. "Marge, just do it for my sake?" her mother pleaded. In fact, they were half way home when Marge finally gave in—but just for that night! Then they would go to the Pocono Manor.

At first, Pinebrook confirmed her worst fears. The girls all looked so plain. The cook had just quit and Crawford himself was trying to make dinner and had burned the spaghetti. Someone even threw a dishrag at her and said, "Wipe the tables!" Taken aback, Marge instead offered to treat everyone to dinner in town. But when they got back to camp and Mrs. Smith asked her daughter to meet Percy Crawford, Marge icily replied, "Forget it. I don't want to meet him," and walked away. Yet as the night wore on, Marge relaxed a bit. The music at the evening service was good and Marge loved good music.

The quartet was about the best she had ever heard. The four young men sang with a sincerity and excitement that was very different from the men in Jack's band. Yet they also cut up and had fun. "These are Christians? I can't believe it. They're having so much fun," she thought. Best of all, there was no preaching. At the end of the meeting, however, Marge could no longer avoid Percy Crawford. "Tomorrow morning when I preach," he said to her, "if you don't accept the Lord I don't want you to stay any longer. I know you're having a good time, but I don't want you hardening your heart to the Lord. That is dangerous!"

Tuesday morning came and Marge found her seat in the auditorium. As Crawford preached she had the distinct feeling that someone had told him all about her—and in fact, that he was preaching *directly* to her. The message was brief, no more than fifteen minutes. But it was about hell, and Crawford had a way of pointing his finger and getting his message across with tremendous impact. As Marge listened she alternated between sneering and trembling. Yet with Crawford's unique way of giving an invitation, she couldn't refuse. As the others were praying, Marge looked up and saw that a small boy had gone forward to be converted. "If that little kid has the courage to do it, what's wrong with me?" she told herself. At last she slipped out of her seat to go forward. But now there were twenty young people who were also standing at the front. The other campers, who had affectionately been calling Marge the "Fifth Avenue Belle," were thrilled to see her come forward. But while the others at the altar were weeping and crying, Marge stood there like a sphinx. "Well, Percy, I guess I'm not saved," Marge said when the two shook hands after the service. After all, she had not yet felt anything. She was not emotional or crying. How could she be converted? But Crawford looked her straight in the eye and declared, "I know you are saved. You are going to do great things for God. He is going to use you." Not until Marge went back to her room did the dam finally burst. She fell on her bed as the tears filler her eyes. The full impact of what she had done, publicly confessing her sins and coming to Christ, now hit her. Then her mother walked into the room. "Marge," she said, "I want you to write a letter to your boyfriend. I want you to tell him that you have received the Lord as your Savior and that you're a Christian. Tell him that you are not interested in getting married to a dance band leader."

And so, even in her first hour of her conversion, Marge was faced with choosing between the old and the new. Yet she knew what her choice must be and, not knowing about Jack's conversion, she began to write him a letter: "Honey, I am saved, and I want you to be saved. But don't get saved until I get home because I want to save you. Marge." Then she enclosed a tract on "How to be Saved." Within a few days a telegram arrived at Pinebrook addressed to Marge. Mail call was in the dining room and, in keeping with the spirit of fun at Pinebrook, Percy Crawford made anyone who received a letter stand up and read it aloud. So Marge got up on a stool and, to everyone in the dining room, read the words of the telegram: "Dear Marge, Praise the Lord! I have been saved for the last few months but I've been afraid to tell you. I'm so thankful that the Lord has saved you. Jack." At that, everyone in the room broke into loud cheers and applause. Knowing Marge's situation, they had been praying for her boyfriend. Now for the second time at Pinebrook she was weeping. "What are you crying for?" Crawford asked. Marge answered, "I'm crying because I didn't save him. I wanted to get home and save Jack. I didn't want anybody else to save him." Nevertheless, she was happy. In the end, the "Fifth Avenue Belle" stayed at Pinebrook not for one night but for two weeks. Instead of dreaming about evening gowns she offered to clean tables. She had never done anything like it before and everyone was surprised. But Marge loved the work and, even more, "I showed them when you're in Christ you are a new creature."

Jack, however, continued to struggle against his old habits and attitudes, especially in overcoming a short temper. At the Merchant's Fire Insurance Corporation his boss, Mr. Jenkins, was an atheist who openly mocked everything Jack said about God. "After I was saved, one night working late in the insurance company," he later recalled, his boss "went just too far. We were both working, just the two of us, and I guess that made us both tired ... and I swore at him and used the Lord's name in vain." To Jack, it was like he had just thrust a dagger into his own side. He excused himself and "went out to the men's room and I cried like a baby. I said, 'Lord, I guess I'm a Judas Iscariot. I'm a phoney. I've denied you.'" Then he remembered how a friend had challenged him to memorize 1 John 1:9, "If we confess our sins, He is faithful and just to forgive us our sins, and to cleanse us from all unrighteousness." It was only the second Bible verse Jack had ever memorized, after 2 Corinthians 5:17, "Therefore, if any man be in Christ, he is a new creature: old things are passed away; behold, all things are become new." Alone in the washroom, his eyes wet with tears, Jack sobbed out his confession before the Lord: "God, you said if I confess it [you'll forgive]. And God, I'm a stinker. I've used your name in vain. I've cursed you. And yet, you've said you'll not only forgive me but cleanse me." With that, he walked back into the office and went to see his boss. "Mr. Jenkins, I want to apologize," Jack said. "You must think I'm a big phoney, using the name of the Lord I've been talking about in vain." The older man looked at Jack and answered, "You know, now I'm beginning to think that you're for real." To Jack's knowledge his boss never became a believer, yet afterward Mr. Jenkins never let anyone speak against Jack and defended his right to share his faith.[33]

In the months that followed, Jack started to read and memorize more of the scriptures. Each morning he had an hour's ride on the subway to his office on Wall Street. "In rush hours it's really packed in, so you stand erect," Jack later explained. "In New York City, everybody put the *Daily News* on your back. So I put the Bible on their backs and started to read it. And New Yorkers are the nosiest people in the world. They're looking over your shoulders to see what you're reading, and I had some verses that had to do with salvation underlined so they'd see them."[34] One such subway patron was Bill Wiley, an office boy at the New York Stock Exchange. He asked if Jack was preparing a Sunday school lesson and, since they both got off at the Wall Street station, the two young men struck up a conversation. Wiley wanted to know more and, in the coming weeks as they became friends, Jack invited him to a Percy Crawford meeting in New York. That night Jack led Bill Wiley to Christ—his first convert.

Yet in the months since he had been converted, Jack was still having a hard time making the break from his old circles. Now that his girlfriend Marge was a believer and everyone knew about Jack's conversion, it was becoming more difficult to straddle the fence between his old life and the new. The issue came to a head in October 1933—a year since Jack had come to Christ—when he and Marge attended a campers reunion at Pinebrook. Jack was assigned to room with Stanley Kline, who would later become a missionary to Africa. As they were talking one night about spiritual things, Jack asked Stanley, "Do you think it is all right for a Christian to play in a dance band and live for the Lord too?"[35] To Jack, the band was only a way to make some good money on the side. It was only a job, like his insurance job, and so the thought of quitting this kind of employment did not occur to him at first. Yet now, as he grew in his faith, Jack was starting to feel uncomfortable with the party scene. Stanley opened his Bible and asked Jack to read Colossians 3:17, "And whatsoever ye do in word or deed, do all in the name of the Lord Jesus, giving thanks to God and the Father by him." Then Stanley gave Jack a gentle but pointed challenge: "Jack, if you as a Christian can do this and do it in the name of the Lord Jesus Christ and be happy, then it's one thing. But if you cannot, then you better quit." Yet Jack still hesitated. He had worked hard to get his band, the "Silver Moon Serenaders," where it was. The struggle continued for two months until the night of December 3, 1933, Jack had an experience that would mark his life forever.

> The last place I played in was the Hotel Ambassador on Park Avenue in New York City. That afternoon, [Marge] and I were going to the Army-Navy football game in Philadelphia.... I can still remember getting in my tux, taking the subway to New York City, trombone under my arm and, just to ease my conscience, walking through the train giving our tracts. And I got there to lead the dance band ... at about one o'clock in the morning. It was a sorority dance.[36]

Soon after the dance started, it was apparent that something was wrong. The sorority girl who hired Jack took a look at him and asked, "You don't feel well, do you? What's the matter? You don't play or sing like you usually do."³⁷ The real truth, however, was that Jack was coming under intense conviction. He had dreamed long and worked hard to get the Silver Moon Serenaders where they were. He didn't want to give all that up. At last, about three in the morning, the dance was over. Jack could relax and put his misgivings behind him. So when a friend and his date offered to give Jack a ride home, he was glad to accept. As the car pulled out onto the avenue, Jack decided to make some conversation. "How's your brother?" he asked his friend. "Oh," the young man replied, "didn't you hear? Two weeks ago tonight he was killed in an automobile accident on the way home from a fraternity dance." The friend paused a moment, then went on with the tragic story. "Hit a tree and was gone. A few drinks too many."

Automatically, Jack blurted out, "Was he saved?"

"What do you mean?"

So Jack explained to him the whole "plan of salvation," how eternal life is a free gift to all who believe that Christ's death on the cross atoned for their sins.

"How long have you known this?"

"Several months," Jack answered.

To his dying day, Wyrtzen would never forget what happened next. His friend turned toward him, looked him in the eye and cried, "Then, if my brother is in hell, it's your fault! Why didn't you tell him?" When the ride was over, Jack got out of the car. He didn't even say goodnight. Instead he went upstairs to his room and, once again driven to his knees, poured out his heart to God. It seemed as if he could still feel the beat of the bass drum in his band. "God, I'm through," he sobbed. "No more of this stuff. No more one foot in the world and one foot on God's side. I'm finished." The next morning, December 4, 1933, Jack sent a telegram to Stanley Kline: "Praise the Lord. Dance band finished. Signed, Jack."³⁸

From then on, things began to happen. A week later, on December 10, George Schilling summoned Jack to his first street meeting in Philadelphia. All Jack could say was the only Bible verse he knew at the time, 2 Corinthians 5:17. But now he could speak of being a "new creature" in Christ with true conviction. Back home, Jack and George counted fourteen churches in their neighborhood but none that were evangelical. In fact, when Jack and Marge attended her parents' church and opened their Bibles to follow the sermon, the minister was startled and became red in the face. "What did you do that for?" he asked them after the service. "Were you checking up on me? Never before has anybody ever pulled a Bible out in this church on me. I don't like that!"³⁹

So that winter Jack and George, along with Ray Studley and their mutual friend Henry Hutchinson, formed a men's fraternity they called Chi Beta

Alpha for "Christians Born Again." When Bill Wiley came to Christ, the former beer garden trumpet player joined Jack and George in a brass ensemble they dubbed the "Christian Harmony Trio." Quickly, Chi Beta Alpha grew to twenty-one members. Jack's mother, who was active in politics, got them a meeting room at the local Republican Club. Then Al Kunz, a Bible teacher who later became international director of the Pocket Testament League, heard about the fraternity. He became a mentor and met with the group in his home each Tuesday night to study the Bible. But the zeal of Chi Beta Alpha could not be contained for long and the group voted to hold its first street meeting. The vote was twenty to one—with Jack casting the lone dissenting vote. He was afraid because everyone in town knew them. Yet the street meeting went ahead and was held in Brooklyn under an elevated subway track. Chi Beta Alpha won its first convert, a Methodist minister's daughter. Jack and his fraternity brothers were emboldened to keep preaching. At one street meeting in Huntington, Long Island, the crowd grew so large that a policeman broke up the gathering and hauled Jack before the local judge. "Officer," the judge declared, "take these men back to town. Block off the whole street and give them whatever assistance they need to conduct their meetings. I know the same Jesus they speak of, and that's exactly what this town needs."[40] More than five hundred eventually thronged the street.

In May of 1934 Chi Beta Alpha decided to hold a banquet. Admission was seventy-five cents for the meal and everyone was required to bring an unconverted friend. Percy Crawford had even agreed to be the speaker. Forty or fifty young people showed up and, at a meeting held afterward in the Baptist church, several were converted. Buoyed by their success these "Young Men for Christ," as they billed themselves in public meetings, were ready to take the next step and schedule a series of weekly rallies. Since none of the fourteen churches in their town held Sunday evening services, Jack was appointed by Chi Beta Alpha to approach the Lutheran church, with its large building, and ask permission to use the sanctuary for Sunday night youth meetings. As his friends prayed outside, Jack went before the deacon board to make his request. The room was filled with tobacco smoke as one of the deacons turned to Jack and said, "What do you want, sonny?" So Jack explained, then was asked to leave the room for a few minutes and summoned back for the deacons' decision. "We've decided not to give you the auditorium," they told him, "but we will let you use the large Sunday school room for October, November, and December."[41] Delighted, Jack went back to share the news with his excited friends.

The night of the first meeting, more than two hundred people thronged the church. "We didn't know anything about evangelism, how to run meetings or anything," Jack confessed later. "We got there and we said, 'Well, who's going to preach?' And somebody said, 'Well, there's only four of you guys that have one sermon.' So we had enough sermons for [October]. We actually flipped a coin and I lost, and the loser had to preach." The only sermon Jack knew was one entitled "Jesus Stood With Them" that he had memorized out of the Percy Crawford magazine, *Youth Today*. "So I preached," he recalled, "and I remember asking for hands to be raised, like Percy Crawford did. And I can still remember the twenty-two hands." But the group was so unschooled in evangelism that Jack didn't know what to do and simply dismissed the meeting without even a closing prayer. "Goodnight, everybody!" he exclaimed. "Come back next week!"[42] By the fourth Sunday, more than four hundred young people were jamming the church—and the four original "Young Men for Christ" had run out of sermons. So they called in several guest preachers and, by the final rally in December, attendance had topped six hundred. Even a women's sorority, Phi Gamma (it was Percy Crawford's idea), was formed to complement Chi Beta Alpha. The meetings were written up on the front page of the local paper—the same paper Jack used to sell for a nickel as a kid. But most important to Jack, in the three months of rallies scores of young people converted to Christ.

The next summer Jack and Marge returned to Pinebrook and at a camp service dedicated their lives to Christian service.[43] When Jack heard a speaker issue a call to the mission field of Africa, his hand shot up. Yet Marge's heart sank. "Well, there goes our wedding," she thought, "because I'm not going to any mission field." Always frail, her health simply would not stand up to the rigors of the foreign field. Seeing her discomfort, Jack put his hand down. The speaker, however, approached the couple while the campers were singing an invitation hymn. "Jack, I want you to know that if you mean it and if you are dedicating your life to the Lord, it might mean breaking up with Marge. However, it could mean if Marge would dedicate her life to the Lord along with you, that God could completely change your lives so that you could do something for the Lord." As the young people continued to sing "Where He Leads Me I Will Follow," Jack and Marge each prayed about what they should do. Marge especially was torn. "Lord," she prayed, "when I said that I wanted to become a Christian, did it also mean I have to sacrifice everything? Do I have to change all my plans?" But she felt that God was giving her an assurance and a peace about fully surrendering her life to him. She turned to Jack and whispered, "Jack, I'll stand with you. I'll surrender all to the Lord. I'll go with you even to the mission field. If need be, I'm ready to lay down my life for the Lord." With that, the two of them walked together down the aisle.

The next years were eventful ones for Jack and Marge. They walked another aisle together on April 18, 1936, when they were married by Al Kunz. (Jack was late for the wedding. He had been playing baseball that morning, broken a tooth, and had to see the dentist.) The soloist was George Beverly Shea—who later became a celebrated singer for the Billy Graham organization, but at the time was in the insurance business and had sold Jack his first life insurance policy. As time went by, however, Jack and Marge recognized that God was not leading them into foreign missions. Jack's ministry with Chi Beta Alpha was prospering beyond all expectation. When he realized that twenty-five million people lived within the New York metropolitan area, he knew his calling lay at home. Evangelistic teams were formed to minister at jails, rescue missions, street corners, and Civilian Conservation Corps camps. Many of the workers were recruited by Percy Crawford who, when he held meetings in the New York area, would refer converts to Jack for follow-up. "There would not be Word of Life if it weren't for Percy Crawford," Jack readily admitted later. "He was our hero. We listened every week on the radio. We got all our material to preach ... from the speakers [at Pinebrook camp] and we wrote down everything they said. And any books that Percy Crawford would announce, we bought everything. I had a library I was reading morning, noon, and night. He was a great inspiration to us."[44] Encouraged by Crawford and inspired by growing numbers, by the late thirties Jack was maintaining a full schedule of meetings. While still working each day at the Merchant's Fire Insurance Corporation, he also "preached every noon hour, almost every night, weekend, vacation. I even preached nine times on my honeymoon!"[45]

Over time, one question became more and more insistent: Should Jack go full-time into evangelism? The case against such a move was emphatically stated by Uncle Chester, the rich relative in Marge's family. One day in 1941 he looked Jack straight in the eye and declared, "You know, you've got a wife and you've got a little girl baby. And you're going to quit this company that's owned by a lot of millionaires! You're going to make a fool of yourself. You're going to starve to death. Don't look at me. I'll never give you a dime!"[46] On the other hand, Chi Beta Alpha had outgrown the modest aims of a small men's fraternity and had recently been incorporated as Word of Life Fellowship, the name taken from a phrase in Philippians 2:16, "Holding forth the word of life." If Jack would come and work full-time, the organization would try by faith to scrape together thirty dollars a week for Jack and his family. Yet at the same time, another evangelistic organization was offering Jack a salary of sixty-five dollars to go with them—plus a parsonage and a car. Both were full-time ministry opportunities, though both paid far less than the insurance business. Complicating the decision was not only Uncle Chester's admonition but, for a very different reason, the caution urged by Al Kunz. "Jack, don't do it if you can possibly help it. But if you have to, go ahead. Remember that you are already having a fruitful ministry."[47] As a respected insurance executive Jack was uniquely effective in such lay organizations as the Pocket Testament League, the Gideons, and the Christian Business Men's Committee. Only if he could no longer keep up with both his job and his ministry, Kunz advised, should Jack go into evangelism full-time.

At last Jack believed the time had arrived. He and Marge prayed about the matter and, on a Monday, believed that God was confirming their decision to go with Word of Life. The next day, Tuesday, it was time for Jack's weekly radio broadcast on WBBC. He would make the big announcement on the radio, that he was now doing the Lord's work full-time and available for meetings. But when he arrived at the Brooklyn station that morning, he and Marge saw a sign on the door: "Out of Business." What would he do now—with no job, no radio program, and no way to spread the word about his ministry? Immediately he considered what other station could carry his broadcast, perhaps a more powerful station. And if he was going to do that, then why not broadcast live from Times Square—and have a giant youth rally there every Saturday night? Again, Al Kunz advised caution: "Jack, I wouldn't do it. Who ever heard of having a Saturday night rally? That's not a church night. That's the night young people go out for fun. Jack, I know you have a tremendous vision, but that sounds like a dream to me."[48] Yet Jack was under the conviction that God was leading him in that very direction. He continued to ponder the pros and cons that final week as he finished out his employment at the insurance company. That Friday, he said,

> I remember they gave me a big farewell party ... and they gave me a pen with a diamond in it. I thought that was pretty nice. But when I walked out I had peace in my heart. I'd done the right thing. I was invited to hold a campaign up in Putnam, Connecticut [the following week].... And this Tuesday night, here I'm in the middle of my first campaign. I'd quit my job.... I was going to go out in faith to support my wife and baby. Somehow God was going to do it.[49]

That Tuesday night while Jack was conducting his Connecticut campaign, he tuned in the radio just in time to hear news commentator Lowell Thomas make his evening report: "Merchant's Fire Insurance will probably go bankrupt, and here's the reason..." Jack was stunned. *That was the company I worked for!* Without hesitation he got down on his knees and shouted, "Thank you, Lord! *You'll* never go broke!"[50] Soon afterward Jack was off to his first road trip for Word of Life. He and Marge headed out to Chicago where some students had invited them to speak at Moody Bible Institute. First they drove to Buffalo for a week of church meetings, except Jack's contact hadn't followed through and only a Sunday service was planned. By Sunday Jack and Marge were out of money but received a ten-dollar check from the church to help them get to Chicago. Arriving at Moody Bible Institute, no one at the school knew Jack was coming because he had only been invited by some students. After a few days, Jack and Marge headed toward home and stopped in Cleveland, where Jack preached at a meeting and some converts were won. Their final meeting was scheduled the next day at a small country church in Binghamton, New York. The pastor and his wife were so destitute, however, Jack knew that God would have him return the offering. That was the first evangelistic campaign for Jack Wyrzten and Word of Life. But Jack believed that God had brought him out and back; even if he had only broken even, Jack reasoned, God had taken care of his needs along the way. And if he could do that, then why couldn't he take care of a Saturday night radio youth rally in Times Square?

Yet the Word of Life radio broadcast on the now-defunct WBBC had given little reason to believe the group could pull off a live program from Times Square. Every Tuesday morning Jack and the other young people around him would assemble at the studios of WBBC in Brooklyn. However, at the last minute the women's "quartet" would often become a trio—and the "men's" brass ensemble would have to borrow its trumpet player from the women's quartet. But the station manager consoled them by saying, "In the first place, you are only human. In the second place, it will keep you humble. And in the third place, nobody listens to this station anyway!"[51] Undaunted, Jack wrote a letter of inquiry to the manager of WHN, a powerful five thousand-watt station. The letter was not answered. So Jack called in a favor from a business friend at Western Electric who secured for Jack a meeting with the WHN manager. The cost for a half hour was $450 with no discounts, even if a contract were possible. But the manager flatly stated that he wanted no religion on WHN, believing it was not in the best interests of the station.

Two or three weeks later, a new salesman at WHN came across Jack's original letter of inquiry. Eager to generate new accounts and unaware of the manager's refusal, the salesman wrote back and invited Jack to "come in and talk it over." He offered Word of Life a contract for thirteen weeks—with a discount—if Jack would pay half the money upfront. That came to $1,750, due before the first broadcast. Could God supply such a large sum so quickly? The week before the broadcasts were set to begin, Word of Life had already scheduled its annual fall banquet. Carlton Booth, the organization's tenor soloist and songleader, provided the music and then brought the message. During the evening Jack happened to see a verse he had underlined in his Bible, "Every place that the sole of your feet shall tread upon, that have I given unto you" (Joshua 1:3). The radio oppotunity was announced at the banquet, an offering was taken, and a total of $1,760 was collected, exactly ten more dollars than was needed. Thus, with the funding in hand, an auditorium was needed and Jack secured the Alliance Gospel Tabernacle at 44th Street and Eighth Avenue. Located in the heart of Times Square, the church had been built by A.B. Simpson, founder of the Christian and Missionary Alliance. It was the same church Paul Rader attended after his conversion one night beneath an electric sign on Times Square in 1911.

"From Times Square, New York, we bring you the Word of Life ... on the air!" With those words the first *Word of Life Hour* was underway, October 25, 1941. As the opening theme, the natural choice was Philip Bliss's popular revival hymn, "Wonderful Words of Life."

> Sing them over again to me,
> Wonderful words of life;
> Let me more of their beauty see,
> Wonderful words of life.

Unlike the improvised broadcasts on WBBC, the Word of Life program was now precisely timed. And rather than a crew of young volunteers, Jack gathered around himself an experienced team. Two-hundred fifty young people turned out that first night for what was billed as a "Youth for Christ" rally. The first half hour was aired live over WHN, featuring a variety of music and testimonies followed by Jack Wyrtzen's message. After the broadcast portion concluded, the rally continued with singing and testimonies and a guest speaker. Attendance fell the second week to one hundred fifty, but by coincidence WHN soon afterward increased its power from five thousand to fifty thousand watts. Word of Life was now reaching a potential audience of twelve million listeners. By the end of January the rallies were packed. The contract with WHN for the *Word of Life Hour* was renewed and in 1942 the rallies were moved to the Mecca Temple which could seat three thousand. Still the rallies grew and Carnegie Hall was rented, and even then up to three thousand people had to be turned away at the door. An Irish policemen told Jack he should take the rallies to Madison Square Garden—which Jack did for a special Victory Rally on April 1, 1944. By then, the *Word of Life Hour* was being broadcast coast-to-coast over the Mutual network. That day, twenty thousand thronged the arena and ten thousand listened on speakers set up on the sidewalks outside. At the invitation, more than eight hundred converted to Christ.

Three more Madison Square Garden rallies were held in 1944, 1945, and 1946. The last featured George Beverly Shea as soloist and a message from Charles Fuller—who also led the crowd in singing his own radio theme song, "Heavenly Sunshine." More than a thousand decisions for Christ were recorded at each of these events. In May 1946, Jack embarked on a preaching tour of the British Isles and broadcast each week from a different city, London, Cardiff, Glasgow, and Belfast. By 1947, mail was coming to the *Word of Life Hour* at a volume of up to five thousand letters per week. In 1948 the youth rallies reached their crescendo. That February, Jack gave the closing services at the famous Founder's Week Conference of the Moody Bible Church in Chicago, filling the four thousand seats of the Moody Church. Then on April 3, Jack and his team hit the road again for a "super rally" at the Philadelphia Convention Center. Nearly twenty thousand attended, and more than three thousand went forward to accept the call to Christian service. The next month, on May 8, similar results were achieved when a *Word of Life Hour* radio rally filled the famous Boston Garden arena. The year-long series of events reached their climax on June 19, 1948, when the *Word of Life Hour* Eighth Anniversary Rally came home to New York's Yankee Stadium. Crowds thronged the stadium and, when Jack gave the invitation, more than eleven hundred people gathered on the baseball diamond to pray and be converted.

During the decade of the 1940s, the best-known members of Jack Wyrtzen's team were songleader and tenor soloist Carlton Booth, organist and songwriter Norman Clayton, and pianist Harry Bollback. To the listening public and to those who attended the rallies, after Jack himself these three men were the most identified with the *Word of Life Hour*. F. Carlton Booth, known to everyone as simply "Carl," already had a full ministry when he agreed to be musical director of the Saturday night rallies in 1942.[52] Head of the music department at Providence Bible Institute (founded by former Paul Rader staff associate Howard Ferrin) of Rhode Island, he also directed music for the school's Sunday morning *Mountain Top Hour* broadcast that originated from Boston. For the past couple of years Booth had helped Wyrtzen at Word of Life banquets, chartered boat rides, and occasional rallies. When Jack asked him to come on as music director for the *Word Life Hour* that meant a long trip from Providence each Saturday, planning music for the broadcast and rehearsing a four thousand-voice choir, then driving to Boston in time for his own *Mountain Top Hour* on Sunday mornings. "Give me three days to pray about it," Booth replied to Wyrtzen's request. In that time he thought of a tragic car accident in which his life had been spared while that of a dear friend and fellow Christian worker had been taken. If God had spared his own life, then certainly he must not spare in his efforts to serve Him. After three days his answer to Jack was "Yes!"

In the years that followed, Booth served not only as songleader, soloist and choir director, but was frequently a speaker at the rallies held after the broadcasts. When he was not speaking, he could always be seen taking voluminous notes of the messages. Booth was also popular for his large sense of humor and good-natured spirit, which were vital to the smooth working of the Word of Life team. In his solo work, Booth was often asked to sing "My Sins Are Gone," "Jesus Gives Me a Song," "Singing," "Living Above," "Holy, Holy Is What the Angels Sing," and "We Shall See His Lovely Face." But by all accounts his signature song was "The Stranger of Galilee." At one rally he introduced the song by sharing the testimony of his own salvation.

> I never will forget one rainy, foggy night, as a boy fifteen years of age, attending a gospel meeting in Seattle, Washington. The message struck home to my heart. I was

the only one who responded to the invitation. But, my what a change when the Lord Jesus Christ came into my life! For since that meeting the Lord Jesus has been my nearest and dearest Friend, and He's no longer a stranger to me. "Not much of a meeting," someone might have said. "Just that little towhead at the altar, and he probably didn't know what he was doing." It was as if I had been going alone down life's pathway pell-mell in the wrong direction, and that night I met the Savior and He said, "Now, Carlton, we'll go together, but we'll face in the opposite direction!" Conversion was truly a right-about-face. And Christ is no more a stranger to me.[53]

And with that introduction Booth began the familiar refrain: "In fancy I stood by the shore one day of the beautiful murm'ring sea; I saw the great crowds as they thronged the way of the Stranger of Galilee...."

Norman Clayton was among the premier gospel songwriters of the golden age of radio.[54] Yet before the year 1930, when he was twenty-seven years old, no one would have guessed he might become a composer. Converted at an early age, as a boy he dabbled at the piano and played "both hands the same," as he put it. In time he apprenticed himself as a bricklayer and, when the Depression caused a slowdown in construction, he found work at a New York bakery. After work Clayton would go to the piano and work on his playing. In addition, he would take old hymns and give them new melodies—and then give those melodies new words. As a songwriting method it was unique, but it worked. When Percy Crawford heard these songs he instantly recognized the young composer's talent. Introduced to the public through Crawford's radio broadcasts and Pinebrook chorus books, Clayton's songs quickly became favorites. Clayton and Wyrtzen first met in the late thirties when the evangelist conducted a Brooklyn meeting in which Clayton was the pianist. The two men quickly became friends and, in time, associates in the ministry. Over the years as Clayton penned hundreds of songs, he readily admitted his ideas were not born out of unique experiences or inspiration. Yet he knew more than a thousand Bible verses and their citations by heart. Furthermore, to keep them fresh he committed to reviewing at least sixty verses a day. Thus his songs were steeped in the scriptures, sometimes by metrically transliterating entire Bible passages.

If the story of how Clayton's songs were written is not dramatic, how they first were printed—including his best loved song, "Now I Belong to Jesus"—is interesting. In the early 1940s as the Word of Life rallies and broadcasts began to reach national audiences, Clayton felt burdened to produce a songbook for the ministry. But in that era before computers or phototype, the complexity and cost of setting music type was high. Word of Life lacked the funds and music publishers were reluctant to back a new venture. At the time, music type was set by hand. Tiny bits of metal type, each containing a musical note or symbol, had to be picked out of large case and painstaking positioned on the printing grid. Customarily the work was only done by a master printer. Could Clayton do it himself? He looked in several founder's catalogs for a set he could purchase but music type was so rare that none could be bought. At last he borrowed money from three supportive Christian women and purchased a set from a very skeptical printer. The task was so daunting that the case of music type lay unused in Clayton's basement for an entire year. But finally he determined to begin. Each day after working at the bakery he would come home and set a few more measures of musical type. Bit by metal bit, working entirely by hand, he positioned the words and music of the now familiar song: "Now I belong to Jesus, Jesus belongs to me."

The new songbook, "Word of Life Melodies No. 1," was released in 1943 and not only earned back the initial investment but soon became a favorite with evangelicals everywhere. Clayton himself believed that "Now I Belong to Jesus" was his best composition, and this initial success fueled demand for more songbooks—though Clayton no longer had to set the type himself. "Word of Life Melodies No. 2" was published in 1945 and introduced what is perhaps the second Norman Clayton song that has come down to the church today, "My Hope Is in the Lord." Its rousing refrain declares, "For me He died, for me He lives."

Still more songbooks followed: "Melodies of Life" and "Low Voice Melodies" (both 1946), and "Word of Life Chorus Melodies" (1947). Then the composer launched his own Norman Clayton Publishing Company, becoming an important force on the evangelical music scene and helping many new songwriters—including John W. Peterson—get their start. In the fifties the company was acquired by the Rodeheaver Hall-Mack Company, which in turn was bought by Word Music in the 1960s. During his years of association with the *Word of Life Hour*, Clayton also served as music director of the Bellerose Baptist Church near his home in Malverne, New Jersey. Yet despite his success, he recognized that there was no sure-fire secret to songwriting. "Songs are unpredictable. What you may think is the best may gain little attention," he stated in 1948, noting that one his personal favorites, "For All My Sin," had remained "largely overlooked." Yet in later years, as appreciation for Clayton's contribution to church music increased, the song enjoyed new popularity.

The radio broadcasts continued through the fifties and beyond (continuing through 2011 as the quarter-hour *Word of Life Today* daily devotional program). But by the fifties, the golden age of radio was coming to close. In 1947 Word of Life opened a Christian youth camp at Schroon Lake in the Adirondack Mountains of upstate New York. The camping programs and Bible conference facilities expanded through the fifties and remain a focus of the ministry today. Word of Life Clubs for local churches were launched in 1959 and a Bible institute in 1971. In the late fifties the ministry began to support its own missionaries. (One of the first was Harry Bollback, who got up from his piano bench at a Word of Life rally and accepted the call to Brazil. From his experience with the first Word of Life overseas youth camp came his popular 1958 Christmas song, "Ring the Bells.") Today the Word of Life youth ministry concept—summer camps feeding into church youth clubs, in turn producing Bible school students who become national workers—is carried on by more than 1,300 missionaries in nearly seventy countries. Marge Wyrtzen, who stayed home to raise five children as her husband often traveled, passed away on New Year's Day 1984. Jack's passing was April 17, 1996, having guided Word of Life through its fiftieth anniversary in 1990 and entering semi-retirement the following year. Though the era of the great mass rallies was over by the fifties, Jack never lamented their passing. Weekly radio rallies and one-time mass meetings were exciting and, he believed, God accomplished much. But his decision to shift the focus of the ministry reflected a realization that youth camping and clubs were more suited to the times and could have a more lasting influence.

Torrey Johnson and Youth for Christ

The phone rang in Torrey Johnson's study at Midwest Bible Church.[55] On the other end was George Beverly Shea. "Torrey," he said, "we've got to do something in Chicago like Jack Wyrtzen is doing in New York!" Shea had worked frequently as a soloist for Jack Wyrtzen's "Youth for Christ" rallies, broadcast live as the *Word of Life Hour* each Saturday night from Times Square. The two men had both been insurance salesman in Manhattan and known each other for years. Shea had sung at Wytzen's wedding—and sold Wyrtzen his first life insurance policy. Now he was in Chicago working as an announcer for WMBI, the Moody Bible Institute radio station, and he keenly missed the excitement of the big weekly rallies.

Johnson was less enthusiastic. Shea had called him repeatedly, to which Johnson replied, "I can't do it. I'm too busy." But Shea was persistent. It was 1944 and Chicago was the railroad hub between east and west. Literally thousands of young servicemen walked the streets of the city each night, en route to Europe or the Pacific. And because of gasoline rationing, all the young people of Chicago couldn't drive and had nowhere to go. Saturday night youth rallies would work in Chicago, Shea insisted, and they would be work big. "Well, I'll see what I can do, but I'm busy," Johnson maintained, hanging up the receiver and hoping to get Shea off his back. Yet his friend kept agitating and Johnson at last gave in. "Well, if God will give us an auditorium," he said, hedging his bets, "then we'll do it."[56]

In calling his friend Torrey Johnson, George Beverly Shea was calling the right man. Although president Will Houghton of Chicago's Moody Bible Institute had a big heart for youth, he had recently been pastor of New York's Calvary Baptist Church and—though he had supported Jack Wyrtzen—generally felt that youth events should be attempted first within the church before organizing them independently. And Clarence Erickson, who taken the reins from Paul Rader at the Chicago Gospel Tabernacle in 1933, already had a large and effective ministry. But Torrey Johnson was a young man, still in his thirties, and definitely on the move. Born March 15, 1909, and named for evangelist Reuben Archer Torrey, the young Torrey Johnson was one of six children. His parents both immigrated from Norway to Chicago, where they met and married. Over the years his father piloted ships on the Great Lakes, painted the superstructure of the Chicago Loop elevated railway, and sold coffee and real estate. Yet his parents' Christian faith was always a constant as they raised the family in the Evangelical Free Church. Their pastor, C.T. Dyrness, later became a founder and president of The Evangelical Alliance Mission.

As a boy, Johnson earned money at a variety of jobs—in a Chinese laundry, a print shop, a glove factory, as a tinsmith, and then working his way through college as an iceman. On Saturdays he often helped his father in the coffee business, going down to the barn, hitching the horse, and riding with his father on the delivery wagon. Johnson was also impressed by the excitement of the 1918 Billy Sunday Chicago Crusade in which his father was an usher. "And my father was a great admirer of Paul Rader," he later recalled, "so that while I was going to my own church, getting into my late teens and twenties, I took every opportunity I could to hear Paul Rader preach."[57] Like many young people, however, Johnson had not yet appropriated his parents' faith as his own. Once when he was eleven or twelve, the well-known evangelist Harry Vom Bruch had preached in his church and the young boy went forward at the altar call. But as time passed he felt no assurance of salvation or a desire to live for the Lord. Upon graduating from high school in 1926 Johnson enrolled in nearby Wheaton College, chiefly because of his father's acquaintance with the president of the evangelical school. As his major Johnson chose science and set his sights on becoming a dentist and oral surgeon. He made it through his first term with adequate grades, then after the winter holiday returned for the start of his second semester. Johnson had been crititcally ill during the break, coming down with the flu while working the mail train between Chicago and Des Moines to earn some money. "But the Lord touched me and strengthened me," he remembered later, "and I came back to school." Arriving in Wheaton on the third Sunday of January 1927 and with nothing to do until Monday, Johnson sauntered over to the evening church service. Maybe by the time church was over his college buddies would be back on campus and they could have some fun.

So I went to church that night and I sat in the balcony ... and Evan Welsh, who was my friend and with whom I played football the year before, was there. And when the invitation was given, he put his arm around me and that was all I needed. Evidently from the weakness of being sick at the holidays, and perhaps pondering something about life and what all it meant, had gotten to me in the subconscious person. And God prepared me so that I can't tell you what the man preached.... [But] I walked down the aisle that night and received Christ. I was the only one that came [forward] that night and I often wondered what people thought afterward. "Well, just one came. It wasn't much of a meeting." But I always said it was the best meeting ever because I got in![58]

The next fall Johnson transferred from Wheaton to the dental school at Northwestern University. But though he did well and enjoyed his studies, an inner conflict was steadily growing. The debate came to a head when he heard a sermon by Harry Rimmer, a prominent preacher and former medical student. "I was going to be a doctor," Rimmer testified, "and I got into my fourth year in medical school. And I thought to myself, 'I'll minister to these peoples' health and strength, and then one day they'll die. That's the end of it. But if I preach the gospel, they'll have eternal life.'" That started Johnson on a train of thought. He could be a dentist, he had the ability. *But maybe there's something more*, he thought. The notion would not go away and the inner struggle intensified. So he tried to bargain with God. "Lord," he prayed, "if I become a dentist and I become successful, I'll make money and send somebody in my place. Lord, I'll send two. I'd be a poor missionary." At last, however, he believed in his heart that God was saying, "I want *you*." With that, he gave up the fight. Torrey Johnson would do whatever God wanted him to do. He could see now that "there was no other way to go, so I surrendered to the Lord."[59]

After a year of study at dental school, in 1929 Johnson returned to Wheaton College. The next two years (during which time Percy Crawford was a classmate) left an indelible mark on the young student. "I was almost a disciple of Paul Rader. He had a vision for the world," Johnson observed later. "He was very daring. He was a great promoter. He had a great deal of imagination.... I received my vision of the world from Paul Rader.... I saw the world and I wanted the world and I dared to believe for the world." When he was married in 1930, Johnson recalled that he and his wife "went to hear [Rader] while we were on our honeymoon. He was going to India on a missionary [trip] and we gave him our honeymoon money [so he could] go.... There wasn't much in that, but we gave him that."[60]

Upon completing his science degree in 1930, Johnson began a pastorate at the Messiah Church in Chicago. Then in 1933 he accepted the challenge to organize a new nondenominational church on the northwest side of Chicago, a part of the metropolitan area with few evangelical churches. Starting with twenty-six charter members in a private home, Midwest Bible Church moved to a storefront, then constructed and soon outgrew its first building, and in time served a thousand members in a church complex that occupied ten buildings on Chicago's Cicero Avenue. Over the ensuing years Johnson's own activities also steadily grew. He earned a 1936 doctorate from Northern Baptist Seminary and taught four years as an adjunct instructor in New Testament Greek and world history. He also served four years as president of the Wheaton College Alumni Association and, in 1942, was named Midwest regional representative for the newly founded National Association of Evangelicals. And like his mentor Paul Rader, Johnson believed that radio could be a boon to the church. His church board, however, was less sure about expanding into radio. "Gentlemen," declared Johnson to his board members, "I feel led to go on the air and broadcast on Sunday afternoon from five to six. I know that we don't have the money, but I want you to know that the church will not be responsible financially for it. If it fails, I will personally assume the financial obligation." Put like that, the church board had nothing to lose and everything to gain. "Well, if we're under no obligation," they at last replied, "and if you'll assume any obligation in regard to it, we'll go along."[61] By 1940, with Midwest Bible Church having become a strong and growing ministry, Johnson stated that,

> I felt, under God, that I had a message, not only for the local congregation, but beyond the local congregation, first in the Chicago area, and then beyond the Chicago area as God would open the door. That was the reason why I went on the radio to begin with the *Chapel Hour*. We took an old two-car garage building, and reworked it and made a studio out of it.... Radio was still somewhat of a novelty and so people would come from various places to that service, after which we served a dinner and then we had the evening service at seven o'clock.[62]

Since most Chicago area churches in those days did not hold Sunday evening services, Johnson reasoned, most churchgoers had nowhere to go on Sunday nights. "If you have an attractive service on Sunday night, there was the potential of drawing them and others in," he believed, "and then others who don't go to church at all on Sunday morning might come on Sunday night." In the end, his hunch proved right as the weekly *Chapel Hour* radio broadcast helped Midwest Bible Church build a strong evening attendance that was even larger than its morning services. As was the customary format of the day, the *Chapel Hour* featured a variety of Christian music and testimonies, followed by a short evangelistic message and a gospel invitation. From the start, the radio broadcast and evening services flourished, so that in time Johnson thought, "What about Sunday night?" Paul Rader had aired a late-night broadcast on Sundays, the *Back Home Hour*, as listeners across the country would tune in after returning home from their own churches. "He had a great grip on people, and they would sit by their radio sets, even beginning with the crystal sets," Johnson noted. And since Rader had gone off the air in 1933, "there was a vacuum, and I thought maybe we could fill that vacuum."⁶³

Thus in 1943 *Songs in the Night* was born, a program still heard in national syndication on evangelical radio today. A powerful clear-channel station, WCFL, was engaged to carry the broadcast. "In those days," Johnson said, "people used to try to see how far they could reach with their radio, how far they could hear from home. And if you could get a station from Chicago in New York that was quite an exciting thing." *Songs in the Night* was aired live from ten fifteen to eleven. Because AM radio signals travel farthest at night, the program—with five to eight minutes of speaking, a spiritual application drawn from a current event, a testimony, and quiet music—soon attracted a wide listenership. "Some people," Johnson remembered, "would even say, 'I went to bed with your program and then I went to sleep.' And people would come from everywhere just to sit in and be a part of it. It was that kind of a broadcast." By the 1940s, radio was less of a novelty so that letters no longer arrived by the bushel as they had in Rader's day. "But we had enough to keep us encouraged," Johnson remarked, "and know that there was a good audience out there."⁶⁴

So in 1944 when George Beverly Shea started calling his friend Torrey Johnson on the telephone, Johnson was already pastoring a thousand-member church, conducting two live radio services each Sunday night, and traveling as a representative of the National Association of Evangelicals. "Torrey, we've got to do something in Chicago like Jack Wyrtzen is doing in New York!" Understandably, even as Bev Shea persisted, Johnson just as firmly said no. The Word of Life "Youth for Christ" rallies were a phenomenon—and a phenomenal undertaking. How could he do it? The thought was absurd, wasn't it? When at last Johnson gave in—on the condition that God would provide an auditorium—he asked a friend from the church to investigate the possibilities: "Go downtown and see what kind of auditorium there is. If there's some auditorium downtown, we'll take it." Kimball Hall was available, but it would only seat five hundred. Too small. What about Orchestra Hall? Instantly, Johnson felt that must be the answer. In Chicago, Orchestra Hall was the equivalent of Carnegie Hall in New York or the Philharmonic in Los Angeles. Once the spring concert season was finished, the hall was largely vacant during the summer. In fact, it would be available every Saturday night for twenty-one weeks starting the third week in May—at a cost of five thousand dollars, "I knew God wanted me to do it," Johnson believed. "I said, 'We'll sign up.' I didn't have the money. I couldn't ask the church for the money ... but I did sign up for it."⁶⁵

The first "Chicagoland Youth for Christ" rally was set for May 27, 1944, the last Saturday of the month. Johnson called together representatives from the Christian Business Men's Committee, from the Breakfast Club and the Christian Endeavor (two lay organizations), and from different youth fellowships around the city. "I called them all together and told them what I was going to do," he recalled. "I didn't consult them now. I knew I was going to do it, but I wanted their help as far as they could give it." Word of the Saturday night Youth for Christ rallies at Orchestra Hall was spread through Johnson's improptu committee, as well as through printed fliers distributed by members of Midwest Bible Church and on the *Chapel Hour* and *Songs in the Night* radio broadcasts. George Beverly Shea offered to be the soloist. Johnson's associate pastor and brother-in-law, Bob Cook (who later became president of The King's College after the death of Percy Crawford), was enlisted to be the songleader. His church music director, Doug Fisher, was called upon to the play the organ. As the pianist, Johson recruited his friend Merrill Dunlop from the Chicago Gospel Tabernacle. Help even came from unexpected sources. The vice president at WCFL, the clear-channel station that broadcast *Songs in the Night*, was a Christian and "a very fine fellow," Johnson recalled.

> He looked at me with tears in his eyes in his office one day and he said, "Torrey, you've got Youth for Christ.... When are you going to have 'Old Men for God' for fellows like me?" I can see him now. His name was Mr. Holt. I thought of that many, many times. He was very valuable to us in opening up WCFL for a broadcast in connection with Youth for Christ in the early part of the Saturday evening service. And that was exciting. To think that you were broadcasting in connection with Youth for Christ ... was a novel course and that made it exciting.[66]

The auditorium was booked, publicity set, music lined up—and a big radio station had agreed to broadcast the rallies, just like Jack Wyrtzen's meetings. These things were important. Reflecting the mood of that first mass media generation, Johnson maintained that

> [We needed] new things at that time, innovative things. And all of it added up to the salvation of souls. [You had to] attract attention—for what purpose? Not for a selfish purpose, but to get the ear and the eye of people for the gospel. You're alive! You're doing something! You're not a part of the fossil age. You're with it.... Percy Crawford did it. Jack Wyrtzen did it. Charles Fuller was in the Civic Auditorium.... You've got to get the attention of people before they hear what you're saying, and I think that was a part of it. And then too, the unreached or the untouched would come to something like that. Not to hear the gospel. They would come for other reasons, and then they would get the gospel.[67]

Everything—the radio, the rallies, the music, the excitement—all pointed to the single purpose of gaining a hearing for gospel. But who would bring the message? Chicago was blessed with many prominent and effective preachers, Johnson not the least. But he chose a struggling young pastor from suburban Chicago whose small congregation had built itself a basement but couldn't yet build the whole church. Many members of Johnson's organizing committee opposed the selection and urged that a better-known evangelist be brought in. But Johnson wanted Billy Graham because—even if he had a habit of wearing red socks—the young man "had lots of potential." And so the day for the first Saturday night rally arrived, May 27, 1944. As Dunlop described it,

> I remember the suspense that we all had, wondering how many people might go up for that first meeting in Orchestra Hall ... and there was much prayer that went on preceding that opening rally. And [when] we arrived at Orchestra Hall that night we were just simply, happily stunned.... Orchestra Hall, the main floor and that first big balcony section were filled.... [T]hat was a tremendous crowd! And the opening rally was just a great one. Everything had been perfectly timed and Torrey Johnson had presented Billy Graham for the message.... But I mean, he had such fire and exuberance and fidelity to the Word of God ... it was just electrifying.[68]

In all, more than three thousand young people turned out for that first Youth for Christ rally. Graham preached a message on Belshazzar's feast from Daniel 5:27, "Thou art weighed in the balances, and art found wanting." At the invitation more than forty young people came forward to be converted. "At that time World War II was on," Dunlop later said in explaining the success of the event, "and there was the war spirit, of course, in the nation.... We were all aware of that, and of course in the big rallies they used to sing songs about the boys in the service overseas like 'God Bless Our Boys.'" But even more important, Dunlop believed, was that the "Youth for Christ movement was surely of the Lord's leading. Men just can't program things on that basis. It takes the blessing of God upon it, in addition to all that men can do to produce what was produced then."[69] As the twenty-one weeks went by, the crowds grew so that two rallies—one at seven, the other at nine—had to be held each Saturday night. "We had people on the street inviting the servicemen in," Johnson said, "and we had novel programs, arrangement for some of them to call home from the platform, and those kinds of things."[70] From Dunlop's seat at the piano, he recalled that "music was a great feature at Youth for Christ. We had all kinds of musical features and music groups. We used the organ and the concert grand piano." There was a large band with ninety pieces and even uniforms bought by some of the businessmen. A large choir was formed, Dunlop added, and "[we] would make awards to different Youth for Christ groups that came from different parts of the city. [We] had talent contests and would feature certain ones who had been selected as the ones who had won certain contests." Dunlop conducted auditions every Saturday night. "We were constantly putting the spotlight on the best we could find in music. We'd have quartets and ensemble groups and youth choirs and so forth. Talented young instrumentalists, cornetists. Of course our band provided great music."[71] In time, Youth for Christ rallies across the country popularized a form of song called a "chorus." Percy Crawford used them to great effect—short songs with catchy words and melodies, essentially a refrain or chorus but without any accompanying verses. Indeed, with some of the older songs that became YFC favorites such as Paul Rader's 1921 "Only Believe," the verses were omitted from the songbooks and only the chorus was sung. Another favorite chorus, "O It Is Wonderful," written by Merrill Dunlop in 1944 and introduced during that first year of YFC rallies in Chicago, captures the spirit of the style with its rousing affirmation that it is "thrillingly wonderful that Jesus died for me."

After the music and testimonies, each Saturday night rally featured a different guest speaker. "Not necessarily a youth himself," Dunlop recalled, "but speakers who were often men of great renown. And we had speakers from all over the country who would be coming through." But Dunlop could also see how some preachers were unaccustomed to tailoring their presentations to the requirements of mass media.

> [T]here was a number of times when some of these preachers ... had come expecting to preach a full length sermon, when what was wanted was about fifteen to eighteen minutes ... a direct scriptural presentation, a gospel appeal, and an invitation. Not a long three-point sermon, as a pastor might preach on Sunday morning.... And I heard many times that criticism voiced, "Well, these Youth for Christ boys, they don't know what they are doing. They're trying to run the message out and just put a lot of music and features in." But the philosophy of it was to appeal to young people with all of these features and get them to hear the message and hook them with it.[72]

When the twenty-one weeks at Orchestra Hall were over, Johnson asked his committee, "What do we do next?" Some believed the rallies should stop for the winter and begin again the next May. "But God didn't let us do it," Johnson said. "It's not that we were so smart. We were just carried along by the Holy Spirit, and there was a great momentum." Once again Johnson looked to Jack Wyrtzen, who in April and September 1944 held hugely successful rallies in New York's Madison Square Garden. Indeed, the Word of Life rally in April was the inspiration that prompted George Beverly Shea to pick up the phone and call Torrey Johnson in the first place. Now, seeing the results of Wyrtzen's September rally, Johnson declared, "If Jack can do it in New York, with God's help we can do it Chicago!"[73] So Youth for Christ rented Chicago Stadium—at the unbelievable cost of five thousand dollars. But on the day of the rally, the thirty thousand seats of the stadium were jammed to capacity and thousands more were turned away at the gate.

By the end of the summer, president Will Houghton of the Moody Bible Institute had seen the effectiveness of the Youth for Christ rallies and gave the group his full support, allowing the rallies to be aired over WMBI. And the Moody Church (a separate ministry from the Institute), which could seat four thousand, agreed to host the Saturday night rallies when Orchestra Hall was not available. That arrangement, using Orchestra Hall in the summer and Moody Church the rest of the year, continued for several years. As 1944 came to a close, Youth for Christ groups were springing up independently in cities all over the country—St. Louis, Indianapolis, Detroit, Minneapolis, Philadelphia. Johnson did everything he could to support the local efforts and in January 1945 hired Billy Graham to come on as a full-time YFC evangelist, traveling to rallies in the different cities. By the time YFC approached its one-year anniversary in May 1945, the group estimated that between three and four hundred rallies were being held across the country with a weekly attendance of between three and four hundred thousand.

And the momentum kept building. With Memorial Day 1945 approaching and the weekly rallies set for a return to Orchestra Hall, Johnson had an idea. Why not kick off the summer season with a big rally, a *really* big rally? Not at Chicago Stadium and its thirty thousand seats, but at legendary Soldier Field which could seat nearly one hundred thousand people. Yet the rent was not five thousand dollars but twenty-two thousand. Johnson asked one of his board members if YFC should pay an additional ten percent for rain insurance. The man, who originally opposed the idea as impractical but agreed to support the majority decision, gave a simple reply: "Torrey, did you ever read about Elijah?" The scriptural reference was clear. The prophet had prayed and it didn't rain. "That's all I needed!"[74] Johnson exclaimed. On the day of the rally, not only was the weather dry and sunny. A crowd of more than seventy thousand arrived for the event—which had been promoted by YFC's field representatives in more than one hundred fifty cities. At the time, it was the largest evangelical youth rally in history. The program for the day featured a three-hundred-piece band; a choir of five thousand voices; several popular soloists, including George Beverly Shea; a flag ceremony with four hundred marching nurses and a wreath-laying by four hundred high school students; an appeal to buy war bonds; a parade of missionary volunteers wearing national costumes; testimonies from a war hero and a collegiate boxing champion; and an exhibition lap by record-holding miler Gil Dodds. Fittingly, the main speaker was Percy Crawford. After his message, youths by the hundreds signed cards attesting that they had converted to Christ. Then the stadium was darkened and a spotlight turned on, panning the crowd to remind them of the duty to be "the light of the world." Following a benediction, a neon sign blazed forth the words "Jesus Saves" as the choir closed by singing "We Shall Shine as Stars In the Morning."[75]

When newspaper mogul William Randolph Hearst (four years before his famous order to "Puff Graham!") saw what happened at the 1945 Soldier Field rally, he wired the editors of all his big-city dailies to "Puff Youth for Christ"[76] because "it would be a good thing for our papers to be the promoters of it" and to "please develop it in every way possible."[77] Suddenly Johnson saw coverage of YFC meetings appearing on front pages and Sunday supplements in New York, Boston, Los Angeles, San Francisco, Chicago, Seattle, and more. In a signed editorial, Hearst even applauded Youth for Christ as a "powerful antidote" to the scourge of juvenile delinquency and urged every community to support the movement. When President Truman attended a rally in Olympia, Washington, he exclaimed that Youth for Christ was what America needed.[78] Another admirer of Youth for Christ was Nell Sunday, widow of the late Billy Sunday. "If you can ever fill up the Billy Sunday Tabernacle for a Youth for Christ rally," she told Johnson, referring to the famous Bible conference grounds at Winona Lake, Indiana, "I'll give you five thousand dollars!"[79] Johnson took the challenge and scheduled the "First Annual Convention of Youth for Christ International" for July 22–29, 1945. The occasion marked the formal incorporation of YFCI as thousands of young people packed the Tabernacle. A delighted Ma Sunday wrote out a check for five thousand dollars. Under the new organization, local groups would continue to operate autonomously but Johnson was elected president to head a central office that could provide coordination and support. In his first address as YFC president, which Johnson entitled "Acceping the Challenge," he declared to the assembled convention,

> The job that needs to be done is bigger than any man in this room—it's a hundred times bigger than all of us put together. But I have faith in God that it can be done. The thing that burdens me is that it must be done lest we who are here will be held responsible for the greatest tragedy in human history—we are headed either for a definite turning toward God or the greatest calamity ever to strike the human race.... I think of the five hundred cities [where YFC groups have held rallies] with an attendance of five hundred thousand young people—and that is a conservative figure—as compared with thirty-seven million young people [in the entire country]. What we've reached is only a drop in the bucket. There are the United States, Canada, and the English-speaking people of the world. There are vast areas that haven't been touched with a movement to present Jesus Christ to young people. I'm not interested in establishing Youth for Christ everywhere in America—I'm interested in reaching young people for Jesus Christ everywhere! ... We must keep our eyes on this as the ultimate in all we do. We want to reach American youth for Christ! We want a revival in the United States. We want to reach youth in other lands. But with it all, there must be that deep spiritual undertone and we must challenge young people with the job that needs to be done around the world. Let's get out to do the work that others have tried and failed.... Let's trust God not for what we can see and do, but for what we cannot do and cannot see and what we believe God wants to do![80]

It was a call to service attuned to the idealism of the youth of the forties, who had grown up during war and with an awareness of the outside world introduced to them through radio. As the 1945 "Youth for Christ" theme song proclaimed, "You for Christ, and Christ for Youth!" Rallies continued to grow in size and number across the country, carrying the slogan, "Geared to the Times, Anchored to the Rock" (or alternately, "Old-Fashioned Truth for Up-to-Date Youth"). In 1946 the movement hit its peak with nine hundred weekly rallies across America attended by an estimated one million young people. Johnson himself continued as pastor of Midwest Bible Church and in 1945 his *Chapel Hour* broadcast was picked up by the newly-formed ABC network. In 1946, to further his dream of winning the youth of the world, he made a European tour for YFC. More super-rallies were held at Chicago Stadium, as well as at stadiums and arenas in other cities. Throughout the forties and fifties, YFC exerted a profound (and sometimes controversial) effect on the development of evangelical popular music.[81] YFC rallies offered a venue for new musical talent and launched the careers of men such as Ralph Carmichael, Kurt Kaiser, and Harold DeCou who became influential songwriters in the 1960s. Evangelical young people could read album reviews in *Youth for Christ Magazine*, hear the music performed at YFC events and in sound tracks for YFC evangelistic films, and then buy the records at Saturday night rallies. Through the YFC book and record club, teens could even sell records to their friends and earn money to attend their YFC state convention. The annual international YFC convention in Winona Lake served as a showcase for the top evangelical singers and musicians of the day. New talent could vie for top honors at local and regional YFC music competitions, then progress to the finals at Winona Lake. Categories included vocal and instrumental soloists and groups, gospel pianists, and songleaders.

By 1948, however, the number of rallies began to drop off. That year the movement's two most popular youth evangelists resigned for other pursuits: Billy Graham to enter independent ministry and Chuck Templeton to enroll in Princeton Seminary. In 1948, Torrey Johnson too resigned as YFC president to devote more time to his pastorate and a growing work as an evangelist in his own right. In 1953, after twenty years at Midwest Bible Church, he entered full-time itinerant evangelism and preached across the United States and in Europe, South America, Africa, and the Far East. From 1967 until his retirement in 1982, Johnson was pastor of Florida's Bibletown Community Church and president of Bibletown Bible Conference. He went home to be with the Lord on May 15, 2002, at the age of ninety-three. Merrill Dunlop, whose lifelong association with Johnson extended from their Tabernacle days in the 1920s to Youth for Christ in the forties—and at Bibletown in the eighties—said of his friend,

> Not only is he a fine preacher.... I think of him as a promoter [and] administrator. Every Monday morning [after the first YFC rallies] we sat down together in his office at Midwest Bible Church ... and we'd knock ourselves out just trying to find our what we had done wrong and what we could do better, and [yet] ... I've never

seen him in a spirit of anger, and that is perhaps unusual for a man of Torrey's influence and greatness. I think that he has genuine Christian love in his heart. And he's always on the job, speaking to somebody about Christ.... It's not just a professional thing with him, it's personal sincerity.[82]

Youth for Christ continues to this day. By the 1950s, however, the days of Saturday night rallies were done. In time the focus shifted to organizing local Bible clubs, then in the late 1960s the concept of campus-based ministries was adopted. Yet as Johnson had envisioned in his opening address to the first YFC convention at Winona Lake, today more than twenty thousand local Youth for Christ leaders serve in more than one hundred countries and report more than a hundred thousand conversions each year.[83]

Billy Graham and the Hour of Decision

It was Sunday night at 10:15 and, as the director gave the cue to begin, the strains of the familiar opening theme lofted skyward over the airwaves: "There's a song in my heart that the world cannot sing...." *Songs in the Night* was on the air. From the platform of Chicago's Midwest Bible Church, where the forty-five-minute program originated live each week, pastor Torrey Johnson looked out over the scores of people in the pews.[84] *Songs in the Night* was a boon to the church, attracting people from across the region who came to watch the broadcast. Thousands more listened across the nation over clear-channel WCFL. As Johnson sat in thought, he could hear the musicians on the chorus of the show's opening theme: "Songs in the night, songs in the night, The Lord giveth songs in the night...." While the organ played softly and the announcer welcomed listeners to the program, Johnson regretted having to give up the program after only a year on the air. But what else could he do? It was 1943 and, in addition to his pastoral duties, he served as Midwest representatives of the National Association of Evangelicals. In addition, his one-hour *Radio Chapel Hour* program was aired each Sunday from five to six. Something had to give, but it would be a shame to simply cancel *Songs in the Night*. Why not let another church and pastor take over the program. But who?

Some days later, Johnson was driving down a Chicago street when he spied a car approaching in the opposite direction. He knew the driver. His name was Billy Graham, a young pastor at a struggling suburban church.[85] Though Graham had just graduated that spring from Wheaton College, Johnson had heard of him through NAE circles. Earlier that year, in April 1943, Graham had preached in Cicero, Illinois—where Johnson's Midwest Bible Church was located—at the citywide rally of the Fundamental Young People's Fellowship. Now Johnson pulled up his car beside Graham's and motioned him over.

"You're Billy Graham?" asked Johnson.[86]

"Yes, sir," Graham replied

"I'm Torrey Johnson."

Graham's eyes widened. "Oh, yes," he answered enthusiastically, "I've heard you lots of times on the radio."

"I'd like to talk with you," Johnson continued.

"Certainly, any time," was the young pastor's response.

Some days later Johnson picked up the phone and gave Graham a call. Graham was just out of college, just getting started in the ministry. But Johnson believed the North Carolina-born preacher had potential and that having a radio program might help him out. "I've got too many things on my plate with a large, growing church and my main radio program on Sunday afternoon," explained Johnson over the phone. "I have another radio program called *Songs in the Night* and I'd like to give that to you. I've prayed about it and thought about it, and I think you're the one who should have it." Graham paused a moment on the other end of the line, then answered that he too would pray about Johnson's offer and discuss it with the deacons of his church. "Okay," Johnson concluded, "call me when you've made a decision."

Less than a decade earlier, in the summer of 1934 when Billy Graham was a boy of fifteen, he was mostly interested in playing baseball. Born November 7, 1918 (four days before the armistice that ended the First World War) he grew up on the Graham family dairy farm near Charlotte. Though raised in a Christian home, young Billy had little interest in religion—and certainly not in hearing any evangelist, even if he was famous. So when Mordecai Ham came to Charlotte that August for a three-month campaign, Billy told his mother and father that he wouldn't go. Then at one of the meetings Ham announced he had proof, including signed affadavits, of moral perfidy at the Charlotte central high school. News traveled fast among the teen crowd and some talked of creating disruptions at the next meeting or even attacking the evangelist himself. Billy wanted to be there if anything happened and so he agreed one night to come with his parents to the specially built tabernacle on Pecan Avenue. Despite himself, he was spellbound by Ham's powerful oratory.

In the weeks that followed, young Billy faithfully attended the meetings each night. The campaign stretched into November and yet the tabernacle remained filled every evening. At each service, as he heard Mordecai Ham's powerful warnings of hell and judgment, the boy came under increasing conviction that he too needed a Savior. At last, sometime around his sixteenth birthday, Billy Graham could contain his conviction no longer. Once again that night, Ham inveighed against sin but then gently closed with the good news that "God commendeth His love toward us, in that, while we were yet sinners, Christ died for us" (Romans 5:8). The songleader then led the congregation in four stanzas of "Just As I Am." Still Graham hesitated. The songleader then had the crowd begin another well-known song of invitation, "Almost Persuaded, Now to Believe." It was the last song and Graham hung back until the last verse. By then, three or four hundred people had come forward to the altar. So he too made his way to the front of the tabernacle. Yet he was confused. All around him, others were weeping as they converted to Christ, but he felt nothing. Then a friend of the family, a local tailor who was a dedicated believer, put his arms around Graham and explained to him from the Bible how to be born again. Even then, he felt no special emotion. But that night in his room, kneeling beside his bed, Graham for the first time in his life prayed earnestly to God without being told. "Lord," he said, "I don't know what happened to me tonight. *You* know, and I thank you for the privilege I've had tonight." Though it would be some time before the young Graham knew the Bible well enough to explain the way of salvation to others, he immediately discovered "that the world looked different the next morning when I got up to do the milking, eat breakfast, and catch the school bus. There seemed to be a song in my heart."[87]

Whenever Graham had stopped to think about his future, he vaguely assumed that he would finish Sharon High School and, despite his modest grades, go on to University of North Carolina. But in the year and a half between his conversion and high school graduation, the Grahams often attended various evangelistic meetings around the Charlotte area and sometimes hosted the evangelists in their home. One of these became a special friend of the family and took Billy to jails and missions where Graham shared his testimony, his first public utterances about his faith. The evangelist encouraged Graham to pursue a Christian education. So after a year (1936–37) at Bob Jones College in Cleveland, Tennessee, and two years (1937–39) at Florida Bible Institute near Tampa, he transferred to Wheaton College to complete his undergraduate degree. There he met and married Ruth Bell. In his senior year as president of the Wheaton Christian Student Union, he spoke at small churches across the upper Midwest and served for a time as student pastor of the Wheaton United Gospel Tabernacle.

One day in early 1943 the Wheaton College chapel service featured a local Christian businessman named Robert Van Kampen. After the service he and Graham struck up a conversation. On hearing that Graham planned to be a preacher, Van Kampen extended an invitation to speak at his own Baptist church in the Chicago suburb of Western Springs. The small congregation was impressed enough by Graham's sermon to call him as its pastor. In June 1943, the same month that he graduated from Wheaton, Graham accepted. Western Springs Baptist Church met in an uncompleted building, actually a roofed-over basement. But with his marriage to Ruth approaching in August, Graham felt a need to ensure that he could support his new bride.

In time, he persuaded the deacon board to rename the church since so few Baptists lived in the predominantly Lutheran and Congregationalist neighborhood. As the Village Church, membership grew slowly as Graham sponsored such outreaches as a businessmen's dinner series featuring leading evangelical speakers.

Yet he and Ruth never viewed Western Springs as anything but a temporary assignment. It was 1943 and Graham, like most young men, wanted to do his part for the war. Ready at first to join the armed services, his Wheaton professors convinced him that he could do more good as an Army chaplain. Though he had twice been rejected for lack of experience—and for being underweight—Graham planned to eventually reapply. But since his Wheaton degree was in anthropology, he intended first to receive some seminary training. Then too, Graham found pastoral work constraining. "Billy's not a pastor," Robert Van Kampen once told his friend Torrey Johnson, "he's an evangelist." As Johnson later recalled from the conversation, "Billy wasn't doing very well because he was not a pastor as far as visitation work and deacons meetings and those kinds of things. They were very difficult for Billy, not to *do* so much but to *like*. He would rather preach ... [and] be in association with other men who were preaching and learn from them.... [So] I thought Billy needed help."[88]

And thus, having decided to give up his *Songs in the Night* radio broadcast, when Johnson saw the struggling young pastor driving down the street one day, he pulled his car beside Graham's and motioned him over. Graham did not have to think long about Johnson's offer. A radio broadcast immediately appealed to his instinctive desire for a broad evangelistic outreach, and perhaps as a way to build church membership quickly without the laborious work of door-knocking and visitation. The weekly cost of airtime on WCFL for *Songs in the Night* was one hundred fifty dollars. But though the entire pledged income of the church was only $86.50, Graham pressed ahead. When Van Kampen offered to provide the start-up funds for the initial thirteen-week contract required by WCFL, the deacon board went along.

But how to make the program succeed? Midwest Bible Church was a large and thriving work, while Torrey Johnson was well-known and a friend of many fine evangelical singers and musicians from around the Chicago area. By contrast, Graham and his church were unknown and lacked contacts. What the broadcast needed was a big name, one that would draw attention. As Graham thought the matter over, an idea, though perhaps a crazy one, formed in his mind. What about George Beverly Shea? The handsome bass baritone was certainly famous. After singing on NBC in New York, he was now in Chicago at the Moody Bible Institute radio station, WMBI. In fact, Graham often listened to him at eight fifteen each morning on the *Hymns from the Chapel* broadcast. People would probably tune in *Songs in the Night* if they could hear George Beverly Shea. At that, Graham drove into downtown Chicago, walked onto the Moody campus, and strode into the radio station office on the top floor of the main Institute building. He could see the famous singer through the glass door of his office but was told by his secretary that Shea was in a meeting. Not willing to waste a trip downtown—or to take "no" for an answer—Graham waited until he saw Shea briefly open his door. Then Graham brushed past the secretary and marched into Shea's office.

"Mr. Shea, I'm sorry to intrude," Graham boldly declared, "but I just have a quick proposal for you. My name is Billy Graham and I'm pastor of the Village Church in Western Springs."[89]

Taken aback by Graham's unannounced entrance, Shea cautiously responded, "I've heard of you."

"Torrey Johnson has asked us," Graham plunged on, "to take over his Sunday night radio show. And I'm convinced that the program would be more successful if you would agree to appear on it."

"Well, I don't know," Shea stammered out.

Undeterred, Graham outlined his plans in his powerful, rapid-fire manner. And even years later, he conceded, "I think [Shea] agreed to give it a try only because he could see that that was the only way he was going to get rid of me."

Throughout his subsequent career, Shea was widely acclaimed as America's most beloved gospel singer. Yet after more than half a century of ministry with Billy Graham, today George Beverly Shea is primarily known for his association with the even-more-famous evangelist. So it may be difficult to visualize, when in 1943 Graham burst into Shea's office at WMBI, just how audacious was his request. Graham was a nobody, just out of college and in his first pastorate, a Southern-accented boy in urban Chicago. Shea, by contrast, was already a well-known singer who had appeared on national network radio, had written songs and made recordings, and worked with many prominent evangelists as a featured soloist at citywide campaigns.

Born Ferbuary 1, 1909, Shea was the son of a Wesleyan Methodist minister in Winchester, Ontario. When he was eight the family moved to Houghton, New York, where his father took up a brief ministry of evangelism and church planting. Though the Sheas later returned to Canada, their sojourn in the United States made an impression on the boy. For in Houghton he was introduced to Clara Tear Williams, a noted hymn writer. The young Shea got to know Williams, who was also a Wesleyan Methodist, and was endeared by the elderly woman's sweet Christian manner. Later, when his father accepted a pastorate in Ottawa and moved the family back to Canada, Shea had memorized some of Williams's hymns. "Satisfied" and "All My Life Long" were two favorites when, encouraged by his mother who was the church pianist, he began in his late teens to sing publicly. A second mentor that Shea credited as an influence on his unique singing style were the early recordings of Homer Rodeheaver, which Shea first heard as a youth of fourteen. "I loved to listen to Homer Rodeheaver singing," he remembered later. "He was an early inspiration. Long ago Homer would [also] sing every week on the radio when the radio was America's only source of entertainment."[90]

In the late twenties the family returned to New York where, in 1928–29, Shea attended Houghton College. But when the stock market crashed in 1929 and a depression followed, finances forced Shea to drop out of school and find a job. He ended up as a clerk in the Mutual Life Insurance Building on Wall Street. There he met a young Jack Wyrtzen, who was also in the insurance business, and sold Wyrtzen his first life insurance policy. New York was the center of the radio world at that time and exerted a great pull on a young and talented singer such as "Bev" Shea. So he auditioned for a popular amateur hour broadcast hosted by comedian Fred Allen. After securing a spot on the show, he placed second in that week's talent contest (beaten by a yodeler). Yet the experience got Shea thinking about a singing career. He started practicing his piano and took voice lessons from Gino Monaco on the top floor of the Metropolitan Opera building. In time, Shea got a job on the staff of the Allen program. He sang popular music and was soon acclaimed by critics and fans who heard him coast-to-coast each week over the NBC network. Yet he was nagged by the thought that he should do more for Christ than to be a pop singer. As he pondered the direction of his life, one Sunday morning he found a poem left on the piano by his mother. She collected inspirational poems, quotations, and literary passages. Wanting to guide her son spiritually and knowing he liked to practice his piano after rising each morning, she would often leave selections there for him to see. On this morning in early 1933, Shea found a poem entitled "I'd Rather Have Jesus" by Rhea Miller.[91] Reading the words, he was overcome with emotion. "Upon reading it over," he later recalled, "a second verse just hit me. I began playing in the key of B flat and just started singing the poem. I didn't know Mother was in the next room having her Sunday morning devotional. I didn't know anyone could hear me. I just sang the song the way it was given to me."[92] Overwhelmed by her son's powerful song, Shea's mother urged him to sing it at his father's church service that day. He agreed. For the song, even then, was working on his heart and would later lead to the conviction that he should dedicate his life to Christian service. But in 1933 he was still unsure of what he should do and so he made no effort to publish the song. He just wasn't ready.

As the thirties went on, Shea would sing at evangelistic meetings around the New York area, including those organized by his friend Jack Wyrtzen. In addition to network radio, plus frequent appearances on Percy Crawford's

Young People's Church of the Air, Shea was also heard locally as chief soloist for the *Meditations in the Psalms* program with evangelical businessman Erling Olsen. During the day he would sell insurance and once a week he continued to sing on the radio. Then a turning point came in 1938 as he left New York to audition for a CBS show that originated from Chicago. When he wasn't selected, the now-married Shea found himself needing a job. But he also found a friend in Will Houghton, president of Moody Bible Institute. Houghton was formerly a New Yorker, having pastored that city's famed Calvary Baptist Church, and took an interest in Shea. Would he come and work as an announcer and singer at WMBI? Shea accepted, and in the months that followed the desire to serve Christ with his singing gifts deepened into a conviction. His daily *Hymns from the Chapel* morning program with organist Herman Voss became a WMBI favorite. Soon afterward, in 1939, he published "I'd Rather Have Jesus." In the years to come his favorite scripture verse, one he would usually attach to his signature, remained Psalm 71:23, "My lips shall greatly rejoice when I sing unto Thee; and my soul, which Thou hast redeemed."

WMBI in those days of the late thirties and early forties was a hub of evangelical activity. Houghton knew the power of radio; his former church, Calvary Baptist, was pioneer in the medium. Under his predecessor, John Roach Straton, Calvary became the first church in America to broadcast services over its own radio station, WQAQ, in 1923. Though the station was later closed, Calvary Baptist aired a highly successful program over New York's WHN. Houghton launched a year-long campaign to celebrate the 1937 centenary of Dwight L. Moody's birth, an effort that ultimately enrolled the participation of 2,300 churches with an attendance of more than four hundred thousand. In 1938–39 he followed up with a series of special *Let's Go Back to the Bible* broadcasts over the Mutual network. Then in 1940, a *Miracles and Melodies* series featuring George Beverly Shea and others debuted on sixty-seven stations across the country. By 1942 the program was aired on 187 stations in the U.S. and Canada. Shea himself had begun making records through Al Smith's Singspiration music company. And in June 1944 he went on national network radio, singing gospel songs on the *Club Time* program, so named for the Club Aluminum company owned by evangelical businessman Herbert J. Taylor.

That was the George Beverly Shea whose office was invaded by Billy Graham in the fall of 1943. Yet the singer agreed to give *Songs in the Night* a try. In January 1944, on the first anniversary of the program, Torrey Johnson officially turned it over to Graham in a final broadcast from Midwest Bible Church. The next week, Ruth Graham helped with the scripts—handwritten because the church had no typewriter—and Bev Shea rigged up some colored lights for the table where Billy would sit to deliver his radio messages. In time, Graham developed a radio speaking style that attracted a following. Under Torrey Johnson, messages delivered on *Songs in the Night* took their cue from current events. Graham picked up on that format, one that he continued to use in his crusade preaching throughout his career. As Johnson explained, Graham would "usually start out with something—an earthquake, a flood, a leakage of poisonous gas, a battle of a war, something that would immediately attract attention—and then move on from that to some kind of spiritual application."[93] The broadcast was built around brief spoken vignettes by Graham, interspersed among musical selections by Shea and a women's quartet, the King's Karrolers, from Wheaton College. From the first, Graham was proved correct in his confidence that a radio program could put the Village Church on the map. People came from all over Chicago to see Shea in person. The church could seat 125 and, from the first week, every pew was full. After the first program, Graham even had to escort Shea out through an exit door in the rear furnace room. Donations quickly rose to cover the cost of airtime, with enough left over to retire the church's mortgage.

Despite the success of *Songs in the Night*, the church deacons grew restive over Graham's frequent invitations to speak at meetings throughout the Midwest. Though they had agreed to this when Graham was called—and though his official title was pastor/evangelist—his absences created some discontent within the church. The controversy only got worse after Torrey Johnson invited Graham to speak at the first Chicagoland Youth for Christ rally in May 1944, his first foray into big-time evangelism. The appearance was hugely successful and soon scores of invitations to speak at youth events in other cities were pouring in. For his part, Graham was encouraged by the growth of the Village Church and its outreaches. Perhaps, he thought, the church might serve for several years as a base for his ministry. He even turned down opportunities to pastor large churches in Chicago and Fort Wayne, Indiana. But the controversy over his speaking absences, and news of his acceptance into the Army chaplaincy program, dampened his desire to remain in Western Springs. Graham believed the war had made the world ripe for the gospel and that made him restless with the pastorate.

Then in September 1944, Graham came down with a raging case of the mumps. Two weeks of expected bedrest turned into two months as the mumps developed into a case of orchitis. With Graham's temperature rising to 105 degrees, the doctors had some fear for his life. The illness also prevented him from attending that year's required Army chaplaincy school at Harvard University. Graham decided to resign his pastorate in October, though he continued as speaker for *Songs in the Night*. A radio listener heard about his illness and sent a hundred dollars to pay for a Florida vacation. Graham desperately needed to recover his strength and, as soon as he was able, gladly accepted the offer. In December, Graham scheduled YFC appearances in

Tampa and Miami. Then he and Ruth rented a room in a small Miami hotel, about a block from the beach. To their delight, they discovered that Torrey Johnson and his family were vacationing at another hotel on the same street. Graham sought out his mentor, to thank him for the radio and rally opportunities, and Johnson invited him to go fishing.

As the two men hired a deepsea boat and headed out on the ocean, Graham looked forward to a day of relaxation in the sun. But as they bobbed on the ocean surf, the fishing was forgotten as Johnson launched into his idea for a bold evangelistic outreach. Youth for Christ was becoming a nationwide movement with rallies springing up in cities across the country. Johnson believed the movement could be even larger and more effective if a central office were established to provide support for local groups. Johnson was asking his church, for the next year, to let him work half-time on the fundraising aspects. Would Graham be willing to come on board as a YFC staff evangelist, available to travel and speak and help organize more local groups? "I think you're the man to become our first full-time employee," Johnson said confidently. "Would you pray about becoming our national—and international—organizer?"[94] When the Army chief of chaplains agreed that Graham could minister more effectively to young servicemen as a youth rally speaker and granted a discharge, Graham could see that his course was set. Thus in January 1945 he walked into the first-ever YFC office on Wells Street in the Chicago Loop and reported for work as the first-ever YFC employee at a salary of seventy-five dollars a week. During that first year of 1945 Graham visited forty-seven states, logged some 135,000 miles, was named United Airlines' top civilian passaenger for the year, and was dubbed by the press as the "Bobby-Soxer Evangelist" (referring to the current slang term for teenage girls).

At the end of 1945 Graham stepped down as speaker for *Songs in the Night* (the church later turned the program over to the Moody Church, which has continued the broadcast to the present day). Then his pace accelerated in 1946 and 1947 as Graham conducted preaching tours of the British Isles both years. The meetings reached out to young and old alike, giving Graham his first experience with citywide evangelistic campaigns. In September 1947 Graham conducted his first citywide crusade in the United States at the city of Grand Rapids, Michigan. Then followed a two-week revival in November at his hometown of Charlotte. The dynamic young Cliff Barrows had joined his team as songleader the previous year. Now George Beverly Shea—who since June 1944 had become nationally prominent as a gospel soloist on his own *Club Time* radio program over the ABC and Armed Forces networks—also decided to travel with Graham on a full-time basis.

Graham's star had risen far and fast. Youth for Christ was then the most dynamic development in American evangelicalism. Its leaders, especially

Graham and Torrey Johnson, were looked on as the next generation of leadership for the nation's evangelical movement. For that reason the aging William Bell Riley, affectionately regarded as the "Fundamentalist pope," became convinced that Graham or Johnson was the man to take over the college he had founded. Johnson had politely but firmly declined. So Riley set his sights on Graham. Northwestern Schools in Minneapolis had been established by Riley in 1902 and had grown to encompass a full liberal arts curriculum and seminary. Now in 1947, as Graham later recalled, he was summoned to Riley's home "where he was lying on a couch. Raising his head from the pillow, the eighty-six-year-old man fixed his clear eyes on me and lifted a frail hand in my direction. With great certainty in his voice, he announced that I would wear his mantle as Elisha had worn the Old Testament prophet Elijah's. His words seemed like a patriarchal blessing."[95] Graham must succeed him as Northwestern's next president, Riley insisted, or at least accept designation as "vice president at large." For his part, Graham did not feel comfortable at this prospect. He himself was only four years out of college and his only academic credential was an undergraduate degree in anthropolgy. "But Dr. Riley," he stammered, "I can't accept this responsibility. God hasn't shown it to me. But if it'll ease you, I'll take it on an interim basis until the board can find a permanent president." And with that, upon Riley's death on December 5, 1947, Graham's "interim" commitment turned into four years as the nation's youngest college president.

Though Graham cut back his YFC travel schedule, neither was he deskbound. Since he accepted no salary from Northwestern and continued on the YFC payroll, his evangelistic travels for the youth ministry continued. During the years 1948–49, Graham continued his dual role as educator and evangelist. At Northwestern he raised funds to complete an unfinished major building project, recruited substantial numbers of new students (enrollment rose from 700 to 1,200 during his four-year tenure), and even conducted the nation's first evangelical radio "sharathon" in launching a new station, KTIS (now flagship of the 15-station Northwestern Media network). Perhaps most important to Graham's later ministry, he inherited Northwestern business manager George Wilson to serve the same function for his own burgeoning enterprises.

Despite his love for Northwestern (today known as University of Northwestern), the call to evangelism was stronger. By 1948 as the momentum of the great Youth for Christ rallies began to subside, Graham scheduled more of his own independent citywide crusades—Augusta, Georgia, and Modesto, California, in 1948; then in 1949 Miami, Baltimore, and Altoona, Pennsylvania. By the summer of 1949 he had preached his last YFC meeting and in September embarked upon the greatest venture of his young career, the "Christ for Greater Los Angeles" crusade. Yet as Graham approached his greatest opportunity, he experienced his greatest crisis. "My very faith was under siege," he remembered. "The particular intellectual problem I was wrestling with, for the first time since my conversion as a teenager, was the inspiration and authority of the Scriptures. Seeming contradictions and problems with interpretation defied intellectual solutions, or so I thought. Could the Bible be trusted completely?"[96] As president of Northwestern Schools, Graham felt a need for "broadened reading habits" and to "keep abreast of theological thinking" by such leading theologians as Karl Barth and Reinhold Niebuhr. His growing doubts about the trustworthiness of the Bible were further fueled by a close friend, Chuck Templeton, a dynamic young pastor from Toronto who was having similar struggles. Along with Torrey Johnson and Billy Graham, Templeton was the third man at the head of the YFC movement. Hugely popular as a YFC speaker, he toured Europe with Graham in 1946. Later, however, he had begun to feel that the YFC rallies were shallow and emotional. So he resigned his Toronto pastorate and enrolled at Princeton Theological Seminary, searching for deeper intellectual grounding. "I talked with him," Graham said, "two or three times that winter of 1948–49—his first as a graduate student—and discovered he was undergroing serious theological difficulties, particularly concerning the authority of the Scriptures. My respect and affection for Chuck were so great that whatever troubled him troubled me also." For his part, Graham's most recent crusade in Altoona, Pennsylvania, had seemed to him a failure. "In fact," he admitted, "I pondered whether God had really called me into evangelism after all." By the spring of 1949, Graham was giving serious consideration to taking a leave of absence from Northwestern and, like Templeton, pursuing a Ph.D. of his own.

In the late summer of 1949, Graham carried these doubts with him to the annual College Briefing Conference at the Forest Home retreat center near Los Angeles. The event was headed by Henrietta Mears, who had been a key Sunday school worker at William Bell Riley's First Baptist Church in Minneapolis. Now as director of religious education at First Presbyterian Church of Hollywood, she had built a Sunday school program that drew 4,500 people a week. Speakers for the conference included Graham as president of Northwestern Schools, the Oxford-trained evangelist and missionary J. Edwin Orr (who wrote the song "Search Me, O God"), and Chuck Templeton. Coming up to Graham early in the week, Templetpon exclaimed, "Billy, you're fifty years out of date. People no longer accept the Bible as being inspired the way you do. Your faith is too simple. Your language is out of date. You're going to have to learn the new jargon if you're going to be successful in your ministry." As the next days went by at Forest Home, Graham "ached as if I were on the rack" with the sensation of being stretched in two different directions. Then one evening he knew that he had reached an hour of decision. "With the Los Angeles Campaign galloping toward me," he later recalled, "I had to have an answer. If I could not trust the Bible, I could not go on." That night Graham went out for a walk in the woods that surrounded the retreat center. As he gazed out over the nearby San Bernardino Mountains, the moon cast long shadows among the darkened trees.

> Dropping to my knees there in the woods, I opened the Bible on a tree stump in front of me. I could not read it in the shadowy moonlight, so I had no idea what text lay before me.... I could only stutter in prayer. The exact wording of my prayer is beyond recall, but it must have echoed my thoughts: "O God! There are many things in this book I do not understand.... I can't answer some of the philosophical and psychological questions Chuck and others are raising." I was trying to be on the level with God, but something remained unspoken. At last the Holy Spirit freed me to say it. "Father, I am going to accept this as Thy Word—by *faith!* I'm going to allow faith to go beyond my intellectual questions and doubts, and I will believe this to be Your inspired Word."[97]

When at last Graham got up from his knees that August night, "My eyes stung with tears. I sensed the presence and power of God as I had not sensed it in months. Not all my questions were answered, but a major bridge had been crossed. In my heart and mind, I knew a spiritual battle in my soul had been fought and won."[98]

As the time of the Los Angeles Crusade approached, press coverage was nil. The only mention were the ads in the church section of the *Los Angeles Times* paid for by the Christian Business Men's Committee, the group that had invited Graham and was sponsoring the campaign. The committee had enlisted the support of more than two hundred churches, tripled its original advertising budget, and hired a professional public relations director from the local Salvation Army. But as far as the media was concerned, "Christ for Greater Los Angeles" was a non-event. The crusade was slated to begin September 25, 1949, and run for three weeks. Shortly before the starting day, Graham got his first promotional break. Henrietta Mears invited him to speak at the Hollywood Christian Group, a fellowship of actors and actresses that met in her Beverly Hills home. Mears, who came from a wealthy family, had become well known in the entertainment community. So her Bible study attracted a number of important Hollywood stars. Among them was Stuart Hamblen, a cowboy songwriter and actor who appeared in movie westerns opposite such names as John Wayne, Gene Autry, Roy Rogers, Tex Ritter, and Randolph Scott. Hamblen was not a believer and attended the Bible study for the sake of his wife Suzy. Yet Graham took an instant liking to rawboned, earthy actor from Texas whose father had been a circuit-riding Methodist preacher. As a result of their meeting, Hamblen asked Graham if he would like to be a guest on his *Sawdust Trail* radio show.

Hamblen's two-hour program was heard daily in several states and he himself was the top-rated radio personality on the West Coast. In the days after the crusade began, Graham found himself mulling over Hamblen's invitation. Attendance in the early days of the crusade was running about three thousand a night, a good crowd but not nearly filling the large tent on the corner of Washington Boulevard and Hill Street. More than that, Graham sensed that he was preaching mainly to the already converted. Maybe appearing on *Sawdust Trail* with Stuart Hamblen, thought Graham, might help his crusade break through the press blackout and boost attendance. It was a risk, however. Hamblen's show was sponsored by a tobacco company and some people on the crusade committee might object to Graham being a guest. But he decided to give it a try and took Bev Shea with him. The show went well as Graham and Hamblen swapped stories and Shea sang some gospel songs. Then to Graham's great surprise the cowboy actor blurted out an endorsement, encouraging listeners to "go on down to Billy Graham's tent and hear the preaching." Even more surprising, he followed that up by saying, "I'll be there too!"

Suzy Hamblen had long been praying for her husband's conversion. He was a regular on the Hollywood studio party circuit, well-known for his drinking and gambling and love of the fast life. Yet on that first night Hamblen attended the crusade, he came under deep conviction about his sins and need for Christ. Confused and troubled, he got angry and stormed out of the tent. But Suzy encouraged him and, two or three nights later, he came back. Over the next two weeks Hamblen would alternately stay away and then return, and then become angry and even shake his fist at Graham as he stalked out of the meeting. In the week before the crusade's scheduled closing on October 16, Graham and some members of the sponsoring committee felt led to consider an extension of the campaign. Yet others opposed such a move, noting that the workers were getting tired and that attendance might start to dwindle. Such an anti-climax might risk losing much of the good things that the crusade had already accomplished. What should they do? Graham, Shea, and Barrows prayed for God's direction. As Graham remembered,

> At last we decided to follow the example of Gideon in the Old Testament and put out a fleece, asking God to give us a decisive sign of His purpose. It came at four-thirty the next morning. I was awakened in my room at the Langham Hotel by the jangling of the telephone. In a voice broken by tears, a man begged to see me right away. It was Stuart Hamblen.... By the time I was up and dressed, Stuart and his praying, godly wife Suzy were at my door. We talked together and prayed, and the rugged cowboy gave his life to Christ in a childlike act of faith. He came forward in the next service. The first thing he did after he received Christ was to call his father, who was an old-fashioned Methodist preacher in west Texas. I could hear his father shout with joy over the phone! ... I knew that we had our answer about continuing the Campaign.[99]

Not only did Hamblen publicly testify of his conversion in the next tent service, he went on the radio to tell all his thousands of listeners. The cowboy actor and radio personality was a household name all along the West Coast. As a songwriter he had enjoyed several bona fide country-and-western hits. News of his conversion made the papers and the airwaves. Then one night a crowd of reporters and photographers showed up at the "Canvas Cathedral." They told the evangelist that their publisher, the legendary newspaper mogul William Randolph Hearst, had ordered them in a telegram to "Puff Graham" (as he had done four years earlier for Youth for Christ). The next morning Graham's crusade headlined the *Los Angeles Examiner*, followed by a front page spread in the *Los Angeles Herald Express* evening newspaper. Both were owned by Hearst, whose papers in San Francisco, New York, Chicago, and Detroit also picked up the story. Soon, competing papers were also covering Graham and his campaign. The press gallery was full as reporters eagerly covered the conversion of Olympic track star and war hero Louis Zamperini (whose story was dramatized in the bestselling 2010 book and 2014 film *Unbroken*) and then West Coast mobster Jim Vaus. Graham's picture appeared on the covers of *Time, Life,* and *Newsweek* magazines. He was even offered a Hollywood screen test. As media interest multiplied, so did the crowds. A second extension of the campaign was decided and, by the time the Greater Los Angeles Crusade closed after its eighth week, total attendance had exceeded a third of million people. Thousands had "rededicated their lives to Christ" and nearly three thousand made first-time decisions for salvation. As for Stuart Hamblen, he began a new radio show called the *Cowboy Church of the Air*. And he started sharing his newfound evangelical faith to his many Hollywood colleagues and friends. One of these was John Wayne. As a result of their conversation, Hamblen wrote the song, "It Is No Secret (What God Can Do)." Sung and recorded by Bev Shea and many others, it soon became a hit—the first of many, as Hamblen went on to become one of the top Christian songwriters of the fifties and sixties.

Boston was the next stop for Graham and his crusade team, with meetings scheduled the first two weeks in January 1950. And there, over the radio, he heard the news that on January 11, 1950, one of his role models had unexpectedly passed away. Walter Maier, a pioneer in religious radio and speaker on *The Lutheran Hour* worldwide radio broadcast, had suddenly suffered a heart attack and died at the age of fifty-six. At the time of his death, Maier had preached to more people than any man in history. "I was so jolted," Graham later said, "that I knelt in my hotel room and prayed that God might raise up someone to take his place on the radio."[100] With all three major networks—NBC, CBS, and Mutual—closed to paid religious broadcasts since the mid-1940s, Maier's *Lutheran Hour* and Charles Fuller's *Old Fashioned Revival Hour* were virtually the only evangelical programs that had maintained a broad national radio presence. Another evangelical leader shaken by the death of Maier was Theodore Elsner, who in 1950 had just been elected president of the National Religious Broadcasters. What use was access to the airwaves, Elsner thought, without the effective testimony of men like Maier? Elsner himself had been broadcasting nearly as long as Maier, since 1931 when he launched the first daily evangelical broadcast in Philadelphia from his pulpit at the Gospel Tabernacle. But he readily admitted that, in the public mind, it was Maier and Fuller who were the twin pillars of religious broadcasting.

Elsner believed one of the vital issues facing NRB was the vacuum left by the loss of Maier. The thought was on his mind that summer of 1950 when Elsner decided to take a vacation. He knew a small cottage that was available for rent in Ocean City, New Jersey. So he drove in early one morning to spend some time alone with God before his family arrived. As he prayed, pouring out his concern over a replacement for Walter Maier, he felt a clear conviction that God was impressing a name upon his heart. As it happened, Ocean City was not only a seaside resort but also home to Methodist camp meeting center. Graham had just come to preach there at a conference, but didn't mind the chance to slip away one morning and play a few holes of golf with Cliff Barrows and another friend from the conference. Then to top off the morning, the three men drove down for lunch to a little diner on the edge of town for some good food and quiet fellowship. Graham and his two companions were happily shooting the breeze over in a corner of the diner. Then out of the corner of his eye, Graham spotted a man coming toward them. Tears filled the man's eyes and he was obviously in the grip of some great emotion. He walked straight over to their table and, as Graham wondered what the man could want, he blurted in a loud voice, "What an answer to prayer! I was just sitting here praying that I would meet Billy Graham, and in you walk! I didn't even know you were on the East Coast."[101] There was confusion for a moment, then the man introduced himself. His name was Theodore Elsner.

When Elsner had finished praying that morning in his rented cottage, he had gotten in his car and driven down to the diner for lunch. Even behind the wheel, he was still in an attitude of prayer, asking God who could fill the shoes of Walter Maier as a national radio voice for the gospel. Then as he walked into the diner, Elsner couldn't believe his eyes. It was Billy Graham, the very name God had placed upon his heart. Of all the places in the world, on that day and hour, Graham was in Ocean City in the little diner on the edge of town. Elsner explained who he was, that he was president of National Religious Broadcasters and a radio preacher for nearly twenty years from Philadelphia. Then he shared his burden and his definite conviction that this meeting was divinely ordained. Now it was Graham's turn to get excited. Soon he was pacing up and down the diner, peppering Elsner with questions about how to get started in network radio. Elsner gave him two suggestions. The first suggestion was to meet Walter Bennett, a powerhouse in mainstream radio whose agency had also promoted *The Lutheran Hour* and other evangelical programs. The second was to meet Fred Dienert, Elsner's son-in-law and partner in the Walter F. Bennett Advertising Agency. Graham thanked Elsner for the reference and, after lunch was over, left the diner with a promise to look into the idea.[102]

Two weeks later Bennett and Dienert introduced themselves to Graham at a Bible conference in northern Michigan and offered to help him start a radio ministry. But in the days since Ocean City, his duties as a college president and conference evangelist had been as pressing as ever. Recently, on July 14, 1950, he had even been invited to the White House for a meeting with President Truman. Graham had quite enough to do and informed the two advertising agents he lacked the time for a regular radio program. Cliff Barrows and Bev Shea agreed it was out of the question. Yet Bennett and Dienert persisted, showing up a week later at Graham's home in Montreat, North Carolina, with some great news. A desirable time slot on Sunday afternoons was available on the ABC network. They could have coast-to-coast coverage for thirteen weekly broadcasts at a cost of only ninety-one thousand dollars. Bennett and Dienert were hoping for an enthusiastic response, but they were soon disappointed. "That kind of money I know nothing about," declared Graham, who then abruptly ended the meeting.

At the end of July, Graham was off to his next crusade in Portland, Oregon. He was surprised—and annoyed—when the two ad men kept pursuing him by long-distance telegram and telephone. Bennett and Dienert explained the weekly program cost was only seven thousand dollars, and that twenty-five thousand was enough to get it on the air. Then listeners would pay for the broadcast thereafter. Graham was irked by their talk and said the money was "twenty-five thousand dollars I don't have!" The amount was equal to the entire budget of the Los Angeles Crusade. So when Bennett and Dienert arrived in Portland, Graham refused to see them. When they would wait for him in the hotel lobby, Graham used the rear elevator or fire escape to avoid them. When a staff member gave them an appointment, he escaped to a nearby resort for a day off. But then Graham received a telephone call that day at the resort. A wealthy friend had heard he might be interested in radio and offered two thousand dollars to set up a fund. That got Graham thinking. Was God at work here? He returned to Portland that evening and called Bennett and Dienert over to his hotel room. Was the network's Sunday slot still available? Could wealthy donors be contacted in time to book the broadcast? The two advertising executives told Graham it was risky to depend on "a lot of big people" and instead suggested he take an offering at the crusade that night. At Graham's request the three men knelt in prayer. The evangelist pledged all he owned if God called him to a radio ministry. "But I want you to give me a sign," he prayed, "and I'm going to put out the fleece. The fleece is for twenty-five thousand dollars by midnight."

The crusade attendance that night was estimated at more than seventeen thousand people. But as the offering was taken, Bennett and Dienert were surprised when Graham made no mention of radio. Only after the offering did the evangelist describe the opportunity. Anyone who would like to take a part could see him at the close of the service. When the sum of twenty-five thousand dollars was mentioned, a few ripples of laughter floated out from the crowd. Then Graham finished his sermon and brought the meeting to a close. Bennett and Dienert were glad to see that hundreds of people had streamed down the aisles to be converted. But they could not help feel a bit discouraged. Graham would be counseling and praying with the new converts for a long time yet. Few people, they thought, would wait around to see him about a radio program. Dejected, they headed toward the airport for a flight they had booked that night to Chicago. Yet much to their surprise, and to Graham's also, a crush of people were waiting outside the arena office door. When the evangelist arrived, a staff member was holding a shoebox containing cash, checks, and pledges scribbled on crusade programs and songsheets. One businessman said he hoped Graham would pick up the torch left by Walter Maier and pledged a thousand dollars. Altogether the contents of the shoebox, together with the original telephone pledge, came to twenty-four thousand dollars.

Was this the sign they had been seeking to go on the radio? "No, it's not a miracle," Graham demurred. "The devil could send twenty-four thousand dollars. It's all or nothing!" Downcast, the evangelist and his team went to dinner at a Japanese restaurant and then returned to the hotel. It was a few minutes before midnight when the clerk at the front desk called out, "There are two letters for you, Mr. Graham." Graham opened the first one. It was postmarked two days earlier from a businessman in another city who felt burdened to start a radio fund so that Graham's sermons could be heard regularly over the air. Inside was a check for five hundred dollars. With a trembling hand, the evangelist opened the next envelope. It too had been postmarked two days ago and contained a check from a businessman who believed Graham should be on the radio. The amount? Five hundred dollars. Graham looked up at the clock, just a minute or two shy of midnight, and exclaimed, "Now I'll grant it's a miracle!" Overcome with emotion, Graham bowed his head in silent prayer and then turned to the hotel elevator. Who then should he see in the hotel lobby? Walter Bennett and Fred Dienert. While at the airport, the two men felt God was telling them not to get on the plane. Graham placed a hand on each man's shoulder and told them, "Sign us up for radio for at least thirteen weeks. God has answered our prayer. We have the twenty-five thousand dollars. We'll take this as a step of faith."

That faith was tested, however, when Bennett and Dienert arrived the following Saturday at ABC headquarters in New York to sign the contract. The only person they could find, however, was a junior executive who informed them that the ABC board had just decided not to allow any more religious programming on the network. "You *promised* it," protested Bennett and Dienert. "We've guaranteed this young man, Billy Graham, that he has a network. To change your minds now is very unfair to us. Get hold of the board." But the junior executive refused. The board members were all playing golf and couldn't be consulted until Monday. Then, declared Bennett and Dienert, "we'll set here until this thing is resolved!" With that, the executive picked up the phone and, at last, succeeded in reaching one of the board members on the eighteenth hole. The decision was changed and *The Hour of Decision* was saved.

The radio contract was signed in August. Meanwhile, the 1950 Portland Crusade was extended through the first week of September, by which time more than half a million people had thronged the meetings. And the shoebox collection that had been taken for radio also had another lasting consequence. At previous crusades donations had always gone toward expenses. Now here was twenty-five thousand dollars unrelated to any campaign. George Wilson suggested that a Billy Graham Evangelistic Association be incorporated, and in September Wilson left his post at Northwestern to become Graham's full-time business manager. It was decided to call the radio program *Hour of Decision*, a name suggested by Graham's wife, Ruth. The first broadcast was set for Sunday, November 5, 1950, while Graham was crusading in Atlanta. The evangelist decided not to adopt the folksy approach of Charles Fuller, but rather the fast and intense speaking style of Walter Maier. This not only suited his own manner of speech but was the style employed by the day's highest-rated newsmen, such as Walter Winchell and Drew Pearson. Like his old *Songs in the Night* broadcast, Graham's *Hour of Decision* programs started with illustrations taken from current events. For awhile, he even kept a teletype machine in his home.

Carried over the one hundred fifty stations of the ABC network, that first year *Hour of Decision* generated more than two hundred thousand letters—all received at "Billy Graham, Minneapolis, Minnesota." In a short time, the broadcasts were self-sustaining through listener donations. By the second year *Hour of Decision* drew larger audiences than the Sunday newscasts, with mail volume running at three to four thousand letters a week. In 1954 the NBC network was added, bringing the total station count to eight hundred. By 1955 the weekly audience totaled an estimated fifteen million listeners over a network of more than a thousand stations. That same year *Hour of Decision* debuted on radio in 1950, Graham began exploring other ways to use mass media. Even as *Hour of Decision* went on the air, others were going behind the camera to film his crusades and make them into motion pictures and a series of *Hour of Decision* telecasts aired between 1950 and 1954. This was a radically new technique in mass evangelism. But as Graham and a few others were now discovering, the visual media could be a powerful tool to capture and transmit the preaching of the gospel. The picture of evangelism was changing and in 1957 the *Hour of Decision* debuted on national TV.

In the decades since Billy Graham emerged as a national figure he has been acclaimed an American cultural icon, the friend of presidents and revered religious statesman. (Yet he has also been controversial, splitting the former unity that until the fifties existed among evangelicals as his crusades welcomed the participation of mainline churches he once opposed.) Seldom remembered is how much Graham was a creation of mass media and especially radio. His early mentor, Torrey Johnson, was a disciple of Paul Rader. Johnson himself was catapulted into prominence by radio, later giving Graham his *Songs in the Night* broadcast that (with the help radio personality George Beverly Shea) first brought the young evangelist to public notice. Graham's entry into big-time evangelism came through Johnson and Youth for Christ, a movement born in the earlier radio work of Percy Crawford and Jack Wyrtzen, and then nurtured by press coverage from the Hearst newspaper empire. Then it was Hearst again, along with radio's Stuart Hamblen, who rescued Graham's struggling Los Angeles Crusade at the critical moment. The resulting triumph turned the evangelist into a national figure who then became a broadcaster himself. In turn, response to the *Hour of Decision* radio program became the foundation of Graham's mailing list and donor base. None of this would have been possible if Graham were not a gifted speaker. But he is also a prime example of the impact of mass media on the practice of evangelism and the rise of evangelical popular culture.

Throughout the fifties, Graham and his team had a profound impact in shaping and showcasing the evangelical popular music of the day. Many of the great hymns of the church were rediscovered under the songleading of Cliff Barrows. Others, such as "To God Be the Glory" and "Great Is Thy Faithfulness," were popularized for the first time. George Beverly Shea, by a wide margin, became America's best loved and most recorded gospel singer. On the recommendation of Stuart Hamblen, in 1951 Shea was signed to a recording contract by RCA Victor. (His first album, *Inspiration Songs*, included Hamblen's "It Is No Secret" as a way to say thanks.[103]) And with the success of "I'd Rather Have Jesus," he kept on writing more songs. In 1955, when the crusades and the *Hour of Decision* radio outreach were at their height, Shea boarded the ocean liner S.S. *United States* en route to meetings in Scotland. A fellow passenger, who was a music publisher, struck up a conversation and asked him about the typical program sequence at a Billy Graham crusade.

Shea described how the meetings were conducted, but then "I found myself at a loss for words when I tried to describe the responses that usually accompanied Mr. Graham's invitations to become a Christian." Turning to the other passenger, he exclaimed, "What happens then never becomes commonplace, watching people by the hundreds come forward. Oh, if you could just see the wonder of it all!" The other man wrote the phrase on a card and handed it to Shea. That sounds like a song to me," he said, and challenged Shea to write one.[104] Later that night, as Shea watched the sun set over the ocean, he was inspired to rough out a melody and to write down the words of a song he entitled "The Wonder of It All." In eight years traveling with Billy Graham, he had seen much. Yet to Shea the most remarkable was not the adulation, fame, and immense public and media interest. "The wonder of it all," his lyric proclaimed, is "just to think that God loves me!"

Al Smith and Singspiration

Al Smith was due that night at a meeting in Oneonta, New York.[105] But before turning west on State Route 23, he decided to stop in the small town of Catskill on the Hudson River. Smith asked where he might find a local resident, a Mr. George C. Stebbins, and was directed to a small brick house on High Street. He drove to the address indicated and, as he approached the door, heard the sound of typing. *He must have a secretary*, Smith thought to himself as he knocked. But it was Mr. Stebbins himself who answered the door. It was he who had been typing, yet he was very glad to welcome the young Smith and invite him in. The year was 1938 and Stebbins was then ninety-four years old. He had been a gospel song composer and friend of Dwight L. Moody, Ira Sankey, Phillip Bliss, Fanny Crosby, and many others. Now he was the only one left. Smith had always loved the old gospel songs and wanted to know the stories of how they came to be written. And that afternoon, for the next three hours, the young Smith was not disappointed as Stebbins regaled him with tales of yesteryear—of the way Fanny Crosby laughed, of how Moody the famous evangelist sang on one note, and of the tragic death of Phillip Bliss in the Great Ashtabula Train Wreck.

Though Stebbins lived another nine years and told Smith many more stories, on that day in 1938 the young visitor believed their meeting was likely to be the last. As he climbed into his car, turned away from High Street and then headed on to Route 23, Smith found himself talking to God. "Lord, if I could only write one little song that would inspire people as much as Mr. Stebbins," he said. It was about seventy-five miles to Oneonta, and as the time passed Smith thought of how the great gospel songwriters of yesteryear had desired to bless others rather than to seek personal blessing. A growing conviction came upon Smith to let his own life be used of God in the same way. At the same time, as he sat behind the steering wheel he started to hum a simple melody. By the time he reached Oneonta the now-familiar words and music—all but one phrase—were in place. Smith had just enough time to stop at the home where he would be staying the night, put down his bags, and then jot down the melody and words of his new song, before rushing to the church meeting. His hosts were two sisters, Grace and Frances Townsend. Because Grace was an invalid, Frances stayed home from the meeting to take care of her sister. She spied Smith's scribbled song script which he had left on the piano and noticed something. Being an English teacher, she immediately saw that her guest had left out a phrase. Like she had done with so many class assignments, Frances took the pencil Smith had left on the piano and, in the empty space, wrote in the words, "What glory that will be!" As Smith readily confessed in later years, if God had not used Frances Townsend to fill in the missing phrase, "I feel sure that I would have put the song aside and perhaps never gotten around to finishing it." Yet from its first publication, just as Smith had prayed that day in 1938 on the road to Oneonta, "For God So Loved the World" has been widely popular.[106]

Born November 8, 1916, in Midland Park, New Jersey, Smith was a young man of many talents. An only child, he excelled at the violin. But even as he was being selected concertmaster for the New Jersey All-State Orchestra and youth soloist for the New York Symphony, Smith earned another coveted honor—as an all-state varsity football player for his high school. But if music provided an outlet for self-expression, his spiritual life did not. The family attended a mainline church that, Smith believed, was stuffy and staid. Then Smith and his mother decided to try a new church that met nearby, the Hawthorne Gospel Tabernacle (where a young Jack Wyrtzen later attended Bible school). Services were held in a tent because the church had no building. In his old church, for music they sang the psalms which Smith had trouble understanding. Now for the first time, the old gospel songs made the way of salvation plain in a manner Smith could understand. One song in particular, entitled "One Day," made a special impression.

> Living, He loved me; dying, He saved me;
> Buried, He carried my sins far away;
> Rising, He justified freely forever:
> One day He's coming—oh, glorious day!

Smith had never before heard such music. Then, in an afternoon service one day, Pastor Herman Braunlin challenged his congregation to make the scriptures even more personal—ironically, by using the same verse that would later inspire Smith's most famous song. "For God so loved the world," the preacher quoted from John 3:16, "that whosoever believeth in Him should not perish but have everlasting life." Then he added, "Now just take that 'whosoever' out and put your own name in there." That was the moment that Smith came under the conviction that Jesus died for him and he needed to convert to Christ.

After high school, Smith went on to study at New York's Juilliard School of Music under the renowned violin pedagogue Leopold Ahuer. Yet even while at Juilliard he took time to help lead songs at Percy Crawford's Pinebrook camp in the Poconos (and was present the day in 1936 that Jack Wyrtzen's wife Marge was converted and Jack dedicated his life to Christian service.) Then, from that day in 1938 on the road to Oneonta when he composed "For God So Loved the World," Smith felt certain that God was leading him into full-time music ministry. So he enrolled at Moody Bible Institute in Chicago to obtain his Bible certificate and then entered nearby Wheaton College to earn a Bible degree.

One semester at Wheaton his roommate was another young student named Billy Graham. The two traveled together throughout their Wheaton years as a team, with Smith leading songs and Graham preaching. Always a man with an entrepreneurial bent, in 1941 Smith conceived the idea of publishing a gospel songbook called *Favorites* that would compile music especially suited for evangelistic meetings. The venture would help the work by enhancing the song service, generating funds for further outreaches, and blessing those who purchased the volumes. As a student, however, Smith lacked the start-up funds to print the songbooks. He and Graham had just received honoraria of one hundred dollars each for an evangelistic meeting and Smith's share was all he could afford to put into the project. Then he and Graham were directed to a Mr. Beck at the college who might be able to help, and the two students paid a call. Smith explained his plans, to which Mr. Beck replied, "Well, Al, how much money do you have?" Not able to lie, Smith confessed he had just a hundred dollars. At that, Mr. Beck reached for one of the drawers in his desk and took out an envelope. It seemed, he explained, that two women had given five hundred dollars to Wheaton College, money to use for something special other than the regular offering. After hearing of Smith's plans, Mr. Beck believed that God would have these funds go toward the cost of printing the songbook. And so it was, with that six hundred dollars, Smith published his first songbook.[107] Two years later, in 1943, he founded the Singspiration Publishing Company. And *Favorites* became a series of songbooks that ultimately were sold the world over and launched Smith on his life's work as a songbook publisher and preserver of evangelical popular music.

Those years in Wheaton, as a student and then after graduation, were eventful ones for Smith. More Singspiration songbooks followed and, through a distribution agreement with the evangelical Zondervan publishing company, were sold by the thousands. Consistent with Smith's desire to help the music ministry of others, the books were used to introduce new songwriters—including a young John W. Peterson whose first successful song, "He Owns the Cattle on a Thousand Hills," debuted in the Singspiration series. Smith also branched out into recordings and was the first to introduce George Beverly Shea and the Old Fashioned Revival Hour Quartet to the record-buying public. Meanwhile, his travels with Billy Graham increased as the young evangelist became in demand. "At the beginning of 1945," Graham later recalled, "in addition to Atlanta and Norfolk, I was preaching all over the Midwest. One day, as I was boarding a train with Al Smith, who was leading my singing, someone handed me a telegram from Chicago. I put it in my pocket, got onto the train, and was well on my way to Indianapolis before pulling it out." It was from Graham's wife. "Ruth is expecting!" the evangelist declared, to his songleader's hearty congratulations.[108]

By 1945, the Youth for Christ movement had rocketed to national prominence. Huge YFC rallies were being held each Saturday night in Chicago and in cities across America, and Al Smith was in demand as a songleader. "He was a tremendous platform man," confirmed Peterson:

> He could hold an audience riveted with his stories. And he was a great songleader and a fine singer. He could really sing a song.... He had a warmth, a believability about him. And when he got a song that he liked, he knew how to sing it and really get the message across. He was one of the best at that. Al was just a great communicator. He had a real gift of communicating with song.[109]

In his role as a YFC songleader Smith had a wide influence on the music that became popular at the rallies, and by extension among evangelicals nationwide. "If a song was used in Youth for Christ," Peterson said, "it became quite popular." By the same token, YFC was a boon to Smith. "Al put together a thirty-two page collection of choruses popular in the Youth for Christ movement and published it," explained Peterson. "The Wheaton students carried it home to their churches and the book took off like a prairie fire. Then came a second book, and a third. They launched Al as a publisher and became the foundation for the Singspiration Publishing Company."[110] Smith made a lasting impact, Peterson believed, when "he started to sing the [short] choruses in the Youth for Christ movement.... Well, that really gave [the chorus style] a great impetus. So I think that was a key thing he did. When he first started Singspiration, he impacted the country, no question about it."[111] Smith's own "For God So Loved the World" was an instant favorite as a rally chorus. Another enduring example of the style is "With Eternity's Values in View," a 1941 composition that urged believers to take the long view and "do each work for Jesus with eternity's values in view."

Another turning point of those years was his marriage to Catherine

Barron, a Wheaton College classmate. The young couple was soon blessed with two children, Barbara and Gordon. But then Catherine began to suffer with ill health and was diagnosed with multiple sclerosis. Though Smith's ministry as songleader for the Billy Graham crusades was just starting to take off, he made the difficult decision to leave traveling evangelism and focus on music publishing. With his wife gravely ill and two small children to care for, Smith moved the family moved back to New Jersey, to be close to his parents. Another great comfort was his favorite Bible verse, "For me to live is Christ and to die is gain" (Philippians 1:21). Difficult as the trial might be for his wife and himself, Smith relied on the biblical promise that God would cause all things to "work together for good" (Romans 8:28).

Living in the New York City metro area, however, proved to be a challenge. The busyness and traffic of city life were a strain and the commuting distances made it difficult to obtain reliable help in caring for Catherine. To get away from these pressures, Smith and his parents would take two weeks each summer to vacation at the famed Montrose Bible Conference in rural Pennsylvania. By the early fifties, Smith had fallen in love with the town of Montrose, its white clapboard homes with green shutters and its quiet tree-lined streets. He bought a home there and ultimately moved Catherine and the children to the country. Moreover, within twenty-five miles of Montrose had lived some of the great gospel songwriters of the nineteenth century, including Daniel Towner, James McGranahan, and Philip Bliss. The notion of basing his own Singspiration publishing company in the very shadow of these musical giants greatly appealed to Smith.

During Smith's days in Wheaton when he was a songleader in the Youth for Christ movement, his chorus books had introduced John W. Peterson as a songwriter to the public. But the two men had never met. That only happened later when, in the late 1940s, Peterson had joined the staff of WMBI and Smith was invited to lead singing at the Moody Bible Institute's annual Founder's Week Conference. "Then was when our friendship developed," Peterson recalled.

> Eventually I started to publish some books on my own through Moody Press, a series called *Melody-Aires* that was somewhat similar to Al's Singspiration books. Now, Al did not have any knowledge of harmony and had to depend on others to write things out for him. Eventually his first editor left and in the interim I had started to publish my own songbooks. Well, one day Al came into my office and said, "John, how about you joining me and becoming my editor?" He needed help for one thing. Secondly, I think maybe he was a little concerned that I would establish some competition to his Singspiration books![112]

At the time, Peterson believed that God was leading him out of radio work and that Smith's offer was God's way of allowing him to concentrate on songwriting. So he accepted the invitation to join Singspiration and in 1955 moved his family to Montrose. "It was a cultural shock for me, coming from Chicago," Peterson confessed. "Al owned a big home there, a white frame house with green shutters. There was an apartment in the back of the home. So when my family first came, we moved into that apartment until we were able to buy a home of our own." Having once been a summer home for a wealthy family, Smith's property had a stable in the back. "He renovated that stable and that's where we put the Singspiration offices, in a renovated stable in the back," Peterson laughed, "and it was rather nice! Al and I worked well together. Singspiration was associated with the Zondervan Brothers, who were the distributors. And we would go to Zondervan each year and line up the books that we were going to do the following year, and they would advance the money. It was a great time, and very successful."[113]

With Peterson doing the arranging and editing, and Smith handling the business side of the company, the two men were busy and seldom had time to work together musically. "Al's gift was more in being an entrepreneur," Peterson believed. "If he were going to write a song, he would have to sing it and then you would have to write it down for him. Since I was occupied with my own writing at the time, there were probably no more than half a dozen little tunes we worked together on during those years."[114] Yet one of those "little tunes," Peterson allowed,

> became quite well known, "Surely Goodness and Mercy." That was the one! I was at the piano one day when Al came into the studio there at Montrose. And I just started to play it and we started to sing together. Before you know it, we had the chorus. It just came! Then I wrote the words and music for the verses later. But we sang and wrote that chorus together. It was just a beautiful thing.[115]

From Smith's perspective, the story behind "Surely Goodness and Mercy" began when he visited the small town of Rome, Pennsylvania. Once the home of Philip Bliss, the noted nineteenth-century songwriter is buried in the town cemetery under large marble shaft that bears the inscription, *In memory of Philip P. Bliss, author of "Hold the Fort."* After Bliss's tragic death in a train wreck, Dwight L. Moody led a campaign to erect the monument with pennies collected from children's Sunday schools in both England and America. Descendants of Bliss still lived in the area and, when Smith inquired about memories of their famous relative, one day he received a note.

> Dear Mr. Smith—
>
> Here's a little true and quaint story about Uncle Phil which you might enjoy having. Uncle Phil, when he was a barefoot boy about six years of age, went to the little one-room schoolhouse for the first time. As he entered the schoolroom his heart skipped a beat when he saw the teacher. She was very petite, less than five feet tall, and red hair, blue-green eyes and her name was Miss Murphy. To little Bliss, he had never beheld anything quite so beautiful and needless to say he fell in love with his

teacher. She must have been a wonderful teacher, Dr. Smith, for the first thing she did with the class was to take her own Bible and from it teach the class to memorize the 23rd Psalm. As the class progressed in the Psalm and they came to "Surely goodness and mercy shall follow me all the days of my life," little Bliss, who of course couldn't read as yet, thought for sure it said, "Surely good Miss Murphy shall follow me all the days of my life!" What a joyous prospect for his little heart—of course it wasn't long before he found out that it didn't say that at all.[116]

"The recalling of the incident," Smith explained later, "gave us the seed-thought for a song. I remarked to John W. Peterson, who was working for me at the time, 'John, that would make a good title for a song—not 'Surely Good Miss Murphy' but 'Surely Goodness and Mercy.' He agreed and before the day was out, together, we had written a song." The lilting and simple title chorus echoed the Twenty-third Psalm: "Surely goodness and mercy shall follow me ... all the days of my life."[117]

In time, Smith's wife Catherine passed away. Then some investments turned sour and, needing money to pay his debts, in 1963 he was compelled to sell the Singspiration company to Zondervan. Peterson remained on, as the operation moved from Montrose to the Zondervan headquarters in Grand Rapids, Michigan. But for Smith, a new phase of his music ministry began that took him back to his love of songleading and itinerant evangelism. His second wife Nancy, a woman from Montrose whom he married in 1967, traveled with him and observed,

> He was happiest when he was out in churches doing the Lord's work. He never minded if it was a little church or a big church. He never once asked for an honorarium. It was strictly an offering basis. Sometimes he'd get enough money to meet his expenses, sometimes he wouldn't. But the Lord always made up for it. He loved the local church. He loved to minister to the people and help the choir director. Quite often he would have a meeting Friday night, then Saturday evening have a choir banquet and give pointers.[118]

One of Smith's best-loved songs was written during such a trip. In 1965 he was in a service at a small Baptist church as announcements were being given and an offering taken. "It was often my custom in those days," he recalled, "to use this time to write an original song with a title supplied by someone in the audience." A teenage girl suggested "His Banner Over Me Is Love" since the phrase occurred in the second stanza of the hymn, "Faith is the Victory," which the congregation had just sung. Since the church was small, the offering did not take long to collect and Smith had only a few minutes to jot down an impromptu song. Though the congregation responded enthusiastically, he went away feeling it was simply a one-time wonder. Yet the young people in the church continued to sing and share the song with others, and soon Smith was receiving numerous requests for the music. At first, copies of the manuscript were simply run off on a duplicator with Smith's original notation, "B.C. Laurelton." The designation helped him keep track of where the song had been written—Baptist Church Laurelton. Four years later when music plates were made for printing, Smith adopted "B.C. Laurelton" as a pen name. "This has proven both an enjoyment and embarrassment," Smith admitted. Though he enjoyed the popularity of "His Banner Over Me is Love" with children, he was frequently embarrased "when folks ask the address of Mr. Laurelton so that they may write and thank him for the song!"[119]

After the sale of Singspiration, Smith's music publishing continued. In time, he formed Better Music Publications to produce songbooks and hymnals. Recordings were made and radio programs produced. In a popular and widely sold book, *Al Smith's Treasury of Hymn Histories*, he preserved the many stories that he had collected from gospel songwriters of the past. "That was his real desire," Nancy confirmed, "to keep those old songs coming. Because a lot of the songs today just don't say much of anything." The nineteenth-century gospel lyricist Fanny Crosby was a special favorite of Smith, who in 1969 gave Crosby's old hymn lyric, "Be Thou Exalted," what became a popular new setting. "He loved Fanny Crosby," Nancy recalled.

> He sang so many of her songs. Everywhere we went, people would say, "Oh, did you know Fanny Crosby? Did you go to school with Fanny Crosby?" Well, the Lord took Fanny Crosby just a little bit before Al was born, so he did not know her personally. But he enjoyed so much taking her poems and maybe just switching a few words around here and there, and giving it a new tune.[120]

Al and Nancy Smith went on to have four children—Rebecca, Sarah, David, and Jonathan. In 1984 the family moved to Greenville, South Carolina, so that the children could attend school there. The work to which he dedicated his life, that day on the road to Oneonta in 1938, continued. "I don't think I've ever met anyone who was more dedicated to the ministry of the gospel song than Al Smith," concluded John W. Peterson. "Christian music has done a one hundred eighty-degree turn. It broke his heart. And he always felt that he wanted to try to stem the tide. Because he felt, which I think is true, that there's a great body of people in the churches across America that still love the old gospel songs."[121] Nancy Smith saw how that dedication and drive never left her husband:

> When he worked on projects, he was busy from morning until into the night. It didn't matter what time it was. He'd get something in his mind that he was working on and he'd just work at it. And he didn't too much care whether he ate or what he did. He was just consumed by that idea. And I said jokingly that when the Lord came to call my husband home, that he was just going to say, 'Well, Lord, I just have this *one* more project. Will you let me finish this *one* more project?' And he did in fact have a couple of books that he had compiled and they were waiting to go and be printed when the Lord took him home.[122]

That homegoing took place August 9, 2001. But not before one final trip that, for Nancy Smith, summed up the life and ministry of her husband.

> One of the favorite stories Al loved to tell was about Vance Havner, the preacher, meeting the famous evangelist Gypsy Smith. And Dr. Havner asked, "I've heard you so many times and now you're over eighty, and yet you preached with such force and enthusiasm. What's your secret?" And Gypsy Smith said, "I have never lost the wonder of it all." And Al wrote a song about that. And you know, that's true about the story of his own life. He just never lost the wonder of it all. He just felt like he just had to keep going. In fact, the last meeting we were in, he was so sick, dying really. But he was just determined to go. And as I was packing I just kept saying, "Lord, I just don't see how we can do it!" Well, he got there and he sang Monday night, Tuesday night, Wednesday night, Thursday night, and Friday night. And you know, the Lord just did that. Because that was the first week of June. Two weeks later we started full-time care, and seven weeks later he was with the Lord.[123]

Through more than six decades of music ministry, Nancy concluded, Al Smith "never lost that passion. He never lost the passion of getting good music out, so that people might come to know Christ as their Savior. He never lost the wonder of it all."[124] Smith expressed that sentiment himself in a 1973 song whose title chorus concludes, "I have never lost the wonder of it all!"

Blackwood Brothers and The Statesmen

At the start of the forties professional gospel quartets lived—as they had since the first Vaughn quartet hit the road in 1910—on the salaries they were paid to represent the major music publishers and sell their songbooks. By the end of the decade quartets could make a living as independent performers, the basic system of the evangelical popular music industry today. The difference? Like the youth rallies of the era, gospel music too had moved from church meeting halls and been propelled by radio into the concert auditoriums of America.[125]

That journey was typified by the decade's premier quartet, the Blackwood Brothers and its leader, James Blackwood. Born August 4, 1919, on a cotton farm in the Mississippi Delta, as a boy Blackwood aspired to sing gospel music after listening to the twice-daily Vaughn Quartet show on WSM from Nashville. His sharecropper parents couldn't afford a radio, so the young Blackwood walked a mile to a neighbor's farm for both the morning and evening broadcasts. "I couldn't wait to get old enough to sing," he said.[126] Blackwood got his wish in 1929 when he joined his eighteen-year-old brother Doyle in attending a nearby singing school. At the end of the ten nights of the school, the instructor recognized the brothers' talent and asked the two boys to join him and another man in a new quartet. The foursome called themselves the Choctaw County Jubilee Singers. By 1934, James and Doyle were joined by brother Roy and his son R.W. to form the first Blackwood Brothers quartet. A typical engagement might be a schoolhouse singing contest, which were popular then in the Depression-era South. If they won first prize, the four might take home some flour, lard, or cornmeal to divide among the family.

The Blackwoods' career might have continued that way had they not seized on a new opportunity—radio. While stations had been broadcasting in the big cities for years, only later did radio come to the rural heartlands of America. Kosciusko, Mississippi, finally got its first radio station in 1934. WHEF was small, only two hundred fifty watts, and its owner was the only employee. With no access to network programming or electrical transcription discs (which had only just been introduced) of recorded music, the owner-manager-announcer needed live talent—not an easy job in Kosciusko. The Blackwoods walked into WHEF one Sunday, offered to sing right then and there, and the owner gave them fifteen minutes. After two songs, the phone started to ring with requests. At the end of fifteen minutes the owner excitedly motioned for the brothers to keep going. Another hour later, the station had logged dozens of local calls and sixty long-distance requests. That was when the Blackwood Brothers decided to try and sing for a living.

An agreement was signed to represent the Vaughn Music Publishing Company and a commission would be paid on songbook sales. But the rest of the Brothers' living expenses were their own affair. At the time, professional quartets did not take radio jobs so much for the modest salary, but to build a following and announce where they would be singing. So in 1937 the Blackwoods moved to Jackson, the state capitol of Mississippi, in hopes of landing a show on five-thousand-watt WJDX. The best they could get was permission to sing one song a day on a country music show. But when the Blackwoods started getting more mail than the show's headliner, the quartet was soon given its own broadcast.

Still, the Blackwoods only scraped by financially. When their old Ford was repossessed, the Brothers could only continue singing when an engineer at WJDX offered to sign a note for them at the bank. Then in 1939 came the break that novice gospel groups still hope for today—a chance to appear on stage with the big-time professionals. It happened at the annual Mississippi State Singing Convention where the headliner that year was the Frank Stamps All-Star Quartet. On hearing the Blackwoods, Frank that night phoned his brother V.O. Stamps at the Stamps-Baxter Music headquarters in Dallas. The next day, V.O. Stamps called the brothers and offered them a contract to represent his company. He would furnish a car and give them a salary of $18.50 per man, per week. If their weekly songbook sales and concert proceeds exceeded that amount, they would send the overage to Dallas. The Blackwood Brothers accepted on the spot. Soon afterward the quartet performed at the Louisiana State Singing Convention. While in town, the group auditioned for its own show on KWKH in Shreveport. Impressed, the ten-thousand-watt station offered them a contract to do two live broadcasts each weekday. Sixteen months later, however, the Blackwoods were on the move again—this time to KMA in Shenandoah, Iowa. They four men had never been out of the South before and thought that Iowa must be a kind of exile. The Frank Stamps All-Star Quartet had pioneered the area and was generating excellent response. But V.O. Stamps was near death and Frank was needed back at Dallas. He recommended that the Blackwood Brothers take over the twice-daily KMA show and the move was made in August 1940. Soon the wisdom of the assignment was clear. KMA was strategically located and could be heard in seven major cities. Mail arrived from twenty-seven states and Canada. The Blackwoods' parents could even listen from their Mississippi cotton farm.

The quartet broke up during World War II when R.W. Blackwood was drafted and James, Doyle, and Roy moved to California for jobs in the aircraft industry. But when the conflict was over, the four men regrouped and picked up on KMA right where they left off. By the end of the 1940s the Blackwood Brothers were in constant demand on radio, records, and the church concert circuit. If the Blackwood Brothers could at last make a living with their music, however, the group was still dependent on the music company that sponsored them. The system used with the Vaughn and Stamps quartets, which had been in place for nearly forty years, was still the norm. Salaries were set and songbooks had to be sold. Because overnight lodging was an added expense and the roads of the day were poor, quartets were often limited to personal appearances within a day's drive.

That system, however, started to change on November 5, 1948. Wally Fowler had sung lead in the legendary John Daniels Quartet which—like the Blackwoods—had first worked for the Vaughn company and then been coaxed to join the Stamps-Baxter empire. During those days when his quartet was in Texas, Fowler struck up a friendship with V.O. Stamps, who had taken a liking the young lead singer. Stamps was then a sick man and Fowler would often drive for him. By the late thirties, the final night of the annual Stamps-Baxter School of Music each June was being broadcast locally over powerful KRLD and nationwide over the CBS network. For the night, Stamps rented the Dallas Sportatorium and put on a show he called the "All-Night Broadcast." KRLD carried the entire eight-hour extravaganza while CBS aired the first half-hour. Always the entrepreneur and promoter, Stamps dreamed of staging All-Night Broadcasts across the country and even around the world. He had told this to no one else, but confided it to the young Fowler. Stamps's wishful thinking planted a seed, but soon the war intervened. Fowler spent much of the war years in Nashville, singing with the John Daniels Quartet on the *Grand Ole Opry* show over WSM. Then he left to start his own broadcast on Knoxville's WNOX. Each Saturday morning his new quartet gave benefit concerts for fifteen hundred youngsters whose parents worked on the atomic bomb project at nearby Oak Ridge Laboratories. In the children's honor Fowler named his group the Oak Ridge Quartet. Two months later, after the atomic bomb was dropped, the name was a keeper.

The next year, 1946, the group moved to Nashville to be on a WSM show headlined by Red Foley—who each week introduced the quartet as the "Oak Ridge Boys." Yet the idea for an "All-Night Broadcast" remained in Fowler's mind, waiting for the right time to sprout. That moment came at the Alabama State Singing Convention of 1948. Though many churches held all-day singings, and statewide singing conventions were annual events throughout the South, singers were paid on an offering basis. Yet audiences often treated the events as discount entertainment and the collection was divided among all the singing groups. To make their expenses, quartets often had to depend on sales of their songbooks and 78 rpm records. That fall of 1948, Wally Fowler and the Oak Ridge Boys made the long drive from Nashville to Birmingham, Alabama. Six thousand people attended the annual state convention, but the collection was only three hundred dollars. "Folks, we sure are short," the organizer apologized to the singers. "I don't know why we didn't get more money out of this. But I'll pay for your gas, anyway." Fowler spoke up and forcefully told the man, "Get back out there and tell those people that they don't mind paying so much to go to ball games or for theater tickets. Ask them what's wrong with them here today!"[127] The organizer agreed to take another offering and, after exhorting the audience, returned with three thousand dollars.

On his return to Nashville, Fowler was determined give his mentor's old dream of an All-Night Broadcast a try. First he did as Stamps had done with his Dallas events—sign up the best radio station in town. Since Fowler's Oak Ridge Boys were regulars on WSM, he convinced the program director to carry the first hour of the all-night event. Next he rented the Ryman Auditorium, then the site of the Grand Ole Opry (still broadcast over WSM today). Next, his Oak Ridge Boys hit the streets, visiting supermarkets and businesses and neighborhoods to sell one-dollar reserved-seat tickets to what was billed as an "All-Night Singing." By the day of the performance—Friday, November 5, 1948—the quartet sold 1,836 of the Ryman Auditorium's 3,214 seats. Despite heavy rains, that night every seat was sold while an additional three hundred chairs were set up on stage and more than a thousand persons were turned away at the door. And no wonder, for the talent on the platform that evening was a "who's who" of gospel music—the Frank Stamps Quartet, the Stamps

All-Star Quartet, the Vaughn Radio Quartet, the Speer Family, the Oak Ridge Boys, the Sunshine Boys, and more.

The program began at eight and the WSM broadcast cut in at eleven. The WSM announcer who emceed the All-Night Singing then offered to read a few telegrams from the stage if listeners would call in. Every telephone line to the station and to the Ryman Auditorium was quickly jammed. "We don't have people to answer the phones, this program has made such an impact," the announcer exclaimed. "We're hearing from all over the United States and Canada."[128] Indeed, the signal of WSM could be heard all across North America, east of the Rockies. By 11:45, fifteen minutes before WSM was due to cut away from the auditorium, more than four hundred telegrams had arrived. If a hundred more were received by midnight, the station offered to extend the broadcast an additional hour. By twelve, exactly 213 more messages had come through. Then, after the radio coverage ended at 1 a.m., the groups kept on singing until three in the morning when a halt was reluctantly called to the event.

When Fowler planned his next All-Night Singing at the Ryman Auditorium for New Year's Eve, the WSM manager contacted the NBC network and arranged to carry an hour of the event, coast-to-coast. More than six thousand letters and telegrams were received that night. Soon the All-Night Singing concept swept across the South—then as far as St. Louis and Detroit, and expanded into the Southwest. The old system of company-sponsored quartets started to wane. Big-time professional quartets could make a living on their own, performing in city auditoriums before crowds of thousands, rather than depending on songbook sales at local churches and conventions. In the new system created by the All-Night Singings of Wally Fowler (and his many imitators) two quartets reigned supreme. One was the Blackwood Brothers. The other was a new quartet out of Atlanta. They were called The Statesmen and had been created especially with the new realities in mind.

Hovie Lister wanted the "perfect" quartet—not just four men who got together and sang but, in essence, a quartet that was professionally staffed. Each man would be the best in the business, classy, a gentleman above reproach. They would be dedicated to the highest standards. Even the way they walked on and off stage would be rehearsed. Lister had been around quartets for most of his young life. At twelve he played the piano for his father's group, the Lister Brothers Quartet, in their hometown of Greenville, South Carolina. In 1941 when he was fourteen and the famed evangelist Mordecai Ham came to the city for a campaign, Hovie was asked to be the accompanist for Ham's songleader—the equally famous gospel songwriter, C. Austin Miles. Two years later Hovie attended the annual Stamps-Baxter School of Music in Dallas. Word soon spread of Lister's ability. Then in 1945 another

Greenville native, Connor Hall, offered Hovie his first paying job as pianist for the Homeland Harmony Quartet out of Atlanta. A year later when he was only nineteen years old, Lister joined the Rangers Quartet, one of the biggest gospel groups of the day. Soon afterward the quartet moved from Atlanta to Charlotte for a daily show on WBT. But Atlanta was then the capital of the quartet-singing world, the place where the action was. So nine months after joining the Rangers, Lister was back in Atlanta to play for the Lefevre Trio which sang on WGST. By 1947 Lister was also playing gospel records as a deejay for WEAS and making vague plans about starting a quartet of his own, a group that would be new and different.

When Lister shared his dream with Barry Howell, his friend knew exactly what to do. His father, Major Howell, was chief stockholder of *The Atlanta Constitution* newspaper—and as Barry explained, was "fixing to put in a new five-thousand-watt radio station soon as they get the building finished." Since nearly every radio station in the South had its own quartet, the new WCON would need one too. Barry Howell hurried his friend over to the *Constitution* and, leaving a half dozen secretaries in their wake, stepped into his father's private office and pulled Hovie along behind him. Upon hearing Lister's plans for a new quartet, Major Howell was immediately interested and replied, "When do you want to start?" Could he have the group put together by the time WCON was ready to sign on the air? Hovie regretfully admitted it was not likely he could have a quartet assembled so soon. But that was all right with Major Howell. "You can just play records until you do get it organized."[129] With his backing assured, Lister approached the best singers in gospel music, men he idolized, to join his quartet—and was turned down by them all. Understandably, the men were not attracted to the idea of leaving their established groups and throwing in with a brash twenty-year-old.

What to do now? Across the street from the *Constitution*, at Rich's department store, the gospel songwriter Mosie Lister (no relation to Hovie) worked as a piano tuner. He could also sing and accepted Hovie's invitation to come on as the lead. Then he telephoned an old quartet friend from Chattanooga, Bobby Strickland, who was glad for the chance to be in Atlanta and agreed to sing tenor. Bobby in turn knew a baritone and bass, Bervin Kendrick and Gordon Hill, and also brought them along. Now Hovie Lister had a quartet and even a salary from the *Constitution* of fifty dollars per man, per week. But he didn't have a name. Always interested in politics and wanting a name that suggested greatness, he pondered "The Congressmen" and "The Senators." But people might associate those names with politics and elections. How about "The Statesmen"? They were above parties, revered for their proven character. Hovie even approached the governor of the state of Georgia, who published a newspaper called *The Statesman*, for permission to use the name. Herman Talmadge not only gave his okay, he was excited about the possibilities for publicity and became a big fan.

When Hovie Lister and The Statesmen debuted on WCON in October 1948 they were an immediate favorite with listeners. Each weekday they broadcast live at 6 a.m. and noon. On top of that, their show was advertised almost daily in the *Constitution*. But Lister was not satisfied. The four men in his quartet were talented, yet the necessary ingredients for the "perfect" quartet still eluded him. He wanted a foursome that was so professional they could hear a song and then sing it in any kind of style. One of the groups he most admired, the Melody Masters Quartet, could do everything from pop to western and straight gospel to modern harmony. After a few months on the air, Mosie Lister went back to songwriting and piano tuning, and Gordon Hill hit the road for a different kind of job as a truck driver. Later that year, 1949, Bobby Strickland decided to organize a quartet of his own in Birmingham, Alabama. Much to Hovie's delight, *three* of the Melody Masters—Jake Hess at lead, James Wetherington at bass, and Cat Freeman at tenor—ultimately agreed to join The Statesmen.

Lister believed that rehearsals were as important as concerts and attendance was mandatory. As true professionals the men responded, for everyone knew their success and livelihood depended on it. And successful they were. Not dependent on sponsorship by any music company, The Statesmen incorporated as a business with each of the five men owning a share. Office space was acquired in a downtown Atlanta hotel and equipped with a complete music room for rehearsals. A corporate advertising deal was signed with Nabisco, which would sponsor the quartet's radio show and a *television* show. Further, The Statesmen purchased other music companies and developed a publishing business of their own. The venture generated income and enabled the Statesmen to nurture new songwriters to help them keep the hits coming. Hired to run the publishing operation was a young man from Asheville, North Carolina. In later years Eldridge Fox launched his own publishing company and quartet, The Kingsmen. Personnel changes are frequent in gospel music to this day. But by 1953, Hovie Lister had assembled the lineup for which The Statesmen are most renowned: Jake Hess at lead and James "Big Chief" Wetherington (a Lumbee Indian) at bass, with Doy Ott (also a Native American) singing baritone and Denver Crumpler at tenor. Lister believed he had put together the one and only perfect quartet, and more than half a century later many southern gospel music fans still agree.

The Statesmen and Blackwood Brothers were, by the early fifties, easily the biggest draws at the All-Night Singings promoted by Wally Fowler and others in cities across the country. The two groups therefore appeared together often and in 1952 had an idea. Why not do joint bookings? They tried it at the Birmingham Central High School in 1952 and drew a standing room-only crowd. Concert promoters saw that The Statesmen and Blackwood Brothers guaranteed a successful event. So while other quartets commonly received fees ranging from $225 to $275 per night, The Statesmen and Blackwoods split fees of between one thousand and fifteen hundred dollars. Both quartets were so professional and their repertoires so large, they could sing in the best cities—such as Atlanta, Birmingham, and Nashville—once a month. Even Northern cities such as Chicago, Indianapolis, and Detroit hosted "the team" four times a year. In addition, The Statesmen and the Blackwoods recorded for RCA Victor, one of the nation's major labels. So dominant were The Statesmen and Blackwood Brothers that all other quartets had to schedule around their concerts. New groups breaking into the business, if they wanted promoters to book them, often had to get a good word first from Hovie Lister or James Blackwood. By the same token, many new quartets benefited because such a reference was all they needed to start receiving bookings.

By this time the Blackwoods had moved their home base from Iowa back to the South, to sing on WMPS in Memphis. Like The Statesmen, they formed their own Gospel Quartet Music publishing company and signed a deal with Dixie Lily Flour to sponsor a television program, *At Home with the Blackwood Brothers*. Roy and Doyle Blackwood came off the road to manage the group's growing business enterprises, so that by 1952 the quartet's lineup featured James and R.W. Blackwood at lead and baritone, Bill Lyles at bass and Bill Shaw at tenor. When Shaw joined the quartet in 1952 he brought along an idea. The Blackwoods had conquered the gospel music world and only one obstacle held them back. No one had figured out a way to conquer distance. Roads were often poor and the interstate highway system had not been built. Then Shaw suggested, Why not fly? James Blackwood embraced the idea and bought two airplanes, an eight-seat Cessna and a smaller plane as a backup. Now they group could cover a far wider territory and perhaps open up the West Coast for the first time.

James hired a pilot until R.W. got his own license and Bill Lyles learned to be co-pilot. The Blackwood Brothers soon were convinced that flying was faster than driving—and safer. All of gospel music had mourned when the Rangers Quartet lost one of its members in a 1951 car accident. Then in 1953 Bobby Strickland, the one-time Statesman, perished in a tragic automobile crash. The year 1954 promised to be the best ever for the Blackwood Brothers. That summer the group was vaulted into nationwide fame when they appeared June 11 on the popular *Arthur Godfrey's Talent Scouts* television program from New York. The quartet won the talent competition by singing, "Have You Talked to the Man Upstairs?" As first prize, they were invited to perform all that week on Godfrey's daily network radio broadcast. While they were in New York, RCA Victor had the Blackwoods record their prize-winning song, which became a Top Ten hit that summer.

The Blackwood Quartet was figuratively and literally flying high when, on the morning of June 30, the group flew into Clanton, Alabama. They were to appear with The Statesmen at the Chilton County Peach Festival. The airstrip runway was short but R.W. got the Cessna down in good shape. The quartet performed at a civic club luncheon, then returned in the afternoon to set up for their evening concert at the Old Airport Hangar. Before it got dark, however, R.W. wanted to take the plane out and get a better feel for the runway. The airstrip not only was short but unlighted, so after the concert they would be taking off in the dark. R.W. and Bill Lyles climbed into the Cessna, taking along the eighteen-year-old son of a local banker for the ride. The plane lifted off and then circled the runway. To land again, R.W. Blackwood had to clear a small hill and then drop the Cessna onto the sod field. He couldn't quite make it on the first pass and so circled around again for a second try. Again the plane had trouble dropping onto the short runway. Without letting the wheels touch the ground, R.W. gunned the twin engines to keep going for a third approach. But then the plane suddenly dropped onto the turf and subsequently bounced high into the air. R.W. Blackwood pushed the forward throttle wide open and retracted the landing gear in an attempt to regain control. In the confusion, however, he failed to retrim the tabs. The plane shot nose-up into the air, stalled, then plunged onto the runway in an explosion of flame. James ran out to rescue his beloved nephew, but it was too late. All three occupants had been instantly killed. To keep James Blackwood out of danger he had to be bodily restrained by Jake Hess of The Statesman.

R.W. Blackwood was thirty-two years old and Bill Lyles thirty-three. Their funeral was held in Memphis; members of twenty-seven professional quartets formed a choir. James thought of calling it quits but decided to continue with Cecil Blackwood taking the baritone spot and then hiring J.D. Sumner of the Sunshine Boys to sing bass. But the Blackwoods were forever through with flying. James sold the backup plane and bought a limousine. A year later, the Blackwoods found an even better way to conquer distance, one that remains the standard in gospel music today. Five men traveling together in a limousine soon seem cramped. Sound equipment, along with records and other sale items, had to be loaded and unloaded into a trailer. More time was lost by having to find lodging on the road each night. Then J.D. Sumner, the group's new bass singer, had a brainstorm. Why not travel by bus, not a commercial bus but their own customized coach? When James Blackwood gave the go-ahead, Sumner sold the quartet's brand-new Cadillac limo and bought a used 1937 Aerocoach from Trailways. Then with a hammer and saw, and with sheets of three-quarter-inch plywood, he installed four bunks in the back of the bus. The sleeping area was partitioned off, and reclining chairs for each singer were placed in a sort of "living room" in the front half of the bus. Now the Blackwood Brothers could sleep comfortably on the road and travel greater distances to concerts, with plenty of room to haul their equipment and records. Sumner even went into the bus business, fixing up and selling vehicles to other quartets. Soon everyone in gospel music was traveling by bus, as they are to this day.

It was also Sumner who founded the National Quartet Convention in 1956, which the Blackwoods underwrote financially to get the event started, and that continues today. Then in 1959, Sumner teamed up with Jake Hess of The Statesmen to form the Skylight Recording Company, the first label dedicated exclusively to southern gospel music. Both men owned music publishing companies and Skylight provided a means to record the songs they held. Fittingly, the Blackwood Brothers' first Skylight album was entitled "Give the World a Smile" after the first hit record of the original Stamps quartet in 1927.

The Blackwood Brothers and the Statesman continued to dominate gospel music through the 1960s. The two groups even co-produced a one-hour television program, *Singing Time in Dixie* (later *The Glory Road*) that was syndicated on as many as a hundred stations and hosted by James Blackwood and Hovie Lister. The two men and their quartets were active and on the road full-time into the 1980s, though the personnel around them changed many times over the years. Both Blackwood and Lister died in 2001. Because the two quartets' careers were so long and their repertoires so large, neither is associated with a particular song. But in their heyday, both groups employerd bass singers who were also accomplished gospel songwriters. Both J.D. Sumner of the Blackwoods and Big Chief Wetherington of The Statesmen wrote more than five hundred gospel songs during their tenures with the quartets. The Big Chief sang with The Statesmen until the day he died—the morning after performing with the group at the National Quartet Convention in October 1973. Among the hundreds of songs he wrote, perhaps the best known and most recorded is one of the simplest, "Tenderly." The lyrics describe God as gentle, quiet, even motherly, as "Tenderly He watches over me, tenderly."

Sumner's first composition was (unfortunately) entitled "Working in the Sawmill for Jesus," but happily his output got better from there. If James Blackwood wanted a new song about the Jordan River, Sumner would sit in his easy chair on the bus and write four or five that same afternoon. "The Old Country Church" is one of Sumner's best-known songs today, but others include "Walking and Talking with My Lord," "I Want to Tell the World About His Love," "He'll Put a Little Heaven in Your Soul," "I Believe in the Old Time Way," "If You Only Know the Lord," and one of the most recorded in its time, "The Greatest of These Is Love."

In 1964, Sumner became associated with the Stamps Quartet when Frank Stamps, shortly before his death, sold his Stamps Quartet Music Publishing company (different from his brother's Stamps-Baxter empire) and quartet to the Blackwood Brothers. A year later Sumner took over the Stamps Quartet, ultimately bought it from James Blackwood, and (with a hiatus in 1982–87 to join Hove Lister and James Blackwood in a group called The Masters V) sang with the Stamps until his death in November 1998. A trouper to the last, he passed away while performing on the road in Myrtle Beach, South Carolina. In the fifties while with the Blackwoods, he wrote about his anticipation of a heavenly home in a frequently recorded song. When "my life is finished" and "at last by the river I stand," Sumner wrote, "I'll not fear death's crossing" because, as the title phrase affirms, "My God won't ever let me down."

Four

The Fifties
Words and Music

IN 1954 RADIO WAS SURPASSED by television in total advertising revenue for the first time.[1] Although the national networks offered a record amount of radio programming for the 1953–54 season, the end of the golden age was at hand. By the middle of the decade, network radio programming began to drop sharply. Many of the popular stars and shows were first "simulcast" on TV and radio, and then dropped from radio altogether. By the end of the decade, network radio was over. Last to go were the daytime radio soap operas which were finally canceled in the 1960–61 season. "Goodbye, and may God bless you," declared Ma Perkins as she signed off the air for her 7,065th and final broadcast, after thirty consecutive years on network radio. By then, however, the major radio networks offered little more than news at the top of the hour plus breaking bulletins, and special events such as sports or political conventions that were also aired on television. As late as 1952, half of all AM radio stations were still affiliates of one or more national networks. In 1960, though the FCC had licensed about a thousand new stations, only a third of all AMs maintained any network affiliation. Hardest hit was the Mutual network, which changed ownership six times between 1956 and 1959, and lost 130 affiliates. With little programming or advertising support to gain from the networks, local radio stations were on their own.

Yet the idea that radio in the fifties began to lose money, while television made money, is not true. Radio may have made less money and its share of national advertising revenues decreased, but the medium found ways to adapt and remain profitable. Most stations in the fifties still employed a "middle of the road" format that, as in the heyday of the networks, offered a little of something for everyone. But by the late fifties a large number of stations had switched to "formula" radio by specializing in a certain kind of music targeted to a particular audience. That chiefly meant rock n' roll aimed at the millions of postwar Baby Boom teenagers who were coming of age. However, country-

and-western formatted stations also boomed in the late fifties. By the end of the decade, songs were ranked on charts by the amount of airplay they received. Thus radio became the arbiter of what was considered a "hit." The "Top 40" format was so popular and "disc jockeys" held so much power, that a major scandal erupted in 1959. The discovery that some deejays accepted bribes to play certain songs, a practice called "payola," led to a government investigation and FCC crackdown.

Nevertheless, radio in its new localized and musically specialized incarnation continued to grow. Where stations once advertised their network affiliations, now their call letters became their primary "brand" name. Station identification, mandated by the FCC and traditionally just a formality, now evolved into an artful blend of catchy slogans and musical jingles. Also by 1960, other encouraging trends emerged that boded well for the future of radio. Transistors replaced tubes so that radios could be truly lightweight, portable, and reasonably affordable. Then, too, nearly seventy percent of automobiles had radios. Unlike television, radio could take advantage of the America's increasing suburbanization and car culture. By contrast, FM radio lagged through most of the fifties. Late in the decade, however, FM stereo was developed and an FCC standard adopted in 1961. Even more important, broadcasters were finding that the AM band had become saturated. The dial was full and, in the nation's major cities, new stations simply could not be squeezed in. FM was the only way to get a new station in a major market. In 1957, FM license applications at last outpaced the number of FM stations going off the air. In 1960, some 750 commercial FMs were on the air (compared to 3,500 AM stations). The chicken-and-egg dilemma was thus solved as enough FM stations were on the air to create a market for the manufacture of FM sets. In 1959, FM receiver sales topped one million, and then two million in 1960. Transistor technology boosted the attractiveness of FM sets, which had previously experienced "frequency drift" as they warmed up. Prices for combined AM-FM radio sets came down to about thirty dollars, only ten or fifteen dollars more than AM-only radios.

The fifties were also a time of transition for evangelical radio and evangelical popular music. As network radio faded, so did the national influence of such venerable network religious programs as the *Old Fashioned Revival Hour* and *Young People's Church of the Air*. Yet locally owned religious radio stations were still too few to be a factor. In 1950 only about ten religious stations were licensed in the entire United States, though the numbers grew slowly throughout the decade. Not until the 1960s did the notion of a chain or network of religious stations start to emerge. And not until the 1970s did enough syndicated evangelical programming exist to permit significant numbers of stations to even adopt a full-time religious format.

For songwriters the new situation presented a challenge. With the demise of network radio they no longer had the national showcases of Charles Fuller, Percy Crawford, and others to introduce their songs. They no longer had legions of evangelical radio listeners ready to buy *Old Fashioned Revival Hour* and *Young People's Church of the Air* songbooks. They no longer had huge crowds, all clamoring to sing the new songs, at the giant rallies which the network radio ministries had once mobilized. And television? Charles Fuller, Percy Crawford, and Jack Wyrtzen all tried weekly broadcasts. But production costs were too high, especially in relation to the limited number of TV stations and viewers in much of the fifties. By the time that television expanded nationwide at the end of the decade, the cost to purchase airtime on a network was out of reach. Not until the 1970s did religious television reach full flower, when enough independent stations were on the air to permit syndication of evangelical programs on a widespread national basis. So gospel songwriters of the fifties were on their own. Yet it could be a blessing as well as a challenge. If they no longer had the network religious radio programs to popularize and publish their songs, neither were they dependent on the make-or-break power of a handful of large radio ministries. With the rise of music-formatted radio stations, a writer who could get songs played on the air might make a living as an independent artist.

But how could a songwriter convince mainstream radio stations to play popular evangelical songs? Two avenues were open which explain much of the evangelical popular music that was written during the fifties. First, in that decade when most Americans at least nominally identified with Christianity, a song that expressed faith in a simple and inoffensive manner, with a catchy melody and singable lyrics, could still be popular. For example, after cowboy actor and songwriter Stuart Hamblen was converted at a Billy Graham crusade in 1949, his first gospel song hit the charts by following that formula. For the same reason Stuart K. Hine's hymn, "How Great Thou Art," was widely popular when published in the mid–1950s and remains popular today. In the fifties as now, the tune and lyrics are infectious.

A second way of success in the fifties was to have a song performed and recorded by a popular gospel music group. In this milieu, groups such as the Old Fashioned Revival Hour Quartet, which were associated with network radio preachers, did not fit the bill. They may have attracted a following on network radio, but as recording artists these radio quartets had only limited appeal. As the major record labels saw it, such groups had not only lost their network radio platforms. Neither were they on tour giving public concerts to expose their music. Further, mainstream radio would not play their records since the groups' repertoires of slow-paced sacred hymns and revival anthems had limited appeal and did not fit the stations' music formats. Gospel music, however, was a different matter. In the fifties the term "gospel music" denoted what today is regarded as "southern gospel" (though today's southern gospel reflects a far greater pop influence than its fifties predecessors). Here were groups such as the Blackwood Brothers and Statesmen quartets that toured the country more than two hundred nights a year, filled large auditoriums for their concerts, had local radio shows in major cities, and whose gospel records were played on the country-and-western radio stations of the day. For example, Mosie Lister was a charter member of The Statesmen quartet in 1948 but his heart was in songwriting. In time he left The Statesmen but continued to write and arrange songs for the quartet. As the group gained in popularity Lister was able to quit his day job as a piano tuner and make his living as a songwriter. By the mid-1950s his songs were recorded not only by The Statesmen but other gospel groups that were receiving radio airplay.

As it turned out, the fifties were a last window of opportunity for evangelical popular music in the golden age of radio to receive mainstream airplay. By the mid to late 1960s rock music came to completely dominate radio, as it did popular culture. Not until the 1980s was it possible to speak of airplay on "Christian radio" stations as a significant factor in popularizing new evangelical songs. Yet that twilight decade of radio's golden age produced evangelical popular music from the pens of mature and gifted songwriters who had the freedom and independence to create a memorable genre of words and music.

John W. Peterson

In 1933 anyone with a radio listened to *Major Bowes and His Original Amateur Hour*. So when Marie Peterson heard that the show's talent scouts were coming to Salina, Kansas, she urged her twelve-year-old brother John to audition.[2] But the boy was reluctant. Born November 1, 1921, and fatherless since the age of four, John was small in stature and almost painfully thin. He lacked the confidence of his four older brothers. Yet he had a clear and beautiful voice, lately honed by his sister's faithful coaching and encouragement. With his sister beside him at the piano, he found great satisfaction in singing for others and thereby gained a measure of compensation for the insecurities he felt in all other respects. But when John left his home in Lindsborg and arrived at the radio studios of KFBI in Salina, he froze. A large crowd of would-be singers, musicians, and vaudevillians had gathered for their own chance at fame and fortune. He had only agreed to come with much coaxing and prodding from his sister, and now he almost turned and went home. As it was, he hung back until everyone else had auditioned and was the last to try out. Yet to his great surprise, he won the contest and received a contract to appear on national radio. Even more, the manager of KFBI offered John his own local fifteen-minute show as "The Singing Farm Boy." The manager even lined up the local Electrolux Vacuum dealer to sponsor the broadcast and pay him a small salary.

"The Singing Farm Boy" aired for only a season. But that year Peterson was eventful in his life when, at the age of twelve, he converted to Christ at an evening service of the Salina Bible Hall. Earlier, his adult brothers Bill, Bob, and Ken had also come to Christ. During his teenage years John watched while his brothers traveled to churches across the Great Plains as the Norse Gospel Trio while also broadcasting their own Sunday morning program on KFBI. Later the trio moved to Tulsa, Oklahoma, where they broadcast over KVOO, a powerful clear-channel station heard in more than half a dozen states. One summer, Peterson went to stay with his brothers in Tulsa and traveled to many of their church meetings. At one meeting in the small Oklahoma panhandle town of Goltry, the tiny church was so packed that the Peterson brothers had to climb in through a back window behind the platform. Later at the parsonage, Peterson was impressed by the pastor's dedication to God, despite his obvious poverty, and his great interest in radio. The pastor's name was Theodore Epp and, a few years later in 1939, God led him to Lincoln, Nebraska, where Epp launched the nationwide *Back to the Bible* broadcast. During those Tulsa days the Peterson brothers became friends with a twenty-year-old radio announcer who often accompanied the trio to church meetings. In time the brothers converted the young man to Christ and later helped him get a job back at KFBI in Salina. Their friend did well, eventually moving to Chicago and becoming a network broadcaster. His name was Paul Harvey (which is, of course, "the rest of the story").

Because of his radio appearances on the *Original Amateur Hour* and as "The Singing Farm Boy," Peterson's brothers gave him increasing opportunities to join them in leading songs for their meetings. The Norse Gospel Trio maintained a full-time schedule and the young Peterson, still in high school, was much in demand. "But in the process," he later recalled, "I put such a terrific strain on my faltering voice, through overuse and inexperience, that I damaged it beyond repair. When I fully realized what had happened, that my voice would never again be beautiful, I suffered such an emotional shock that it was months before I recovered. Singing, I had had the power to thrill people, and suddenly it was all gone." During those months Peterson arrived at two turning points in his young life. First, upon reading the biography of missionaries John and Betty Stam—who had recently been martyred by Chinese Communists after refusing to renounce their faith—Peterson pledged his life to serve God in whatever direction He might lead. Second, he turned his attention to something that before had been just a hobby, the writing of gospel songs. "With my voice damaged," he remembers, "I turned more and more to writing and that talent was allowed to emerge and develop. What at first seemed a tragedy was used for good."[3]

Not long after his high school graduation in 1939, Peterson moved to Wichita, Kansas, when his brothers decided to leave full-time singing and start a church in that city. Later, after Bob Peterson moved his own family to Colorado, John took his place in gospel trio. Along with establishing the Independent Bible Church, the threesome also broadcast a weekly program from a local Wichita radio station. And after many rejections—from the likes of Percy Crawford, Wendell Loveless, and Homer Rodeheaver—Peterson sold his first song, "Yet There Is Room," in 1940 for eight dollars to R. E. Winsett, a Tennessee-based music publisher (who in 1942 wrote the classic gospel song, "Jesus Is Coming Soon"). Even if the printed songbook mistakenly credited the song to "John Patterson," it was a start.

Like most men of his generation, Peterson was drafted into the armed services and in 1942 assigned to the new United States Army Air Force. During flight training he evangelized other cadets with a portable radio and making "a point of listening to Dr. Fuller and the *Old Fashioned Revival Hour,* the *Young People's Church of the Air,* and similar broadcasts, turning up the volume in the hope that others in the barracks would become intrigued."[4] After two years, first in training and then as a flight instructor—and after marrying his hometown sweetheart Marie during a 1944 furlough—he was posted as a pilot to fly the famed "China Hump." The long and dangerous route began at the Allied air base in Burma and traversed the Himalaya Mountains—the "Hump"—to resupply American and Nationalist Chinese forces fighting the Japanese in China. By the end of the war more than nine hunred planes were lost over the Hump—including one tragic incident that deeply impacted Peterson's life.

The jungle base camp in Burma seemed wild and exotic compared to the wheatfields of his native Kansas. Peterson enjoyed the surroundings as well as the company of his Air Force buddies. One evening he stopped at a neighboring tent to talk with a friend, a handsome and outgoing officer whom everybody liked. The two men were soon laughing and chatting, when the friend slyly reached under his cot to pull out a piece of paper. "Hey, John, take a look at this," he said. It was a dirty picture.[5]

"You don't need this," Peterson replied, and then explained how conversion to Christ could fill any human void.

"John, I believe everything you tell me," the friend answered. "I don't have any question about it. I really want to become a Christian." Yet as the two buddies talked long into the night, the man could not make a decision and at last ended the conversation by declaring he "just wasn't ready." The very next day his plane headed over the Hump and was never seen again. Over the years that tragic incident continued to haunt Peterson until at last, in the song "God's Final Call," he found the words to express his sorrow: "This could be it, my friend, if you but knew: God's final call."

Peterson's days as a pilot over the China Hump also inspired the song that "made" his career and which for many people remains the best-loved of his many compositions. "Flying the Himalayas gave me a feeling of tremendous exhilaration," he wrote many years later. "Though I was lonely and wanted to be at home, it filled me with a towering sense of power to be at the controls of a big airplane, knifing through the clouds over areas so remote and fearsome that many of them remained uncharted. The savage beauty of those peaks and valleys stirred my poetic soul. That landscape was the greatest display of God's handiwork in nature that one could find anywhere on earth."[6] Four years later in 1948, while sitting in a Moody Bible Institute lecture, the professor's talk reminded Peterson of what he saw as the miracle of his own conversion and God's guidance ever since. "My thoughts raced to the flights over the Himalayas," he recalled, and "the spectacular power of God revealed in those electrical storms, the majesty of the mountains themselves, the incredible variety of the jungle, and the star-filled nights of dazzling beauty high in the air. As the scenes flashed through my memory, I began to focus on the element of the miraculous in all of God's work, creation and redemption."[7] Even before the bell rang to end the class period, Peterson had already worked out the chorus of a song, "It Took a Miracle." In moments he had raced over to an empty studio in the campus music building, where he fleshed out the full hymn.

Peterson came home from the war in December 1945 just in time for Christmas, and the next year used his GI Bill benefits to enroll in the one-year certificate program at Moody Bible Institute of Chicago. He even wrote a song, "He Owns the Cattle on a Thousand Hills," to express his confidence that God would provide for the needs of his wife Marie and their infant daughter. The song was soon published by Al Smith and, when the Petersons arrived in the Windy City to start school, the tune was already enjoying great popularity at youth rallies across the area. At Moody, Peterson met George Schuler and Harry Dixon Loes, both music instructors at the Institute, as well as Merrill Dunlop who was organist and music director at the famed Chicago Gospel Tabernacle founded by radio evangelist Paul Rader. He also received a note from the campus radio station, WMBI, asking him to audition for a program. Though he had grown up admiring the music of the WMBI station director and songwriter Wendell Loveless, he didn't know how the station had heard about *him*. Later he discovered that a staff member had heard, through a mutual Kansas friend, about Peterson's days as "The Singing Farm Boy" on KFBI in Salina. As it turned out, more than fifty other students had also received invitations to audition. They all crowded into the radio studios and, typically, Peterson waited until the very last to try out—though this time as a guitar player rather than a singer. The manager liked the sound and offered him a twice-weekly spot on a fifteen-minute hymn program for a salary of fifty cents per broadcast.

That year the radio evangelist Percy Crawford, who was also a pioneer in television, came to Chicago to do a telecast. He had lunch with Harry Dixon Loes and the Moody professor told Crawford about the songwriting skills of his pupil John Peterson. Afterward Loes urged, "John, why don't you send him some of your songs. After what I said about you, he'll be expecting them." The very thought sent Peterson's head spinning. Crawford's national radio program, the *Young People's Church of the Air*, was heard by millions and his songbooks were big sellers. So he crossed his fingers and mailed the evangelist a dozen of his songs including "It Took a Miracle." The reply wasn't long in coming. Crawford liked the songs. What would it cost to buy them? Peterson would have gladly *given* the songs to Percy Crawford. But forty dollars would pay a month's rent, so he asked for that amount—minus four dollars, which would be his tithe to Crawford's ministry. Soon, a check arrived for thirty-six dollars. And from the first time "It Took a Miracle" was heard on the *Young People's Church of Air*, the song was an instant favorite, soon recorded by both gospel and popular recording artists. Other publishers then began clamoring for Peterson's songs. One of those was Norman Clayton, pianist for evangelist Jack Wyrtzen's *Word of Life* crusades and radio broadcasts, who had also set up a music company of his own. He offered Peterson a contract to supply forty songs a year, from which Clayton was obligated to buy twenty songs at twenty-five dollars apiece. In time, Clayton published nearly a hundred of Peterson's songs—including "No One Understands Like Jesus"—and the money was just enough to get Peterson through school. Meanwhile, Peterson's WMBI music show became so popular that it was drawing more listener mail than any other station broadcast. So when his one-year Bible program was finished, the manager offered to give him his own daily program at three dollars per broadcast. That was five days and fifteen dollars a week, which seemed like a fortune to Peterson. And it would help pay the bills while at he studied at Chicago's American Conservatory of Music over the next three years.

In those days Peterson shuttled between the Conservatory and the Moody radio station. His daily WMBI program, *Familiar Hymns*, was also syndicated on other stations across the country and around the world. Whenever well-known gospel songwriters and artists would come through Chicago, he would have them as guests on the broadcast. In that way he met many of era's most famous gospel songwriters such as B.D. Ackley and Phil Kerr. In addition to producing *Familiar Hymns*, Peterson served as assistant talent director and hosted a daily morning show called *Cheer Up* as well as the weekly *Shut-In Hour*. One year, in the fall of 1953, Peterson was listening on a speaker at the radio station to a live broadcast from the famous Founder's Week Conference at Moody Bible Institute. As a WMBI staff member, he himself was unable to attend. The songleader was Al Smith and, at one of the afternoon services, he ended the session with the audience singing Fanny Crosby's revival hymn, "All the Way My Savior Leads Me." So overcome was Smith by the moment, he asked the assembled host to softly repeat the final phrase, "This my song through endless ages, Jesus led me all the way." Peterson and Smith met shortly afterward and Peterson told his friend how much he had been blessed by listening to the service, especially by hearing the final song. "Thanks, John," replied Smith, who was publisher of the Singspiration songbook series. "By the way, why don't you write a complete song using Fanny's last line as the title for yours?" Some days later, Peterson completed a new composition, "Jesus Led Me All the Way," and send Smith the manuscript: "I will tell the saints and angels as I lay my burdens down, 'Jesus led me all the way.'"[8]

By 1950 Peterson's family was complete with the birth of his third daughter. And in 1953 he signed a contract to produce a new "Melody-Aires" songbook series for Moody Press. That same year Peterson wrote a song called "Over the Sunset Mountains." WMBI listener response was so strong that he cut a demo record and sent it to several music companies. A mainstream publisher, knowing the "cross over" success of "It Took a Miracle," offered a contract for the new song and raved about the potential royalties and demand for more recordings. But the publisher had one small "suggestion" about the lyrics. The first line of the chorus, "Over the sunset mountains Heaven awaits for me," was fine; but the second line, "Jesus my Savior I'll see," was too sectarian. To avoid offending anyone, the publisher asked if Peterson could "eliminate the reference to Jesus and develop the idea of heaven further?" Though Peterson was torn by his dream for a hit song, "I knew I could not compromise myself as a gospel songwriter. I could not shun the name of Jesus.... On the way home I felt disappointed but confident that I had made the right decision. Suddenly a new song began to take shape in my mind, and when it was completed it became my public answer to the request that I water down the gospel. I called it simply 'My Song.'"[9] The lyric proclaimed his commitment, "I have no song to sing but that of Christ my King."

Peterson continued to seek God's guidance and, as he later recounted, received it in a way he did not expect. After serving a year as assistant talent director at WMBI, when the director left Peterson seemed in line for the job. To his dismay, however, another man was hired for the position from outside the station. Crestfallen, he went home to his small apartment "wondering why the Lord would allow this, quite sure He had abandoned me and that I was on the shelf forever." Then a thought came to his mind: "God understands. He knows I'm suffering. I'm not alone in this."[10] As the bitterness left him, he plunked out on the piano the music and words to a song, "No One Understands Like Jesus."

Though Peterson and the talent director become good friends and workmates, Peterson felt himself being pulled out of radio and into new directions. In 1955 he joined Al Smith to edit the popular Singspiration series of songbooks. Scores of Peterson's songs remain popular, from "Heaven Came Down" and "I Believe in Miracles," to "Jesus Is Coming Again," "Springs Of Living Water," and many more. Soon he also began to write choral music and cantatas for choirs, and to conduct church choral clinics and workshops. Then in 1971 he made the reluctant decision to leave Singspiration. Freed from administrative and travelling responsibilities—and making a new home in Carefree, Arizona—he could concentrate once again on his first love, writing songs which proclaim that, as the title of his 1976 autobiography put it, *The Miracle Goes On*. Peterson was inducted into the Gospel Music Hall of Fame and enjoyed a long career until his passing in 2006. Ultimately he composed more than a thousand songs, while more than ten million of his cantatas and musical have been published and sold.[11] Today the Scottsdale-based John W. Peterson Music Company continues to manage the songwriter's extensive catalog of original songs, cantatas, musicals and copyrighted arrangements.

Stuart Hamblen

Everyone in Hollywood liked Stuart Hamblen.[12] Amiable, outgoing, just to know him was to be his friend. Hamblen was a cowboy movie actor who co-starred with some of the best in the business, as well as a popular country and western songwriter. More than that, he was a favorite among the community of movie stars who knew him as a great companion and drinking buddy on the Hollywood party scene. So Hamblen had no problem finding guests for his daily radio program, *Sawdust Trail*, heard locally in the Los Angeles area. Each morning during the thirties and forties, stars and celebrities would stop by for some talk and perhaps some music. But one morning in 1949, Hamblen's guests were a bit different than his usual fare. They were celebrities, but one was an evangelist and the other a gospel singer. When Billy Graham and George Beverly Shea came into the radio studio that morning for *Sawdust Trail*, Hamblen was both repelled and attracted by the two men. Graham's crusade in Los Angeles was the talk of the town—and among Hamblen's movie star friends, the talk was mostly ridicule. The evangelist preached in an old circus tent they laughingly dubbed the "Canvas Cathedral." Yet as Hamblen interviewed Graham and sang some songs with Bev Shea, he saw a warmth and genuineness that was appealing.

Hamblen remembered his childhood as the son of a Texas preacher. Born in Kellyville on October 20, 1908, he would often travel with his father on horseback as they would ride from church to church. During the long hours on the trail he listened to his father, an old-fashioned Methodist, tell Bible stories and stories of the Old West. It was the Old West tales that the boy liked best, and so the young Hamblen dreamed of someday becoming a cowboy movie actor and a friend of all the Hollywood stars. By the mid twenties, Hamblen was making a living in Dallas as a cowboy singer. In 1928 he moved to New York in hopes of being "discovered" and landed a recording contract with the Victor Talking Machine Company. That provided the stepping stone he needed to reach Hollywood. When he wrote "Out on the Texas Plains," a country-and-western song that became a national hit, his place in the entertainment world was secured. By the mid-1930s, Hamblen was acting—usually as the bad guy—and singing in motion pictures beside the likes of Roy Rogers, Gene Autry, Tex Ritter, and Randolph Scott. John Wayne was one of his best friends. Hamblen also had his own radio show, was married to a glamorous starlet, and invited to all the studio parties. He continued to turn out more hit songs including "Remember Me, I'm the One Who Loves You," "My Mary," "Brown-Eyed Texas Rose," "Golden River," and "Little Old Rag Doll." Despite the Depression and then the war years, he lived the good life—big home, fast cars, fine dining, and plenty of money for drinking, gambling, and partying all night.

On that morning in 1949 as Hamblen interviewed Graham and Shea, he again recalled his boyhood days riding the Texas range with his preacher father. Billy Graham and Bev Shea had the same kind of faith. So did his wife Suzy who had recently come to Christ. In his heart, Hamblen knew he didn't deserve such a patient and devoted wife. She was part of a Bible study fellowship called the Hollywood Christian Group that met in Beverly Hills. Many stars went to the study and, as a favor to Suzy, Hamblen went too and played the role of "Christian husband." That's where he first met Graham, when the evangelist was invited to speak at the fellowship just before his crusade started. The two men seemed to hit it off and Hamblen invited his new acquaintance to appear on *Sawdust Trail*. And now, at the end of the program, Hamblen found himself urging listeners to "go on down to Billy Graham's tent and hear the preaching." Then, surprising his two guests, Hamblen exclaimed, "I'll be there too!"[13]

Hamblen was curious to see for himself what was happening under the big revival tent. But what would his Hollywood friends say? He could just imagine the ribbing he would get if they ever found out he had actually gone to one of Graham's meetings. Then again, Hamblen often went to check out the "acts" of the guests on his radio show. It was a professional thing, he convinced himself. When he told Suzy, she was naturally supportive. So Hamblen begged off the party scene for one night, got in the car with Suzy, and drove over to the corner of Washington Boulevard and Hill Street. The tent was stuffy and the unreserved seats were nothing more than hard, wooden folding-chairs. Yet the message and music reminded Hamblen of his father's meetings so long ago. Unlike then, however, Hamblen for the first time was starting to come under the conviction that he needed Christ. When Graham gave the invitation, Hamblen felt deeply convicted over his sinful lifestyle. But unable to understand what he was feeling, he refused to walk down the aisle. Instead he angrily got up and walked out. For two or three nights Hamblen stayed away, but then decided to come back. Over the next two weeks he would show up for a service, get angry and vow not to return, and then return a day or two later. Sometimes he would get so upset that he would shake his fist at Graham as he stalked out of the tent. At one service, the evangelist even had the temerity to say from the platform, "There is someone in this tent who is leading a double life. There is a person here tonight who is a phoney."[14] It was a veiled reference to Hamblen's posturing with the Hollywood Christian Group. Yet through his anger, he knew Graham was right.

Now that he was coming under conviction, Suzy's urging for her husband to convert seemed like nagging. Hamblen had to get away. So he scheduled a hunting trip in the mountains with a group of buddies. The men got drunk that night and Hamblen most of all. But in the middle of their fun, a terrifying storm suddenly came up over the mountains and burst upon them. Scared within an inch of his life, Hamblen beckoned the men to get back in their car and flee before it was too late. Suddenly, Hamblen felt he needed desperately to talk with Billy Graham. It was near the end of the crusade's scheduled closing after three weeks, but the evangelist was still in town. So at four-thirty in the morning, he and Suzy drove downtown and rang the evangelist's room at the Langham Hotel. Tearfully, Hamblen begged to see him and Graham agreed. But when the evangelist open the door of his room, Hamblen staggered in, fell on his knees, grabbed Billy around the legs, and with slurred speech asked Graham to help him. "Stand up, Stuart," Graham told him sharply. "You're drunk. You don't know what you're doing." Hamblen admitted his condition but still pleaded for help, and so the two men went to the kitchen table where Graham opened his Bible. After a long talk and many tears and prayers, the cowboy actor said he "heard the heavenly switchboard click." The next thing Hamblen did was to use the hotel switchboard and call his father. And even Graham could "hear his father shout with joy over the phone!"[15]

That night he came forward at the tent service. The next day, he testified of his conversion on his radio show, even telling listeners not to drink and smoke the products advertised on his program. Since *Sawdust Trail* was sponsored by a tobacco company, Hamblen's stand cost him his job. News of his conversion quickly spread in Hollywood. Not only was he well known in the entertainment community and was the number-one radio personality on the

West Coast. People across the nation watched his movies and bought his records. Was his "religion" for real? But when Hamblen stopped his drinking and gambling and parties, and even sold his prized race horses, everyone could see he was serious. He even launched a new Sunday morning radio show, *Cowboy Church of the Air*. As for Graham, news of Hamblen's conversion began to attract reporters to the crusades, which had previously been ignored by the press. Newspaper mogul William Randolph Hearst ordered his two Los Angeles papers and other big-city publications to "Puff Graham." Attendance at the tent meetings, which had been modest, now started to swell. Eventually the crusade was extended to eight weeks, attracted a third of a million people, was supported by seven hundred churches, and overnight turned Graham into a national media figure.

Later, Hamblen ran into his friend John Wayne on Hollywood Boulevard. "Hey, I heard what happened to you," said Wayne. "I guess it's no secret," Hamblen replied with a smile. At that, Wayne laughed, "That sounds like a song to me!" The two men kept talking as they walked down the street and Hamblen shared his newfound faith: "You know, John, what God has done for me, He can do for you."[16] That night Hamblen reflected upon his meeting with John Wayne. His concentration was only interrupted when the clock on the mantel struck midnight. Snatching up a piece of paper, he began to write the words of song. Working through the night, by dawn he had finished "It Is No Secret (What God Can Do)," soon to become one of the first true "crossover" hits.

When "It Is No Secret" was recorded and released in 1950, the song sold a million records, rocketed to number three on the country-and-western chart, and made the Top Forty on the pop chart. But more important to Hamblen were the doors that opened to share his faith. He went on the road for months at a time with Graham and other evangelists, singing and giving his testimony. He worked extensively at youth meetings while also witnessing Christ on the movie lots and rodeo circuit. And the *Cowboy Church of the Air* became an effective evangelistic outreach and outlet to introduce new gospel songs. In time, Hamblen won many of his Hollywood friends to Christ. He was asked many questions and, as a "newborn Christian," did not always have the answers. Yet he wrote a song—perhaps the one which is most sung in the church today—that expressed his faith that God would someday make everything clear. With that promise, he wrote, believers could confidently keep the faith "Until Then."

During his career Hamblen scored several cross-over favorites. "It Is No Secret," "His Hands," and "Open Up Your Heart and Let the Sun Shine In" all ranked high on the charts. And with "This Ole House," Hamblen racked up a number-one hit when popular singer Rosemary Clooney recorded and released the song in 1955. It stayed at the top of the charts for three weeks, brought Hamblen international fame, and sparked a gospel song fad in the mainstream recording industry. Ever since then, "This Ole House" has been sung as an upbeat tune. But Hamblen, whose own 1954 recording made it to the Top Ten, meant the song to be somewhat slower and more reflective. Indeed, the story behind the song is poignant. It began when Hamblen took a group of friends on an extended hunting trip. Often on such trips he would go out for weeks at a time. John Wayne was a frequent companion as both men loved wide open spaces, hiking into remote areas, and talking into the night beside a campfire. On this particular trip, Hamblen and Wayne and their party had found a solitary cabin among the trees, deep in the Sierra Nevada mountains of California.

Curious, the men made their way to the tiny log shack. Despite the heavy winter snow, there was no smoke in the chimney. Hamblen shouted a greeting but the only reply was the barking of a dog from inside the cabin. The men stepped onto the porch, out of the wind, and could hear the animal pawing at the front door. Hamblen knocked and called repeatedly but no one answered. At last, he and Wayne forced the door. The cabin was unlit. As their eyes adjusted to the darkness, the men could see that the old hound dog was near starvation. In the far corner of the one-room shack, lying on a bed was an old prospector. He had been dead a long time, yet still wore a peaceful expression on his face. Arranged around the bed were the items that had been most important to the old miner—yellowed photographs of loved ones and an open Bible. "He has gone to a better home," Hamblen said quietly to the others. The men buried the prospector beside his cabin, gathered up any special items his relatives might want and then departed, taking the dog with them. In the days that followed, Hamblen found himself deeply moved by the experience. The prospector had known, when his time was come, what things were truly important: "Ain't a-gonna need this house no longer—I'm gettin' ready to meet the saints."

After his conversion Hamblen lived another forty years before his passing in 1989. Not long after his conversion, in 1953, he reflected on what his first day in heaven might be like. Always a dreamer, even since his boyhood days on the Texas range when he dreamed of being a movie star, Hamblen now conjured up a very different vision—one that has since become a gospel music standard—of "Your First Day in Heaven."

Ira Stanphill

As Ira Stanphill read the letter he clutched in his hands, he stared at the words in disbelief.[17] What would he do now? He looked over at his son Butch, asleep in the corner bed of the small hotel room they were sharing that night.

What would happen to his son? At that moment, Stanphill could not think of what might happen to his own ministry and career. He was too overwhelmed with a sense of personal failure. The letter he held in his hands was a divorce paper. Stanphill remembered when he and Zelma were married, before the war. For such a beautiful and talented woman to join him in the work seemed the greatest of all gifts. They had even worked together on a song, "Room at the Cross for You," that was now used for altar calls at evangelistic meetings nationwide. The title had been suggested to him at such a meeting when, as was his custom, he invited the congregation to submit titles for a new song that he would compose by the end of the evening. Later that night as he cleaned out his pants pockets, he found the title "Room at the Cross for You" scrawled on a scrap of paper. Struck by the phrase, he quickly sketched out some words: "Though millions have come, there's still room for one—Yes, there's room at the cross for you."

Ira Stanphill was born February 14, 1914, in Bellview, New Mexico, on land his parents homesteaded after journeying by covered wagon from Arkansas. He converted to Christ at the age of twelve while attending a church service. Though he had only a year of formal music lessons, he soon taught himself to play the piano, organ, ukulele, and accordion. Later the family moved to Coffeyville, Kansas, where his father was a telegraph operator and young Stanphill attended junior college. At age seventeen he wrote his first song for his church youth group, and would travel as a music assistant to various evangelists. Five years later, at age twenty-two, he preached his first revival meeting in Arcadia, Kansas. From 1930 to 1934 Stanphill sang on a daily program over local Coffeyville radio station KGGF, then in 1936 entered full-time evangelism. Music publishing became a part of his ministry when in 1938 Stanphill founded his own Hymntime company. Ultimately, over his lifetime Stanphill would compose more than six hundred gospel songs and minister as a singing evangelists in more than forty nations.

The war years brought increased opportunities for Stanphill to travel as an evangelist, songleader, and composer. One of those meetings was in Dallas with evangelist Gene Martin, just after the war ended in the late summer of 1945. Across the country, joyous feelings of relief mingled with sorrow among the many families that had lost loved ones in the conflict. To encourage the audience, a local businessman testified at one of the evening services about his own experience in overcoming great loss and personal devastation. The man had been wealthy and prosperous, but when the stock market crashed in 1929 he nearly lost everything. In the years of Depression that followed, the man lost his home, was grieved to let go of his faithful employees, and was confronted with the agonizing decision of whether to dissolve his business in the face of mounting debts. Then one day in desperation, to be alone with his thoughts and frustrations, the man got into his car and simply kept driving for hours on end without caring where he was going. Dallas was far behind when, late in the day, the man found himself on a dirt road in the rolling Texas hill country. The way was too narrow to turn around and, given the deep ruts in the road, he had no choice but to keep going. At last the man realized he was utterly lost and, it seemed, utterly alone. Still he pushed on, finally coming to a tiny ramshackle house that seemed to have been abandoned long ago. Debris littered the small yard, which was overgrown with weeds and scrub grass.

Yet to his great surprise a young girl came out to greet him. She had on ragged old clothes and clutched a broken doll, but wore a broad and joyful smile. Curious how anyone could live like this, the man asked the girl how she could be so happy. The child replied that she was looking forward to the day when, as her father had promised, he would build her a new house on the hilltop. Touched by the girl's innocent optimism, the man bid her farewell and turned his car around with renewed hope. After many years and much work, together with much prayer, he eventually rebuilt his business. Hearing the man's testimony, the audience was indeed encouraged by his story of faith in overcoming the Depression. But Stanphill was struck most by the childlike faith of the little girl who trusted her father's promise. That night after the service he went home, then arose the next morning and in one sitting composed what became an instant gospel music favorite, "Mansion Over the Hilltop."

By the mid 1940s, Stanphill was recognized as a leading gospel songwriter and evangelist. He traveled nationwide to conduct meetings and often teamed with prominent preachers of the day. His compositions were frequently recorded and heard on the radio, so that his published songbooks and sheet music were in great demand. To all appearances, he and Zelma were a model Christian couple and often sang duets together at services. It seemed that Stanphill had everything. After their son Butch was born, Zelma stayed home while her husband traveled. These were the war years and a time when Stanphill's meeting schedule was rapidly expanding. In her new role, however, Zelma grew bored and restless. Not long after Butch was born, she entered into an affair with a servicemen she met at a church service near their home in Los Angeles. A series of affairs with other servicemen then followed, but each time Stanphill forgave his wife and the two vowed to start over. To remove Zelma from further temptation, Stanphill decided to give up his pastoral position in Los Angeles and move the family to the East Coast. But within a few months Zelma was involved in another affair. Again he moved the family, this time to Springfield, Missouri, the place where he and Zelma had met. Maybe this environment would provide the positive reinforcement his wife needed to turn her life around.

Summer was a busy time for revival meetings and Stanphill was booked throughout the season. Zelma opted to stay home but asked her husband to take Butch, since the boy was now old enough to accompany him. Stanphill agreed—and it was during one of his summer campaigns that the surprised songwriter was served with divorce papers. In the weeks that followed Stanphill grieved over his broken family. Sadly, his son Butch might never know the kind of loving home in which Stanphill himself had grown up. Memories of his childhood in New Mexico and Kansas came to his mind, simple memories of daily family life that are often the sweetest to recall. One image stuck in his mind. Day after day, he and his brother Ray would go out to play in a friend's yard. Oblivious to the cares of the world, the boys would play happily until sunset. Then they would hear their mother's voice calling out, "Ira, Ray, come home, it's supper time." As that memory came into focus, Stanphill took up a pen and some manuscript paper. His mind was transfixed by a thought: When he was a boy, his mother had called him home to supper at the end of the day. Now as a Christian he looked forward to the moment when, at the end of all days, God would call him home to heaven and to the great Marriage Supper of the Lamb. Quickly he wrote out the words and music to what became one of his most recorded gospel songs, "Suppertime."

In time, Stanphill decided to continue on with his gospel ministry and accepted a staff position at the Bethel Temple in Dallas. The church was well known as the site of the annual Stamps-Baxter School of Music and so, throughout the year, Stanphill worked with some of the best talents in evangelical popular music. He met many people at Bethel Temple and his attention was soon drawn to a vibrant and talented woman named Gloria. Since she seemed to return the interest, many of Stanphill's friends urged him to marry her. Gloria had all the gifts, spiritual and musical, that would make her an ideal complement to his ministry. Nobody would blame him for remarrying. The divorce with Zelma was not his fault. Yet Stanphill felt convicted that he should stay true to his marriage oath. Zelma had been with several men since the divorce and was singing in a nightclub. Yet perhaps someday his ex-wife would renounce her lifestyle and seek reconciliation and restoration. The prospect seemed remote, but while she lived Stanphill must keep his vows and was not free to remarry. Stanphill explained his conviction to Gloria and even urged her to find someone else. But though they agreed to cut off contact with each other, he could tell their feelings had already deepened into love. What should he do? More than once, Stanphill was ready to give up on his vows to his ex-wife. Why must he face a choice between being lonely in order to stay in the ministry, or leaving his life's work to marry the woman he loved?

One morning as Stanphill drove to work at Bethel Temple, he silently prayed to God about his dilemma. Doing what was right could mean a life of misery, but to follow his heart meant living with guilt forever after. In the car, as he poured out his sorrow about seemingly intractable circumstances that he could not understand, Stanphill began to sing a little tune about trusting in God to guide his steps. By the time he reached Bethel Temple, he rushed to the piano to complete the song. When he did so, a quiet peace came over his spirit for, as the title of his new song proclaimed, "I Know Who Holds Tomorrow."

Five years went by after Stanphill's divorce and still he held to his marriage vows. In his own heart and mind he now felt a peace and contentment, not seeking to remarry and entrusting his future to God. Then came the sad news that Zelma had died in a car accident, leaving Butch without a mother. Stanphill tried to fill her place in his son's life but could not be a mother as well as a father. As it happened, however, soon after his ex-wife's passing Stanphill in his travels crossed paths again with Gloria. The two had not seen or communicated with each other in some years and their meeting was not planned. In time they were married and, just as important to Stanphill, Gloria also loved Butch as her own son. Stanphill had grieved that Butch might never know the blessing of a home "united in Christ." And so, one evening when his new bride was preparing dinner, Stanphill shed quiet tears of joy when he heard Gloria call out, "Butch, come home, it's supper time!"

Ira Stanphill had been through, as he wrote in "I Know Who Holds Tomorrow," the flame and flood of spiritual and emotional turmoil. The tragedy that befell him is something no one would wish. Yet he believed God used his trial to bring a new depth and feeling to his songwriting. Over the ensuing years he held pastorates in Florida and Pennsylvania, then returned in 1966 to Texas as pastor of the Rockwood Park Assembly of God in Fort Worth. His Hymntime company remained an important force in evangelical music publishing until Stanphill sold it to Zondervan in 1967. Yet he continued to write songs. A favorite of Sunday school children everywhere, "Happiness Is the Lord," was composed in 1968 after Stanphill was driving home from his church office and was disturbed to hear a radio ad extolling the "happy hour" of a local bar. At last, he passed away in 1994. But not long after his second marriage, Stanphill looked back upon the trials God allowed in his life. He was moved to write a song that expressed not only his own story but, through its many recordings over the years, has encouraged those who can also say "He Washed My Eyes with Tears (That I Might See)."

Mosie Lister

Rich's Department Store in downtown Atlanta was a full-service enterprise. In the music department, staff not only sold pianos but made house calls to repair and tune their customers' instruments. That is what Mosie Lister liked best about his work, visiting people's homes and helping them get the most from their investments.[18] Back at the store, Lister also enjoyed listening to the daily gospel show on WCON. That year, 1948, the station had just been built by *The Atlanta Constitution* newspaper whose office building was across the street from Rich's. The young disk jockey, Hovie Lister (no relation), once played the piano for the famous Rangers Quartet. So he knew how to pick the best songs for his daily show. One day, however, Mosie got to hear his favorite deejay in person when Hovie Lister paid a call. Just about every radio station in the South had its own quartet and the *Constitution* was backing Hovie to start a new group for WCON. Hovie didn't have a name yet for the quartet. But the paper had promised him two radio shows a day, fifty dollars a week per man, and extensive advertising support in the *Constitution*. So they'd have a steady salary and could announce their upcoming concerts over the air. Mosie had to admit it was a good set-up. So when Hovie offered him the job of singing lead, Mosie was persuaded.

Converted at age seventeen, Mosie Lister had been bitten by the quartet bug before the war when he joined the Sunny South Quartet out of Tampa, Florida. Now, after returning home from the Navy to his home state of Georgia, Hovie's offer was the kind of opportunity he was looking for. In October 1948 the new WCON quartet signed on the air as The Statesmen—the name was taken from Hovie's interest in politics—and from the very first, the group was successful. Soon they were doing not only a live radio show in the morning (which was transcribed and rebroadcast in the afternoon), but performing concerts nightly throughout the Southeast. Mosie was a good lead singer and dedicated quartet man. He could see that The Statesmen were starting to have an impact. But he could also sense that his heart was not completely in it. All the days that The Statesmen spent on the road were tiring and exhausting. Not only was Mosie away from home and family, he also found himself desiring more and more to spend his time writing songs rather than in traveling to sing them.

Yet in the late 1940s, how could a gospel songwriter make it on his own? If he wasn't singing in a group, how would his music ever get noticed or published? Mosie pondered the question and, after a bout with pneumonia that damaged his throat, decided in 1949 to leave the Statesmen. Besides, if he was going to try and make it someday as a songwriter, he could never do it on the kind of travel schedule that a big-time quartet demanded. When he told Hovie about his decision, Hovie was supportive and wanted to continue using his friend's songwriting and arranging skills. Mosie gladly agreed to maintain a working relationship. So even as he returned to Atlanta and resumed his old day job as a piano tuner, Hovie would often call him to get help and advice for The Statesmen.

Those who knew Mosie Lister could understand his decision to leave the road and concentrate on songwriting. Born in 1921 in Cochran, Georgia, his father was a singing teacher and choir director. By the age of five, young Lister could read music but, to his parents' dismay, was also tone deaf. Yet by studying the piano, violin and guitar, the boy's ability to distinguish sounds gradually improved. His father and mother were great lovers of gospel music and had formed their family into a gospel group that sang regularly in local churches. So when other boys would listen to ballgames on the radio, Mosie Lister would listen to symphonies. Instead of reading comics or adventures, he read every book on music he could find and virtually memorized them. "I grew up on a farm. As a child I would walk around the fields and in my mind I could hear choirs singing and orchestras playing. I wanted so much to write songs that those choirs would sing and the orchestras would play. I prayed, 'God, I'd like to be a songwriter.' I prayed that prayer for a whole year."[19]

By his late teens, Lister was performing with his family's gospel group and singing solos as well. In 1939, at the age of eighteen, he studied at the Vaugn School of Music in Tennessee. After a brief stint with the Sunny South Quartet in the early 1940s, he spent the war years in Florida and North Africa with the U.S. Navy. Following his discharge, Lister at first studied engineering at New York's Rensaeller Polytechnic Institute. But the desire for a career in music was too strong. He rejoined the Sunny South Quartet for brief stint, before forming his own Melody Masters Quartet and enrolling in Middle Georgia College to earn a degree in harmony and counterpoint, specializing in piano and organ arrangements.

So by 1949, after a year on the road with The Statesmen, life as a piano tuner could seem dull by comparison. Yet Mosie persevered, honing his skills by helping his friend Hovie Lister and maintaining his contacts with other gospel groups he had met on the road. Three years went by, and then in 1952 came a breakthrough with his first real hit, "I'm Feelin' Fine." The lyrics expressed his own feeling of "joy in my soul 'cause I knew my Lord had control." He shared the song with the Lefevre Trio who, unbeknownst to Lister, recorded it soon after.

> A month or so later I heard it being sung on the radio. I was surprised when I heard my song being sung in a fast tempo—really fast. My response was one of shock. I thought they had completely ruined my song. But they sounded as if they were enjoying it. And it moved along quite well. They started including it during personal appearances. Other groups began to sing it.[20]

Then, when the Blackwood Brothers visited New York to sing on radio's *Arthur Godfrey Show*, "they carried my song and used it during the week that they were there," Lister recounted. "From there the song began to spread."[21]

Yet despite the popularity of "I'm Feelin' Fine" and a growing reputation as a gospel songwriter, "I hadn't yet made a step of faith and given my life completely to writing," Lister later recalled. But in that year of 1952 came a turning point in his career.

> As a part of my job with the store I made calls on customers, worked on their pianos in their homes and, when I'd gotten the instrument tuned or fixed, I'd sit in front of the keyboard and play something to get a feel for how it sounded. Although I don't know why, on a day when I was playing in this one home, I lost myself in the keyboard. I just kept playing a melody that was new to me. I had never heard it and I had no idea for words to go with that melody. I just knew I liked it and I kept playing it over and over again.[22]

Over the next year, as he visited homes and tuned his customers' pianos, each day he would end his work by playing that melody. At last, one woman asked him the name of the song. "I told her it was something I had been playing for awhile," he recalled, simply "an unfinished work." Yet the woman's question, and her disappointment at hearing no words to go with the captivating melody, filled Lister with a sudden urge to finish the song. The woman's home was about sixty miles from his own house in Atlanta. Driving home that evening, Lister repeated the melody in his mind, over and over, but the words simply would not come. So he began to talk with God as he drove until, overcome with emotion, he pulled the car to the side of the road. "Lord," he prayed, "you understand me, I believe this song is something You want me to write. I need some help writing the words. Please reach out to me." When he reached home, Lister quickly got out of the car, walked in the front door, and rushed to grab a pen and paper. "I still don't know the process," he later remembered. "I don't know how the words came to me. As I wrote them down I just knew that God was real and He was answering my prayer. I called my wife into the room and told her I wanted to sing my new song for her. She thought it was beautiful."[23] After a few finishing touches, Lister showed "His Hand in Mine" to The Statesmen. The slow ballad describes how the believer, even if unable to comprehend "why He loves me so," can nevertheless "feel His hand in mine, that's all I need to know." At the time, however, The Statesmen were looking for an uptempo song and passed on the introspective new composition. So Lister contacted Bobby Strickland who had sung with Lister as an original member of The Statesmen. Strickland had left the group to form a quartet of his own, the Crusaders Quartet out of Alabama, and was glad to take "His Hand in Mine."

In the four years since Lister himself had left The Statesmen, he felt God calling him to establishing a full-time music publishing business. As a piano tuner, "I found the job I was doing was a genuinely rewarding experience," he said. "Yet as much as I enjoyed my work, I felt the Lord had something else in mind for me. I thought he wanted me to do more for Him."[24] Lister was barely keeping ahead of the bills as he saved money to someday launch a music business of his own. At last in 1953, with two children to feed and nothing but his own savings to live on, he made his decision. Later he recalled, "I started a music publishing effort, and I quit my job to do it. At this time we had the twins. Those were two mouths to feed beyond my own and my wife's, and we had bills to pay. So striking out on my own was not a smart move. But I genuinely believed I was called by God to go into Christian songwriting and publishing. Because I believed that, I also believed He would take care of us and supply our needs."[25]

In the months that followed, to promote Mosie Lister Publications he was constantly on the road, traveling to church concerts, conventions, and all-night singings. But despite all the days away from home, the goal of getting his business established seemed no closer. Then on the way home from South Carolina one night, he stopped at an all-night concert in Macon, Georgia.

> While I was there, I talked to friends and listened to music. When the concert ended, I got into my car and began driving toward home. I wasn't really thinking about anything. I just began to sing a chorus. At first I didn't realize that it was one I had never heard. Without knowing it, I was writing a new song. I sang it over and over, time and time again so I wouldn't forget it. The more I sang it, the more I was overcome with a spiritual feeling. After a while it seemed that I wasn't alone, that I had a voice in the car with me, with an orchestra playing the music. It was an incredible experience![26]

As soon as Lister arrived home, he wrote down the words and music to the chorus. But the verses were another matter. As with "His Hand in Mine," an entire year went by as he struggled to find the right lyrics. The new song he had made up on the way home from Macon had been so easy to begin, yet seemed impossible to finish. But as Lister continued the struggle to establish himself as a songwriter and publisher, he turned to the Bible for sustenance. One day in 1956,

> I stumbled upon the story of David and I identified with it strongly. I began to see David as a sinner who was feeling sorry for his sins and asking God to forgive him. I tried to take on the attitude of what I thought King David might have been feeling at that time. He was sitting alone in his palace knowing how wrong he had been. He was surrounded by the riches of the world, everything he could desire, but he was all by himself. It didn't make any difference that he was a ruler, what mattered was he was separated from God. David must have realized that nothing was worse than that. With that picture in mind, I began walking around the block, and by the time I got back I had two verses sketched out in my head.[27]

The finished song, "Where No One Stands Alone," expresses the believer's heart-cry to God, "Take my hand, let me stand where no one stands alone." Lister's trust in God was, as he later told the story, ultimately rewarded. After the Crusaders Quartet recorded "His Hand in Mine" in 1953, a year later it came to the attention of the Blackwood Brothers—and from there, Lister's success was assured. The Statesmen then recorded "His Hand in Mine" and by 1955 nearly every gospel quartet in America was using the song. When Elvis Presley chose "His Hand in Mine" as the title track for his first gospel album, suddenly Lister was getting airplay on radio stations nationwide and earning royalties from two dozen foreign countries. For the rest of the decade a string of hits flowed from the pen of Mosie Lister including "Goodbye, World, Goodbye" (1955), "Then I Met the Master" (1956), and "How Long Has It Been?" (1956) which gospel songwriting legend Albert Brumley proclaimed "is the greatest gospel song." Lister's own perspective on "How Long Has It Been?" starts with his recollection of how as a child he learned to say bedtime prayers. "It occured to me one day that there were no doubt many adults who grew up with that kind of experience. I wondered if I couldn't say something in a song that would ask if they still remembered that God heard those prayers, if they remembered telling God, 'I love you.' I thought about asking, 'How long has it been since you prayed like that? How long since you really prayed?'"[28] Realizing that was the very phrase he needed to express in song, Lister began to write "as fast as I could. I had the words and music in little more than ten minutes, and before much longer had the whole song completed. Later I felt disappointed with one chord and changed it, but that was the only change I made."[29] Within five years "How Long Has It Been?" sold more than a million copies in sheet music form and continues to be sung and recorded today.

Over his long career Lister eventually wrote more than a thousand songs, becoming "by far the most influential gospel songwriter of the 1950s from the standpoint of the developing gospel quartets" through work that "complemented the growing professionalism of the gospel music industry" and pioneering the practice of writing songs with particular artists in mind.[30] In addition to the scores of gospel groups that used his work, pop and country singers that recorded Lister's songs included Elvis Presley, B.J. Thomas, Porter Waggoner, Merle Haggard, Jimmy Dean, and Loretta Lynn. In 1969 his Mosie Lister Publications merged with the Lillenas Publishing Company, freeing him from administrative duties to instead concentrate full-time on songwriting from his home in central Florida—and even, despite being a reluctant speaker, to be ordained in 1970 as a Southern Baptist minister.

In 1958 when he was at the height of his popularity, Lister was asked to write a song for Mahalia Jackson. It was a time of growing tension in America over racial issues and civil rights. As Lister, a Georgia-born white southerner, prayed about a song for the legendary African American gospel singer, he felt God leading him to write words of hope "'Til the Storm Passes By." "I feel that this is something God gave me to say," he later recalled.[31] As it happened, Jackson never recorded the song—but many others did.

Bill and Gloria Gaither

By 1960, when Bill Gaither wrote his first song, the golden age of radio was at an end.[32] The change had come gradually and, at the time, most people did not notice. Gaither himself was still an heir of the radio days, his musical roots in the gospel songs and groups that had been popularized by radio. "My brother and sister and I enjoyed listening to the great southern gospel quartets on radio and even got to some of their concerts when they sang anywhere close to us," he later recalled of his childhood in Alexandria, Indiana.[33] Inspired by what he had heard, he adds, "As soon I graduated from high school in 1954, I went after my dream" and joined a quartet that sang each noon on a daily quarter-hour broadcast over WRFD in Worthington, Ohio.[34] But by the mid-1950s a local radio show was no longer a guarantee of success. Gaither's dream ran into reality; by 1959 he was back in Indiana, working as a junior high school teacher and directing the local church choir. Yet as he pondered over the words and music of his first song, "I've Been to Calvary," he was drawn to a vision of something new.

> After a couple of years of teaching and directing the choir, I started to notice what I considered a hole in Christian music. There seemed to be a gap in the area of personal expression; ideas needed to be communicated, but no songs existed to express them. Many of the songs of that time [the fifties] were good, and some were just okay. Others seemed as if they had some good elements, but I thought leaned toward the sentimental and needed more solid doctrine or theology.[35]

With the end of radio's golden age, evangelical popular music reached a crossroads. Ever since radio first emerged in the 1920s and '30s, preachers and musicians had been compelled to match the lush musical quality and stylings of the era's radio and motion picture orchestras. They also learned that success in network radio required musical variety as well as brevity. Similarly, the mass youth rallies of the forties favored short and easily memorized choruses. As a result, evangelical popular music of the radio days had developed to supply the need for short and catchy songs. Yet with the rise of television in the 1950s, network radio—and network religious programs—were in decline. Because local religion-formatted radio stations were nearly nonexistent, evangelical songwriters lacked a showcase for their work. Since exposure could only come through mainstream record companies, the pressure to produce "juke box hymns" was great.[36] Indeed, in 1950 when Stuart Hamblen's "It Is No Secret (What God Can Do)" unexpectedly sold a million records, the industry rushed to capitalize on the trend.

Soon Americans were listening to "inspirational" balads by artists from Mario Lanza ("I'll Walk with God," 1952) to the Crew Cuts ("Angels in the Sky," 1955). Pop singer Rosemary Clooney hit the top of the charts with an up-tempo

1957 version of Hamblen's "This Ole House." Tennessee Ernie Ford had a smash hit with the folksong "Sixteen Tons" but was equally acclaimed for his albums of old hymns. Music fans could buy the bestselling single "Church Twice on Sunday" and, on the flip side, also get the sultry "What Lola Wants" from the musical *Damn Yankees*. Americans of the fifties were invited to come on a nostalgic trip to "The Church in the Wildwood" and reveled in the popular song "I Believe." Such juke box hymns fit popular religious sentiments in 1950s America. After the war and strife of the previous decade the nation longed for a return to normal life and to the high living standards and traditional religious values that typified the American Way. Membership in mainline Protestant denominations grew faster than the population, even in the midst of a postwar baby boom. Interest flourished in liturgical worship, gothic architecture, and other reassuring symbols of religion. In 1950 the National Council of Churches was established. Politicians openly extolled the nation's religious heritage in contrast to the claims of atheistic Soviet communism. To reinforce the point, on Flag Day of 1954 Congress added the words "under God" to the Pledge of Allegiance. Popular religion also found expression at the movies with such box-office hits as *The Robe* and *A Man Called Peter*. The nation's bookshelves were similarly filled popular religious bestsellers including Norman Vincent Peale's *A Guide to Confident Living* (1948), *The True Joy of Positive Living* (1950), and *The Power of Positive Thinking* (1952).[37]

It was in this climate that Bill Gaither decided to try his hand at writing a song. The catchy choruses once popular on network religious radio programs and mass rallies no longer seemed to fit the needs of the day. Writing a "juke box hymn" might score a popular hit but seemed an empty exercise. The "rock 'n' roll" craze was in full swing, yet few evangelical songwriters at the time felt comfortable adopting the style. (Not until 1969, for example, did a survey of local Youth for Christ directors find that a majority endorsed the use of folk and folk-rock styles to appeal to teenagers.[38]) Instead, Gaither determined to find an alternative. Observing that most songs then popular with evangelical Christians were either about salvation or heaven, he noted that "between those two realities we have a lot of living to do in this old world." Though he later admitted "it may seem presumptuous to think that despite the huge history of Christian music through the years there was something only I could contribute, [nevertheless] most new ideas are brought into existence because of that felt need."

> Finally, in 1960, I decided to try to write a song, a personal testimony about the fact that though I had never been to the Holy Land, spiritually I had been to Calvary. I saw it as a new birth song. The words and music seemed to come together over a few hours, and I painstakingly picked them out and jotted them down. For all the insecurities I had as a pianist and singer, when I finished my first composition, I felt a quiet confidence.[39]

The song, "I've Been to Calvary," was intended by Gaither to describe the kind of faith that sustains the believer. Since conversion comes through hearing the Word and then taking a metaphorical journey to Christ's cross at Calvary, the convert "can say I've seen the Lord ... through the witness of His Word." Soon the song was performed by his friend Jim Hill (writer of "What a Day That Will Be"), whose Golden Keys Quartet introduced the song to immediate acclaim. When Ben Speer of the legendary Speer Family heard it, he immediately called Gaither and offered a contract to publish the song through his own Ben Speer Music company. Not long afterward, the Speer Family also recorded "I've Been to Calvary" for the southern gospel-only Skylight Records label. Ironically, Gaither recognized that the success of his first song—and of his attempt to try something new—probably "would not have [happened] if I had become an overnight success at nineteen or had hooked up quickly with a big touring gospel group. No, this had come about because of what I thought had been a colossal failure in my life."[40]

The story of Gaither's "colossal failure" began with his dream, a dream shared by many evangelical youth in the forties and fifties, to sing with a quartet like the ones he heard on the radio. "I loved the music as early as I can remember," he later remembered.[41] Though his hometown of Alexandria, Indiana, had a population of only six thousand, a good radio receiver could bring in broadcasts from Tennessee, Kentucky, Ohio, Illinois, and Missouri. Born March 28, 1936, his early memories include getting a bath from his mother each Saturday night as they listened together to the *Grand Ole Opry* over WSM from Nashville. As a youth of fourteen he heard a record of the Blackwood Brothers for the first time. Later he recalled, "I can't begin to tell you the impression those records made on my young life. I couldn't wait to get home from school in the evening to play them. I had many dreams to one day be able to sing like that."[42]

His father was a toolmaker and his mother a homemaker, and the family of five attended the Nazarene Church in Alexandria. The weekday routine began at dawn when Bill, the oldest child, and his brother Danny would milk the family cows. But Gaither most looked forward to taking piano lessons and singing with Danny and their sister Mary Ann at church services and school musicals. Once, after his voice had changed, Bill got a standing ovation at the high school variety show for his rendition of "Old Man River." Encouraged by such acclaim, Gaither "set my sights on a career as a musician. My dream was to play or sing with a well-known gospel group.... I enjoyed being in front of a crowd, and I dreamed of traveling and performing with the heroes of my youth. Mostly I wanted to be on stage." As soon as Gaither graduated from high school in 1954, he turned his back on college and instead joined a group of young men in a quartet they called The Pathfinders. In time they moved to Columbus, Ohio, and were hired by WRFD for a daily fifteen-minute radio show sponsored by the Pennington Bread Company. Broadcasts were taped each morning and aired at noon. "We hoped our show would get people to invite us to their churches," Gaither recalls.[43]

Yet it proved prophetic that The Pathfinders were sponsored by a bread company. Over the next year, much of the time Gaither and the group lived on toast and coffee. As a local radio quartet, however, they got to share the stage when such groups as the Blackwood Brothers and The Statesmen came to Columbus. Gaither sustained himself with the hope that "one of those groups [would] discover me. I was sure they'd fire whoever they needed to, to make room for me. I was nineteen and I was ready." But after several months went by and the church invitations failed to materialize, he remembers, "A sense of foreboding set in when we realized—and I especially—that it wasn't happening for us." The low point came in 1955 when The Pathfinders were scheduled to appear in the 4-H building of the county fairgrounds at Van Wert, Ohio. Ticket sales for the concert that night "were so thin that if I had been less stunned I might have laughed," Gaither recounted. "I needed to be alone, so I made my way out behind the auditorium and cried bitter tears."[44]

"For the first time in my life," Gaither recalled of that tearful time behind the 4-H building in Van Wert, "I had to stare my dream in the face and realize that I was about to wake up. I didn't have it. My vocal skills and keyboard skills were not good enough for me to make it in the music business, and that was that. 'God,' I prayed, 'there has to be more life than this.' I committed myself to do whatever He wanted, even though I had no idea what that was." In fact, though he was a believer—and though he had "worn a path to the altar in our church" every time an evangelist came to town—his failure that day in 1955 led Gaither to one of his first "real" encounters with God. Until then his spiritual experiences "had been mostly emotional" and even his dream of singing with a gospel group, he admits, "had been more to make a living at what I enjoyed than to have any ministry." Now with his dream of a music career seemingly ended, Gaither had reached what he calls "the lowest point in my young existence, I had nowhere to turn. I was a failure, my hopes shattered."[45]

As the lyrics to "Something Beautiful" put it, "My dreams turned to ashes, my castles all crumbled, my fortune turned to loss." Yet despite the raw wound Gaither felt in his soul, he told God "that if music was not what He wanted for me, I was willing to give it up." Indeed, in Gaither's mind his music career was now over: "I realized I was empty and how little I had to offer. [Yet] then and there I told the Lord, 'I want to be totally Yours.'"[46] As he would sing many years later, "All I had to offer Him was brokenness and strife" in the hope that God could make "something beautiful of my life."

Gloria Gaither also recounted how her husband described the experience: "It wasn't very long before the glamor and the glory of his dream began to wear into the stark reality of bookings and food to eat and bills to pay. There were empty hours to spend trying to discover what was wrong."

> There were the usual internal struggles inside the group ... trying to find new styles, new songs, new arrangements, new methods. But all the while, the Holy Spirit was dealing with the young pianist about *why* he wanted to sing: what his motives were.... Should he just use his abilities and go on working to become a success at what he loved—or should he risk the possibility of giving up what he loved to be God's total person, whatever that meant? ... He had come face-to-face with a problem that had to be resolved: the problem of the Lordship in his life.[47]

The next morning after the concert Gaither packed his bags and went home to Alexandria. For a time he worked at Cox's supermarket, then he enrolled as a day student at Taylor University in Upland, Indiana. The campus was about twenty miles away and, in those days before interstate highways, the daily commute was a grind. "But during the drive every morning," he recalls, "I tuned in fifty-thousand-watt WOWL [from Fort Wayne] and listened to the Weatherford Quartet's morning show, and that was the only thing that made that year at Taylor bearable." Gaither still loved gospel music and, subconsciously, his dream lingered. In contrast to the daily delight of listening to the Weatherfords, his classes as an English literature major seemed dry and unprofitable: "I didn't like that I didn't understand most of my classes and had to work hard just to make C's." Yet the greatest test of his resolve was still to come. "In the middle of all that, what could have been the break of a lifetime came right to my doorstep," Gaither remembered. The Weatherfords were one of the nation's big-time quartets (both Glen Payne and George Younce, later of The Cathedrals, got their starts with the group). After listening all those months to the Weatherfords on the radio, Gaither was a huge fan. Then to his surprise, "One day Earl Weatherford and his wife stopped by and offered me a job in their group. They had heard me play and thought I was what they needed at the keyboards. They offered me a lot more money than I had been making to travel with them. 'Do I want a job? Of course! I'd love to do that.' I told them I would talk to my parents and call them."[48]

Yet his father and mother had watched their son struggle over the past year with The Pathfinders. Would traveling with the Weatherfords be any more secure? The Gaithers were hard-working Germans and his father, a factory worker and son of a factory worker, wanted his own child to get a college education. "My dad, who was always gentle and soft-spoken, rarely said no," Gaither recalled, "but now he did: 'You started out the year at Taylor and you'll finish out this year.'"[49] But by then the Weatherfords would have already hired a new pianist. Such an opportunity was unlikely to come again. Yet he honored his father's wishes, finished his freshman year at Taylor, and then transferred the next fall to nearby Anderson College.

When Gaither began his sophomore year, he soon noticed that something had changed: "For some reason, maybe because I was at peace with myself about my potential in music, things started to gel for me." He made friends at school, started to understand his classes better, and was able to make B's and C's. "The academic atmosphere became exciting to me as it never had before," he explained. Encouraged, he decided to earn a teaching degree with a major in English and minor in music. Meanwhile, on weekends he sang at local churches with his brother Danny and sister Mary Ann in the first Gaither Trio. By his junior year Bill could quit his supermarket job and pay for his schooling through part-time singing. Ironically, the trio did better than the Pathfinders ever had. Audiences felt they were not simply seeing a show or concert, but that "something was happening spiritually when we sang." Looking back later at the initial success of "I've Been to Calvary," Gaither admitted his songwriting career probably would not have been launched if he had gone instead with the Pathfinders or Weatherfords. For one thing, he believed his setbacks "had put me in place where I had been forced to study literature and English poetry, and where I had been exposed to a broader range of music" and equipped to try the new kinds of songs that he envisioned. More importantly, Gaither felt, his complete surrender to the Lord put him in a place where God could truly use him.[50]

In 1960, as far as Gaither knew, God's plan was to use him as a public schoolteacher and Christian layman. Even when his pastor asked him to lead the church choir, he recalls, "I didn't feel choral directing was my strength, but I agreed to do it anyway. I was not trained in formal church music, and my first love was singing in a group, but I knew that was a dead issue."[51] Though he wrote a few more songs and began to receive invitations to sing them at nearby churches, Gaither discovered that "I enjoyed teaching more than anyone might have predicted from my own academic background. Reading philosophy and broadening my worldview was new to me after having given up my dreams of a performing career. While I never considered myself an intellectual, I grew to really enjoy literature, language, and interacting with students and colleagues."[52] That was how Gaither, after he had transferred to Alexandria High School, met a young substitute French teacher in January 1962. "That's Gloria Sickal from Battle Creek, Michigan," another teacher told Gaither when he asked who she was. "Her dad's a pastor up there and she's a student at Anderson College."

"Is she married?"

"Nope."

"Why don't you introduce us?"

Bill and Gloria met for the first time in the high school cafeteria, where the two ate lunch together and discussed current events and literature. Gloria was attractive, articulate, and an English major like Bill. In fact, she had a double major in sociology and a minor in French. The couple hit it off and, after several dates, Bill invited her home one evening to play and sing some of his songs for her. "You write this stuff?" she asked. Gloria did not consider herself to be musical and the two had never discussed the subject. Bill admitted the songs were his, to which Gloria exclaimed, "It's pretty good!" Less than a year after they met, December 22, 1962, the two were married.[53]

While Gaither continued to enjoy schoolteaching, "I was also becoming more and more interested in getting good new music to other people." When he personally underwrote a record album with his own church choir, entitled *The South Meridian Sings* and featuring many of his songs, he was astonished to see it sell more than a thousand copies—enough to justify a second album, *The South Meridian Sings, Volume 2*. The assistant pastor of the church, Paul Hart, was also a musician and took an interest in helping expand Gaither's ministry. Thus Hart introduced him to a soloist named Doug Oldham from the Church of God, a denomination based in nearby Anderson, Indiana. At the time, Gaither had fulfilled his initial contract with Ben Speer Music by writing three more songs: "In the Upper Room with Jesus," "Lovest Thou Me More Than These?" and "Have You Had a Gethsemane?" Oldham was immediately captivated by the contemplative and heartfelt quality of the compositions, especially "Have You Had a Gethsemane?" Oldham was going through the midst of his own "Gethsemane," his marriage broken because of his own failures. What was more, nobody wanted to hear a gospel singer who was not "walking the walk." Oldham admitted to Gaither that he had come to the end of himself, so that the words of the song penetrated into his soul.

As Christ had done at Gethsemane, Oldham said, he too decided "not my will, but Thine." Soon he was invited to sing at the upcoming 1963 Church of God convention. Then as now, Church of God members enjoy lively gospel music. "Usually the big, loud songs with the fancy endings turn on the crowd the most," Gaither said, "but when Doug sang 'Have You Had a Gethsemane?' a holy hush fell over the place." Oldham also sang "In the Upper Room with Jesus" and "Lovest Thou Me More Than These?" At the end of the evening, Oldham's father came up to Gaither and said, "Bill, those are good songs; they're not run-of-the-mill." Since the elder Oldham was a well-known radio preacher, musician, and evangelist for the Church of God, Gaither knew the compliment was more than just being polite. In fact, Gaither began to play the piano for Doug Oldham at many of his father's revival services. Encouraged by the reception for his songs, Gaither decided to copyright his own work and start a small a publishing venture, the Gaither Music Company. During the 1960s he penned such songs as "Joy in the Camp," (1964), "The Longer I Serve Him" (1965), "I Could Never Outlove the Lord" and "Going

Home" (1967), "I'm Free" (1968), "Thanks to Calvary" and "I Will Serve Thee" (1969). The relationship with the Oldhams also led to what Gaither considered his "breakthrough" song. In 1963, en route to a preaching service in Huntington, Indiana, the senior Oldham turned to Gaither and exclaimed, "You ought to write a song called 'He Touched Me' about how God changes lives." The next Sunday morning before church, Gaither went to the piano. By Gaither's count it was his fiftieth song, and the words and music quickly came to him. Despite his burden of guilt and shame, he wrote, "the hand of Jesus touched me and now I am no longer the same."[54]

"The following Tuesday night," Gaither remembered, "we were at another of Dr. Oldham's meetings. I handed Doug a copy of the music and suggested, 'Sing this one tonight.' We ran through it a few times, and he loved it. When he sang it for the people, something happened." Throughout that night's song program Oldham returned again and again to the simple chorus, "He touched me, oh, He touched me. And, oh, the joy that floods my soul." Soon the audience picked up on the simple words and melody: "Something happened and now I know He touched me and made me whole." Gaither quickly published the sheet music for "He Touched Me" and the song was soon picked up by evangelist Kathryn Kuhlman for use on her radio broadcasts. Ben Speer was next to discover the song and started performing it with the Speer Family. He called Gaither and ordered three hundred copies of the sheet music—then the very next day called again and blurted, "We're out! Send us five hundred more!"[55]

As early as 1963, the elements were falling into place for a new direction in evangelical popular music. Unlike the dream of the Pathfinders Quartet in 1954, this emerging pattern did not require a radio show. The music spoke to a new generation, not only of salvation and heaven, but of the realities of Christian living in this present world. The songs were shared not in mass rallies or radio programs, but in evenings of live worship. The experience moved beyond entertainment to praising God. Music could serve not only to set up a spoken message but could also be "sermons in song." And where evangelical popular music had once been sustained by radio, now retail stepped into the picture through record album and sheet music sales.

The Gaither Trio, which had started out with siblings Bill and Danny and Mary Ann, also took shape during the 1960s. When Danny left to sing full-time with the Golden Keys Quartet, Gloria reluctantly agreed to fill in even though she did not consider herself a singer. "She had a pleasant enough blending voice," Bill admits, "but she was not a professional and had a limited range." When Gloria became pregnant, she dropped out and Danny returned. Then Mary Ann left the trio to get married. His sister's departure left Bill Gaither in a bind. He had accepted an invitation for the trio to sing on a Sunday night in Springfield, Ohio, at the Maiden Lane Church of God. Gaither auditioned a few singers to take Mary Ann's place but none worked out. "The Gaither Trio had unraveled," Bill said. Yet with the Springfield date approaching, he recalled, "I begged Gloria to step in with Danny and me as third voice." His wife protested, "I can't sing," but at last agreed to help. What happened next, Bill Gaither remembered, astonished everyone.

> We called ourselves the Gaither Trio, but we were really Danny and the Schoolteachers. We opened with a Henry Slaughter tune called "I Never Loved Him Better Than Today" and followed with Doris Akers' "Sweet, Sweet Spirit." Then I asked Gloria to pray.... [She] has a way of articulating the passions of the heart. She was not praying for effect, but what an effect it had! ... People all over the auditorum were weeping. God had annointed that place and that crowd and His three singers, even though two of us were truly weak.... It was nine years past the day when I had shelved my dream, and Gloria had never pretended to be a vocalist. Yet in spite of our limitations, the Spirit of the Lord took control.[56]

Later the pastor confided to Bill that he had seldom seen such audience response even in many evangelistic campaigns. Many people came to Christ that evening. After the event, the Gaithers sold every record and piece of sheet music they had brought with them. Soon Gloria was well known for her "readings" or spoken interludes during songs. The trio recorded three more albums, substituting a professional vocalist for the female singing parts but using Gloria for the spoken interludes. In time, however, the Gaithers heard frequent reports that people were skipping over the music and going right to Gloria's readings. Even in concerts, fans often encouraged the trio to do less singing and more talking—or rather, to let Gloria do more talking. At last, in 1970 the Gaithers' Nashville record producer, Bob MacKenzie, told Gloria she would also do her own singing on the trio's next album. He had seen her in concert at the First Baptist Church of Elkhart, Indiana, and witnessed how the audience had been impacted by a new song Gloria and Bill had co-written, "There's Something About That Name," and especially her spoken interlude. "Jesus. The mere mention of His name can calm the storm, heal the broken, raise the dead. At the name of Jesus, I've seen sin-hardened men melted, derelicts transformed, the lights of hope put back into the eyes of a hopeless child...."[57] "You're singing in person" at live performances, MacKenzie told her, so "when people buy the records, they think they're getting you. You've got to sing on the records."

But Gloria still demurred. "I'm not a singer," she replied.

"I know you aren't," MacKenzie answered, "but I'll help you. Trust me. You're good enough for a concert; we'll make you good enough in the studio."[58]

In the end, Gloria trusted MacKenzie and joined in the vocals for the Gaither Trio's 1970 album, *Back Home In Indiana*. Tracks included "There's Something About That Name" with Gloria's narration, plus another new song entitled "The King Is Coming." By 1970, the two Gaithers had become a songwriting team, taking the respective roles of composer and lyricist. "Because of Gloria's involvement," Bill stated, "the lyrics of my songs began to develop some real depth." The two often got their inspiration from a phrase or snippet they heard in sermons or from friends. The idea for "The King Is Coming" came when a friend told them about a service he had recently attended.[59] The evangelist, Jim Crabtree, ended his message by running down the church aisle and shouting, "The King is coming!" Struck by the thought, the Gaithers soon wrote the song and then introduced "The King Is Coming" on *Back Home in Indiana*.

At the time, any Christian record that sold more than ten thousand copies was considered a huge success. Thirty or forty thousand was almost more than anyone could imagine. The Gaithers' previous albums had done well enough at six to eight thousand in sales. So the trio was thunderstruck when, almost overnight, sales of *Back Home in Indiana* topped ten thousand—then twenty thousand, then fifty and a hundred, and at last tallied three hundred thousand units. For the Benson label which released the album, it was easily their biggest project ever. The two songs, "There's Something About That Name" and "The King Is Coming," became instant standards in evangelical popular music. "This was by a trio," Gaither recalls, "that included two people who didn't consider themselves singers, and one of these had never done a serious record before! All that showed me was the truth of Scripture that it's 'not by might, nor by power, but by My Spirit, says the Lord.'"[60]

Nor was the success of *Back Home in Indiana* due to radio. Virtually no stations existed in 1970 that featured an evangelical music format. How could they? The music to supply such stations did not yet exist. Exclusively evangelical music labels had only recently begun to emerge—and with them, a means to develop and support exclusively Christian artists. Moreover, FM radio did not attain its current role as a music medium until the late seventies and eighties. When the Gaither Trio recorded *Back Home in Indiana,* the old system of the radio days was over. Gone was network radio. Gone were the network radio preachers who had given evangelicval popular music its platform. Gone to television were the audiences who had once tuned in gospel quartet shows on local radio. Gone was the interest of mainstream music labels such as Columbia and RCA Victor to record evangelical groups that no longer had national radio exposure. Gone was the popular religiosity of the fifties that had sustained even the genre of juke box hymns.

Yet a new system was taking shape. With the success of *Back Home in Indiana,* explained Gaither, "Up to that point we had been singing in large churches, [and] we then started appearing in high schools that would seat a thousand or so. When those venues began selling out in advance and we had to turn people away, we booked civic auditoriums that could accommodate two and three thousand people, and finally moved our concerts to the twelve- and fifteen-thousand-seat arenas."[61] Here was a synergy between concert touring and retail sales that could sustain evangelical popular music and nurture evangelical artists. The emerging new industry enabled Bill Gaither to leave schoolteaching and realize his original ambition of full-time music ministry. As a disillusioned teenager in 1955, he recalled, "I had hit a brick wall in my life and had to conclude, 'Bill, you're not good enough to make your living with your fingertips and your vocal cords.' Now the very dream I gave to God and put on the shelf, He gave back to me, in effect saying, 'I think I can trust you with this now.'" The difference was not in his voice or keyboard skills, he believed, but because he had "matured emotionally and spiritually, and was doing what He had planned for me—composing."[62] The freedom afforded to Bill and Gloria Gaither by their record sales allowed the couple to concentrate on their songwriting. What followed was a burst of songs still beloved in evangelical churches today. In 1970 alone, the couple wrote multiple songs that remain standards including "There's Something About That Name," "The King Is Coming," "I'm So Glad I'm a Part of the Family of God," "That's What Jesus Means to Me," and "The Old Rugged Cross Made the Difference." Those early years of their full-time songwriting also produced the gospel classics "Because He Lives" and "Something Beautiful" (1971), and "Let's Just Praise the Lord" (1972).

The latter was written after a concert in New Jersey. An enthusiastic crowd clamored for an encore, yet Gaither desired to close the event by pointing the audience to God rather than to himself and the trio. On the spur of the moment he slid to the piano bench and struck up the old hymn, "Oh, How I Love Jesus," and then asked his brother Danny to sing. At once he sensed the people lifting their hearts toward God. Afterward he remarked to Gloria, "Honey, we need a song of our own that sums up the evening and ends the concert on a note of praise and worship." As he recalled it, "That was all she needed to hear. Fresh from the experience, she wrote the perfect lyric to a song that would close our programs."[63] The simple chorus, "Let's Just Praise the Lord," invites worshippers, "Let's just lift our hands toward heaven and praise the Lord!"

One member of a Gaither audience who was impressed by the spiritual experience was Ron Huff, a leading arranger and producer who often came as the guest of Bob MacKenzie. Huff took several Gaither songs, reworked and rearranged some of the musical and spoken parts, and helped create a musical called "Alleluia! A Praise Gathering for Believers." A demo tape was produced to help churches and choirs know how to stage the musical. But response was so great that the demo was released as an album and ultimately became a gold record on its own. With the wide acceptance of "Alleluia," says

Gaither, "I discovered what life was like in a fishbowl." Bill and Gloria Gaither did not think of themselves as celebrities, yet their outreach had expanded nationwide by pioneering a new approach to evangelical popular music. Thus when brother Danny Gaither left the trio in the mid–1970s it was not the end of the act. Though Bill was "ready to hang it up and quit," MacKenzie offered an alternative: "Bill, do you really want to give up your public platform at this age?" he asked. "You don't have to. I'll help you put something else together." With that, Bill and Gloria Gaither started using a series of guest artists to join in their concerts. They called the venture "Gaither and Friends" and launched an annual "Praise Gathering for Believers" in Indianapolis to further showcase the new singers. "We put together the New Gaither Vocal Band with Gary McSpadden, Steve Green and others, [and] added Gary to the trio," Bill Gaither explained, "and began introducing new talent at all our concerts—people like Don Francisco, Sandi Patti, Carman, and more.... The names and the chemistry kept changing, but the ministry continued."[64]

The Gaither Music Company expanded in the mid-1970s, a development that was close to Bill Gaither's heart. In concerts, he noted, "We might minister before thousands, but that was nothing like the influence our records could have on hundreds of thousands, or even millions, if we packaged it correctly." Another watershed was reached in 1975 when Bob MacKenzie joined the Gaithers in forming the Paragon publishing company. Their goal was to answer the question, "Can we do something in a hymnal that's never been done?" The result was a hymnal interspersed with spoken readings—the first of its kind—and entitled *Hymns for the Family of God*. The concept, Gaither said, was to create "a hymnal with lots of our music in it [that] would allow churches to replicate what we would otherwise have to bring to them live or on a record."[65] Fans could now hear the Gaithers in person, buy their albums, and even duplicate the experience in church. Today the Gaithers' influence is wider than ever as the Gaither Vocal Band and the Gaither Music Company's *Homecoming* video series, begun in 1990, and "Homecoming Friends" concert tours have been immensely popular.[66] Yet even in the late sixties and early seventies, all the elements were in place. The modern evangelical music industry was being born. Just as radio in its golden age had been the shared experience of the evangelicals across America, over time new forms of evangelical popular culture emerged that continue in their essentials to the present day.

Five

Other Notable Songwriters

IN ADDITION TO THE BIGGEST NAMES, the midcentury evangelical popular music scene was populated by a constellation of working songwriters, lyricists, and editors who churned out a steady stream of material for Christian music publishers. No doubt some readers will review the names below and, remembering a favorite church song from childhood days, wonder at the omissions. Though the literature on twentieth-century evangelical songwriters is small compared to the number of works on hymn writers of earlier eras, many useful volumes nevertheless turned up.[1] After reviewing these sources, two criteria for inclusion emerged. First, which songwriters were at their peak during radio's golden age? Second, which ones were covered in the extant literature with enough information to construct a story?

Some songwriters (such as Thomas Chisholm, William Runyan, George Bennard, and C. Austin Miles) lived and wrote songs during the radio days but did their best-known work before 1920. Since their signature songs were released in the pre radio era, the literature contains little information about their careers after 1920. Futher, most books in the hymn-story genre tell the stories behind famous songs rather than describe the overall careers of the writers. Thus, a host of prolific radio-era gospel songwriters are excluded because they wrote no "famous" songs and, therefore, no information exists about them in the hymn-story literature.

Alfred and Benton Ackley

The Ackley Brothers, Alfred H. and Benton D., were two of the most prolific gospel songwriters of radio's golden age whose songs are frequently included in hymnbooks today. Their father, a Methodist pastor in rural Springhill, Pennsylvania, was musically gifted and gave his boys their first music lessons at home. Alfred, the younger brother born January 21, 1887, went on to study harmony and composition in New York and at the Royal

Academy of Music in London. He specialized in the cello and in time became first cellist for a prominent orchestra. A call to preach led Ackley into the ministry, where in 1914 he was ordained a Presbyterian minister and held pastorates in Elmhurst and Wilkes-Barre, Pennsylvania, and Escondido, California. But he never stopped writing music, composing more than a thousand songs in his lifetime and contributing often to hymnals and songbooks of The Rodeheaver Company.

He often found inspiration in the simple things of life. "The Little White Church on the Hill" (1935) honored the memory of his father's church in Springhill. Similarly, "At the End of the Road" (1930) was written after a visit to Alfred's favorite boyhood fishing hole on Wyalusing Creek. The fish were not biting that day and, in his disappointment, Ackley recalled how his father once told him, "Remember, you won't always see your reward here. But don't forget, God keeps accounts and at the end of the road He won't forget you!"[2] On the walk back to Springhill, the words and music formed in his mind.

Alfred Ackley's best known song, "He Lives," was inspired by listening to the radio. While shaving on Easter Sunday morning in 1932, he tuned in the NBC network and heard an Easter greeting from a well-known liberal preacher. The speaker claimed that Christ's resurrection did not matter since His teachings remained to guide mankind. "It's a lie!" shouted Ackley at the radio set. He recalled how in recent weeks he had been talking with a young Jewish man who kept asking, "Why should I worship a dead Jew?" Ackley's reply had been, "That's the whole point. He isn't dead, He's alive!" Still angry at the minister on the radio, that Sunday morning and evening Ackley preached with special fervor. But that night he was still seething about the way Christ's resurrection had been denied. His wife suggested he get the matter off his chest by writing a song. "Heeding her advice," Ackley recalled, "I went into my study. I once again turned to the resurrection story as found in Mark 16:6 and reread the words, 'He is risen; He is not here!' A thrill filled my soul, a glorious experience I will never forget." Soon he wrote the words which proclaim, "I know that He is living whatever men may say." In a short time, the remaining stanzas fell into place. Then Ackley sat down at the piano and, that night, composed the chorus and the melody just as they appear in hymnbooks today.[3]

Benton Ackley, born September 27, 1872, as a boy would often travel to play the piano and a portable organ for his father's evangelistic meetings—and even mastered several brass and wind instruments so that he could play in his father's fourteen-piece band.[4] At the age of sixteen he went to New York to learn stenography while serving as a church organist in Brooklyn. During those days, in 1892, Ackley published his first song. His musical and business training were both useful when in 1907 Ackley joined the Billy

Sunday evangelistic team as pianist and secretary. Later he was employed by Homer Rodeheaver, Sunday's former songleader, as music arranger and hymnal editor at the Philadelphia office of the Rodeheaver Company. Over his long career Ackley composed some 3,500 hymn tunes and collaborated with many of the nation's best known songwriters. One fruitful partnership was with Oswald Smith, the Toronto pastor and prolific writer of hymn texts. Ackley set more than a hundred of Smith's songs to music including "Joy in Serving Jesus" (1931), "The Glory of His Presence" (1935), "God Understands" (1937), "Beyond the Shadows" (1946), and "The Man of Galilee" (1950).

On occasion the Ackley brothers would collaborate. Their first joint venture, "Somebody Knows," was inspired when the two men were walking together down the street in Pennsylvania. Benton had received some bad news and, turning to Alfred, declared, "Isn't it encouraging that Somebody knows?" Both were immediately struck by the phrase and, passing a local music store, they went inside and asked to use a piano. Before they left the song was essentially complete. Another simple experience led to perhaps the Ackleys' best known collaboration, "I Am Coming Home."[5] One day Benton was riding the train home from an evangelistic meeting. Longing to see his three-month-old daughter, he listened to the rhythmic click of the wheels over the rails until a phrase entered his mind. Over and over, to the rhythm of the rails, he began repeating, "I am coming home, I am coming home." Then he was struck by the thought that his Heavenly Father was ever waiting for His children to come home. Benton Ackley composed a melody, one suggested by the rhythm of the train, and sent it to his brother Alfred with some suggestions for lyrics. Alfred completed the song and, upon publication, it soon became a favorite.

> Jesus, I am coming home today,
> Never, nevermore from Thee to stray;
> Lord, I now accept Thy precious promise,
> I am coming home.

The brothers' deaths occurred within two years of each other. Benton Ackley passed away September 3, 1958, in Winona Lake after serving more than thirty years with The Rodeheaver Company. Alfred followed him July 3, 1960, passing away in Whittier, California, after years of service as a pastor and songwriter.

Eugene Bartlett

Born Christmas Eve 1885, Eugene Monroe Bartlett was raised in the Ozark hills near Waynesville, Missouri. In those days, few children in rural

America completed more than an elementary education. But Bartlett's ready mind and musical gifts marked him for further training as he studied at the Hall-Moody Institute and William Jewell Academy. In 1914 he entered full-time music ministry, traveling to churches and singing conventions throughout the South. Four years later while living in Hartford, Arkansas, he founded his own Hartford Music Company. Like all his endeavors, it was a success from the first. Not only did Bartlett publish his own songs, he introduced many new songwriters, including a young Albert E. Brumley.

In the twenties and thirties, Bartlett's gospel songs were widely sung across the country. He himself was renowned as a singer and composer, teacher of singing schools, and publisher of the *Herald of Song* magazine. Over the years he became associated with both the Stamps-Baxter and James D. Vaughn music companies. Radio spread even further the popularity of such songs as "I Heard My Mother Call My Name in Prayer," "He Will Remember Me," and "Everybody Will Be Happy Over There" (still a gospel music standard today). As the thirties wore on, despite the Depression and his own advancing years Bartlett maintained a full travel schedule with no sign of slowing down. Indeed, he was the eternal optimist. His sunny disposition and infectious humor were expressed in such novelty songs as "Take an Old Cold Tater and Wait" (which actually became a big country music hit), "You Can't Keep a Good Man Down," "The Old Razor Strop," and "The Men Will Never Wear Kimonos By and By."

Then in 1939 Bartlett, who had always tirelessly pushed himself, suffered a stroke that left him partially paralyzed and unable to travel. Instead of begrudging his confinement, he busied himself with Bible study—and tried to write at least one more song. Words and music no longer came easily to his once-sharp mind and writing them down required great effort. In fact, within two years of being stricken Bartlett died, on January 21, 1941. Yet as his body weakened, his faith increased and "Victory in Jesus," published in 1939, became his most enduring legacy.

Virgil and Blanche Brock

The husband and wife team wrote more than five hundred gospel songs, among them "He's a Wonderful Savior to Me" (1918), "Resting in His Love" (1928) and, inspired by one of Homer Rodeheaver's favorite poems, "Sing and Smile and Pray" (1934). But the Brocks are, by far, known best for their hymn, "Beyond the Sunset."

In the summer of 1936 the couple was in Winona Lake, Indiana, assisting Homer Rodeheaver with his annual School of Sacred Music. Interestingly,

Virgil Brock later gave three accounts of how the song came to be written. In one version[6] the couple had been invited, along with Virgil's cousin Horace Burr and his wife Grace, to a music school faculty dinner at Rody's home on Rainbow Point. That evening the group witnessed an especially breathtaking sunset over Winona Lake. Then Horace Burr, who was blind from birth, exclaimed suddenly, "My, that sure is a wonderful sunset! Thanks so much for picturing it for me. I sure would have missed a lot if you folks hadn't been here to describe it." Another dinner guest then raised the question, "I wonder what's beyond all of this?" Virgil Brock, in this telling of the story, was immediately struck how his blind cousin had "never seen the glory of an earthly sunset yet was blessed as we tried to describe it to him. So we too, as Christians, have never seen what is beyond. But God in His love and promise has told us in the Bible of the glory that is awaiting us beyond." Within the hour the Brocks were back at their own apartment, soon composed the song, and as a final touch dedicated "Beyond the Sunset" to Horace and Grace Burr.

In the second account,[7] like the first, the Brocks marveled at the sunset over Rainbow Point. But in this version, storm clouds were threatening overhead and they returned to their own home with the Burrs for dinner. Though the Brocks lived year round in Indianapolis, they had a combination summer home and restaurant in the back of the Billy Sunday Tabernacle. As the foursome ate their meal, Horace declared, "I have never seen such a beautiful sunset!" Virgil then told his cousin, "People are always amazed when you talk about seeing." To that Horace replied, "I can see. I see through other people's eyes, and I think I can see more clearly because I see beyond the sunset." That thought, together with the inflection of Burr's voice, struck Virgil Brock so forcibly that he started singing a few measures of words and music. "That's beautiful!" Blanche exclaimed. "Please go to the piano and sing it." The first verse was quickly completed, describing the "glorious dawning" of that "blissful morning" as toil ends and heaven begins "beyond the sunset when day is done."

According to this version of the story, the Burrs then participated in writing the following stanzas of the song. "You should have a verse about storm clouds," Horace urged, and so Virgil and Blance composed the second verse: "Beyond the sunset no clouds will gather, no storms will threaten, no fears annoy." Then recalling how Horace in his blindness always walked hand in hand with his wife Grace, the Brocks wrote a third verse that declared, "Beyond the sunset a hand will guide me to God, the Father whom I adore." Then, said Virgil in this account, "Before the evening meal was finished, all four stanzas had been written and we sang the entire song together." The third account,[8] however, is a mixture of the first two—in which the Brocks write the first verse of "Beyond the Sunset" during dinner at Rody's home, then return to their own dwelling and write the remaining three stanzas.

Born January 6, 1887, near Celina, Ohio, Virgil Brock was the sixth of eight brothers. His parents were devout Quakers and Brock was converted at the age of sixteen during a church revival meeting. Feeling a call to preach, he was ordained at age nineteen and later went on to study at Fairmount Friends Academy and Earlham College in Indiana. Over these years he pastored several small Quaker churches. While attending college and pastoring the Christian Church in Green Forks, Indiana, he met Blance Kerr, who was known as the "Belle of the Community." Born February 3, 1888, the daughter of a local physician, for a brief time she was a schoolteacher. But her musical gifts led her to study voice and piano at the Conservatory of Music in Indianapolis and the American Conservatory in Chicago. As early as age twelve she played the piano for church meetings. When she met Virgil Brock at Earlham College, Blanche was serving as a pianist and soloist for a traveling evangelist.

The two were initially drawn together because they had both been Sunday school teachers and had directed church choirs and orchestras. They were married in 1914 and soon became known as "The Singing Brocks," traveling and ministering at churches in and around their home state of Indiana. When evangelists would come to the area for revival or evangelistic meetings, Virgil would often handle the advance work and both he and Blance would direct the musical program. As a songwriting team, the respective strengths of Virgil and Blanche complemented one another. Melodies were always flowing out of Virgil's heart, but he readily admitted that "after I had written a melody I could not have read it, if I had not known the tune. To me the theory of music seems more complicated than building a spaceship." Instead it was Blanche, with her musical training, who notated and scored the couple's more than five hundred songs. From 1922 to 1936 the Brocks ministered in evangelism for their denomination throughout Indiana. Then in 1936 the couple decided to enter the wider field of independent itinerant evangelism. That is why, in the summer of 1936, they were at the Winona Lake Bible Conference where they wrote "Beyond the Sunset."

Twenty-two years later Blanche was again in Winona Lake, when she died of cancer on January 3, 1958. Virgil later remarried and stayed active in music and evangelism almost until his death at the age of ninety-one. His traveled to evangelistic campaigns throughout the United States and Canada, and was known for improvising choruses during a service or writing custom songs for special occasions. Brock lived out his final days at Youth Haven Ranch, an outreach to underprivileged children in Rivers Junction, Michigan. At the end of his life, as in the final verse of "Beyond the Sunset," he looked forward to that "glad reunion with our dear ones who've gone before; in that fair homeland we'll know no parting, beyond the sunset forevermore!"

Albert E. Brumley

Albert E. Brumley wrote so many classic gospel songs that even a partial list of favorites does his body of work little justice.[9] Some of the most recorded include "I Will Meet You in the Morning," "I Will Meet You by the River," "If We Never Meet Again," "The Sweetest Song I Know," "Little Pine Log Cabin," "Did You Ever Go Sailing?," "He Set Me Free," "Go Right Out," "Jesus, Hold My Hand" "When We Sing Around the Throne Eternal," "Heaven's Radio Station is On the Air," "'Twill Be Glory There for Me," "Bound for That City," and "God's Gentle People." For these and his more than eight hundred other songs—including "I'll Fly Away" and "Turn Your Radio On," his two greatest hits—Brumley was named by the Smithsonian Institution as "the greatest white gospel songwriter before World War II." At the height of his career he was acknowledged as the most recorded songwriter in the world. "I'll Fly Away" alone has been recorded more than five hundred times—the most of any gospel song—and for that achievement he was inducted in 1986 into the SESAC Hall of Fame. Altogether, Brumley's songs have been printed an estimated fifteen million times in sheet music, songbooks, and hymnals.[10]

His beginnings were less auspicious. Oklahoma was not yet a state—it was called Indian Territory—when Brumley was born October 29, 1905, on a cotton farm near the hamlet of Spiro in LeFlore County. Yet his musical ability was evident as a youth, when he learned to play the pump organ. When he was sixteen Brumley met some songwriters while attending a nearby singing school, but was most inspired when the teacher drew a musical scale on the blackboard: "When he said ... that all the songs and melodies that had ever been written had come from that little scale up there on that blackboard ... and all that ever would be written could be found in that scale ... that set me afire! That's when I decided if other people could do it, I could do it."[11]

In 1927, at the age of nineteen, he realized his boyhood dream by attending Eugene Bartlett's famous Hartford Music Institute in Hartford, Arkansas. But after a year of study his first composition, "I Can Hear Them Singing Over There," was rejected for publication and, discouraged, he returned to the family cotton farm in Rock Island, Oklahoma. There in 1929 while picking cotton and singing the then-popular song, "If I Had the Wings of an Angel," Brumley was struck by a sudden thought. "Actually," he recalled later, "I was dreaming about flying away from that cotton field when I wrote 'I'll Fly Away.'"[12] The song was still incomplete when, that same year, he returned to the Hartford Music Institute. Having no money, he was befriended by Bartlett himself. The famous gospel songwriter even invited Brumley to stay in his home and study by his side. "Telling me to go to his house meant more to me than being invited to the White House to live with the President!" Brumley later exclaimed. Over the next two years he traveled and sang with the Bartlett company's Hartford Quartet and taught singing schools throughout the Ozarks. At one of these schools in Powell, Missouri, he met and in 1931 married his wife Goldie. The couple settled in Powell where they ultimately raised their six children—Bill, Al Jr., Bob, Tom, Jack, and Betty.

Goldie encouraged her husband to try and have at least one of his songs published. By then, "I'll Fly Away" was completed and in July 1932 Brumley mailed it to the Hartford Music Company. Bartlett bought the rights and published it in a new songbook, *The Wonderful Message*. Soon the song gained national recognition and numerous other publishers were paying royalties to have "I'll Fly Away" printed in their own hymnals and songbooks. At the time, Brumley was working for a dollar a day in his father-in-law's general store, while teaching music and tuning pianos on the side. But on the strength of "I'll Fly Away" he was hired by Hartford Music as a staff writer.

For the next thirty-four years Brumley was employed as a staff writer for the Hartford and then the Stamps-Baxter music companies. By the mid-1930s his compositions were so popular that his friends and neighbors in Powell, Missouri, took justifiable pride in their town's most famous citizen. They would eagerly listen to the radio to hear the best-known quartets in America sing the newest Brumley songs. When one of these came on the air, they would rush to the phone. "They would call me whenever they heard anyone singing one of my songs," Brumley recalled. "The first thing they would always say was, 'Albert, turn your radio on.'"[13] And of course, that phrase provided the inspiration for his 1938 song of the same name, "Turn Your Radio On."

Though Brumley's songs were popular, he was not financially secure until Bartlett, upon his death in 1941, willed the rights to "I'll Fly Away" back to his former pupil. In time, Brumley prospered enough to establish his own Albert E. Brumley & Sons Music Company—and later, purchased Bartlett's old Hartford Music Company. Still under family ownership today, Brumley Music continues to do a brisk business. The company's annual Albert E. Brumley Memorial Gospel Sing, held each summer, is the largest such outdoor event in the nation. Meanwhile, Brumley remains one of the most widely recorded gospel music composers in America. "I'll Fly Away" has been recorded by artists ranging from Ray Charles to Andy Griffith, and even the Boston Pops. A rendition by Aretha Franklin was included in the 1997 *Princess Diana Tribute Album*. But most important to Brumley was not the popularity, but the truth, of his messages in song. As James Blackwood observed, "I think one of the marks of a truly great man is his humility and this is clearly evident whenever you meet Albert E. Brumley. He was completely unassuming, always reluctant to be in the limelight. He was shy to receive the honors that he so bountifully deserved."[14] Brumley passed away on November 15, 1977.

Avis Christiansen

Ranked by hymn historian Kenneth Osbeck as "one of the most important gospel hymn writers of the twentieth century,"[15] Avis Christiansen was born October 11, 1895, in Chicago. Over her long life of ninety years Christiansen wrote the words to hundreds of gospel hymns and songs, and also published several volumes of poetry. Her collaborators included many leading evangelical composers from radio's golden age—Harry Dixon Loes ("Blessed Redeemer," "Love Found a Way"), Merrill Dunlop ("Only One Life"), Wendell Loveless ("Precious Hiding Place"), Haldor Lillenas ("Jesus Has Lifted Me"), Harry Clarke ("Believe on the Lord Jesus Christ"), Homer Hammontree ("Fill All My Vision"), Lance Latham ("Only Jesus"), and George Schuler. In fact, her first two songs were published with music by the famed nineteenth-century gospel song composer Daniel Towner. They appeared in *Tabernacle Praises* in 1915, four years before Towner's death.

Christiansen started writing poetry as a girl, having grown up in a devout home and being converted at an early age. After graduating from high school in Chicago, she attended secretarial school and later enrolled in evening classes at Moody Bible Institute. Her husband, Ernest Christiansen, was affiliated with the Institute for nearly forty years. Together they were longtime members of Moody Memorial Church, having joined the congregation in 1915 when Paul Rader was its pastor. Not surprisingly, her lyrical gifts were well known among the circle of songwriters who in radio's golden age gravitated around Moody Bible Institute (Loveless, Loes, Schuler) and Rader's Chicago Gospel Tabernacle (Dunlop, Latham). These men would compose melodies and send them to Christiansen to write an appropriate text. "Love Found a Way," for example, was written after Harry Dixon Loes heard Paul Rader preach a sermon at the Moody Church. Using John 3:16 as his text, Rader declared that "love found a way" for God to bring men back to Himself, and that Way was Jesus Christ. Similarly, "Blessed Redeemer" was inspired when Loes heard a Rader sermon on Christ's atonement. In both cases he composed a melody and sent it, with a suggested title, to his friend Avis Christiansen. She herself did not attribute the writing of her hymn texts to any unusual experiences. Instead, she credited her daily relationship with God as the inspiration for her lyrics.

> Blessed Redeemer, precious Redeemer!
> Seems now I see Him on Calvary's tree,
> Wounded and bleeding, for sinners pleading,
> Blind and unheeding, dying for me!

Cleavant Derricks

In 1977 an elderly man walked into the Nashville offices of Canaanland Music and declared to the woman at the front desk, "I have written some songs and I am looking for a publisher." Before the woman could give her standard put-off, the visitor pressed on. "I live in Washington, D.C., and I believe that I have written some songs a gospel music publisher might be interested in." When the woman asked him if he had ever had any songs published before, the finely dressed black preacher replied, "As a matter of fact, I have even had a few recorded." When the woman asked if she might know any of them, the man smiled and said, "Have you ever heard of a song called 'Just a Little Talk with Jesus'? I wrote that and some others too." The woman couldn't quite believe her ears. "Just a Little Talk with Jesus" had been one of the most famous gospel songs of all time for at least forty years. "What is your name, sir?" she stammered out. "I am Cleavant Derricks," he responded, "but most people call me Rev."[16]

The story of Cleavant Derricks begins in the Depression-era South, a place of poverty and hopelessness where he pastored a small black church in Alabama. To cheer his flock, most of whom had little prospect of betterment, he wrote songs of eternal hope. One of his earliest, written in 1934, declares that "We'll Soon Be Done with Troubles and Trials" in that heavenly home where no sorrows ever come. "Just a Little Talk with Jesus" followed in 1937.

Encouraged by the entusiastic reception of his songs, he contacted the Stamps-Baxter Music Company in Dallas. At the time, Stamps-Baxter was the largest publisher of gospel music in the world. Incredibly to Derricks, they liked his songs and offered to supply his church with fifty new hymnbooks in exchange for publishing rights. In the thirties and forties it was common practice for writers to sell their songs outright to publishers for a flat fee. Derricks was overjoyed at the new hymnbooks, which his church greatly needed but could never afford. Yet soon after its publication as a "spiritual" in the Stamps-Baxter *Harbor Bells No. 6* songbook, "Just a Little Talk with Jesus" became one of the hottest songs in gospel music. Year after year it was recorded by groups of every description. Yet Derricks never made a penny. "We'll Soon Be Done with Troubles and Trials" also became a standard, along with Derricks' 1944 song, "When God Dips His Love in My

Heart." But despite having nothing to show but fifty hymnals, he continued to minister as "the Rev" to the churches he pastored. Fame was not important to Derricks—which was just as well, since few people outside the industry even knew his name and, by 1977, many assumed he must be dead. "I got to meet him a couple times," recalled George Younce of The Cathedrals Quartet. "He was such a gentleman. He came backstage and was very humble. Not very many people even knew who he was. Yet he was such a great writer. I always thought it was a shame that he wasn't out in the spotlight for the great songs he had given to the world."[17]

On the day in 1977 when Derricks walked into Canaanland Music seeking a publisher, even the company executives had to be convinced he was really Cleavant Derricks. But once they knew the truth, the company helped Derricks recover some of his rights and secured back payments for the past six years of royalties. The amount was fourteen thousand dollars, more money than the Rev had ever seen in his life. Some months later Derricks had moved to Knoxville, Tennessee, and brought his family to meet the record company executives. The group included his wife, twin sons, daughter, and a cousin—and they sang so well, Word Records immediately signed them to a contract. After the family recorded some of Derricks' unpublished songs, the producer asked for a favor. Would the Rev sing "Just a Little Talk with Jesus"? Derricks agreed and, as his rich baritone voice brought the words to life, tears began to stream down his face. A lifetime of Christian service was summed up in that moment, that song. Not long afterward, Derricks passed away.

Thomas Dorsey

Widely regarded as the greatest African American gospel songwriter, Thomas Dorsey was on the platform at a 1932 St. Louis revival meeting when a telegram arrived. It was from his home in Chicago and, when his friends signed for the telegram and read its content, they were at loss about what to do. But at last, while the meeting was still in progress, they informed Dorsey of the awful news. His wife Nettie had died giving birth to their first child. Dorsey rushed to the telephone to confirm the tragic message. He had hesitated to make the drive to St. Louis, fearing to leave his wife in her ninth month of pregnancy. But Nettie had persuaded him to go on with a friend to the revival meeting. On the road to St. Louis in his Model A Ford, he had even turned back. "After driving about twenty miles, I discovered I didn't have my music briefcase, so we returned," Dorsey later remembered. "Nettie was still asleep and I thought, 'I won't wake her,' so I slipped the briefcase out from under the bed and went on to St. Louis."[18]

Now devastated and too distraght to drive, Dorsey was taken home by a friend to Chicago, where he was the music director of Pilgrim Baptist Church. Twice before, he had forsaken a career in mainstream popular music to serve God. For awhile, at this latest terrible blow, he got angry with God and thought of giving up the ministry. "God, you aren't worth a dime to me right now!" he cried.[19] Then upon returning home, Dorsey was greeted with more devastating news. His child, who had seemed healthy, had died unexpectedly during the night. Mother and child were laid together in the same coffin. "I was very despondent for several days as I mourned," Dorsey recalled. "I was severely tempted by Satan to go back to the world's music. But the Lord helpd me up and strengthened me."[20]

In the days following the funeral, Dorsey drove his car aimlessly around the Chicago streets. And in his distress, the germ of a song began to form in his mind. A few weeks later he visited a friend, Theodore Frye, a fellow gospel singer. Sitting at a piano in the basement of an old hairdressing college in the city, Dorsey started to play and sing, "Blessed Lord, take my hand...." After going over the new song several times, he stopped and turned to his friend.

> I said, "Come here, Frye. How do you like this song?" and I went over it again for him. He said, "The words are good, but that 'Blessed Lord' won't work. Call him 'Precious Lord.'" I agreed. "That does sound better," and so we went over it once more. The next Sunday morning Frye's choir sang it at the Ebenezer Baptist Church, and I played the accompaniment. It tore up the church.[21]

With that, the plaintive yet powerful song, "Precious Lord, Take My Hand," born out of tragic personal loss, went on to become the most popular of Dorsey's gospel compositions. "Although Dorsey's songs were first written for the black congregation, they also struck a responsive chord with whites," oberved music historian Don Cusic. "Two top publishers for white churches, Stamps-Baxter and R. E. Winsett, began anthologizing Dorsey tunes in the late thirties and his two biggest songs, 'Peace in the Valley' and 'Precious Lord, Take My Hand,' were major hits in the white market."[22]

Born July 1, 1899, in Villa Rica, Georgia, Dorsey grew up in Atlanta as the son of an itinerant Baptist preacher. His mother played a portable pump organ and, by the age of twelve, young Dorsey had learned the instrument and mastered the piano as well. That same year he converted to Christ. But the South offered little opportunity for a young black man like Dorsey. Impressed by the jazz musicians he heard in Atlanta as a teenager, by age sixteen he began playing the piano in the city's jazz clubs and bordellos. A year later, drawn by the lure of a music career, he drifted to Philadelphia, then to Gary, Indiana, and then in 1918 to Chicago. By World War I, the Windy City was emerging as a mecca for African Amercan blues and jazz. Playing the piano in bars and brothels on city's South Side, in 1920 Dorsey used his earnings to enroll in the Chicago School of Composition. That same year he wrote his first hit song, a blues number, "If You Don't Believe I'm Leaving, You Can Count the Days I'm Gone." Yet the pressure of performing and touring, in addition to his music studies, led to illness and breakdown. Dorsey dropped out of music school and despaired of his life. But in September 1921 an uncle took him to the National Baptist Convention, the annual gathering of the historically black denomination. Dorsey was profoundly moved and, on hearing the gospel song "I Do, Don't You?," he dedicated his life to writing gospel music. Soon after, he penned his first gospel song, "If I Don't Get There."

In 1921, however, the idea of gospel songs inspired by the African American experience and influenced by the blues style was new and encountered resistance. As Dorsey explained his approach, "If a woman has lost a man, a man has lost a woman, his feeling reacts to the blues; he feels like expressing it. The same thing acts for a gospel song. Now you're not singing blues; you're singing gospel, good news song, singing about the Creator; but it's the same feeling, a grasping of the heart."[23] But bringing blues inflections into the church was shocking to many. "I got thrown out of some of the best churches in those days," Dorsey later recalled.[24] Moreover, black composers in all music genres had trouble getting their work published. Finding no takers for his songs, within a year Dorsey was back in the Chicago nightclub scene playing the blues. This time, he began to have some success. Songs such as "Muddy Water Blues" and "I Just Want a Daddy I Can Call My Own" gained him a growing reputation. By 1924 Dorsey, under the name "Georgia Tom," formed his own "Wild Cats Jazz Band" that toured with legendary blues singer Ma Rainey. Other well-known blues singers, including Bessie Smith, also performed his songs. Dorsey married Nettie Harper—Ma Rainey's wardrobe mistress—in 1925 and his future as a blues musician looked bright. But in 1926 another breakdown thwarted his ambition to establish himself as a successful solo act on the nightclub circuit. Later Dorsey admitted that he seriously contemplated suicide and that the friendship of a local black minister saved his life. Dorsey found renewed faith, again dedicating his songwriting gifts to religious music and taking an appointment as choral director at Pilgrim Baptist Church.

Publishers, however, were still not ready to accept his African American gospel songs. Now married and desperate for income, Dorsey again turned his talents to writing the blues. Yet in those Depresssion days, he earned enough royalties—his career output totalled more than 150 blues compositions—to keep the wolf from the door. One song, "Tight Like That," written and recorded for the Paramount label in 1928 with slide guitarist Hudson "Tampa Red" Whitaker, sold seven million copies. The duo teamed up as "The Famous Hokum Boys" and recorded more than sixty songs over the next four years.[25] With that respite from economic distress, he at last surrendered his songwriting gifts fully to God. As his songs became known, Dorsey soon rose to the top of black church music circles. By 1932 he formed the Dorsey House of Music, the first independent publisher of black gospel music. As his style of songwriting became popular, Dorsey traveled almost every week to revival meetings and conventions, singing (and selling) his work.

That is how Dorsey found himself in St. Louis when the tragic telegram arrived in 1932. But this time, even at this most terrible blow of all, he vowed to remain true to the precious Lord who now took his hand. By the mid-1930s he was recognized as the nation's leading African American gospel song composer, and his compositions were starting to be sung by white artists as well. Over the years, "Precious Lord, Take My Hand" was recorded by Elvis Presley, Mahalia Jackson, Aretha Franklin, B.B. King, Johnny Cash, Tennessee Ernie Ford, Roy Rogers, and scores of others. It was a favorite of Martin Luther King, Jr., and, after being sung at the civil rights rally in Memphis the night before his 1968 assassination, was reprised at his funeral by Mahalia Jackson. President Lyndon Johnson also requested that "Precious Lord, Take My Hand" be sung at his own funeral in 1973. Dorsey's other best-known work, "Peace in the Valley," was composed in 1938 while he was on the road:

> Just before Hitler sent his war chariots into Western Europe, I was on a train going through southern Indiana on the way to Cincinnati, and the country seemed upset about this coming war that [Hitler] was about to bring on. I passed through a valley on the train. Horses, cows, and sheep were all grazing together in this little valley. A little brook was running through the valley, and up the hill I could see where the water was falling from. Everything seemed so peaceful with all the animals down there grazing together. It made me wonder what's the matter with humanity? What's the matter with mankind? Why couldn't man live in peace like the animals down there?[26]

At the time, it so happened that Dorsey had recently been singing to himself an old spiritual, "Walk Through the Valley of Peace." Now he himself, inspired by the biblical prophecy of Isaiah 11:6, took out pen and paper and scribbled down some words. Isaiah had prophesied that when Jesus reigned on the earth, "The wolf also shall dwell with the lamb, and the leopard shall lie down with the kid; and the calf and the young lion and the fatling together; and a little child shall lead them." So the words of "Peace in the Valley" started to take shape as Dorsey set the Old Testament prophecy to music. Four stanzas were ultimately written, along with the title chorus.

Dorsey's song was widely popular during World War II, while hit recordings on the pop music charts were made well into the fifties. Singer Red Foley put "Peace in the Valley" on the country music charts in 1951, while Elvis Presley sang his own balladic version on national television during a 1956 guest appearance on the *Ed Sullivan Show*. Recordings by both artists, as well as by Tennessee Ernie Ford and Pat Boone, all sold more than a million records. Roy Rogers and Dale Evans even recorded a Western-inflected version. Like "Precious Lord, Take My Hand" before it, "Peace in the Valley" remains a favorite in both black and white churches. White gospel artists who have recorded "Peace in the Valley" include The Blackwood Brothers, The Statesmen, J. D. Sumner and The Stamps, and Bill Gaither. Dorsey believed the crossover success of his music was due to universal appeal:

> My business is to try to bring people to Christ instead of leaving them where they are. I write all my songs with a message. If there is no message, there is no need of having a song.... All the songs belong to God. I don't write for races, I don't write for colors, I write for God and all God's people, and I want them all to use it. And I want the blessing to go to everybody. All people are my people.... I try to lift their spirits and let them know that God still loves them. I want them to understand that God is still in business and he's still saving and he can give that power.[27]

Over his career, Dorsey shared this musical mission by writing more than 250 gospel songs (and through his music company, publishing more than four hundred) and founding, in 1933, the National Convention of Gospel Choirs and Choruses.[28] He remarried in 1941 and went on to serve as music director at Pilgrim Baptist Church until his retirement in the late 1970s. By then, the music world began to take note of his lasting contribution as the "father" of black gospel music. In 1979 he became the first African American inducted into the Nashville Songwriters Hall of Fame and, four years later, the documentary film *Say Amen, Somebody* brought Dorsey national recognition when it was released in theaters and then shown in 1986 on public television.[29] In 1993, at the age of ninety-three, Dorsey passed away.

Merrill Dunlop

The career of Merrill Dunlop is interwoven with the stories of Paul Rader and the Chicago Gospel Tabernacle, and of Torrey Johnson and Youth for Christ.[30] Yet his music also brought him into contact with nearly all the great evangelists and preachers of radio's golden age, while his songs became mainstays of evangelical popular music.

His grandfather was a prominent Methodist preacher in Ireland, while Dunlop's father immigrated to Chicago and for a time planned to enter the ministry. "But he decided that was not his calling," Dunlop said, "and he became associated with a woolens company in sales." The elder Dunlop met and married a woman who herself had emigrated from Canada, and the two were blessed with their only child in 1905. They named Merrill Dunlop after a Methodist bishop whom they greatly admired. "My mother was an organist and a teacher of piano," Dunlop recalled. "She had a lot of students, and I just had to learn music. My mother made me. I didn't have any choice in it." Failure to practice brought a spanking, he added, "but she loved me very dearly and wanted me to become a musician. So I was the usual young rebel in the early days when I was five, until I saw I had to do it." When Dunlop was eight years old his mother engaged the English concert organist, Frances Herrington, to be his teacher. Dunlop studied with Herrington up through his college years. At the age of twelve, however, Dunlop was introduced to the music that governed the rest of his life. His grandmother had told him, "Oh, Merrill, you ought to come down to the Moody Tabernacle and hear the music! They have a band and a big choir of two hundred voices and all kinds of music and somebody plays the piano."[31] Paul Rader was then the pastor of Moody Church, but Dunlop's grandmother mostly wanted him to come and hear the music.

> I just sat there kicking the shavings between the wood pine benches, waiting for the music to start. When the service started and the music started, I was just all ears. And then this great big man got up and began to preach with a big white handkerchief he waved around. His name was Paul Rader, but it didn't mean anything to me as a young boy. I didn't care too much about him. But little by little as I began to listen to him, the message of the Gospel began to hit me in the heart. I loved the music so much, I wanted to go back again. I said to my grandmother, "Oh, take me again!" And so Sunday after Sunday we went.[32]

Since Dunlop lived in suburban Oak Park and his grandmother in downtown Chicago, each week he would take the elevated train to her home on Saturdays and spend the night "with the anticipation of going the next day to Moody Tabernacle," he recalled. "We'd spend all day there, just listening to the music.... But I was thrilled with it. The messages of Paul Rader hit my heart and I got deeply under conviction." It was on such a Sunday, when Rader had delivered his message and "was asking people to walk down those aisles and go to the inquiry room," Dunlop remembered, "[that] I was deeply under conviction myself." Everyone around him was singing "Just As I Am" when a pleasant-looking young man with blond hair, one of Rader's personal workers, approached and put his arm around the twelve-year-old Dunlop. "Buddy, are you a Christian?" the young man inquired. Though feeling under great conviction, Dunlop was still undecided. Knowing it was not the truth, he stammered out, "Yes, I am."[33]

> I think he knew I immediately that I was lying to him. All he said was, "Buddy, I'm going to be praying for you." And boy, that really did it as far as I was concerned. I was so deeply under conviction when I went out of that tabernacle that night. And it wasn't long after that I personally accepted Christ. But that was the way it started. So Paul Rader was really my father in the Lord.[34]

Those days during World War I were an exciting time in Dunlop's life. In March 1918 Billy Sunday came to Chicago for a two-month campaign. Meetings were held in a cavernous temporary wooden tabernacle that seated sixteen thousand people. Dunlop was especially impressed by the two-thousand-voice choir and the songleading of Homer Roderheaver, who in later years became a dear friend. "And it was a thrill, just a thrill," Dunlop remembered, "to be there to hear Billy Sunday.... He was a very demonstrative preacher. Sometimes he'd even take a chair, waving it around to make a point. And I even saw him jump on the pulpit one time. And he spoke to the crowds and he had a great invitation and people would come down those aisles by the hundreds." About that time, Dunlop's family joined a new church in suburban Oak Park. "The church was meeting in a store building because it was a new venture," he explained. "Some of the people who were tired of denominational liberalism, which was creeping in, had started Madison Street Bible Church. And I was one of the boys in the Sunday school there." Dunlop had been so impressed by the music of Paul Rader and the Moody Church, "I learned the hymns and amplified them myself, and the people of Madison Street Bible Church liked it so well they asked me to become their church pianist."[35]

Dunlop vividly recalled his first songwriting effort while at Madison Street Bible Church. "I got the idea of writing a song early in my teens," he said. "I remember so proudly working that song out, so laboriously. And we even had a music plate made of it, the choir of the church did, and I was so proud as a young boy in my early teens then." When the church erected a new building in 1921, the congregation invited evangelist James Conant to conduct a special two-week campaign. His songleader was Homer Hammontree, a well-known evangelical songwriter, who quickly took note of the talented young man at the piano. Hammontree was so impressed that he went down to the Moody Church and urged the staff to hire Dunlop. "They called me on the phone and asked me to come down and play for the Moody Tabernacle," he recalled. Paul Rader had recently left the Church and his pianist, Lance Latham, had gone with him. "So they asked me to take his place and I became the pianist of the Moody Church in the big tabernacle, and I was about sixteen years of age."[36]

Later, Dunlop attended and graduated from the Moody Bible Insitute (a separate organization from Moody Church). Then in 1925 he was invited by Rader to join his music staff at the Chicago Gospel Tabernacle. What followed for Dunlop were seven years of fast-paced ministry under his dynamic mentor. Through the Tabernacle's extensive work in evangelism, radio and publishing, Dunlop enjoyed a growing reputation as a musician and songwriter. Until coming to the Chicago Gospel Tabernacle, Dunlop had not done much songwriting. But that soon changed. With a staff of eighteen musicians, he observed, "Music was featured a great deal under Paul Rader.... We had broadcasts on Sundays that went from ten in the morning until midnight. That was fourteen hours. We had to have much, much music. Then every morning we would have an hour on the Columbia network. Where would we get the music? A lot of it we had to write ourselves." Dunlop began to conceive of his music ministry in terms of both playing and songwriting, "and of course you learn by doing." From then on, and for the rest of his career, he continued to turn out hundreds of songs.[37]

The culmination of those early years was Dunlop's 1932 wedding, held in the Chicago Gospel Tabernacle. Shortly afterward, however, Rader left "the Tab" to personally assume its radio debts and prevent creditors from closing the ministry. Rader asked Clarence Erickson, a preacher from Indianapolis, to take over the work. But he would do it on one condition. Erickson came to Dunlop and said, "Merrill, I will only say yes to Paul Rader if you will agree to stay with me and we work together."[38] Dunlop prayed and believed God would have him remain at the Tabernacle, and in time he served there a total of twenty-five years. During the mid to late 1940s he also served as Torrey Johnson's pianist at the Youth for Christ rallies in Chicago and other cities. After leaving the Tabernacle he continued in full-time music ministry through 1977, traveling with evangelists Jimmie Johnson, John Haggai, Ford Philpot, and Ken Campbell. Afterward he entered semi-retirement, working with his old friend Torrey Johnson during the winter season at Florida's Bibletown Bible Conference Center.

Though Dunlop admitted he was influenced musically by the balladic and romantic melodies that characterized popular music in the twenties and thirties, he attributed the greatest influence to evangelical songwriter Robert Harkness. As a boy Dunlop would go through songbooks and hymnbooks, then pick out and learn the songs that appealed to him most. "The [writer's] name of the songs that were my favorites seem to have been the same, Robert Harkness," he recalled. "I think there was something unique about his melodies and about his harmonies. And I got so that I just looked for songs by Robert Harkness." In time, Dunlop developed his philosophy for the role of music in evangelism. There are three types of songs, he believed, including "songs of testimony, songs of praise, and any song that has to do with the redemptive work of Christ. And that is the hardest to find."[39] As he explained,

> Very few people seem to write about the finished work of Christ, what He's done, what His sacrifice really means. There is today so much written that is so light and frothy as far as its message is concerned.... Just because a person uses the word "God" in a song doesn't mean it's a sacred song [or] a gospel song. You've got to have some aspect of the gospel in it to be a gospel song—and that means the death, burial, and resurrection of Christ. So my feeling is that music in evangelism should

portray the very thing we're preaching [but] in another language, that is the language of music.[40]

Over his long career Dunlop published numerous volumes of songbooks featuring his work, and from the 1960 onward was published through the Singspiration company. Among his hundreds of compositions, today the most widely sung are "My Sins Are Blotted Out, I Know" (written in 1927 when a crossing on the ocean liner *Leviathan* brought to mind the prophecy of Micah 7:19, "Thou wilt cast all their sins into the depths of the sea"), "Opened for Me" (1936), "He Was Wounded for Our Transgressions" (1941), and "Only One Life" (1937). The latter is perhaps Dunlop's best-known work and, since his passing in 2002, stands as a testimony of the evangelical faith by which he lived his life: "Consecrated alone to Thy matchless glory, yielded fully to Thee."

Vep Ellis

Vesphew Benton Ellis was born March 11, 1917, in Oneonta, Alabama.[41] Understandly, it was the nickname "Vep" that stuck when he entered the ministry as a pastor, evangelist, and soloist. When he began writing songs in the early 1940s, his work quickly became a favorite for quartets of the day who eagerly awaited his latest compositions. An early hit was "Heaven's Joy Awaits" recorded by The Statesmen, who later scored with another Ellis song, "When I Got Saved." The Harmoneers helped put Ellis on the map as a gospel songwriter with "There Is a Change." Then in 1948 he enjoyed a breakthrough song with "I'm Free Again" that was recorded by nearly every gospel group of the time. From then on, hit songs flowed from his pen including "My God Can Do Anything," "Let Me Touch Him," "Over the Moon," "Heavenly Love," and "At the End of the Trail."

Ellis composed more than five hundred songs and hymns that were chiefly published through the Lillenas Publishing Company and the Tennessee Music and Printing Company. As a singer in his own right, he recorded numerous 78s and 45s, as well as five long-play albums, while self-publishing several songbooks of his own. Yet he considered his main vocation to be preaching and, for forty-nine years, served as a pastor in the Church of God. For six years he also ministered as music director and soloist for the Oral Roberts tent crusades. One of the most enduring songs written by Vep Ellis is the plaintive and prayerful "Do You Know My Jesus?" Still a favorite that is often included in many songbooks and hymnals, the chorus implores very simply, as Ellis himself did through a half century of preaching and evangelism, "Have you heard He loves you, and that He will abide till the end?"

Robert Harkness

The career of Robert Harkness spanned the Gilded Age to radio's golden age.[42] Born March 2, 1880, in Bendigo, Australia, his father was a local minister. In June 1902, when Harkness was twenty-two, evangelist Rueben Archer Torrey and songleader Charles Alexander held a meeting in Bendigo. Alexander chanced to hear Harkness play the piano and invited him to join Torrey's team. More importantly, Alexander won the young pianist to Christ. The two spoke long into the night at Alexander's hotel in Bendigo and, at last, Harkness was converted. For the next six years Harkness toured widely with Torrey and Alexander, and then traveled worldwide with evangelist J. Wilbur Chapman. Throughout his long career, he was recognized as one of the premier sacred music pianists in the world and toured across the United States. In his later years Harkness settled in England and gave solo piano performances throughout that country in a program he called "The Music of the Cross." A correspondence course written by Harkness, *Evangelistic Piano Playing*, was released by the Lillneas Publishing Company and was widely used by thousands of aspiring musicians. Over his lifetime, he composed or arranged more than two thousand hymns and gospel songs.

Chronologically and stylistically, Harkness's compositions range from his 1910 arrangement of "Our Great Savior"—still a staple of hymnbooks today—to the simple chorus, "Are We Downhearted?," a favorite in the Youth for Christ movement of the 1940s. Other songs composed by Robert Harkness include "In Jesus," "No Longer Lonely," "Why Should He Love Me So?," "Thine, Lord," "Only Believe and Live," "When I See My Savior Hanging on Calvary," "Hiding in the Shadow of the Rock," "Sometime, All Sorrow Will Be O'er," "Shadows," "No Burdens Yonder," "He Will Hold Me Fast," and "Such a Love." Harkness remained active in music ministry until his death, May 8, 1961, in London, England, at the age of eighty-one.

Phil Kerr

Music in Evangelism and Stories of Famous Christian Songs, authored in 1939 by Phil Kerr, is perhaps the best contemporary source for the practice of music in crusade evangelism and on evangelical radio during the era.[43] The philosophy behind Kerr's own music is explained on the flyleaf of his 1936 *Phil Kerr's Gospel Songs*: "Atheism is devoid of music, Heathenism has only a few dull notes, such as the thud of the tom-tom. Unbelievers favor jazz, which is composed of a series of conflicting sounds and discordant notes. Christianity alone reaches to the depths of the human soul. Only believers really have anything to sing about."[44]

Kerr was born in Los Angeles while his missionary parents were on furlough from an assignment in the Colorado mining camps and en route to a new work in Mexico. He showed an early gift for playing musical instruments, and then in 1923 obtained work as a radio announcer. Three years later, however, he dedicated himself to full-time Christian service. Over his career Kerr ministered as an evangelist, songwriter and publisher, and gave sacred piano concerts across the United States. Some of Kerr's better-known song compositions, which were extensively used on radio, include "I Love Thee, My Savior," "Melody Divine," "Over in Glory," and "In Love with the Lover of My Soul." In his travels, Kerr would often compose songs publicly during his meetings, and many of these were later published. One interesting song of this type, "Broadcasting for Jesus" (which Kerr composed publicly in Tampa, Florida, in 1931), captured the excitement many evangelicals felt in the early days of radio at "broadcasting the story of a Christ who came from glory."

Haldor Lillenas

Author and composer of more than four thousand hymns and gospel songs, Haldor Lillenas was born November 19, 1885, on the Island of Stord in the fjord region of Bergen, Norway. As a young child he immigrated with his parents to the United States, where for two years the family worked a farm in South Dakota before settling in Astoria, Oregon. His parents were devout Christians and, at the age fifteen, Lillenas was confirmed in the Lutheran church. "Shortly after," he recalled, "my mother passed away and the home was broken up. Not having been born again, my determination to keep my confirmation vows failed and I gave up my profession of religion."[45] Lillenas decided on a career in chemistry. But in 1906 at the age of twenty, he was converted at an evangelistic service conducted by the Peniel Mission of Portland, Oregon. Soon he was writing gospel songs and felt called of God to preach the gospel. While studying at Deets Pacific College in Los Angeles, in 1909 he met and year later married his wife Bertha Mae.

Ordained in the Nazarene church, from 1910 to 1914 Lillenas pastored several small congregations in California. While serving in Pomona in 1913 his health failed and, as he later remembered, "after careful examination and diagnosis, the young doctor advised us that very likely I would not live more than six months at the most. This was indeed unwelcome news. I was young and loved my work. I had a gifted and attractive wife, and a lovely baby girl. Life seemed good to me. I had just begun to live!" A few days later, Lillenas was awakened early one morning by the sound of mockingbirds loudly singing in the orange grove adjoining the church parsonage. Seeing the sunrise over the colorful Mojave Desert, he grabbed a pencil and paper and started to write a poem. The song, "Some Golden Daybreak," was the result. Lillenas wrote confidently that "some golden daybreak I shall reach my home, sweet home," fully expecting that day might be soon. As it happened, however, he resigned his pastorate and returned to Oregon for rest. In time, and against all expectation, he regained his health and a few months later resumed his pastorate in Pomona. Strangely, by then the young doctor who had given Lillenas six months to live had himself passed away.[46]

In 1914, Lillenas and his wife felt called to leave pastoral ministry and enter full-time evangelistic work. Eventually they built their first home, a small three-room bungalow in Olivet, Illinois. "Upon its completion," Lillenas later recounted, "we had scarcely any money left to furnish the little home. Having no piano at the time, and needing an instrument of some kind, I managed to find, at one of the neighbor's home, a little wheezy organ which I purchased for $5.00. With the aid of this instrument, a number of my songs were written which are now popular," including his best known work, "Wonderful Grace of Jesus."[47] Yet as Lillenas remembered of his early songwriting efforts, "Several years passed without receiving any encouragement from anyone, but eventually the song, 'He Set Me Free,' became popular."[48] Still, after entering evangelistic work in 1914, his songwriting output flourished as everyday incidents in his travels provided inspiration for scores of songs. For example, at a 1914 campaign in Pueblo, Colorado, Lillenas wrote "Wonderful Peace" after hearing the evangelist preach his closing message on the peace of God.[49] A year later at a revival meeting in Denver, he composed "I Know a Name" after a local bank refused to cash his check until it was endorsed by a sympathetic local businessman.[50] Then in 1917 while holding meetings in Joplin, Missouri, Lillenas was practicing on an old upright piano when he noticed the white ivory keys bathed in the slanting red light of a stained glass window. Inspired, he wrote the song, "Under the Atoning Blood."[51]

Lillenas reentered the pastorate in 1916, serving the next three years at the Church of the Nazarene in Auburn, Illinois. There at his parsonage, inspecting his flower garden after a rain shower, he was inspired to write "The Peace That Jesus Gives."[52] Yet he continued to travel for meetings and supplied songs to some of the day's leading evangelists, notably Charles Alexander and Homer Hammontree. In 1922 Lillenas accepted a call to pastor in Redlands, California, then two years later returned to the Midwest as pastor of the First Church of the Nazarene in Indianapolis. That same year, 1924, Lillenas founded the Lillenas Music Company in Indianapolis. It was subsequently purchased in 1930 by the Nazarene Publishing Company of Kansas City, where Lillenas served for the next twenty years as music editor. His songs—among them, "The Bible Stands Like a Rock Undaunted," "It is Glory Just to Walk with Him," "Jesus Has Lifted Me," "My Wonderful Lord," and "The Peace That Jesus Gives"—were used extensively in churches, evangelistic work, and on the radio.

The connection between music and radio is suggested by Lillenas' relationship with Paul Rader and the Chicago Gospel Tabernacle. "Wonderful Grace of Jesus," for example, was first introduced in print—for which Lillenas was paid five dollars—in the *Tabernacle Choir Book* released in 1922. (He often lamented that it was sung too fast by most congregations: "A song should be performed in such a fashion that the words can be comfortably pronounced without undue haste."[53]) Meanwhile, his popular invitation song, "Come Just as You Are," was inspired after hearing a 1927 sermon by Rader in which he closed his message with those words.[54]

Lillenas' wife Bertha Mae was a talented songwriter in her own right. Born March 3, 1889, in Hansen, Kentucky, her father went on to become a general superintendent in the Church of the Nazarene. To assist in her husband's pastoral and evangelistic work, she deferred her own songwriting efforts until their children were grown and she herself experienced ill health that prevented her from traveling. Her compositions include "He Will Not Forget," "Leave Your Burden at the Place of Prayer," "Jesus Is Always There," and "Saved by the Blood." They suggest how her gifts might have developed, had she not died April 13, 1945. The last years that Haldor and Bertha Mae Lillenas spent together are reflected in his 1938 song, "My Wonderful Lord." Lillenas was driving down Paseo Boulevard in Kansas City on his way to the office one morning:

> It was a gray day, chilly, with some fog and smoke in the air. Both of our children had married and left home. My wife was very ill and it was with a heavy heart that I had left home that morning. I recalled brighter days, when we were busy in our much-loved pastorates and when we had the children at home. Now I was busy writing songs, compiling and editing books, doing what I felt God had called me to do. But sometimes I wondered how many of them would be sung. Suddenly as I drove along the avenue, it seemed that Someone quietly opened the car door and sat down beside me. I could feel the warmth of His sacred presence and I began to sing quietly: "My wonderful Lord, my wonderful Lord, by angels and seraphs in heaven adored...."[55]

Haldor Lillenas passed away August 18, 1959, at the age of seventy-three. Over his long career he had pastored small churches in rural America prior to the Great War, sang with and wrote music for some of the great evangelists of the prewar era, and lived to see his work spread by through the mass communication of radio and publishing.

Harry Dixon Loes

Though born October 20, 1892, in Kalamazoo, Michigan, Harry Dixon Loes spent his childhood in Chicago—where his father more than once told the boy, "Harry, you are wasting your time trying to write songs."[56] As a child Loes would try out new melodies on the family piano and, as the years went by, never gave up his desire to write music. After a brief time in the employ of the Marshall Field department store, Loes enrolled in Moody Bible Institute and graduated in 1915. That same year he published "All Things in Jesus I Find" which inspired a fellow Chicagoan, Avis Christiansen, to become a songwriter. Later, the two collaborated on many songs including two still-beloved hymns, "Blessed Redeemer" and "Love Found a Way." Of the latter, Loes remembered,

> Many of my ideas for songs came from hearing Paul Rader preach. One Sunday night [in 1915] I head him preach in the old Moody Church in Chicago on John 3:16. He emphasized the fact that man was steeped in sin, and that God had endeavored to find some way to bring man back to Himself, and that "love found a Way" and that "that Way was God's only Son, willing to die on Calvary to bring men back into fellowship with the Father." The phrase, "love found a Way," struck me immediately as a good suggestion for a song. I jotted the pitches on a piece of paper, and a few lyric suggestions for the chorus. Later the complete music, with the lyric suggestions, was sent to Mrs. Avis Burgeson Christiansen, in Chicago. She wrote the stanzas and completed the chorus.[57]

Similarly, "Blessed Redeemer" was inspired when Loes heard a sermon with the same title, composed a melody, and sent it to Christiansen to write a text. Both songs were published in 1921. By then Loes had broadened his musical training by studying at the American Conservatory, the Metropolitan School of Music, and the Chicago Musical College, and received a bachelor of music degree from the Branden Institute of Music in Virginia. From 1927 to 1939 Loes served as music and education director of two Oklahoma churches, First Baptist of Okmulgee and First Baptist of Muskogee. During that time he was also involved in evangelistic work, and in 1939 joined the music faculty of Moody Bible Institute where he taught harmony, voice, and directing. There he joined a Chicago circle of evangelical popular musicians that gravitated around Moody Bible Institute and its radio station WMBI, as well as such nearby Wheaton College and Winona Lake Bible Conference. One of his students in the days just after World War II, John W. Peterson, remembers his professor as one of the "source[s] of my greatest encouragement in my early songwriting."

> Loes wrote scores of songs, and out of that vast body of material were a few songs of enduring quality. He was a wonderful fellow who loved the gospel music field. I studied harmony and composition with Mr. Loes, and he became my friend, collaborator, and champion as well as my teacher. He often gave me tips on where to send my songs and encouraged people in the publishing business to take a chance on me.[58]

Before his passing in 1965, Loes penned some two thousand hymns and gospel songs, among them "Everybody Ought to Love Jesus," "All That I Want Is in

Jesus," and "For Me." Yet the melody inspired by a chance phrase in a Paul Rader sermon, "Love Found a Way," remains among his most enduring.

Audrey Mieir

From 1937 to 1945 Audrey Mieir was on the air daily as staff pianist for the Los Angeles–based broadcast ministries of the International Church of the Foursquare Gospel. The denomination, founded by evangelist Aimee Semple McPherson, enjoyed a wide radio following in southern California and beyond. So Mieir, who was ordained into the Foursquare ministry in 1937, was also active in personal appearances. Yet her work as a songwriter did not emerge until later, not until the fifties, in the twilight years of radio's golden age.

Born May 12, 1916, in Leechburg, Pennsylvania, Mieir ultimately headed west and enrolled in the L.I.F.E. Bible College of Los Angeles. There at the Foursquare school, she met and in 1936 married Charles Mieir. Following her ordination, she ministered on the radio for eight years, then in the years 1946–58 organized a number of professional choirs for evangelistic travel and recordings. Among these was the Phil Kerr Singers, in which she worked in the early fifties with gospel songwriter Phil Kerr. Though she had occasionally tried her hand at songwriting since her teenage years, by the mid to late 1950s Mieir's choral work prompted her to develop her writing gifts. Her work came to the attention of Manna Music in Los Angeles, whose staff writer Tim Spencer became a mentor. In the fifties, gospel choruses were popular and Mieier's writing fit the style well. Two of her best-known efforts from this period of her career are "I'll Never Be Lonely" (1957) and "When You Pray" (1959).

In 1959 Mieir served as director of the Mieir Choir Clinic in Hollywood, then in 1960 became vice president of the Mieir Music Foundation, also of Hollywood. She died in 1996 after a long life and distinguished career. Though Mieir wrote scores of gospel songs, her reputation today rests chiefly on her most enduring work, "His Name Is Wonderful," published in 1959 by Manna Music. Al Smith met Mieir in the fifties when she was still directing the Phil Kerr Singers and recalled, "I'll never forget the inspiration of this young lady and so it was no surprise to me, in later years, that the songs written by Audrey would become top favorites in the Gospel field and particularly 'His Name Is Wonderful.'"[59] Later, Smith reported Mieir's account of how the song was composed.

> Fragrant pine boughs perfumed the air in our [brother-in-law's] little Bethel Union Church in Duarte, California.... Little children sat impatiently anticipating the re-creation of the old, old story—their eyes sparkling, reflecting Christmas tree lights,

> not wanting to miss anything including the Christmas play.... The curtain opened ... [on] the humble manger scene. Mary was a shy teenager, cheeks flushed with excitement, holding someone's baby doll close in her arms. A young Joseph hovered over her, his smooth face discreetly hidden in old drapery. A beautiful angel glittered and shone, out-brillianced only by the flashing smile for mom and dad in aisle two. Her halo had slipped precariously to one side. Eleven-year-old shepherds shuffled down the aisle with unmistakable reticence, their jeans peeking out form under dad's old robe. The procession halted and the choir sang, "Sleep in heavenly peace." Dr. Luther Mieir's voice filled the small church. "His name is wonderful," he said with his hands lifted heavenward. And I—I heard the familiar rustling of angel wings. I did not know at that strangely moving moment that a once-in-a-lifetime experience was about to happen. As I grabbed my old Bible and wrote in it, more than with any other of my songs, I felt as if I were only a channel, as if I were not otherwise involved.[60]

For the evening service, Mieir taught her new song to a chorus of young people who sang it for the first time. Yet, as is the case with many popular evangelical songs, the composer left other accounts that differ somewhat in detail. In one account, her brother-in-law quotes rather than paraphrases Isaiah 9:6, "His name shall be called Wonderful." In another account, Mieir hears her brother-in-law's exclamation and searches the concordance in the back of her Bible for the names given to Jesus in the scriptures.[61] Further, the version of "His Name Is Wonderful" sung by the youth group at that Christmas evening service was not the final published version, so that Mieir in another account said her search for the names of Christ took place sometime later.

> God blessed "His Name Is Wonderful" and it seemed to capture people's hearts. But one day I met [music publisher] Tim Spencer who said to me, "Audrey, it's a good song, but there isn't enough of it. Maybe you could write a bridge for it." (At that time I didn't know a bridge was also a musical term.) He explained the word to me and showed me how I could extend the song and enlarge the blessing of its message. I was just on my way to lunch. After I had ordered my hamburger, I began to think of Tim's suggestion. And so I opened my Bible there in the booth to the concordance and began to run my finger down the list of names given to Jesus in the Scripture. I wrote them down on my napkin. After I had returned to the office, I went to the piano and finished the song.[62]

In the years following its publication, Mieir had opportunity to personally hear "His Name Is Wonderful" sung at meetings in Sweden, Korea, the Philippines, Hong Kong, and in Jerusalem's Garden of Gethsemane. Whatever the details of its writing, Mieir concluded, "The song will outlive the chubby hand chosen to write a few black notes on the five lines and four spaces of the music score, but will never outlive the original composer—God the Father—who glories in His only begotten Son's name and rejoices in our praise of Him, for His name is truly wonderful!"[63]

George Schuler

George Schuler and his colleague Harry Dixon Loes were the twin towers of the Moody Bible Institute music department during the golden age of radio. Al Smith speaks of his former instructor Schuler as a "great influence on my early Christian life" during his student days at Moody in the late thirties.[64] A decade later John W. Peterson studied under Schuler and in his memoirs recalled that

> George Schuler was a tall, handsome man with a flowing mane of white hair. He was dignified, a wonderful organist, and highly sophisticated, fully familiar with the classics as well as with gospel music—the personification of what I thought a songwriter should be. He tried to help me get my compositions published and was responsible for one of my songs being bought by Haldor Lillenas. It was my first publication while at Moody, a song called "Something That He Cannot See."[65]

If Schuler was the personification of a gospel songwriter, he himself had examples to follow. Born April 18, 1882, in New York City, he went on to study under the well-known gospel songwriters Daniel B. Towner, Charles H. Gabriel, and Edwin O. Excell. Yet another pupil of Schuler's, Bert Wilhoit who studied under him at the annual Winona Lake School of Sacred Music, recalled another side of the dignified professor. "In his classroom instruction," Wilhoit remembered, "he had the knack of imitating the students at the keyboard, motivating them to feel more relaxed in their performance."[66] Likewise, Smith remembers how Schuler could regularly be found "doodling" at the piano and in 1935 composed his one of most poular songs, "Overshadowed," during such a reverie.

> One day, as George Schuler was improvising at the piano the thought of God's nearness began to impress itself upon him in a new and deeper way. In his mind's eye he began to relive many of the experiences of the past. Through them he could not help but see the guiding hand of God. At the moment he could almost feel the presence of God with the same protecting power he had experienced all through life. During all of this retrospection he kept on "doodling" at the piano as he later told me. Soon a distinct melody began to take form and with it the words which said, "I'm overshadowed by His mighty love, love eternal, changeless, pure. I'm overshadowed by His mighty love."[67]

In 1914 Schuler joined the music faculty at Moody Bible Institute, his alma mater, and served there forty years teaching piano, organ, notation, and conducting. In those years he was a prolific writer of such songs as "Overshadowed" and "O, What a Day!" Five collections of his song compositions were published over his lifetime, while he also authored the widely used textbooks *Gospel Song and Hymn Tune Composition, Evangelistic Piano Playing, The Accompanist's Manual,* and *Choral Directing.* Yet as often happens, out of this large body of work just one song remains today in widespread use. Ironically (but not untypically) its writing was unplanned and seemingly accidental. "Make Me a Blessing" was first published in 1924 and is a staple in hymnbooks and songbooks today. The words were written around 1909 and Schuler, who later composed the music, explained that

> "Make Me A Blessing" was written in my student days; the poem by a fellow student, Ira B. Wilson. Oddly enough, neither of us can recall how we came to write the song. To this day [Wilson] claims to have had no part in authoring the work, but I know he wrote it. When the song was in manuscript form it was submitted to a publisher. It was rejected as "being unsuited for our need." I had plates made and one thousand copies printed, costing me a sum I could ill afford at the time. George Dibble, well known as an evangelist in those days, introduced the number at an International Sunday School Convention at Cleveland, Ohio. Here it became a great favorite, and it is needless to say that within a short time I received many offers for the song.[68]

For his part, Ira Wilson steadfastly maintained his ignorance of having written the words. In his later career Wilson almost exclusively wrote music rather than words as a composer, arranger, and editor for the Lorenz Publishing Company of Dayton, Ohio. Phil Kerr, in his 1939 book of song stories, told of a visit to Wilson's home in which Kerr and his wife sat at the piano and sang "Make Me a Blessing." Wilson then "listened politely, but it was evident he knew not what we were singing. When we remarked that *he* had written the song, his eyes widened in amazement. Actually, he had forgotten that the oft-used young people's song had come from his pen."[69]

After retiring from Moody Bible Institute, Schuler served for a time on the editorial staff of The Rodeheaver Company and then spent his last years in Florida, and passed away October 30, 1973.

Oswald Smith

Oswald Smith was, and likely remains, Canada's most prolific writer of hymns and gospel songs.[70] Chronicling his life, however, presents a challenge—not from any scarcity of detail but because of its abundance. The twelve hundred hymn and song texts Smith wrote is a large body of work by any standard and many remain in wide use today. These include "Joy in Serving Jesus," "Saved," "Then Jesus Came," "Deeper and Deeper," "God Understands," and "The Song of the Soul Set Free." Yet songwriting was only a small part of his ministry. For Smith was, in his day, internationally prominent as a pastor, evangelist, conference speaker, missionary statesmen, Bible college administrator, Christian author, magazine publisher, and radio broadcaster. His books alone number thirty-five volumes, not including three autobiographies he wrote about his life and a book of his own collected hymn stories.

Born November 8, 1889, in a farmhouse on the outskirts of Odessa, Ontario, Smith was the eldest of ten children. Because his father was a telegraph operator for the Canadian Pacific Railroad, the family moved several times to various railway stations until settling in Embro when Smith was five. As a youth he remembered being interested in religion but did not convert to Christ until the age of sixteen. That year, the famous team of evangelist Reuben Archer Torrey and songleader Charles Alexander conducted a campaign in Toronto. Caught up in the excitement, Smith took the train to the meetings and converted on January 28, 1906.

When he was seventeen, Smith left home to work as an office boy for eight dollars a week at the National Cash Register Company in Toronto. He enrolled in evening classes twice a week at Toronto Bible College and participated in outreaches to the central city prison and several local rescue missions. In fact, at the end of his first college term Smith applied to the Presbyterian mission board. He was turned down as too young and inexperienced. Undaunted, he was accepted by the Upper Canada Bible Society to sell Bibles during the summer of 1908 in the Muskoka region of Ontario. Often that summer Smith was refused food and lodging, and once had to sleep outdoors in a barley field. But a pastor took him in and gave Smith his first opportunity to preach. From that time forward, Smith knew this was his life's work. That fall he was sent by the Bible Society to British Columbia where he ministered among the Native American tribes. A year later he continued his theological education, graduating from Toronto Bible College in 1912 and Chicago's McCormick Theological Seminary—where served in student pastorates—in 1915. Chicago made a deep impression on Smith, especially the services at the Moody Church where Daniel Towner, the legendary gospel songwriter, was choir director. It was Towner who first helped Smith develop his own writing gifts.

> Dr. Towner had already written many famous hymns and, when I began to write gospel songs in the year 1913, I immediately sent them to him. He accepted them without a moment's hesitation and wrote music for a great many of them, most of which were immediately published. It was a great joy to go to Dr. Towner's office in the Moody Bible Institute, where he held the position of Director of Music, and watch him as he played the organ and worked on hymns. Thus I commenced hymn writing with one of the great composers of the day for which I will always be thankful.[71]

Nearly forty years later Smith still recalled, "Never will I forget the thrill that was mine, when I saw the first printed copies of two of my hymns. It was 1914 when I was twenty-four. The music was by Dr. D.B. Towner, and he it was who sent them to me. My whole being was electrified as I gazed at them.

The ecstasy of that moment will never be erased." Nevertheless, he admitted that "in those early years only a few of my hymns ever really saw the light of day. I wrote scores, but for years it was a struggle with many discouraging experiences. True, my hymn poems were accepted by various composers, but for some reason they were seldom used." Both Towner and a former associate of Dwight L. Moody, the noted songwriter George C. Stebbins, encouraged Smith. And Charles Alexander published some of Smith's work for his evangelistic campaigns. But when Towner died in 1919 and Alexander in 1920, "after that for years I did little or nothing and it looked as though my hymn writing was at an end," said Smith.[72] By then he had written more than two hundred hymn poems and in the thirties and forties some became popular. These included "The Finest of the Wheat" and "The Savior Can Solve Every Problem" (1913); "Deeper and Deeper" and "Jesus Only" (1914); "Alone with Thee," "Christ Is Coming Back Again," "Surrender," and "Have I Grieved Thy Holy Spirit?" (1915); "A Revival Hymn" (1916); and "Saved!" (1917).

Ordained in 1915, Smith accepted a call as associate pastor of Dale Presbyterian Church in Toronto. A year later, in 1916, he and his wife Daisy were married. Soon afterward, with the fighting at its height in the First World War, the senior pastor was called into active military duty and Smith was placed in charge of the church. The majority of the congregation, however, were traditionalists and did not appreciate Smith's evangelistic fervor. So in October 1918 he resigned. Two months later, in January 1919, the Chicago evangelist Paul Rader and his songleader Arthur McKee arrived in Toronto for a one-week campaign. As Smith later remembered,

> I had just resigned from Dale Presbyterian Church. I tried to usher, but was turned down. I endeavored to do personal work, but was ignored. Then I started selling hymnbooks in the aisles, praying and hoping that God would use me again. Suddenly one night, Mr. McKee announced that they were going to sing a brand new hymn called "Saved," which had been included in the new songbook they were using. My heart was in my mouth. Pointing down to where I was selling hymnbooks, he said, "That young man down there wrote this hymn!" I turned my back and went on selling books. Then they sang it, 3,400 voices, sang it until it seemed as though they would lift the roof. Mr. McKee led it as only he could. I was now hearing it introduced for the first time. I was often to hear it in after years. Oh, how it stirred me! ... Now, as I was out of everything, I was fearfully discouraged, but that night God spoke to me again and I was inspired and elated. God, I knew, was not going to put me on the shelf.[73]

At the Rader crusade Smith learned of a missionary organization, the Shantymen's Christian Association, which ministered to lumberjacks in the remote camps of the north. The director spoke to Smith of the need to open up the work in British Columbia, where Smith had once traveled for the Bible Society. Over the spring and summer of 1919 he preached among the lumbermen and many were converted. Yet he felt God calling him back to Toronto. On faith he rented an auditorium and conducted a three-month campaign. In time, Smith learned of an opportunity to launch a work in Toronto for the Christian and Missionary Alliance (CMA), of which Paul Rader was president. Thus in January 1921 he was installed as pastor of the Alliance Tabernacle. A year later a permanent building was erected and the dedication service was preached by Rader himself, who became a mentor to the young Smith.

Like Rader's Chicago Gospel Tabernacle, the Alliance Tabernacle was not a church but a citywide center for evangelism. Meetings were held nightly on a continuing basis, while other programs ranging from Bible studies to book publishing were carried on. Smith led the new effort to great success and, after five years, left in 1926 to become CMA superintendent for eastern Canada. In 1927 Smith was appointed pastor of the Los Angeles Gospel Tabernacle. But his heart was still in Toronto. By then, Paul Rader had left the CMA to start his own organization, Christian World Wide Couriers. So in 1928 Smith joined forces with Rader to establish the Cosmopolitan Tabernacle in Toronto, later to be renamed in 1930 and become famous as The People's Church. The church became Smith's base of operations for the rest of his long life. Before he died in 1986 at the age of ninety-six, the People's Church was supporting three hundred fifty missionaries worldwide and he himself had held campaigns in sixty-six countries. As the work flourished in the late 1920s and early 1930s, Smith once again took up his pen and started to write hymns and gospel songs. In 1930 he met a man who would become his musical alter ego for the next twenty-seven years.

> Then one day, in the Churchill Tabernacle, Buffalo [New York], the year I launched the People's Church, when I was forty, I met the world's greatest living composer of gospel music, B.D. Ackley. Again I began to write. Hymn after hymn I sent him, and the music he wrote so fitted the words that they were in immediate demand. They were brought out by the Rodeheaver Company [of which Ackley was music editor].[74]

Until Ackley's death in 1958, the two men collaborated on more than one hundred songs. The first joint effort was "Joy in Serving Jesus," published in 1931 and still a favorite in hymnbooks today. In the thirties and forties the duo's songs were widely popular in songbooks and on the radio, among them "The Savior Can Solve Every Problem" (1932), "Satisfied with Thee" (1932), "A Revival Hymn" (1933), "Have I Grieved the Holy Spirit?" (1933), "Happy Days Will Come Again" (1934), "Where Dreams Come True" (1935), "His Love Is All My Plea" (1936), "The Breaking of the Day" (1936), "God Understands" (1937), "When the Autumn Leaves Have Turned to Gold" (1937), "Let King Jesus Reign" (1937), "The Dawning of the Morning" (1938), "God Is in the Shadows" (1938), "God Is Waiting in the Silence" (1939), "Waiting on

Thee" (1939), "The Broken Threads of Life" (1939), "The Need of the World Is Jesus" (1939), "Deeper and Deeper" (1942), "Surrender" (1942), "Be Thou Near" (1944), "I Will Trust" (1945), "Beyond the Shadows" (1946), "The Finest of the Wheat" (1946), "Forgive Me for Forgetting" (1949), and "My Heart's Desire" (1949). Smith attributed the success of their collaboration to the fact that "Hymns, like people, have to be well married to really live. To B.D. Ackley I owe a debt of gratitude that I will never be able to repay, for he has such a gift of melody that the music fits the words as though the two had been born together."[75] While Ackley composed the music, Smith had his own method for writing the words. "Poets, they say, are born, not made," Smith advised aspiring gospel songwriters. "Well, perhaps so."

> Be that as it may, the gift, I know, has to be developed. When I was in my early twenties I purchased volumes of poetry and read the poems aloud so as to get what is called "rhythm" into my soul. Such works as Milton's "Paradise Lost" and Dante's "Inferno" I read line by line aloud. Tennyson, Browning, Byron, Bryant, Longfellow, Hood, Whittier, Shakespeare, and a whole shelf of others, I literally devoured. These volumes I still have, and they are marked throughout.[76]

Before his passing on January 25, 1986, Smith preached more than twelve thousand sermons, wrote 35 books translated into 128 languages, and published some twelve hundred poems, of which more than a hundred were set to music.[77] As the titles of his songs suggest, noted music historian Kevin Kee, "Smith's songs turned inward, away from the concerns of day-to-day life. Often a stanza dwelling on the sorrow of feeling separated from God was followed by a celebration of the glory and happiness of life in Christ."[78] This spirit is exemplified in Smith's three most popular works, "The Song of the Soul Set Free" (1933, with A.H. Ackley), "The Glory of His Presence" (1935, with B.D. Ackley), and "Then Jesus Came" (1940, with Homer Rodeheaver). Yet the introspective lyricist was an innnovate entrepreneur. As Kee recounted, Smith drew "on all the media resources in his environment [and] succeeded by creating slide shows, movies, radio, magazines, and concerts that presented the gospel in an entertaining format." Services at the People's Church "appeal[ed] to those who could be drawn to a musical extravaganza" as Smith "adjusted his music so that it reflected the style of the 'big band era,' and watched the number of men and women at his services increase."[79] By the thirties, a hundred-voice choir was backed by a forty-piece orchestra that not only performed at Sunday morning and evening services, but also gave a one-hour Sunday afternoon pre-service concert. Then after the evening service, Smith and his musical team broadcast a "religious musical variety show, heavy on entertaining renditions of gospel songs" that was aired coast-to-coast on nearly fifty Canadian stations.[80]

Smith was unafraid to use big band, jazz, and even ragtime renditions on his broadcasts, and often crossed the color line by featuring African American gospel quartets. Indeed, he later confessed, "One of the great surprises in my life was to get into the cowboy world."[81] After preaching a series of meetings—including one in the home of Stuart Hamblen—in Hollywood to a group of entertainers, cowboy movie actor and country music singer Redd Harper set several of Smith's poems to music including "I'm Singing for My Lord" (1952) and "Come with Your Heartache" (1955). Smith's lyrics enjoyed crossover success because, as he explained, "I have never written in a mechanical way just for the sake of writing. As a rule I wait until I am passing through some great crisis, and then I cannot help writing. And because they have born out of personal experience, they appeal to others." Such an experience led to the writing in 1914 of his personal favorite, "Alone with Thee," one of the few songs for which he also composed the music. Smith claimed that his poems provided "a glimpse into the spiritual struggles and mental experiences through which I have passed."[82] The lyrics to "Alone with Thee" recalled to his mind "the sob of the ocean on some lonely shore ... the plaintive cry of the sea bird ... the moaning of the pines ... [until] disappointment gives way to realization, despair to hope, separation and heartbreak to reunion and fellowship, for Christ comes and fills the aching void."[83] In that spirit, his favorite composition testified to his relationship with Jesus: "My burdens all forgotten, when far away I soar alone with Thee."

N.B. Vandall

One evening in 1934, N.B. Vandall was reading the newspaper at home when his wife asked him to call their four boys to supper.[84] Laying aside his paper, Vandall headed toward the front door. Through the door he could hear the sound of children screaming and crying in the yard outside. He rushed down the front porch steps as his son Ted rushed hysterically to meet him.

"What's wrong, son? Here's Daddy. You're not hurt, are you? Come on, now, what's wrong?"

"Oh, Daddy! I'm all right," Ted sobbed, "but it's Paul!"

"Calm down now, son. What's it all about?"

With growing alarm, Vandall heard the story. His son Paul had been playing close to the curb when a car came careening down the street, out of control. The boy was hit and dragged almost the length of the street. "Oh, Daddy," Ted cried, "they have taken him away and I don't know where he is!" Vandall ran to the accident scene, confirmed the account with a neighbor who witnessed the tragedy, and found his unconscious son at a nearby doctor's office. Though an ambulance had been called, the doctor feared it was too late. Neither did the hospital hold out much hope when his son arrived with a brain concussion, fractured skull, broken leg and collar bone, dislocated shoulder, and the scalp missing from the left side of his head. "The boy is badly hurt," the surgeon gently but candidly told Vandall. "We will do the best we can, but do not hope for too much." To make matters worse, Paul had a heart condition and might not withstand the needed operation. His heart could stop at any time, the doctor warned, and so the surgery must be done without anesthesia. As a World War I veteran, Vandall had seen horrible injuries and deaths before. Now he quietly asked to remain in the emergency room, to hold his son's hand and pray, while the surgeon did his work. The doctor agreed and, through an hour and fifteen minutes of surgery, Vandall stayed at his son's side.

When the surgeon was done and Paul transferred to a hospital bed, Vandall returned home to reassure his wife and other three sons—though he himself felt no assurance that Paul would recover. "I fell on my knees and tried to pray," Vandall recalled, but "the words would not come. I remember saying only, 'Oh, God!'" Yet even at that simple prayer, Vandall felt God's presence. "It seemed to me that Jesus knelt by my side and I could feel His arms around me as He said, 'Never mind, my child. Your home will be visited with tribulation and sorrow but, in the afterwards to come, these things shall not be. Your home is in heaven, where tears shall be wiped away.'" Despite everything, Vandall felt at peace and "for the time, at least, I forgot my little boy lying at death's door and, brushing aside my tears, made my way to the piano." There the melody and words of a song came flooding into his mind: "After the toil and the heat of the day, after my troubles are past...." Soon Vandall completed the song and, not knowing if his son Paul would live or die, entitled it "After" and finished with the words, "On His beautiful throne He will welcome me home—after the day is through." Whatever might happen, Vandall and his family felt assured that God would see them through the trial. Unexpectedly, in time Paul did recover from the accident, though with his nerves and eyesight impaired. Yet from the time "After" was published in 1934, it became an immediate favorite in churches and on the radio.

Born December 28, 1896, in Creston, West Virginia, Vandall was "born again" in 1920 at a Methodist campmeeting in Sebring, Ohio. That was big change for a young man who had been without any Christian influence since his mother died when he was a boy. Later, after trying various jobs, he found work as a singer in cabarets and theaters. After serving in the Marines during World War I, he settled down as a businessman in Akron, Ohio. His wife, however, was an evangelical believer and urged Vandall to convert to Christ. Upon his conversion, he soon entered full-time evangelism through singing, preaching, broadcasting, and songwriting. During those early years of his ministry, Vandall encountered financial trials and other obstacles that caused him to question his vocation. Tempted to forsake his evangelistic work and return to the business world, Vandall strove to keep an eternal perspective. A song came to his lips and the words were soon written: "I see the light of that city so bright, my home, sweet home."

Vandall's song, "My Home, Sweet Home," was heard by Haldor Lillenas one day in 1926. The well-known songwriter and music publisher was then pastoring the First Church of the Nazarene in Indianapolis. "We conducted a revival campaign in which a young man with a lovely tenor voice was the soloist. That singer was N.B. Vandall," Lillenas remembered.[85] He was so struck by the song that he published it that same year in *Lillenas' Solos and Duets No. 1*. The release helped bring Vandall to the attention of the evangelical public and opened further doors. In the years that followed he wrote such songs as "I Know He Can Save Me Too," "Just One Glimpse," "He's the One I Love," and a perennial favorite that is likely Vandall's most widely used song today, "My Sins Are Gone." Ironically, the bright and peppy "My Sins Are Gone" was published in 1934, the same year that "After" appeared. The contrast with "After" suggests Vandall's range as a composer. The first verse declares, "You ask me why I'm happy, so I'll just tell you why, because my sins are gone." The remaining stanzas go on to say the devil has departed, temptations and doubts are dispelled, and life is happy and filled with music. Why? The believer's sins are gone, placed "underneath the blood of the Cross of Calvary" and thus into "the sea of God's forgetfulness." Until his death on August 24, 1970, Vandall held to the conviction, "That's good enough for me, praise God, my sins are gone!"

Charles Weigle

Charles Weigle had just come home from evangelistic campaign when he found a note from his wife.[86] "Charlie, I've been a fool," she wrote. "I've done without things long enough. From here on out, I'm getting all I can of what the world owes me. I know you'll continue to be a fool for Jesus, but for me—it's goodbye!" The two had been married for many years and, Weigle admitted, the life of an itinerant evangelist often required doing without. "To some it may have seemed a life of sacrifice," he believed, "but to me the reward of seeing souls saved was worth more than money. God had given me a definite call. I was obeying Him and He promised to keep me and supply all my needs."[87]

Born November 20, 1871, in Lafayette, Indiana, and converted at age twelve, Weigle studied at the Cincinnati Conservatory of Music and went on to become an evangelistic singer. Later God called him also to preach. Haldor Lillenas met him in 1909 and was impressed that Weigle "possessed a rich baritone voice and preaching [that] was eloquent and powerful."[88] By then Weigle had already experienced many trials and difficulties in his work, so that friends and relatives urged him to forsake evangelism and seek secular employment. "This seemed like turning my back on the Lord," he explained, "and such a course was unthinkable. It was at this time [1903] I wrote the song, 'Living for Jesus,' and the chorus became the prayer and determination of my heart."[89]

The lyrics Weigle wrote in 1903 asked God for help to faithfully serve and praise him, and to daily live in his presence without turning. But that had been more than twenty years ago. Through it all, Weigle believed his wife supported him. Now he rushed to find her, to reason with her and plead with her not to leave. He loved her and wanted her at his side. But at the urging of several relatives, her mind was made up. For Weigle, it seemed that the bottom had fallen out of his world.

> One day as I sat on the porch of a cottage in Florida overlooking a lake, I felt so depressed and forsaken I thought, "Why not end it all? Your work is finished. No one cares whether you're dead or alive anyway. Why not walk off the pier?" But through the appalling gloom of that moment, there seemed to flash a voice in my soul that said, "Charlie, I haven't forgotten you. Charlie, I care for you. Let not your heart be troubled." I threw myself down beside my chair and asked the Lord to forgive me for not fully trusting Him, and promised that come what may, from here on out I'd never again let such a thought cross my mind.[90]

Though Weigle was a prolific composer—by his death in 1966 he had written more than four hundred gospel songs—in the years that followed his wife's departure he put down his pen. And yet, he recalled, "I began serving the Lord again. At first it wasn't easy, for some folks did not understand the situation and were reluctant to use me. But slowly the Lord began to heal this hurt also and soon I was again busy for the Lord." Then in 1932, he again received some tragic news.

> One day I received the sad news that my wife had died, and under very heartbreaking and tragic circumstances. She had had less than five years in which to "try the world" and eternity had begun for her. And what did the future hold for me? It was while reviewing the heart-rending experiences of the past few years, and reflecting upon the goodness and love of the Savior who never forsook me through it all, that there was rekindled in my soul a desire to write a song. This song would be the summation of my whole life experience with this wonderful Friend. It was a story the whole world needed to know and it came to me as fast as I could put it down. It was the first song I had written since the day my world seemed to fall apart. Now I wanted the whole wide world to know that "No One Ever Cared For Me Like Jesus."[91]

Upon its publication in 1932, "No One Ever Cared for Me Like Jesus" became an immediate favorite on radio and among evangelicals everywhere, in churches and evangelistic meetings. Its popularity opened the door for Weigle to have wider opportunities for preaching, singing, and publishing. In time he founded True Life Library to publish songbooks, as well as numerous devotional booklets. Some titles included *Quit Worrying, Heaven: A Better Country*, and *The Way of the Cross*. Weigle himself clung for his inspiration to Psalm 40:1-3,

> I waited patiently for the Lord; and he inclined unto me, and heard my cry. He brought me up also out of an horrible pit, out of the miry clay, and set my feet upon a rock, and established my goings. And he hath put a new song in my mouth, even praise unto our God: many shall see it, and fear, and shall trust in the Lord.

"It is not for me to question the testings of the Lord, no matter how hard they may seem to be," Weigle testified. "God, in His love, knows what is best and someday He'll tell me why it happened. Until then I'll go on singing and telling the world that 'No One Ever Cared for Me Like Jesus.'"[92]

Epilogue

BY THE FALL OF 1950, two of America's top religious broadcasters were on network television. Percy Crawford had already completed a full season on ABC and his *Youth on the March* program was well received by critics and viewers alike. Charles Fuller had just gone on the air with an ABC telecast named *The Old Fashioned Meeting* that featured the proven talents of Rudy Atwood and the quartet, plus Leland Green and the choir. A year later, both broadcasts were no longer on network television. Fuller quit after six months, convinced God had not called him to be a television preacher. By then it was clear *The Old Fashioned Meeting* would never pay its own way, while the hot lights and heavy makeup needed for TV in the early fifties were simply too exhausting for Fuller and his team.[1] For his part, Crawford was determined to make television work. But facing costs of up to twenty-five thousand dollars per show, after 1951 he was forced to turn *Youth on the March* into an off-network broadcast.[2]

More was working against Fuller and Crawford than just the high cost of network television. At the time, instantaneous transmission of television programs over a network was not possible; programs had to be copied as "kinescopes" onto movie film and then sent to stations across the country. And while ABC (formed in 1945) aired the two preachers, not until the mid-1950s did NBC and CBS reverse their policies against the sale of airtime for religious programs. The chief factor working against Fuller and Crawford, however, was simply the limited outreach of network television in the early fifties. Production costs are the same whether a program is aired on half a dozen stations or half a hundred. For both *The Old Fashioned Meeting* and *Youth on the March*, their "national" networks were hookups of little more than twenty stations. Most Americans did not yet own a TV set—only 2.3 percent of households in 1949; nine percent in 1950; 23.5 percent in 1951.[3] And these viewers were concentrated in major cities, while the largest audiences Fuller and Crawford had reached on radio were in smaller markets where most Mutual affiliates were located. So Fuller and Crawford, two of the giants in religious radio, did not make it on network television (though *Youth on the March* lasted a respectable three seasons on ABC). But they tried, while most radio preachers did not make the attempt. And to be fair, when it became evident that TV would consume their resources, Fuller and Crawford still had large and effective radio ministries they could not afford to sacrifice. Those who led the way into television, then, were young preachers who had nothing to lose. Rex Humbard went on the local television in 1953, followed by Oral Roberts in 1954 and Jerry Falwell (a Fuller convert) in 1956. By the 1970s there were enough TV stations on the air for these men to purchase airtime on two or three hundred outlets. After the FCC mandated that all television sets be manufactured to receive "UHF" (channels 14–83) as well as "VHF" (channels 2–13) signals, hundreds of independent non-network stations went into operation. On that scale, the economics of television ministry could be successful. At the same time, equipment for shooting and editing broadcast-quality videotapes (which could then be easily shipped to stations) became affordable. The "electronic church" flourished and, in doing so, became a showcase to introduce and popularize the evangelical music of the day.

But what about radio? During the 1960s when network radio ceased to be an outlet for religious programming, evangelical broadcasting was transformed. In 1950 less than a dozen locally owned religious radio stations were on the air; by 1970 that number had grown to more than three hundred.[4] A mutually beneficial "bargain" had emerged. Radio preachers could buy time on reliable evangelical outlets with reliably responsive evangelical audiences, while stations received dependable income that kept them on the air and shielded them from having to compete with mainstream stations for ratings and advertising. Under this arrangement the number of radio programs grew significantly during the seventies. Teaching broadcasts such as *Focus on the Family* with James Dobson, *Insight for Living* with Chuck Swindoll, and *In Touch* with Charles Stanley were started during the decade and quickly set the pace. Even more significantly, the number of religious stations almost tripled in the seventies to nearly a thousand outlets.[5] A few evangelical radio networks had also begun to emerge. And independent "listener-supported" noncommercial religious stations were becoming a factor.

As the nature of evangelical radio changed, so did the programming. During the golden age of radio when Fuller and Crawford and others were heard on mainstream networks, their programs featured a variety format of musical selections and testimonies, followed by a brief message. Then everything changed. Theodore Epp made that discovery when, in 1959, KEAR signed on as San Francisco's first religion-formatted radio station. Response to his *Back to the Bible* broadcast on KGO, one of the most powerful mainstream stations in the Bay Area, dropped off to nearly nothing. Why? All the evangelical listeners were now tuning their dials to KEAR.[6] Within a decade, evangelical programs were mostly heard by evangelical listeners on evangelical stations. Though Epp and Fuller and the other radio preachers had always attracted a largely evangelical audience, during radio's golden age the prospect of *evangelizing* unconverted listeners could not be ignored. If nothing else, being on mainstream networks and stations required at least some effort to broadcast programs that could attract non-evangelical listeners. By the sixties and seventies, however, the emphasis for preachers shifted chiefly to "discipling" listeners who were already believers. From the standpoint of preachers and station owners, this was (and is) not necessarily bad. Broadcasters never viewed themselves as replacements for the local church but rather as supplements, aiding the church by helping to feed the flock during the week. In the meantime, the growing number of stations in the 1970s once again gave radio a key role in introducing and popularizing evangelical music. Top 40 music charts for both Contemporary Christian Music and Southern Gospel music debuted during the decade. These charts were (and are) compiled as radio stations report what they are playing to evangelical music fan magazines. Only when a sufficient number of stations are on the air are such charts feasible. Music charting, in turn, created a marriage between recording, radio, and retail that today has grown ever larger.

This is a role that religious television never fulfilled. Nevertheless, despite the enormous growth of religious radio during the seventies and eighties, "televangelism" attracted the most public attention. That attention peaked in 1987 and 1988 when TV preachers Jim Bakker, Jimmy Swaggart, and Oral Roberts were all embroiled in sexual or financial scandals. While hubris was the fundamental cause, the medium itself was a contributing factor. Unlike radio ministries that primarily solicited donations to pay for airtime, televangelists could show viewers pictures of building projects and mission fields that donors could support. And having built large ministries through television came the pressure to maintain them. Though the televised "electronic church" did not die in late eighties, the genre lost three-quarters of its audience.[7] "Echoes of the [Bakker] scandal reverberated far and wide. Christian ministries across America saw steep declines in giving.... Public disapproval of televangelists rose to more than 90 percent in numerous surveys."[8] Yet in hindsight, this dropoff may ultimately have had more to do with the changing technological landscape of television.

In 1986, prime-time Sunday viewing choices for many Americans were limited to three network shows per hour plus a syndicated televangelist on the local independent station. Those who did not fancy *Our House, Valerie, Easy Street,* or *Murder, She Wrote*—or who did not want to stay up late for the *ABC Sunday Night Movie, CBS Sunday Night Movie,* or *NBC Sunday Night Movie*—often gave the preacher and his musical ensemble a look.[9] Thirty years ago, cable television reached fewer than half of U.S. households and offered only a handful of channels.[10] In the media universe of the 1980s, televangelists such as Jerry Falwell, Pat Robertson, Oral Roberts, Rex Humbard, Robert Schuller, and others were mainstream TV personalities who amassed audiences of up to 7 million weekly viewers.[11] Yet television was on the cusp of major change. During the eighties, the number of cable households tripled from less than 1 in 5 to nearly 3 in 5.[12] Meanwhile, the number of cable TV networks jumped from 28 to 79.[13] As a result, the audience share of over-the-air broadcast television fell from about 90 percent of viewers in 1980 to only 77 percent in 1990. Over the same period, the percentage of households with VCRs rose from 1 percent to 69 percent.[14] Meanwhile, remotely controlled TV sets became widespread and encouraged "channel-switching" by viewers. Still, noted media researcher Stephen Winzenburg, "despite claims ... that these TV preachers would need to shut down ... none of the major ministries would ever go off the air. Every single ministry ... has remained on the air or temporarily left the air only to return later."[15] This was possible because televangelists forged a new business model adapted to the increasingly fragmented media universe that emerged in the 1990s through the expansion of cable television and introduction of direct-broadcast satellite TV services.

Televangelists forsook the old model of building a broad-based audience through first-run syndication on broadcast television. Instead they aimed their programs at religious viewers attracted to religious cable and satellite channels. In part, this trend was accelerated when the Federal Communications Commission in 1996 ordered all local television stations to switch from analog to digital broadcasting within ten years. Scores of independent stations, including over-the-air religious stations, could not afford the multimillion-dollar cost and sold their licenses to larger networks. Thus, while preachers since the nineties have targeted a smaller slice of the pie, the audience fragment they pursue is more reliably supportive. As noted in the Introduction, ninety percent of evangelical Christian adults in the United States consume "Christian media" each month, including 1 in 5 who consume it daily.[16] Compared to three evangelical cable TV networks in the eighties, today a dozen are transmitted via mainstream cable and satellite providers to a potential reach of 100 million U.S. households. In turn, they provide platforms for dozens of independent syndicated televangelists whose telecasts draw up to seven million weekly viewers.[17]

Religious radio was also transformed in the 1990s. Restrictions on how many stations a broadcaster could own were virtually eliminated under the Telecommunications Act of 1996. The effects of the law were immediate as nearly 2,200 stations changed hands in 1996 alone.[18] By 1997, ownership of radio stations was concentrated in the hands of a relative few number of broadcasters in 86 percent of the America's fifty largest radio markets, compared to 18 percent just five years earlier.[19] By 2002, more than 40 percent of U.S. radio stations were under new ownership.[20] Nationwide, the total number of station owners fell by one-third.[21] Between 1996 and 2002, the 21 largest radio groups acquired more than 2,600 stations and, in 2002, owned one-fifth of all U.S. radio stations.[22] Four of the 21 groups in 2002 were evangelical broadcasters. Since then, religious radio has become, like the radio industry generally, "consolidated" or dominated by a handful of evangelical media conglomerates that each own or supply programming for hundreds of stations.[23] This new reality, by driving up the cost for preachers to purchase airtime, favors the largest syndicated programs and has forced scores of lesser-known programs off the air.[24] Production values have markedly increased, but so has homogeneity. Unlike radio's golden age when personalities such as Charles Fuller and Percy Crawford were the focus of evangelical radio, today "the market forces unleashed by [deregulation] ... pushed religious radio into a new era dominated less by faces and more by corporations."[25] All told, some 3,400 radio stations now air religious teaching, talk, or music.[26] Nearly a dozen major national evangelical radio networks are on the air, while more than thirty independent syndicators secure time on up to 2,000 stations each.[27] Meanwhile, "Christian radio" has become the *de facto* "hymnal" of contemporary American evangelical churches, arbitrating what is sung in worship even as market forces diminish the range of this music to catchy "praise" anthems that attract radio listeners and sell product.[28]

In the golden "radio days" when religious programs were carried on mainstream networks, music was means to attract listeners for the message to follow. Thus, it needed to be comparatively "light" and with an emphasis on variety and brevity. Music was intended to be a pleasant and enjoyable "set up" for the sermon. As Wendell Loveless counseled in his *Manual of Gospel Broadcasting,* religious radio programs must avoid being mere "amusement" but did require genuine "entertainment value." "A radio audience may be amused for a half hour without the accomplishment of anything instructive. But the gospel broadcaster, who properly employs entertainment factors, has held the interest of the listening audience and has rendered a constructive service."[29] By contrast, Contemporary Christian Music is largely heard today on stations that feature full-time music formats. Each song is written and recorded as a *devotional* experience for personal worship. A recent ethnography of a contemporary evangelical church, captured this ethos:

> [M]usic is prayer.... Some people stand, eyes closed, palms out and upward, swaying slightly, their cheeks sometimes wet with tears. Some sit and rest their foreheads on clasped hands. Some kneel in prayer.... I have seen people speak intently but silently during the worship [music] period, eyes focused on something no one else can see.... Worship [music] time is understood to be private, personal, a time to commune with God alone while in the presence of others.... Unlike older church hymns,

you do not sing *about* God but *to* God, directly to him in the second person, and with unbridled yearning.... These worship songs suggest that you, the singer, feel [God] in your body.... He is in you, but he is also apart from you, someone whom you love and who loves and cuddles you.[30]

Almost unthinkable today is the idea of contemporary evangelical popular music as *entertainment*. Yet midcentury evangelicals, whether listening on the radio or attending a rally or all-night singing, relished occasions to enjoy good Christian music. It could even be (as Homer Rodeheaver always maintained) fun. Evangelical popular music might at times be enjoyed as entertainment, but it was "entertainment-plus" and certainly better than being entertained by the "world." Thus, one reason that midcentury evangelical popular music is now lost is because its premise no longer exists in the contemporary evangelical church. Listeners who tune in to today's evangelical music radio immerse themselves in a devotional experience. Yet in the decades covered by this volume, evangelicals would gather around the radio each Sunday night and tune in perhaps *The Old Fashioned Revival Hour* or *Young People's Church of the Air* simply to enjoy an entertaining hour of good Christian music.

This spirit is captured in a story from the waning days of network radio. Before television took over, one of the last truly lavish radio productions was simply named *The Big Show*. The variety program debuted in 1950 on NBC and, hosted by Tallulah Bankhead, each Sunday evening presented dozens of big stars. The music director was Meredith Willson, best known today as author and composer of the hit Broadway musical, *The Music Man*. The day before the premier broadcast, Willson still lacked a closing musical theme.

> The broadcast took place on Sunday, so, in searching desperately for a closing-theme idea, the only thought I could get hold of was ... my mother's weekly benediction to her Sunday school class back in Mason City, Iowa: "May the good Lord bless and keep you." Twenty-four hours later I taught the new song to Tallulah, who threw back her long tawny bob and broadcast the first performance from NBC's Studio H.[31]

That song, "May the Good Lord Bless and Keep You," was a nationwide hit and recorded by many popular evangelical artists of the day. Though not biblically profound or even scripturally based, its general outlook instilled hope and encouragement. Today, such a song would never be recorded. It is not appropriate for a worship service. And beyond the fact that musical styles have changed, it is too "light" to be included on any contemporary evangelical album or aired on any station. Yet in those final years when families still gathered around their radio sets at night, many a believer might go to bed with Willson's song whispered softly on the lips: "May the good Lord bless and keep you till we meet again."

Chapter Notes

Abbreviations

BGCA	Billy Graham Center Archives
Drury T5	BGCA. "Collection 492—Rev. William A. Drury. T5 Transcript." http://www2.wheaton.edu/bgc/archives/trans/492t05a.htm.
Dunlop T1	BGCA. "Collection 50—Merrill Dunlop. T1 Transcript." http://www2.wheaton.edu/bgc/archives/trans/050t01.htm.
Dunlop T2	BGCA. "Collection 50—Merrill Dunlop. T2 Transcript." http://www2.wheaton.edu/bgc/archives/trans/050t02.htm.
Dunlop T3	BGCA. "Collection 50—Merrill Dunlop. T3 Transcript." http://www2.wheaton.edu/bgc/archives/trans/050t03.htm.
Johnson T1	BGCA. "Collection 285—Torrey Johnson. T1 Transcript." http://www2.wheaton.edu/bgc/archives/trans/285t01.htm.
Johnson T2	BGCA. "Collection 285—Torrey Johnson. T2 Transcript." http://www2.wheaton.edu/bgc/archives/trans/285t02.htm.
Johnson T3	BGCA. "Collection 285—Torrey Johnson. T3 Transcript." http://www2.wheaton.edu/bgc/archives/trans/285t03.htm.
Johnson T4	BGCA. "Collection 285—Torrey Johnson. T4 Transcript." http://www2.wheaton.edu/bgc/archives/trans/285t04.htm.
Johnson T6	BGCA. "Collection 285—Torrey Johnson. T6 Transcript." http://www2.wheaton.edu/bgc/archives/trans/285t06.htm.
Porter T16	BGCA. "Collection 357—Ruth (Duvall) Crawford Porter. T16 Transcript." http://www2.wheaton.edu/bgc/archives/trans/357t16.htm.
Wyrtzen T1	BGCA. "Collection 446—Jack Wyrtzen. T1 Transcript." http://www2.wheaton.edu/bgc/archives/trans/446t01.htm.
Wyrtzen T2	BGCA. "Collection 446—Jack Wyrtzen. T2 Transcript." http://www2.wheaton.edu/bgc/archives/trans/446t02.htm.
Wyzenbeek T1	BGCA. "Collection 40—Andrew Wyzenbeek. T1 Transcript." http://www2.wheaton.edu/bgc/archives/trans/040t01.htm.

Preface

1. See Armstrong, *The Electric Church*; and Ward, *Air of Salvation*.
2. Rodrigues et al., *Radio Today*.
3. Ward, "Major Networks and Personalities."
4. Ward, "Dark Preachers"; and Ward, "Consolidating the Gospel."
5. Ward, "Major Networks and Personalities."
6. Ibid.
7. Winzenburg, "TV Ministries Use of Air Time."

8. Steinberg and Kincheloe, *Christotainment*.
9. Grossman, "Faith's Purchasing Power."
10. The Nielsen Company, "Spiritual Entertainment."
11. *Ibid*.
12. Box Office Mojo, "Christian Movies."
13. Barna Group, "More People Use Christian Media than Attend Church."
14. Chaffee and Metzger, "The End of Mass Communication?"; Davis, *The Web of Politics*; Havick, "The Impact of the Internet"; Hollander, "Tuning Out or Tuning Elsewhere?"; Iyengar and Hahn, "Red Media, Blue Media"; Mancini, "Media Fragmentation, Party System, and Democracy"; Prior, *Post-broadcast Democracy*; Tewksbury, "What Do Americans Really Want to Know?"; and Tewksbury, "The Seeds of Audience Fragmentation."
15. Sunstein, *Republic.Com 2.0*.
16. For example, see Shires, *Hippies of the Religious Right*; Schäfer, *Countercultural Conservatives*; Schäfer, *American Evangelicals and the 60s*; Shields, "Framing the Christian Right"; Magee, "From Bible Belt to Sun Belt"; and Young, "From Hippies to Jesus Freaks."
17. Ward, "Give the Winds a Mighty Voice," 124.
18. *Ibid.*, 122.
19. Hangen, "Speaking of God, Listening for Grace," 144.
20. Ellwood, *1950: Crossroads of American Religious Life*, 188.
21. Lindlof, "Media Audiences as Interpretive Communities"; and Lindlof, "Interpretive Community: An Approach to Media and Religion."
22. See Kerr, *Music in Evangelism*.
23. For example, see Smith and Seignious, "Medium, Message, and Ministry."

12. See Brereton, *Training God's Army*.
13. Schultze, "The Mythos of the Electronic Church."
14. Balmer, *The Making of Evangelicalism*, 53.
15. Winrod, "Introduction."
16. DeBerg, *Ungodly Women*; and Bendroth, *Fundamentalism and Gender*.
17. Ward, "Give the Winds," 125.
18. Katz, "The Ethic of Expediency."
19. For example, see Emerson and Smith, *Divided by Faith*; and Emerson et al., "Equal in Christ."
20. For example, see Ault, *Spirit and Flesh*; Bartkowski, *Remaking the Godly Marriage*; Bendroth, *Fundamentalism and Gender*; Brasher, *Godly Women*; Gallagher, *Evangelical Identity and Gendered Family Life*; and Griffin, *God's Daughters*.
21. Carpenter, *Revive Us Again*.
22. Rosell, *The Surprising Work of God*, 15.
23. *Ibid.*, 185.
24. *Ibid.*, 185–186.
25. Balmer, *The Making of Evangelicalism*, 5–6.
26. Radosh, *Rapture Ready*. For explorations of contemporary evangelical popular culture see Hendershot, *Shaking the World for Jesus*; Kintz, *Between Jesus and the Market*; Kintz and Lesage, *Media, Culture, and the Religious Right*; and Roof, *Spiritual Marketplace*. For a historical background of religious merchandising see McDannell, "Christian Retailing."
27. Rosell, *The Surprising Work of God*, 16.
28. The literature on media proliferation and audience fragmentation is reviewed and applied to religious media in Ward, "Televangelism, Audience Fragmentation, and the Changing Coverage of Scandal."
29. Sumser, *The Conflict*, 154.

Introduction

1. Marsden, *Fundamentalism and American Culture*, 184.
2. Brinkley, "The Scopes Trial," 274.
3. *Ibid.*, 274.
4. Noll, "God and the Colonies," 101.
5. Stout, "The Transforming Effects of the Great Awakening," 130.
6. Hatch, *The Democratization of American Christianity*.
7. Noll, *America's God*, 9.
8. See Marsden, *Fundamentalism and American Culture*.
9. Starr, *The Creation of the Media*.
10. Evensen, *God's Man for the Gilded Age*, 13.
11. Sandeen, *The Roots of Fundamentalism*.

Chapter One

1. See Armstrong, *The Electric Church*; and Ward, *Air of Salvation*. A slightly different version of the first religious broadcast is related in Siedell, *Gospel Radio*. However, the Armstrong and Ward versions are endorsed by the National Religious Broadcasters association.
2. The account of radio's prehistory is drawn from Sterling and Kitross, *Stay Tuned*; Hilliard and Keith, *The Broadcast Century and Beyond*; and Lewis, *Empire of the Air*.
3. See Silverman, *Lightning Man*.
4. See Gordon, *A Thread across the Ocean*.
5. See Wightman, *Signor Marconi's Magic Box*; and Larson, *Thunderstruck*.
6. Barnouw, *A Tower in Babel*, 8.
7. The account of radio in the twenties is

drawn from Sterling and Kitross, *Stay Tuned*; Hilliard and Keith, *The Broadcast Century*; and Lewis, *Empire of the Air*.
    8. Ward, "Air of the King."
    9. The account of Crawford is drawn from Crawford, *When God and Papa Ganged Up on Me*; Crawford, *Papa and I*; and Armstrong, *Religious Broadcasting Sourcebook*. The author is indebted to Kevin Mungons for giving me a copy of *Papa and I*.
    10. The account of Brown is drawn from Armstrong, *The Electric Church*; Armstrong, *Religious Broadcasting Sourcebook*; Siedell, *Gospel Radio*; Ward, *Air of Salvation*; and Ward, "Air of the King."
    11. Turner, *Standing without Apology*.
    12. See Armstrong, *The Electric Church*; Siedell, *Gospel Radio*; and Ward, *Air of Salvation*.
    13. The account of Rader is drawn from BGCA, "Memorial to Merrill Dunlop"; BGCA, "Jazz Age Evangelism"; BGCA, "Papers of Torrey Maynard Johnson"; Wyzenbeek T1; Chicago Gospel Tabernacle, *Gospel Songs of the Air*; Butler, *Save Them!*; Hangen, *Redeeming the Dial*; Carpenter, *Revive Us Again*; Abrams, *Selling the Old-Time Religion*; Armstrong, *The Electric Church*; Siedell, *Gospel Radio*; Ward, *Air of Salvation*; and Melton et al., *Prime-Time Religion*.
    14. The hospital visit is described in Dunlop T1.
    15. Dunlop T1.
    16. *Ibid.*
    17. Wyzenbeek T1.
    18. Dunlop T1.
    19. Ward, *Air of Salvation*, 28.
    20. Armstrong, *The Electric Church*, 21.
    21. Kerr, *Music in Evangelism*.
    22. Abrams, *Selling the Old-Time Religion*, 37.
    23. Wyzenbeek T1.
    24. Ward, *Air of Salvation*, 29.
    25. Dunlop T1.
    26. Carpenter, *Revive Us Again*, 128.
    27. *Ibid.*, 127.
    28. Johnson T1.
    29. *Ibid.*
    30. Dunlop T1.
    31. Carpenter, *Revive Is Again*, 128.
    32. Johnson T1.
    33. Dunlop T1.
    34. The account is found in Smith, *Al Smith's Treasury*, 49–50.
    35. Johnson T1.
    36. Abrams, *Selling the Old-Time Religion*, 43.
    37. Dunlop T1.
    38. *Ibid.*
    39. Johnson T1.
    40. Armstrong, *The Electric Church*, 21.
    41. The account of Moody Bible Institute and the founding of WMBI is drawn from Getz, *MBI*; Armstrong, *The Electric Church*; Armstrong, *Religious Broadcasting Sourcebook*; Siedell, *Gospel Radio*; Ward, *Air of Salvation*; and the Moody Bible Institute website at http://www.moody.edu (accessed 2003).
    42. Getz, *MBI*, 166.
    43. The account of Loveless is drawn from his file in the Moody Bible Institute Archives Room, including the magazine articles "'Precious Hiding Place' Brings Fame"; Carlson, "Patriarch of Christian Radio"; Cook, "To Me to Live Is Christ"; Albus, "By Air and by Tract"; W. Loveless, "How to Write a Gospel Chorus"; Hoke, "Wendell Loveless"; as well as R. Loveless, "Because of the Grace of God." The author is indebted to Moody Library archivist Corie Zylstra for facilitating access to these materials. Additional details about Loveless are drawn from Getz, *MBI*; W. Loveless, *Manual of Gospel Broadcasting*; and W. Loveless, *Radio Songs and Choruses*.
    44. "'Precious Hiding Place' Brings Fame."
    45. R. Loveless, "Because of the Grace of God," 9.
    46. "'Precious Hiding Place' Brings Fame."
    47. R. Loveless, "Because of the Grace of God," 11.
    48. Carlson, "Patriarch of Christian Radio," 14–15.
    49. R. Loveless, "Because of the Grace of God," 12.
    50. "'Precious Hiding Place' Brings Fame."
    51. Cook, "To Me to Live is Christ," 1.
    52. W. Loveless, *Manual of Gospel Broadcasting*, 67–78.
    53. Carlson, "Patriarch of Christian Radio," 16.
    54. W. Loveless, "How to Write a Gospel Chorus," 30.
    55. From the flyleaf of W. Loveless, *Radio Songs and Choruses*.
    56. The account of Vaughn and the early history of Southern Gospel music is drawn from Terrell, *The Music Men*; Goff, *Close Harmony*; and Cyberhymnal.org (accessed 2003).
    57. The conversation between Vaughn and Green is recounted in Terrell, *The Music Men*, 19–20.
    58. Goff and Terrell differ on whether or not WOAN was the first radio station in Tennessee, on its original wattage, and the date a power increase was granted. Goff's account in *Closer Harmony* cites independent sources and is relied on here.
    59. Terrell, *The Music Men*, 29.
    60. The account of Rodeheaver and Sunday is drawn from Rodeheaver, *Twenty Years*;

Wilhoit, *Rody*; Dorsett, *Billy Sunday*; Bruns, *Preacher*; Rodeheaver, *Homer Rodeheaver's World's Greatest Collection*; Rodeheaver, *Rodeheaver's Radio Songs*.
   61. Rodeheaver, *World's Greatest Collection*.
   62. Rodeheaver, *Rodeheaver's Radio Songs*.
   63. Rodeheaver, *Singing Black*, 9.
   64. Smith, *Al Smith's Treasury*, 157–161. A slightly different, though sketchy, account of the song from its lyricist is found in Smith, *Oswald J. Smith's Hymn Stories*.
   65. Rodeheaver, *Rodeheaver's Radio Songs*.
   66. Smith, *Al Smith's Treasury*, 81; Emurian, *Forty Stories*, 63–64.
   67. Bruns, *Preacher*, 298.
   68. Rodeheaver, *Twenty Years*, 79.
   69. Shea, *Songs that Life the Heart*, 30.
   70. Rodeheaver, *Twenty Years*, 78.

Chapter Two

   1. The account of Maier is drawn from Maier, *A Man Spoke*; Ward, *Air of Salvation*; Armstrong, *The Electric Church*; Siedell, *Gospel Radio*; Melton et al., *Prime-Time Religion*; and Tona J. Hangen, "Man of the Hour."
   2. Maier, *A Man Spoke*, 119.
   3. The account of radio in the 1930s is drawn from Sterling and Kitross, *Stay Tuned*; Hilliard and Keith, *The Broadcast Century*; and Lewis, *Empire of the Air*.
   4. Kerr, *Music in Evangelism*, 82.
   5. *Ibid.*, 82.
   6. *Ibid.*, 83.
   7. *Ibid.*, 84.
   8. *Ibid.*, 84.
   9. *Ibid.*, 85.
   10. *Ibid.*, 88.
   11. The account of Fuller is drawn from Fuller, *Give the Winds a Mighty Voice*; Wright, *The Old Fashioned Revival Hour*; Smith, *A Voice for God*; Marsden, *Reforming Fundamentalism*; Armstrong, *The Electric Church*; Siedell, *Gospel Radio*; Melton et al., *Prime-Time Religion*; Ward, *Air of Salvation*; Old Fashioned Revival Hour Broadcast, http://www.oldfashionedrevivalhour.com (accessed 2003); and Fuller et al., *Old Fashioned Revival Hour Songs*.
   12. Fuller, *Give the Winds*, 23.
   13. *Ibid.*, 37.
   14. *Ibid.*, 37.
   15. *Ibid.*, 86.
   16. *Ibid.*, 93.
   17. *Ibid.*, 121.
   18. The account of the Old Fashioned Revival Hour (OFRH) Quartet, Choir, Rudy Atwood, and Leland Green is drawn from Fuller, *Give the Winds*; Smith, *A Voice for God*; BGCA, "Memorial to Merrill Dunlop"; and liner notes from OFRH recordings *The Old Fashioned Revival Hour*; *Old Fashioned Revival Hour Choir*; *The Distinguished Old Fashioned Revival Hour Quartet*; and *Sweeter as the Days Go By*.
   19. *Dr. Charles E. Fuller Presents*.
   20. Fuller, *Give the Winds*, 143–144.
   21. *Ibid.*, 148.
   22. *Ibid.*, 242.
   23. The account of Crawford is drawn from Bahr, *Man with a Vision*; D. D. Crawford, *A Thirst for Souls*; D. A. Crawford, *Love, Wonderful Love*; Armstrong, *The Electric Church*; Siedell, *Gospel Radio*; Melton et al., *Prime-Time Religion*; Ward, *Air of Salvation*; P. Crawford, *The Art of Fishing for Men*; R. Crawford and P. Crawford, *The Young People's Church of the Air Hymn Book*; P. Crawford, *Pinebrook Choruses*; R. Crawford and P. Crawford, *Pinebrook Melodies*; Crawford Broadcasting Corporation, "History"; BGCA, "Papers of William A. Drury"; BGCA, "Papers of Percy Bartimus Crawford and Ruth Crawford Porter"; BGCA, "Interview with Perry Clark Straw": BGCA, "Papers of John Von Casper 'Jack' Wyrtzen"; BGCA, "'As This is Our First Broadcast'"; and cassette liner notes for Telecasters Quartet, *We Were There When It Happened*. The author is grateful to Hilda Sands, former librarian at Northland Baptist Bible College, who worked at the Pinebrook camps as a teenager and shared her copy of *Pinebrook Choruses*; the volume lists Pinebrook attendance figures and fees, as well as King's College tuition rates.
   24. Bahr, *Man with a Vision*, 7.
   25. The conversations between Crawford and the two women are recounted in Bahr, *Man with a Vision*, 13–14.
   26. Crawford's recollections of his conversion are provided in Bahr, *Man with a Vision*, 17–18.
   27. P. Crawford, *The Art of Fishing for Men*, 16.
   28. *Ibid.*, 16.
   29. *Ibid.*, 28.
   30. *Ibid.*, 29.
   31. *Ibid.*, 29.
   32. Johnson T2.
   33. Bahr, *Man with a Vision*, 42.
   34. Drury T5.
   35. Quoted in D. A. Crawford, *A Thirst for Souls*, 137.
   36. Bahr, *Man with a Vision*, 52.
   37. BGCA, "'As This is Our First Broadcast.'"
   38. Wyrtzen T2.
   39. *Ibid.*
   40. Telecasters Quarter, *We Were There When It Happened*.
   41. D. D. Crawford, *Love, Wonderful Love*, 1.

42. D. A. Crawford, *A Thirst for Souls,* 169.
43. Porter T16.
44. BGCA, "Perry Straw Excerpts."
45. BGCA, "'As This is Our First Broadcast...' Newspaper and Magazine Reaction to *Youth on the March,*" http://www2.wheaton.edu/bgc/archives/exhibits/Crawford/crawford09.htm.
46. D. D. Crawford, *Love, Wonderful Love,* 1.
47. Drury T5.
48. Wyrtzen T2.
49. Wrytzen T1.
50. Bahr, *Man with a Vision,* 47–48.
51. Accounts of the rally are found in Carpenter, *Revive Us Again,* 166–167; and BGCA, "The Greatest Youth Gathering in History." Torrey Johnson (organizer) and Merrill Dunlop (music director) also expound at length about the event in their BGCA oral history interviews. Crawford's participation is highlighted in D. A. Crawford, *A Thirst for Souls,* 234–235; and Bahr, *Man with a Vision,* 64–65.
52. Peterson, *The Miracle Goes On,* 145.
53. D. A. Crawford, *A Thirst for Souls,* 141.
54. BGCA, "'As This is Our First Broadcast...' The Later History of *Youth on the March,*" http://www2.wheaton.edu/bgc/archives/exhibits/Crawford/crawford17.htm.
55. Sterling and Kitross, *Stay Tuned.*
56. Telecasters Quartet, *We Were There.* The announcer's words are reproduced in the group's recording of "The Youth on the March Theme Song."
57. BGCA, "'As This is Our First Broadcast.'"
58. Articles are quoted in BGCA, "Newspaper and Magazine Reaction to *Youth on the March,*" http://www2.wheaton.edu/bgc/archives/exhibits/Crawford/crawford09.htm, and "Get a Television Set," http://www2.wheaton.edu/bgc/archives/exhibits/Crawford/crawford05.htm.
59. Porter T16.
60. Accounts of these initial radio and TV station purchases are found in D.A. Crawford, *A Thirst for Souls,* 287–300; and Crawford Broadcasting Corporation, "History."
61. Reproduced in Crawford, *Love Wonderful Love,* 9.
62. The conversation and scene is recounted in Bahr, *Man with a Vision,* 83.
63. *Ibid.*, 85–86.
64. The college moved in 1999 into three floors of New York's Empire State Building and in 2012 relocated to its current site on Broadway near Manhattan's Wall Street financial district. See The King's College, "History of the King's College," https://www.tkc.edu/about-kings/history.

65. Ward, *Air of Salvation,* 100.
66. Porter's biography is found in BGCA, "Papers of Percy Bartimus Crawford and Ruth Crawford Porter."
67. Porter T16.
68. Telecasters Quartet, *We Were There.*
69. The story of the Norse Gospel Trio's meeting with Epp is recounted in Peterson, *The Miracle Goes On.*
70. Peterson, *The Miracle Goes On,* 69–70.
71. The account of Epp and Webb is drawn from Siedell, *Gospel Radio*; liner notes from the *Back to the Bible* recordings *Back to the Bible Choir and Quartet*; *Back to the Bible Broadcast*; and *The Best Selections of the Back to the Bible Broadcast*; and liner notes from *Music of the Free Methodist Church: Light and Life Hour Choir.*
72. Siedell, *Gospel Radio,* 72.
73. *Ibid.*, 73.
74. *Ibid.*, 80.
75. Liner notes, *Back to the Bible Broadcast.*
76. Liner notes, *Back to the Bible Choir and Quartet.*
77. The author personally heard this announcement in the mid-nineties while working for a Christian radio station in the Washington, D.C., metropolitan area.
78. The account of Myers is drawn from Ward, *Air of Salvation*; Armstrong, *Religious Broadcasting Sourcebook*; and Haven Ministries, "History," http://www.havenministries.org (accessed 2003).
79. The account of Myers's conversion is taken from Armstrong, *Religious Broadcasting Sourcebook,* C-9ff.
80. For a study of nautically themed hymns see Mouw, "Some Poor Sailor."
81. Haven Ministries, "History," op. cit.
82. The account of the Haven of Rest Quartet is drawn from liner notes for *Haven of Rest Favorites*; *Shipmates of Song*; and *Welcome Aboard.*
83. Liner notes, *Shipmates of Song.*
84. Blesh, "Scott Joplin," p. xxiii.
85. The account of Stamps and Baxter is drawn from Terrell, *The Music Men*; Goff, *Close Harmony*; Cyberhymnal.org (accessed 2003); and Southern Gospel Music Association Hall of Fame and Museum, "1997," http://sgma.org/category/sgma-hall-of-fame/1997/.
86. Terrell, *The Music Men,* 47.
87. Rodeheaver's telegram is found in Kerr, *Music in Evangelism,* 208.

Chapter Three

1. "Religious Broadcasting Needs a Checkup," *The Christian Century* (December 15,

1943): 1461; quoted in Fuller, *Give the Winds*, 154–155.
   2. Charles W. Crowe, "Religion on the Air," *The Christian Century* (August 23, 1944): 973–974; quoted in Fuller, *Give the Winds*, 155.
   3. Accounts of the battle over paid-time religious broadcasts are found in Hangen, *Redeeming the Dial*; and Ward, *Air of Salvation*.
   4. Hilliard and Keith, *The Broadcast Century*, 88.
   5. BGCA, "Papers of Torrey Maynard Johnson."
   6. Fuller, *Give the Winds*, 151.
   7. Ward, *Air of Salvation*, 16.
   8. *Ibid.*, 59.
   9. *Ibid.*, 17.
   10. *Ibid.*, 17–19.
   11. See Matthews, *Standing Up*.
   12. Ward, *Air of Salvation*, 62.
   13. *Ibid.*, 62–63.
   14. *Ibid.*, 63–64. Also see Wright, *The Old Fashioned Revival Hour*.
   15. The account of the founding of National Religious Broadcasters (NRB) is drawn from Ward, *Air of Salvation*. The author was editor of the NRB *Directory of Religious Media* and staff writer for the group's *Religious Broadcasting* trade journal in 1993–95.
   16. Ward, *Air of Salvation*, 67; quoting Murch, *Adventuring for Christ*, 174.
   17. Ward, *Air of Salvation*, 20.
   18. *Ibid.*, 20.
   19. *Ibid.*, 70.
   20. *Ibid.*, 109.
   21. The account of Hofer is drawn from Ward, *Air of Salvation*; and Armstrong, *The Electric Church*.
   22. The account of radio in the forties is drawn from Sterling and Kitross, *Stay Tuned*; and Hilliard and Keith, *The Broadcast Century*.
   23. The account of Wyrtzen, Booth, and Clayton is drawn from Jackson and Jackson, *Celebration—Fifty Faithful Years*; Bollback, *The House that Jack Built*; Sweeting, *The Jack Wyrtzen Story*; Forbes, *God Hath Chosen*; BGCA, "Papers of John Von Casper 'Jack' Wyrtzen"; BGCA, "Papers of Torrey Maynard Johnson"; and Booth, *Living Above*. The author worked with Wyrtzen in 1987–92 as publications manager for Word of Life Fellowship.
   24. Wyrtzen T1.
   25. The conversations are recounted in Sweeting, *The Jack Wyrtzen Story*, 21.
   26. Wyrtzen T2.
   27. *Ibid.*
   28. The scene is recounted variously in Forbes, *God Hath Chosen*, 18; Sweeting, *The Jack Wyrtzen Story*, 17–18; and Bollback, *The House That Jack Built*, 10–11.
   29. Sweeting, *The Jack Wyrtzen Story*, 23.
   30. Wyrtzen T2.
   31. Bollback, *The House That Jack Built*, 11.
   32. Marge Wyrtzen's first visit to Pinebrook and conversion there is recounted in Bollback, *The House That Jack Built*, 12–16.
   33. The incident is recounted in Wyrtzen T1.
   34. Wyrtzen T1.
   35. The conversation between Wyrtzen and Kline is recounted in Bollback, *The House That Jack Built*, 18.
   36. Wyrtzen T1.
   37. *Ibid.* A somewhat differently worded version is found in Bollback. *The House That Jack Built*, 21–22.
   38. Bollback. *The House That Jack Built*, 22.
   39. Wyrtzen T1.
   40. Jackson and Jackson, *Celebration*, 14.
   41. *Ibid.*, 14.
   42. Wyrtzen T1.
   43. Jack and Marge's dedication is recounted in Bollback, *The House That Jack Built*, 19–20.
   44. Wyrtzen T2.
   45. Wyrtzen T1.
   46. *Ibid.*
   47. Bollback. *The House That Jack Built*, 25.
   48. *Ibid.*, 26.
   49. Wyrtzen T1.
   50. *Ibid.*
   51. Forbes, *God Hath Chosen*, 48–49.
   52. On Booth see Forbes, *God Hath Chosen*, 89–93.
   53. Forbes, *God Hath Chosen*, 91.
   54. On Clayton see Forbes, *God Hath Chosen*, 93–97..
   55. The account of Johnson is drawn from BGCA, "Papers of Torrey Maynard Johnson"; and BGCA, "Memorial to Merrill Dunlop." Along with these two sources, the account of Youth for Christ is drawn from Carpenter, *Revive Us Again*; Graham, *Just As I Am*; Martin, *A Prophet with Honor*; Pollock, *Billy Graham*; *Youth Rally Songs and Choruses*; BGCA, "The Greatest Youth Gathering in History"; and Bergler, "I Found My Thrill."
   56. The phone conversation is recalled in Johnson T3.
   57. Johnson T1.
   58. *Ibid.*
   59. *Ibid.*
   60. *Ibid.*
   61. Johnson T3.
   62. *Ibid.*
   63. *Ibid.*
   64. *Ibid.*
   65. *Ibid.*
   66. *Ibid.*
   67. *Ibid.*
   68. Dunlop T2.

69. *Ibid.*
70. Johnson T3.
71. Dunlop T2.
72. *Ibid.*
73. Johnson T3.
74. *Ibid.*
75. Accounts of the rally are found in Carpenter, *Revive Us Again*, 166–167; and BGCA, "The Greatest Youth Gathering in History." Johnson and Dunlop also expound at length about the event in their BGCA oral history interviews.
76. Johnson T4.
77. BGCA, "The Greatest Youth Gathering in History: Coverage," http://www2.wheaton.edu/bgc/archives/exhibits/YFC%201945/07%20coverage%2008.html.
78. Carpenter, *Revive Us Again*, 169.
79. Johnson T6.
80. BGCA, "Address given by Torrey Johnson at the first annual convention of Youth for Christ, held in Winona Lake, Indiana, July 26, 1945," http://www2.wheaton.edu/bgc/archives/tmj1.html.
81. See Bergler, "I Found My Thrill."
82. Dunlop T2.
83. Figures reported by Youth for Christ, http://www.yfc.net.
84. See BGCA, "Papers of Torrey Maynard Johnson."
85. The account of Graham, Shea, and Barrows is drawn from Graham, *Just As I Am*; Martin, *A Prophet with Honor*; Pollock, *Billy Graham*; Ward, *Air of Salvation*; and BGCA, "Papers of Torrey Maynard Johnson." Additional details about Shea are drawn from Shea, *Songs That Lift the Heart*; and BGCA, "Papers of John Von Casper 'Jack' Wyrtzen."
86. The conversations between Graham and Johnson are recounted in Graham, *Just As I Am*, 84–85.
87. Graham, *Just As I Am*, 31.
88. Johnson T3.
89. The scene between Graham and Shea is recounted in Graham, *Just As I Am*, 85–86.
90. Davis, *Enriching Hymn and Song Stories*, 205–206.
91. The account of "I'd Rather Have Jesus" is drawn from Osbeck, *101 More*; Collins, *Turn Your Radio On*; and Davis, *Inspirational Song and Hymn Stories*.
92. Collins, *Turn Your Radio On*, 104.
93. Johnson T3.
94. Graham, *Just As I Am*, 93.
95. The conversation between Graham and Riley is recounted in Graham, *Just As I Am*, 115.
96. Graham recounted his crisis of faith in *Just As I Am*, 135–139.
97. Graham, *Just As I Am*, 139.
98. *Ibid.*, 139.
99. *Ibid.*, 148–149.
100. *Ibid.*, 176–177.
101. *Ibid.*, 177.
102. The founding of the *Hour of Decision* broadcast is recounted Graham, *Just As I Am*, 176–181; Armstrong, *The Electric Church*, 93–97; and Ward, *Air of Salvation*, 75–82.
103. Shea, *Songs that Lift the Heart*, 74.
104. *Ibid.*, 91.
105. The account of Smith is drawn from Smith, *Al Smith's Treasury*; Al Smith Ministries, "Al Smith Biography," http://livinghymns.org/bio.htm (accessed 2003); Peterson, *The Miracle Goes On*; and a series of oral history interviews conducted by Robert Sims, then a Bob Jones University student, in October and November 2001 for his senior project in radio and television broadcasting. Shortly after Smith passed away, Sims interviewed his wife Nancy Smith and former colleagues John W. Peterson, Harry Bollback, Brian Donley, and Frank Garlock. The author is indebted to Sims for providing access to this material.
106. Smith, *Al Smith's Treasury*, 179–180.
107. Sims, *The Life and Legacy of Al Smith*.
108. Graham, *Just As I Am*, 94.
109. Sims, *The Life and Legacy*.
110. Peterson, *The Miracle Goes On*, 161.
111. Sims, *The Life and Legacy*.
112. *Ibid.*
113. *Ibid.*
114. *Ibid.*
115. *Ibid.*
116. Smith, *Al Smith's Treasury*, 206.
117. *Ibid.*, 206.
118. Sims, *The Life and Legacy*.
119. Smith, *Al Smith's Treasury*, 28–29.
120. Sims, *The Life and Legacy*.
121. *Ibid.*
122. *Ibid.*
123. *Ibid.*
124. *Ibid.*
125. The account of the Blackwoods and The Statesmen is drawn from Terrell, *The Music Men*; Goff., *Close Harmony*; Davis, *The Legacy of the Blackwood Brothers*; and Taylor, *Happy Rhythm*.
126. Terrell, *The Music Men*, 44.
127. *Ibid.*, 122–123.
128. *Ibid.*, 125.
129. The conversations are recounted in Terrell, *The Music Men*, 111–112.

Chapter Four

1. The account of radio in the 1950s is drawn from Sterling and Kitross, *Stay Tuned*; and Hilliard and Keith, *The Broadcast Century*.

2. The account of Peterson is drawn from Peterson, *The Miracle Goes On*; and Sims, *The Life and Legacy of Al Smith*.
3. Peterson, *The Miracle Goes On*, 72.
4. *Ibid.*, 90.
5. The conversation is recounted in Peterson, *The Miracle Goes On*, 119–120.
6. Peterson, *The Miracle Goes On*, 117–118.
7. *Ibid.*, 144.
8. The account is found in Smith, *Al Smith's Treasury*, 85.
9. Peterson, *The Miracle Goes On*, 156.
10. *Ibid.*, 158.
11. John W. Peterson Music Company, "About Us," http://johnwpetersonmusic.com/about-us.php.
12. The account of Hamblen is drawn from Collins, *Turn Your Radio On*; Davis, *Inspirational Song and Hymn Stories*; Graham, *Just As I Am*; Carpenter, *Revive Us Again*; Martin, *A Prophet with Honor*; and Pollock, *Billy Graham*.
13. Graham, *Just As I Am*, 147.
14. Martin, *A Prophet with Honor*, 45.
15. Because Hamblen's highly publicized conversion was instrumental to the success of the Billy Graham 1949 Los Angeles Crusade, which in turn brought the evangelist to national attention, the conversion story is found in Graham, *Just As I Am*; Carpenter, *Revive Us Again*; Martin, *A Prophet with Honor*; and Pollock, *Billy Graham*.
16. The conversation between Hamblen and Wayne is recounted in Collins, *Turn Your Radio On*, 131–132.
17. The account of Stanphill is drawn from Osbeck, *101 More*; Collins, *Turn Your Radio On*; Davis, *Inspirational Song and Hymn Stories*; and Reynolds, *Companion to the Baptist Hymnal*.
18. The account of Lister is drawn from Terrell, *The Music Men*; Collins, *Turn Your Radio On*; Davis, *Inspirational Song and Hymn Stories*; and Terry, *Stories Behind 50 Southern Gospel Songs, Vols. 1 & 2*.
19. Terry, *Stories Behind 50 Southern Gospel Songs, Vol. 1*, 53.
20. Terry, *Stories Behind 50 Southern Gospel Songs, Vol. 2*, 151.
21. *Ibid.*, 151.
22. Collins, *Turn Your Radio On*, 97.
23. *Ibid.*, 98–99.
24. *Ibid.*, 254.
25. *Ibid.*, 255.
26. *Ibid.*, 255.
27. *Ibid.*, 256.
28. Terry, *Stories Behind 50 Southern Gospel Songs, Vol. 1*, 122.
29. *Ibid.*, 122.
30. Goff, *Close Harmony*, 215–216.
31. Terry, *Stories Behind 50 Southern Gospel Songs, Vol. 1*, 105.
32. The account of the Gaithers is drawn from B. Gaither, *I Almost Missed the Sunset*; and G. Gaither, *Because He Lives*.
33. B. Gaither, *I Almost Missed*, 41.
34. *Ibid.*, 42.
35. *Ibid.*, 46–47.
36. On "juke-box hymns" see Bergler, "I Found My Thrill."
37. On American popular religiosity at mid-century see Ellwood, *1950: Crossroads of American Religious Life*.
38. Bergler, "I Found My Thrill," 145.
39. B. Gaither, *I Almost Missed*, 47.
40. *Ibid.*, 48.
41. *Ibid.*, 41.
42. Davis, *The Legacy of the Blackwood Brothers*, 6.
43. B. Gaither, *I Almost Missed*, 42.
44. *Ibid.*, 42–43.
45. *Ibid.*, 43–44.
46. *Ibid.*, 44.
47. G. Gaither, *Because He Lives*, 65–66.
48. B. Gaither, *I Almost Missed*, 44–45.
49. *Ibid.*, 45.
50. *Ibid.*, 45–47.
51. *Ibid.*, 46.
52. *Ibid.*, 54.
53. *Ibid.*, 55–56.
54. *Ibid.*, 57–58.
55. *Ibid.*, 58–59.
56. *Ibid.*, 60–61.
57. *Ibid.*, 66.
58. *Ibid.*, 66.
59. The account of "The King is Coming" is taken from the March 1997 issue of *Singing News* magazine.
60. B. Gaither, *I Almost Missed*, 68.
61. *Ibid.*, 69.
62. *Ibid.*, 71.
63. *Ibid.*, 90.
64. *Ibid.*, 102.
65. *Ibid.*, 103–104.
66. For analyses of the Gaither Homecoming franchise in evangelical popular culture see Graves, "The Gaither Homecoming Videos"; and Keeler, "Why Do They Love Southern Gospel Music?"

Chapter Five

1. Sources for this chapter include Osbeck, *101 More*; Smith, *Al Smith's Treasury*; Reynolds, *Companion to the Baptist Hymnal*; Davis, *Inspirational Hymn and Song Stories*; Davis, *Enriching Hymn and Song Stories of the Twentieth Century*; Kerr, *Music in Evangelism*; Terrell, *The Music Men*; Collins, *Turn Your Radio On*;

Chapter Notes—Five

Terry, *Stories Behind 50 Southern Gospel Songs, Vols 1 & 2*; Osbeck, *101 Hymn Stories*; Osbeck, *Amazing Grace*; Osbeck, *52 Hymn Stories Dramatized*; Osbeck, *25 Most Treasured*; Lillenas, *Modern Gospel Song Stories*; Smith, *Oswald J. Smith's Hymn Stories*; and Emurian, *Forty Stories*. Unless otherwise noted, the accounts in this chapter are drawn primarily from these sources.

2. Smith, *Al Smith's Treasury*, 135.
3. Ibid., 250–251.
4. Benton Ackley was the chief collaborator with Oswald Smith, who provided helpful details about Ackley in *Oswald J. Smith's Hymn Stories*.
5. Smith, *Al Smith's Treasury*, 281.
6. Ibid., 79.
7. Osbeck, *Amazing Grace*, 220.
8. Emurian, *Forty Stories*, 20–21.
9. The account of Brumley is drawn primarily from Brumley Music, "Biographies," http://www.brumleymusic.com (accessed 2003).
10. Brumley Music, "Biographies."
11. Quoted in Goff, *Close Harmony*, 94.
12. Brumley Music, "Biographies."
13. Collins, *Turn Your Radio On*, 220.
14. Davis, *Inspirational Hymn and Song Stories*, 197.
15. Osbeck, *Amazing Grace*, 107.
16. The scene is recounted in Collins, *Turn Your Radio On*, 146–147.
17. Collins, *Turn Your Radio On*, 241.
18. Dorsey, "Precious Lord," 44.
19. Ibid.
20. Davis, *Inspirational Song and Hymn Stories*, 164.
21. Dorsey, "Precious Lord," 45.
22. Cusic, *The Sound of Light*, 81–82.
23. Harris, *The Rise of Gospel Blues*, 97.
24. Terry, *Stories Behind 50 Southern Gospel Favorites, Vol. 2*, 75.
25. Musician Biographies, "Hudson Whitaker," accessed August 13, 2016, at http://www.musicianguide.com/biographies/1608000662/Hudson-Whittaker.html.
26. Quoted in Desnoyers-Colas and Howard, "Bridge over Troubled Gospel Waters," 139.
27. Dorsey, "Precious Lord," 45–46.
28. The difficulties of reconciling divergent accounts are illustrated in the biography of Dorsey. The present account generally follows Dorsey, "Precious Lord," written by him in 1974 and published in 1976. By contrast, Terry in *Stories Behind 50 Southern Gospel Favorites, Vol. 2*, reported that in 1977 he tape-recorded an interview with Dorsey in which many details were differently recalled. In the Terry version, Dorsey learned to play the piano by age seven (not twelve), was converted at age sixteen (not twelve), wrote about three hundred gospel songs (not 250) and 450 blues songs (not 150), lost his wife and child in 1930 (not 1932), composed "Precious Lord, Take My Hand" in the music room (not the basement) of a local music college (not a hairdressing college), and composed "Peace in the Valley" in 1937 (not 1938) for Mahalia Jackson (not while riding a train).

29. Niernberg, *Say Amen, Somebody*.
30. The account of Dunlop also draws from BGCA, "Memorial to Merrill Dunlop."
31. Dunlop T1.
32. Ibid.
33. Ibid.
34. Ibid.
35. Ibid.
36. Ibid.
37. Ibid.
38. Ibid.
39. Dunlop T3.
40. Ibid.
41. The account of Ellis is drawn from Terrell, *The Music Men*, 174–176.
42. The account of Harkness is drawn from Lillienas, *Modern Gospel Song Stories*, 87; and Reynolds, *Companion to the Baptist Hymnal*, 326.
43. Kerr, *Music in Evangelism*. The account of Kerr also draws from Phil Kerr, *Phil Kerr's Gospel Songs*.
44. Winrod, "Introduction." Winrod was an independent evangelist known for his virulent antisemitic statements. The underlying racism of his comments in the Kerr songbook is evident.
45. Lillenas, *Modern Gospel Song Stories*, 123.
46. Ibid., 23.
47. Osbeck, *101 More*, 314.
48. Lillenas, *Modern Gospel Song Stories*, 123.
49. Ibid., 79.
50. Ibid., 97.
51. Ibid., 81.
52. Ibid., 31.
53. Osbeck, *101 More*, 315.
54. Lillenas, *Modern Gospel Song Stories*, 47.
55. Ibid., 105.
56. Lillienas, *Modern Gospel Song Stories*, 95.
57. Kerr, *Music in Evangelism*, 146.
58. Peterson, *The Miracles Goes On*, 131–132.
59. Smith, *Al Smith's Treasury*, 166.
60. Ibid., 166–167.
61. Farrer, *The Audrey Mieir Songbook*.
62. Smith, *Al Smith's Treasury*, 167.
63. Ibid., 167.
64. Ibid., 253.
65. Peterson, *The Miracles Goes On*, 131.

66. Wilhoit, *Rody*, 109.
67. Smith, *Al Smith's Treasury*, 253.
68. Lillenas, *Modern Gospel Song Stories*, 9.
69. Kerr, *Music in Evangelism*, 148.
70. The account of Smith is drawn primarily from Smith, *The People's Church and Its Pastor*; Smith, *The Story of My Life*; Smith, *What Hath God Wrought*; Smith, *Oswald J. Smith's Hymn Stories*; Hall, *Not Made for Defeat*; and Kee, "Marketing the Gospel."
71. Smith, *Oswald J. Smith's Hymn Stories*, 59.
72. Smith, *What Hath God Wrought*, 111–112.
73. Smith, *Oswald J. Smith's Hymn Stories*, 29.
74. Smith, *The People's Church*, 109.
75. *Ibid.*, 118.
76. *Ibid.*, 199.
77. Kee, "Marketing the Gospel," 107.
78. *Ibid.*, 108.
79. *Ibid.*, 109–110.
80. *Ibid.*, 112.
81. Smith, *The People's Church*, 110.
82. Smith, *What God Hath Wrought*, 112–113.
83. Smith, *Oswald J. Smith's Hymn Stories*, 19.
84. The story is recounted in Osbeck, *101 More*, 25–26.
85. Lillenas, *Modern Gospel Song Stories*, 37.
86. The account of Weigle also draws from Weigle, *I Sing of Thee*.
87. Smith, *Al Smith's Treasury*, 123.
88. Lillenas, *Modern Gospel Song Stories*, 61.
89. *Ibid.*, 61.
90. Smith, *Al Smith's Treasury*, 123.
91. *Ibid.*, 124.
92. *Ibid.*, 124.

Epilogue

1. Fuller, *Give the Winds*.
2. BGCA, "'As This is Our First Broadcast.'"
3. Sterling and Kitross, *Stay Tuned*.
4. Ward, "Air of the King."
5. *Ibid.*
6. This anecdote is found in Wyrtzen T2.
7. Winzenburg, "TV Ministries."
8. Ward, *Air of Salvation*, 175.
9. Brooks and Marsh, *The Complete Directory*.
10. Sterling and Kitross, *Stay Tuned*.
11. Melton et al., *Prime-Time Religion*.
12. Sterling and Kitross, *Stay Tuned*.
13. National Cable and Telecommunications Association, "Cable's Story."
14. Sterling and Kitross, *Stay Tuned*.
15. Winzenburg, "TV Ministries," 9.
16. Barna Group, "More People Use."
17. Ward, "Major Networks and Personalities."
18. Fratrik, *Radio Transactions 2001*.
19. Drushel, "The Telecommunications Act of 1996."
20. Sterling, "The Telecommunications Act of 1996."
21. Williams and Roberts, *Radio Industry Review 2002*.
22. DiCola and Thomson, *Radio Deregulation*.
23. Ward, "Consolidating the Gospel."
24. Ward, "Dark Preachers."
25. Ward, "Air of the King," 111.
26. Rodrigues, Green, and Virshup, *Radio Today*.
27. Ward, "Major Networks and Personalities."
28. Smith and Seignious, "Media, Message, and Ministry."
29. Loveless, *Manual of Gospel Broadcasding*, 21–25, 46–47.
30. Luhrmann, *When God Talks Back*, 4–5.
31. Simon, *Reader's Digest Treasury*, 277.

Bibliography

Primary Sources

Billy Graham Center Archives

ORAL HISTORY INTERVIEWS

"'As This is Our First Broadcast...' Perry Straw Excerpts." http://www2.wheaton.edu/bgc/archives/GUIDES/396.htm.
"Memorial to Merrill Dunlop, 1905-2002." http://www2.wheaton.edu/bgc/archives/mdunlop.html.
"Papers of Andrew Wyzenbeek—Collection 40." http://www2.wheaton.edu/bgc/archives/GUIDES/040.htm
"Papers of John Von Casper 'Jack' Wyrtzen—Collection 446." http://www2.wheaton.edu/bgc/archives/GUIDES/446.htm.
"Papers of Percy Bartimus Crawford and Ruth Crawford Porter—Collection 357." http://www2.wheaton.edu/bgc/archives/GUIDES/357.htm.
"Papers of Torrey Maynard Johnson—Collection 285." http://www2.wheaton.edu/bgc/archives/GUIDES/285.htm.
"Papers of William A. Drury—Collection 492." http://www2.wheaton.edu/bgc/archives/GUIDES/492.htm.

ONLINE EXHIBITS

"'As This is Our First Broadcast': Percy and Ruth Crawford and the Birth of Televangelism." http://www2.wheaton.edu/bgc/archives/exhibits/Crawford/crawford01.htm.
"The Greatest Youth Gathering in History." http://www2.wheaton.edu/bgc/archives/exhibits/YFC%201945/entrance.html
"Into the Big Tent: Billy Graham and the 1949 Christ for Greater Los Angeles Campaign," http://www2.wheaton.edu/bgc/archives/la49.html
"Jazz Age Evangelism: Paul Rader and the Chicago Gospl Tabernacle, 1922-1933." http://www2.wheaton.edu/bgc/archives/cgt.html.

Autobiographies

Crawford, Lois. *Papa and I.* Boone, IA: Self-published, 1981.
_____. *When God and Papa Ganged Up on Me.* Boone, IA: Self-published, 1977.
Gaither, Bill. *I Almost Missed the Sunset.* Nashville, TN: Thomas Nelson, 1992.
Gaither, Gloria. *Because He Lives.* Old Tappan, NJ: Revell, 1977.
Graham, Billy. *Just As I Am.* New York: HarperCollins, 1997.
Peterson, John W. *The Miracle Goes On.* Grand Rapids, MI: Zondervan, 1976.

Rodeheaver, Homer. *Singing Black: Twenty Thousand Miles with a Music Missionary.* Chicago: Rodeheaver Company, 1936.
_____. *Twenty Years with Billy Sunday.* Nashville, TN: Cokesbury, 1936.
Smith, Oswald J. *The People's Church and Its Pastor.* Toronto: People's Press, 1957.
_____. *The Story of My Life.* Toronto: People's Press, 1950.
_____. *What Hath God Wrought.* Toronto: People's Press, 1947.

Books

Crawford, Percy B. *The Art of Fishing for Men.* Chicago: Moody Press, 1950.
Loveless, Wendell P. *Manual of Gospel Broadcasting.* Chicago: Moody Press, 1946.

Song Story Books

Barrows, Cliff. *Crusade Hymn Stories.* Chicago: Hope Publishing, 1967.
Collins, Ace. *Turn Your Radio On.* Grand Rapids, MI: Zondervan, 1999.
Davis, Paul. *Enriching Hymn and Song Stories of the Twentieth Century.* Greenville, SC: Ambassador, 2002.
_____. *Inspirational Song and Hymn Stories of the Twentieth Century.* Greenville, SC: Ambassador, 2001.
Emurian, Ernest K. *Forty Stories of Famous Gospel Songs.* Grand Rapids, MI: Baker, 1959.
Kerr, Phil. *Music in Evangelism and Stories of Favorite Christian Songs.* Glendale, CA: Gospel Music Publishers, 1939.
Lillenas, Haldor. *Modern Gospel Song Stories.* Kansas City, MO: Lillenas, 1952.
Osbeck, Kenneth. *Amazing Grace: 366 Inspiring Hymn Stories for Daily Devotions.* Grand Rapids, MI: Kregel, 1990, rev. 2002.
_____. *52 Hymn Stories Dramatized.* Grand Rapids, MI: Kregel, 1992.
_____. *101 Hymn Stories.* Grand Rapids, MI: Kregel, 1982.
_____. *101 More Hymn Stories.* Grand Rapids, MI: Kregel, 1985.
_____. *25 Most Treasured Gospel Hymn Stories.* Grand Rapids, MI: Kregel, 1999.
Reynolds, William. *Companion to the Baptist Hymnal.* Nashville, TN: Broadman & Holman, 1976.
Shea, George Beverly. *Songs that Lift the Heart.* Old Tappan, NJ: Revell, 1972.
Smith, Alfred B. *Al Smith's Treasury of Hymn Histories.* Greenville, SC: Better Music Publications, 1982.
Smith, Oswald J. *Oswald J. Smith's Hymn Stories.* Winona Lake, IN: Rodeheaver Co., 1963, rev. 1969.
Terry, Lindsay. *Stories behind 50 Southern Gospel Songs, Vol. 1.* Grand Rapids, MI: Kregel, 2002.
_____. *Stories behind 50 Southern Gospel Songs, Vol. 2.* Grand Rapids, MI: Kregel, 2005.

Songbooks

Bock, Fred. *Favorites Number 8.* Grand Rapids, MI: Zondervan, 1975.
Booth, F. Carlton. *Living Above Songs and Choruses.* Grand Rapids, MI: Eerdmans, 1947.
Chicago Gospel Tabernacle. *Gospel Songs of the Air.* Chicago, IL: Chicago Gospel Tabernacle, 1929.
Crawford, Percy B. *Pinebrook Choruses.* Philadelphia, PA: Percy B. Crawford, 1934.
Crawford, Ruth D., and Percy B. Crawford. *The Young People's Church of the Air Hymn Book.* Grand Rapids, MI: Eerdmans, 1932.
Crawford, Ruth D., and Percy B. Crawford. *Pinebrook Melodies.* Grand Rapids, MI: Eerdmans, 1941.
Fuller, Charles E., H. Leland Green, and William MacDougall. *Old Fashioned Revival Hour Songs.* Winona Lake, IN: Rodeheaver Hall-Mack, 1950.

Kerr, Phil. *Phil Kerr's Gospel Songs*. Glendale, CA: Gospel Music, 1936.
Loveless, Wendell P. *Radio Songs and Choruses, Anniversary Combined Edition*. Wheaton, IL: Singspiration, 1951.
Peterson, John W. *Favorites Number 6*. Grand Rapids, MI: Zondervan, 1966.
_____. *Favorites Number 7*. Grand Rapids, MI: Zondervan, 1971.
Rodeheaver, Homer. *Homer Rodeheaver's World's Greatest Collection of Sacred Songs*. Chicago, IL: M. M. Cole, 1933.
_____. *Rodeheaver's Radio Songs*. Winona Lake, IN: Rodeheaver Hall-Mack, c. 1945.
Simon, William L. *Reader's Digest Treasury of Best Loved Songs*. Pleasantville, NY: Reader's Digest Association, 1972.
Smith, Alfred B. *Favorites Number 1*. Grand Rapids, MI: Zondervan, 1943.
_____. *Favorites Number 2*. Grand Rapids, MI: Zondervan, 1946.
_____. *Favorites Number 3*. Grand Rapids, MI: Zondervan, 1951.
_____. *Favorites Number 4*. Grand Rapids, MI: Zondervan, 1956.
_____. *Inspiring Hymns*. Grand Rapids, MI: Singspiration, 1951.
_____. *Living Hymns*. Greenville, SC: Better Music Publications, 1988.
_____. *Victorious Hymns*. Greenville, SC: Better Music Publications, 1975.
Smith, Alfred B., and Homer Rodeheaver. *Youth Rally Songs and Choruses*. Winona Lake, IN: Rodeheaver Hall-Mack, 1945.
Smith, Alfred B., and John W. Peterson. *Favorites Number 5*. Grand Rapids, MI: Zondervan, 1961.
Weigle, Charles F. *I Sing of Thee*. Holland, MI: True Life Library, 1943.

Recording Liner Notes

OLD FASHIONED REVIVAL HOUR

The Distinguished Old Fashioned Revival Hour Quartet. Waco, TX: Word Records, 1965.
Dr. Charles E. Fuller Presents the Old Fashioned Revival Hour Choir. Glendale, CA: Supreme Recordings, 196–?.
The Old Fashioned Revival Hour. New York: RCA Victor, 1958.
Old Fashioned Revival Hour Choir. Northridge, CA: Christian Faith Recordings, 195–?.
Sweeter as the Days Go By. Waco, TX: Word Records, 1969.

BACK TO THE BIBLE

Back to the Bible Broadcast. New York: RCA Victor, 1960.
Back to the Bible Choir and Quartet. Grand Rapids, MI: Zondervan, 195–?.
The Best Selections of the Back to the Bible Broadcast. Grand Rapids, MI: Zondervan, 1964.

HAVEN OF REST

Haven of Rest Favorites. Waco, TX: Word Records, 196–?.
Shipmates of Song. Waco, TX: Word Records, 1965.
Welcome Aboard. Kansas City, MO: Lillenas, 1971.

YOUTH ON THE MARCH

We Were There When It Happened. Bluebell, PA: Young People's Church of the Air, 1989.

LIGHT AND LIFE HOUR

Music of the Free Methodist Church. Waco, TX: Word Records, 195–?.

Secondary Sources

Abrams, Douglas Carl. *Selling the Old-Time Religion: American Fundamentalists and Mass Culture*. Athens: University of Georgia Press, 2001.

Albus, Harry. "By Air and by Tract." *Tract Club of America News* (January 1945): 5–8.
Armstrong, Ben. *The Electric Church.* Nashville, TN: Thomas Nelson, 1979.
_____. *Religious Broadcasting Sourcebook.* Morristown, NJ: National Religious Broadcasters, 1978.
Ault, James. *Spirit and Flesh: Life in a Fundamentalist Baptist Church.* New York: Knopf, 2004.
Bahr, Bob. *Man with a Vision: The Story of Percy Crawford.* Chicago: Moody Press, c. 1961.
Balmer, Randall. *The Making of Evangelicalism: From Revivalism to Politics and Beyond.* Waco, TX: Baylor University Press, 2010.
Barna Group. "More People Use Christian Media than Attend Church." Accessed May 17, 2014, https://www.barna.org/barna-update/article/5-barna-update/183-more-people-use-christian-media-than-attend-church#.VCB2thZaaRk.
Barnouw, Erik. *A Tower in Babel: A History of Broadcasting in the United States to 1933.* New York: Oxford University Press.
Bartkowski, John P. *Remaking the Godly Marriage: Gender Negotiation in Evangelical Families.* New Brunswick, NJ: Rutgers University Press, 2001.
Bendroth, Margaret Lamberts. *Fundamentalism and Gender, 1875 to the Present.* New Haven, CT: Yale University Press, 1996.
Bergler, Thomas E. "'I Found My Thrill': The Youth for Christ Movement and American Congregational Singing, 1940–1970." In *Wonderful Words of Life: Hymns in American Protestant History and Theology*, edited by Richard J. Mouw and Mark A. Noll, 123–149. Grand Rapids, MI: Eerdmans, 2004.
Blesh, Rudi. "Scott Joplin: Black-American Classicist." In *Scott Joplin: Collected Piano Works*, edited by Vera Brodsky Lawrence, xiii-xl. New York: New York Public Library, 1971.
Bollback, Harry. *The House That Jack Built.* Schroon Lake, NY: Word of Life Fellowship, 1972.
Brasher, Brenda E. *Godly Women: Fundamentalism and Female Power.* New Brunswick, NJ: Rutgers University Press, 1998.
Brereton, Virginia L. *Training God's Army: The American Bible School, 1880–1940.* Bloomington: Indiana University Press, 1990.
Brinkley, Alan. "The Scopes Trial: Darrow v. Bryan." In *Days of Destiny: Crossroads in American History*, edited by James M. McPherson and Alan Brinkley, 264–277. New York: Dorling Kindersley, 2001.
Brooks, Tim, and Earle F. Marsh. *The Complete Directory to Prime Time Network and Cable TV Shows, 1946-Present.* New York: Ballantine Books, 2009.
Bruns, Roger A. *Preacher: Billy Sunday and Big-Time American Evangelism.* New York: W.W. Norton, 1992.
Butler, Paul. *Save Them! The Life and Legacy of Paul Rader*, Chicago: EDIT Productions, 2003 [film].
Carlson, Bernice. "Patriarch of Christian Radio." *Sunday School Promoter* (December 1943): 12–16.
Carpenter, Joel A. *Revive Us Again: The Reawakening of American Fundamentalism.* New York: Oxford University Press, 1997.
Chafee, Steven H., and Miriam J. Metzger. "The End of Mass Communication?" *Mass Communication and Society* 4 (2001): 365–379.
"Christian Movies Produced by Christians That Promote or Embody Their Religions: 1980-Present." Box Office Mojo. Accessed January 5, 2016, http://www.boxofficemojo.com/genres/chart/?id=christian.htm.
Cook, Robert. "To Me to Live Is Christ." *Power* (January 1944): 1–3.
Crawford, Dan D. *Love, Wonderful Love: Remembering Ruth and Percy Crawford.* Bluebell, PA: Crawford Broadcasting Corporation, 2000.
_____. *A Thirst for Souls: The Life of Evangelist Percy B. Crawford, 1902–1960.* Selinsgove, PA: Susquehanna University Press, 2010.
Crowe, Charles W. "Religion on the Air." *The Christian Century* (August 23, 1944): 973–974.

Cusic, Don. *The Sound of Light: A History of Gospel Music.* Bowling Green, OH: Bowling Green State University Popular Press, 1990.
Davis, Paul. *The Legacy of the Blackwood Brothers.* Greenville, SC: Blue Ridge, 2000.
Davis, Richard. *The Web of Politics: The Internet's Impact on the American Political System.* New York: Oxford University Press, 1999.
DeBerg, Betty. *Ungodly Women: Gender and the First Wave of American Fundamentalism.* Macon, GA: Mercer University Press, 2000.
Desnoyers-Colas, Elizabeth F., and Stephanie Howard. "Bridge Over Troubled Gospel Waters." In *More than "Precious Memories": The Rhetoric of Southern Gospel Music,* edited by Michael P. Graves and David Fillingim, 131–152. Macon, GA: Mercer University Press, 2004.
DiCola, Peter, and K. Kristin Thomson. *Radio Deregulation: Has It Served Citizens and Musicians?* Washington, D.C.: Future of Music Coalition, 2002.
Dorsett, Lyle W. *Billy Sunday and the Redemption of Urban America.* Grand Rapids, MI: Eerdmans, 1991.
Dorsey, Thomas A. "Precious Lord, Take My Hand," *Moody Monthly* (April 1976): 44–46.
Drushel, Bruce E. "The Telecommunications Act of 1996 and Radio Market Structure." *Journal of Media Economics,* 11.3 (1998): 133–120.
Ellwood, Robert S. *1950: Crossroads of American Religious Life.* Louisville, KY: Westminster John Knox Press, 2000.
Emerson, Michael O., and Christian Smith. *Divided by Faith: Evangelical Religion and the Problem of Race in America.* New York: Oxford University Press, 2000.
Emerson, Michael O., Christian Smith, and David Sikkink. "Equal in Christ, but Not in the World: White Conservative Protestants and Explanations of Black-White Inequality." *Social Problems* 46 (1999): 398–417.
Evensen, Bruce J. *God's Man for the Gilded Age: D.L. Moody and the Rise of Modern Mass Evangelism.* New York: Oxford University Press, 2003.
Forbes, Forrest. *God Hath Chosen: The Story of Jack Wyrtzen and the Word of Life.* Grand Rapids, MI: Zondervan, 1948.
Fratrik, Mark. *Radio Transactions 2001: Where Did All the Deals Go?* Chantilly, VA: BIA Financial Networks, 2001.
Fuller, Daniel P. *Give the Winds a Mighty Voice: The Story of Charles E. Fuller.* Waco, TX: Word, 1972.
Gallagher, Sally K. *Evangelical Identity and Gendered Family Life.* New Brunswick, NJ: Rutgers University Press, 2003.
Getz, Gene. *MBI: The Story of the Moody Bible Institute.* Chicago: Moody Press, 1986.
Goff, James R., Jr. *Close Harmony: A History of Southern Gospel.* Chapel Hill: University of North Carolina Press, 2002.
Gordon, John Steele. *A Thread Across the Ocean: The Heroic Story of the Transatlantic Cable.* New York: Walker & Company, 2002.
Graves, Michael P. "The Gaither Homecoming Videos and the Ceremonial Reinstatement of Southern Gospel Music Performers." In *More than "Precious Memories": The Rhetoric of Southern Gospel Music,* edited by Michael P. Graves and David Fillingim, 153–181. Macon, GA: Mercer University Press, 2004.
Griffith, R. Marie. *God's Daughters: Evangelical Women and the Power of Submission.* Berkeley: University of California Press, 1997.
Grossman, Cathy Lynn. "Faith's Purchasing Power." *USA Today,* December 12, 2006. Accessed January 5, 2016, http://www.usatoday.com/news/religion/2006-12-12-faiths-purchasing-power_x.htm.
Hall, Douglas. *Not Made for Defeat: The Authorized Biography of Oswald J. Smith.* Grand Rapids, MI: Zondervan, 1969.
Hangen, Tona J. "Man of the Hour: Walter A. Maier and Religion by Radio on the *Lutheran Hour.*" In *Radio Reader: Essays in the Cultural History of Radio,* edited by Michele Hilmes and Jason Loviglio, 113–134. New York: Routledge, 2002.

———. *Redeeming the Dial: Radio, Religion, and Popular Culture in America.* Chapel Hill: University of North Carolina Press, 2002.

———. "Speaking of God, Listening for Grace: Christian Radio and Its Audiences." In *Radio Cultures: The Sound Medium in American Life,* edited by Michael C. Keith, 131–150. New York: Peter Lang, 2008.

Harris, Michael W. *The Rise of Gospel Blues: The Music of Thomas Andrew Dorsey in the Urban Church.* New York: Oxford University Press, 1992.

Hatch, Nathan O. *The Democratization of American Christianity.* New Haven, CT: Yale University Press.

Havick, John. "The Impact of the Internet on a Television-Based Society." *Technology in Society* 22 (2000): 273–287.

Hendershot, Heather. *Shaking the World for Jesus: Media and Conservative Evangelical Culture.* Chicago: University of Chicago Press, 2010.

Hilliard, Robert L., and Michael C. Keith. *The Broadcast Century and Beyond: A Biography of American Broadcasting,* 3rd Ed. Boston: Focal Press, 2001.

Hoke, Donald E. "Wendell Loveless—Devotional Writer." *Good Books* (Spring 1945): 3–8.

Hollander, Barry A. "Tuning Out or Tuning Elsewhere? Partisanship, Polarization, and Media Migration from 1998 to 2006." *Journalism & Mass Communication Quarterly* 85 (2008): 23–40.

Iyengar, S. Hanto, and Kyu S. Hahn. "Red Media, Blue Media: Evidence of Ideological Selectivity in Media Use." *Journal of Communication* 59 (2009): 19–39.

Jackson, Dave, and Neta Jackson, eds. *Celebration—Fifty Faithful Years.* Schroon Lake, NY: Word of Life Fellowship, 1989.

Katz, Steven B. "The Ethic of Expediency: Classical Rhetoric, Technology, and the Holocaust." *College English* 54 (1992): 255–275.

Kee, Kevin. "Marketing the Gospel: Music in English-Canadian Protestant Revivalism, 1884–1957." In *Wonderful Words of Life: Hymns in American Protestant History and Theology,* edited by Richard J. Mouw and Mark A. Noll, 96–122. Grand Rapids, MI: Eerdmans, 2004.

Keller, J.D. "Why Do They Love Southern Gospel Music? An Audience Study of the Bill Gaither Nostalgic Concert Video Presentations." In *More than "Precious Memories": The Rhetoric of Southern Gospel Music,* edited by Michael P. Graves and David Fillingim, 201–233. Macon, GA: Mercer University Press, 2004.

Kintz, Linda. *Between Jesus and the Market: The Emotions That Matter in Right-Wing America.* Durham, NC: Duke University Press, 1997.

———, and Julia Lesage, eds. *Media, Culture, and the Religious Right.* Minneapolis: University of Minnesota Press, 1998.

Larson, Erik. *Thunderstruck.* New York: Broadway, 2006.

Lewis, Tom. *Empire of the Air: The Men Who Made Radio.* New York: Edward Burlingame, 1991.

Lindlof, Thomas R. "Interpretive Community: An Approach to Media and Religion." *Journal of Media and Religion* 1 (2002): 61–74.

———. "Media Audiences as Interpretive Communities." *Communication Yearbook* 11 (1988): 81–107.

Loveless, Robert C. "Because of the Grace of God." In *An Evening with Pastor Loveless Appreciation Luau, September 19, 1981,* 3–15. Honolulu, HI: First Chinese Church of Christ, 1981.

Loveless, Wendell P. "How to Write a Gospel Chorus." *Sunday* (March 1945): 30–31, 46–47.

Luhrmann, T.M. *When God Talks Back: Understanding the American Evangelical Relationship with God.* New York: Knopf, 2012.

Magee, Malcolm D. "From Bible Belt to Sun Belt: Plain-Folk Religion, Grassroots Politics, and the Rise of Evangelical Conservatism." *Journal of Church and State* 53 (2011): 506–508.

Maier, Paul L. *A Man Spoke, a World Listened: The Story of Walter A. Maier and the Lutheran Hour.* New York: McGraw-Hill, 1963.

Mancini, Paolo. "Media Fragmentation, Party System, and Democracy," *The International Journal of Press/Politics* 18 (2013): 43–60.
Marsden, George M. *Fundamentalism and American Culture: The Shaping of Twentieth Century Evangelicalism, 1870–1925.* New York: Oxford University Press, 1980.
———. *Reforming Fundamentalism: Fuller Seminary and the New Evangelicalism.* Grand Rapids, MI: Eerdmans, 1987.
Martin, William. *A Prophet with Honor: The Billy Graham Story.* New York: William Morrow, 1991.
Matthews, Arthur. *Standing Up, Standing Together: The Emergence of the National Association Evangelicals.* Carol Stream, IL: National Association of Evangelicals, 1992.
McDannell, Colleen. "Christian Retailing." In *Material Christianity: Religion and Popular Culture in America,* by Colleen McDannell, 222–269. New Haven, CT: Yale University Press, 1995.
Melton, J. Gordon, Phillip Charles Lucas, and Jon R. Stone. *Prime-Time Religion: An Encyclopedia of Religious Broadcasting.* Phoenix: Oryx, 1997.
Mouw, Richard J. "'Some Poor Sailor, Tempest Tossed': Nautical Rescue Themes in Evangelical Hymnody." In *Wonderful Words of Life: Hymns in American Protestant History and Theology,* edited by Richard J. Mouw and Mark A. Noll, 234–250. Grand Rapids, MI: Eerdmans, 2004.
Murch, James DeForest. *Adventuring for Christ in Changing Times.* Louisville, KY: Restoration Press, 1973.
National Cable and Telecommunications Association. "Cable's Story." Accessed January 5, 2016, https://www.ncta.com/who-we-are/our-story.
The Nielsen Company. "Spiritual Entertainment: The Religious Genre in Book, Home Entertainment and Music." Accessed January 5, 2016, http://www.nielsen.com/us/en/newswire/2014/spiritual-entertainment-the-religious-genre-in-book-home-entertainment-and-music.html.
Nierenberg, George T. (Director). *Say Amen, Somebody* [documentary film]. New York: GTN Productions.
Noll, Mark A. *America's God: From Jonathan Edwards to Abraham Lincoln.* New York: Oxford University Press, 2002.
———. "God and the Colonies." In *Eerdmans' Handbook to Christianity in America,* edited by Mark A. Noll, Nathan O. Hatch, George M. Marsden, David F. Wells, and John D. Woodbridge, 1–156. Grand Rapids, MI: Eerdmans, 1983.
Pollock, John. *Billy Graham: The Authorized Biography.* New York: McGraw-Hill, 1966.
"'Precious Hiding Place' Brings Fame to Wendell Loveless, WMBI Director." *Gospel Music* (January 15, 1942).
Prior, Markus. *Post-Broadcast Democracy.* New York: Cambridge University Press, 2007.
"Religious Broadcasting Needs a Check-Up," *The Christian Century* (December 15, 1943): 1461.
Rodrigues, Ron, Jeff Green, and Lauren Virshup. *Radio Today: How America Listens to Radio, 2013 Edition.* Columbia, MD: Arbitron, 2013.
Roof, Wade Clark. *Spiritual Marketplace: Baby Boomers and the Remaking of American Religion.* Princeton, NJ: Princeton University Press, 2001.
Rosell, Garth M. *The Surprising Work of God: Harold John Ockenga, Billy Graham, and the Rebirth of Evangelicalism.* Grand Rapids, MI: Baker, 2008.
Sandeen, Ernest. *The Roots of Fundamentalism: British and American Millenarianism, 1800–1930.* Chicago: University of Chicago Press, 1970.
Schäfer, Axel R., ed. *American Evangelicals and the 60s.* Madison: University of Wisconsin Press, 2013.
Schäfer, Axel R. *Countercultural Conservatives: American Evangelicalism from the Postwar Revival to the New Christian Right.* Madison: University of Wisconsin Press, 2011.
Schultze, Quentin J. "The Mythos of the Electronic Church." *Critical Studies in Media Communication* 4 (1987): 245–261.

Shields, Jon A. "Framing the Christian Right: How Progressives and Post-War Liberals Constructed the Religious Right." *Journal of Church and State* 53 (2011): 635–655.
Shires, Preston. *Hippies of the Religious Right*. Waco, TX: Baylor University Press, 2007.
Siedell, Barry. *Gospel Radio*. Lincoln, NE: Good News Broadcasting Association, 1971.
Silverman, Kenneth. *Lightning Man: The Accursed Life of Samuel F.B. Morse*. New York: Knopf, 2003.
Sims, Robert. *The Life and Legacy of Al Smith*. Unpublished senior thesis. Greenville, SC: Department of Radio and Television, Bob Jones University, 2002.
Smith, L. Ripley, and Mark H. Seignious. "Medium, Message, and Ministry: How Music Radio Shapes Evangelical Culture." In *The Electronic Church in the Digital Age: Cultural Impacts of Evangelical Mass Media, Vol. 1*, edited by Mark Ward Sr., 101–125. Santa Barbara, CA: Praeger, 2016.
Smith, Wilbur M. *A Voice for God: The Life of Charles E. Fuller*. Boston: W.A. Wilde, 1949.
Starr, Paul. *The Creation of the Media: Political Origins of Modern Communications*. New York: Basic Books, 2005.
Steinberg, Shirley R., and Joe L. Kincheloe. *Christotainment: Selling Jesus Through Popular Culture*. Boulder, CO: Westview Press, 2009.
Sterling, Christopher H. "The Telecommunications Act of 1996." In *Museum of Broadcast Communications Encyclopedia of Radio, Vol. 3*, edited by Christopher H. Sterling, 1382–1384. Chicago: Fitzroy Dearborn Publishers, 2004.
_____, and John Michael Kitross. *Stay Tuned: A History of American Broadcasting, 3rd Ed*. Mahwah, NJ: Erlbaum, 2002.
Stout, Harry S. "The Transforming Effects of the Great Awakening." In *Eerdmans' Handbook to Christianity in America*, edited by Mark A. Noll, Nathan O. Hatch, George M. Marsden, David F. Wells, and John D. Woodbridge, 127–130. Grand Rapids, MI: Eerdmans, 1983.
Sumser, John. *The Conflict Between Secular and Religious Narratives in the United States: Wittgenstein, Social Construction, and Communication*. Lanham, MD: Lexington, 2016.
Sunstein, Cass R. *Republic.Com 2.0*. Princeton, NJ: Princeton University Press, 2009.
Sweeting, George. *The Jack Wyrtzen Story*. Grand Rapids, MI: Zondervan, 1960.
Taylor, David L. *Happy Rhythm: A Biography of Hovie Lister and the Statesmen Quartet*. Lexington, IN: LexingtonHaus, 1994.
Terrell, Bob. *The Music Men: The Story of Professional Gospel Quartet Singing*. Asheville, NC: Self-published, 1990.
Tewksbury, David. "The Seeds of Audience Fragmentation: Specialization in the Use of Online News Sites," *Journal of Broadcasting & Electronic Media* 49 (2005): 332–348.
_____. "What Do Americans Really Want to Know? Tracking the Behavior of News Readers on the Internet," *Journal of Communication* 53 (2003): 694–710.
Turner, Daniel L. *Standing Without Apology: The History of Bob Jones University*. Greenville, SC: Bob Jones University Press, 2001.
Ward, Mark, Sr. "Air of the King: Evangelicals and Radio." In *Evangelicals and Popular Culture: Pop Goes the Gospel, Vol. 1*, edited by Robert H. Woods Jr., 101–118. Santa Barbara, CA: Praeger, 2013.
_____. *Air of Salvation: The Story of Christian Broadcasting*. Grand Rapids, MI: Baker, 1994.
_____. "Consolidating the Gospel: The Impact of the 1996 Telecommunications Act on Religious Radio Ownership." *Journal of Media and Religion* 11 (2012): 11–30.
_____. "Dark Preachers: The Impact of Radio Consolidation on Independent Religious Syndicators." *Journal of Media and Religion* 8 (2009): 79–96.
_____. "Give the Winds a Mighty Voice: Evangelical Culture as Radio Ecology," *Journal of Radio and Audio Media* 21 (2014): 115–133.
_____. "Major Networks and Personalities." In *The Electronic Church in the Digital Age: Cultural Impacts of Evangelical Mass Media, Vol. 1*, edited by Mark Ward Sr., 253–284. Santa Barbara, CA: Praeger, 2016.
_____. "Televangelism, Audience Fragmentation, and the Changing Coverage of Scandal."

In *Scandal in a Digital Age,* edited by Hinda Mandell and Gina Masullo Chen, 53–68. New York: Palgrave MacMillan.

Wightman, Gavin. *Signor Marconi's Magic Box.* Cambridge, MA: Da Capo, 2003.

Wilhoit, Bert. *Rody: Memories of Homer Rodeheaver.* Greenville, SC: Bob Jones University Press, 2001.

Williams, George, and Scott Roberts. *Radio Industry Review 2002: Trends in Ownership, Format, and Finance.* Washington, D.C.: Federal Communications Commission, 2002.

Winrod, Gerald B. "Introduction." In *Phil Kerr's Gospel Songs,* edited by Phil Kerr, flyleaf. Glendale, CA: Gospel Music, 1936.

Winzenburg, Stephen. "TV Ministries Use of Air Time, Fall 2004." Accessed January 5, 2016, http://faculty.gvc.edu/swinzenburg/tv_ministries_study.pdf.

Wright, J. Elwin. *The Old Fashioned Revival Hour and the Broadcasters.* Boston: The Fellowship Press, 1940.

Young, Shawn David. "From Hippies to Jesus Freaks: Christian Radicalism in Chicago's Inner-City." *Journal of Religion and Popular Culture* 22 (2010): 1–28.

General Index

Ackley, Alfred H. 52, 219–221, 250
Ackley, Benton D. 52, 191, 219–221, 249–250
Aerial Girls 31
Ahuer, Leopold 167
Akers, Doris 215
Albert E. Brumley & Sons Music Company 226
Albert E. Brumley Memorial Gospel Sing 226
Alexander, Charles 238, 240, 247, 248
All-Night Broadcast 101, 175, 176
Alleluia! A Praise Gathering of Believers (record album) 217
Allen, Fred 60, 151
Allen, Gracie 59
Allen, Joe M. 47, 49
Alliance Gospel Tabernacle (New York) 130
Alliance Tabernacle (Pittsburgh) 29
Alliance Tabernacle (Toronto) 249
Alpha Gamma Omega Christian Fellowship 78, 79
AM-FM radios 185
AM radio 100, 115, 139, 184, 185
American Broadcasting Corporation (ABC) 73, 85, 86, 112, 115, 145, 154, 161, 163, 256, 257
American Marconi Company 20, 80
American Telephone & Telegraph (AT&T) 18, 21
America's Keswick 45
Amos n' Andy 58, 59
Anderson College 212
Angelus Temple 34, 93
Announcers Trio 42
Armed Forces Network 154
Armstrong, Edwin 19, 60
Arthur Godfrey Show 203
Arthur Godfrey's Talent Scouts 180
At Home with the Blackwood Brothers 180
Atwood, Rudy 70–71, 73–74, 256
Autry, Gene 157, 194
AWANA 31
Ayer, William Ward 1–2, 105–106, 107, 111

Back Home Hour 31, 138
Back Home in Indiana (record album) 215–216
Back Stage Wife 60
Back to the Bible x, 8, 11, 89–92, 188, 257
Back to the Bible Missionary Agency 91
Back to the Bible Quartet 3, 62, 91–92
Bakker, Jim 258
Bankhead, Tallulah 261
Baptist Bible Union 65
Barnes Memorial Church 79
Barnhouse, Donald Grey 26, 106
Barrows, Cliff 154, 158, 160, 161, 164
Barth, Karl 156
Bartlett, Eugene 221–222, 225–226
Baxter, Clarice 98
Baxter, J.R. 97, 98, 101
Bell, Alexander Graham 18
Ben Lippen Bible Conference 45
Ben Speer Music 209, 213
Bennard, George 52, 219
Dennett, Walter 161–163
Benny, Jack 59
Benson Music 216
Bergen, Edgar 60
Bertermann, Eugene 110
Bethel Temple 200–201
Bethel Union Church 243–244
Better Music Publications 172
Bible Fellowship Hour 90
Bible Institute of Los Angeles (Biola) 65, 66, 67, 72, 75–77, 89
Bible Women Speak Today 88
Bibletown Bible Conference 145, 236
Bibletown Community Church 145
Biederwolf, W.E. 51
The Big Show 261
Billy Graham Center Archives x, 10
Billy Graham Evangelistic Association 163
Billy Sunday Tabernacle 52, 144, 223
Blackwood, Cecil 181
Blackwood, Doyle 173, 175, 180
Blackwood, James 49, 100, 101, 173–177, 180–183, 227

283

Blackwood, Roy 174, 175, 180
Blackwood, R.W. 174, 175, 180-181
Blackwood Brothers 3, 9, 100, 173-177, 179-183, 187, 203, 206, 209, 210, 233
Bliss, Phillip P. 3, 131, 165, 169, 170-171
Bob Jones College 148
Bob Jones University ix, x
Boca Raton Bible Conference and Church 45
Bollback, Harry x, 132, 135
Boone, Pat 233
Boone Biblical College 22
Booth, F. Carlton 130, 132-133
Boston Pops 226
Bowman, Bob 95, 96
Braunlin, Herman 166-167
Breakfast Brigade 32
Breakfast Club 140
Brinkley, John "Doc" 100
Broadbent, George 71
Brock, Blanche 52, 222-225
Brock, Virgil 52, 222-225
Brown, Kenneth 71
Brown, R.R. 24-25
Brumley, Albert E. 1, 206, 222, 225-227
Brumley, Goldie 226
Brunswick Records 100
Brushwyler, Vincent 111
Bryan, William Jennings 6
Buck Rogers 60
Burns, George 59
Burr, Grace 223
Burr, Horace 223

cable television 259
Cadman, S. Parkes 105
Calvary Baptist Church 2, 105, 106, 118, 136, 152
Calvary Church 65, 66, 67, 68
Calvary Church Radio Bible Class 67
Calvary Episcopal Church 15-16
The Calvary Pulpit (magazine) 105
Campbell, Ken 236
Canaanland Music 228, 229
Cantor, Eddie 59
Captain Midnight 60
car radios 60, 185
Carman 218
Carmichael, Ralph 145
Cash, Johnny 232
The Cathedrals Quartet 101, 211, 229
Cedar Lake Bible Conference 45
Century of Progress World's Fair 35
Chapel Hour 138, 140, 145, 146
Chapman, J. Wilbur 238
Charles, Ray 226
Chatauqua movement 40, 51, 52
Cheer Up 191
Chi Beta Alpha (Christians Born Again) 126-127, 128
Chicago Gospel Tabernacle x, 27, 29-35, 42, 70, 78, 136, 140, 190, 227, 233, 235-236, 241, 249
Children's Bible Hour 45
Choctaw County Jubilee Singers 174
Christian and Missionary Alliance 24, 28-29, 34, 63, 130, 249
Christian Business Men's Committee 129, 140, 157
Christian Century (magazine) 103
Christian Endeavor 140
Christian Faith Records 70, 71, 96
Christian Harmony Trio 126
Christian Life (magazine) 86
Christian Right 9, 11
Christian World Wide Couriers 34, 249
The Christian's Hour 110
Christiansen, Avis 43, 227-228, 242
Church of God (Anderson) 213, 237
Church of the Nazarene (Auburn) 240
Church of the Nazarene (denomination) 241
Church of the Open Door 64, 76, 77
Churchill Tabernacle 249
Clarke, Harry 227
Clayton, Norman 4, 132, 133-134, 191
Clooney, Rosemary 196, 207
Club Time 152, 154
Coleman, Jack 71
College Briefing Conference 156
Columbia Broadcasting System (CBS) 21, 26, 31, 32, 50, 53, 57, 58, 67, 69, 79, 101, 103-104, 105, 108, 109, 115, 152, 159, 175, 236, 255, 256
Columbia Records 52, 100, 216
Columbia Workshop 60
Como, Perry 115
Conant, James 235
Concordia Seminary 57, 58
Confident Living (magazine) 92
Conrad, Frank 20
consolidation (radio industry) 2, 259-260
Contemporary Christian Music 2, 4, 9, 258, 260
Cook, Bob 140
Coolidge, Calvin 21
Correll, Charles 59
Cosmopolitan Tabernacle 249
Coughlin, Charles 103
Country Church of Hollywood 70
Cowboy Church of the Air 159, 196
Crabtree, Jim 216
Crawford, Dan 82, 84
Crawford, Dean x, 82
Crawford, Donald 81, 82, 83, 88
Crawford, Donna Lee 82
Crawford, J. Charles 22-24
Crawford, Lois 22-24
Crawford, Margaret 74, 78, 87
Crawford, Percy ix, x, 3, 8, 9, 36, 45, 62, 74-89, 103, 104, 116, 117, 120-123, 124, 126, 127, 128, 133, 137, 140, 142, 143, 151, 164, 167, 186, 189, 191, 256-257, 260

General Index

Crawford, Richard (Dick) 82
Crawford Broadcasting Corporation x, 87, 88
Crawford Porter, Ruth 81–82, 86, 87, 88, 89
Crew Cuts 207
Crosby, Bing 59
Crosby, Fanny 3, 4, 165, 172, 192
Crowell, Henry 37–40
Crowell, H.P. 37
Crowley, Dale, Sr. 111
Crumpler, Denver 179
Crusaders Quartet 204, 205

Dale Presbyterian Church 248
Darby, John Nelson 8
DeArmond, Lizzie 53, 56
Death Valley Days 59
Deaton, Otis 99
Decca Records 52
DeCou, Harold 145
Deets Pacific College 239
Defenders of the Christian Faith 66
De Forest, Lee 18–19
De Forest Wireless Telegreaph Company 18–19
Dempsey, Jack 20, 99
Derricks, Cleavant 228–229
Dibble, George 246
Dick Tracy 60
Dienert, Fred 161–163
digital mandate 259
dispensational premillennialism 8
Dobson, James 257
Dodds, Gil 143
Dorsey, Nettie 229–230, 231
Dorsey, Thomas 229–233, 271n28
Dorsey House of Music 232
Drury, Bill 80, 83–84
Dunlop, Merrill ix, 4, 27, 29, 32, 33–34, 35, 42, 52, 140, 141, 142, 145–146, 190, 227, 233–237
Durante, Jimmy 60
Duvall, R. Fenton 81
Dyrness, C.T. 136

Earlham College 224
Ebenezer Baptist Church 230
Echols, Odis 99
The Ed Sullivan Show 233
Edison Company 48, 52
electrical transcription *see* long-play (LP) records
Ellis, Vep 237
Elsner, Theodore 159–161
Emerson Radio Company 60
Epp, Theodore 3, 8–9, 61, 89–92, 103, 188, 257–258
Erickson, Clarence 35, 136, 236
European Enlightenment 7
The Evangelical Alliance Mission 136

Evangelical Free Church 136
Evans, Dale 233
Excell, Edwin O. 245

Fairmont Friends Academy 224
Falwell, Jerry 73, 257, 259
Familiar Hymns 191
Family Altar League 42
The Famous Hokum Boys 231
Far East Broadcasting Company 96
Favorites (songbook) 11, 167
Federal Communications Commission (FCC) 60, 105, 111, 112, 114–115, 184, 185, 257, 259
Federal Council of Churches 104–105, 108, 110
Federal Radio Commission (FRC) 22, 38–39, 60
Ferrin, Howard 132
Fessenden, Reginald 18
Fibber McGee and Molly 60
Field, Cyrus 17
First Baptist Church of Elkhart 251
First Baptist Church of Minneapolis 156
First Baptist Church of Muskogee 242
First Baptist Church of Okmulgee 242
First Chinese Church of Christ 46
First Church of the Nazarene (Indianapolis) 240, 253
First Great Awakening 6–7
First Mate Bob *see* Myers, Paul
First Methodist Church of Collingswood 81
First Presbyterian Church of Hollywood 156
Fisher, Doug 140
Florida Bible Institute 148
FM radio 60, 115, 185, 216
Focus on the Family 257
Foley, Red 176, 232
Ford, Tennessee Ernie 208, 232, 233
Forest Home 156
Fort Wayne Gospel Tabernacle 35
45 rpm records 115, 237
Fosdick, Harry Emerson 105
Founder's Week Conference 131, 169, 191
The Four D's 82, 85
Foust, Ira 47
Fowler, Wally 175–177, 179
Fox, Eldridge 179
Fox, Leonard 96
Francisco, Don 218
Frank Stamps All-Star Quartet 99, 174, 175, 177
Franklin, Aretha 226, 232
Free Methodist Church 90
Freeman, Cat 179
Frye, Theodore 230
The Fundamentals (publication) 8
Fundamental Young People's Fellowship 146
Fuller, Charles E. ix, 3, 8, 9, 26, 36, 62–74, 76, 77, 103–105, 106, 109, 112, 116, 117, 131,

General Index

140, 159–160, 163, 186, 189, 256–257, 258, 260
Fuller, Daniel 67–68
Fuller, Grace 3, 63, 64, 65, 68, 72
Fuller, Henry 62–63
Fuller Seminary 73

Gabriel, Charles H. 245
Gaither, Bill 9, 207–218, 233
Gaither, Danny 209, 212, 214, 218
Gaither, Gloria 9, 211, 212–213, 215–218
Gaither, Mary Ann 209, 212, 214–215
Gaither and Friends 218
Gaither Music Company 213, 218
Gaither Trio 214–218
Gaither Vocal Band 218
Gangbusters 60
Gideons 94, 129
The Glory Road 182
Godfrey, Arthur 115, 180, 203
Golden Keys Quartet 209, 214
Good News Broadcaster (magazine) 91
Good News Broadcasting Association 91, 92
Goodman, Benny 115
Goose Creek Quartet 70
Gosden, Freeman 59
Gospel Broadcasting Association 68, 72
Gospel Music News (magazine) 101
Gospel Quartet Music Company 180
Gospel Tabernacle (Philadelphia) 160
Graham, Billy 9, 80, 88, 128, 141, 143, 145, 146–165, 167, 168, 169, 186, 193, 194–196
Graham, Ruth 148–149, 152, 163, 168
Grand Ole Opry 176, 209
Gray, James 36–37, 39
The Great Gildersleeve 115
Green, Fred 47–48
Green, Leland 67, 71, 256
Green, Steve 218
The Green Hornet 60
Griffith, Andy 226
The Guiding Light 60
Gull Lake Bible Conference 45

Haggai, John 236
Hall, Connor 178
Ham, Mordecai 147, 177
Hamblen, Stuart 9, 157–159, 164, 186, 193–197, 207, 208, 251
Hamblen, Suzy 158, 194, 195
Hamilton, J.E. 98
Hammontree, Homer 227, 235, 240
Happy Hour 67
Harding, Warren 1, 15, 21
Harkness, Robert 66, 236, 238
Harlan, Al 70
The Harmoneers 237
Harper, Redd 251
Hart, Paul 213
Hartford Music Company 222, 225–226

Hartford Quartet 226
Harvey, Paul 188
Hauptmann, Bruno 59
Haven of Rest x, 54, 92, 95–96
Haven of Rest Quartet 3, 11, 62, 96–97
Havner, Vance 173
Hawthorne Gospel Tabernacle 166
HCJB 30, 91
Hearst, William Randolph 143–144, 159, 164, 196
Herald of Song (magazine) 222
Herold, Doc 19
Herrington, Frances 234
Hertz, Heinrich 17
Hess, Jake 179, 181, 182
higher criticism 6, 7
Hill, Gordon 178, 179
Hill, Jim 209
Hine, Stuart K. 186
Hofer, David 113–114
Hofer, Egon 113
Hogg, Josiah 70
Hollywood Christian Group 157, 194, 195
Hollywood Presbyterian Church 35
Homecoming Friends 218
Homecoming Videos 218
Homeland Harmony Quartet 178
Hope, Bob 60
Hosier, Herman 96
Houghton, Will 118, 136, 142, 152
Houghton College 151
Hour of Decision 163–164
Howell, Barry 178
Howell, Major 178
Hubbard, David 73
Huff, Ron 217
Humbard, Rex 257, 259
Hutchinson, Henry 125
Hyde, Rosel 111
Hymns for the Family of God (hymnal) 218
Hymns from the Chapel 149, 152
Hymntime Company 198, 201

In Touch 257
Independent Bible Church 189
Inerrancy 7
Insight for Living 257
Institute for Education by Radio (IER) 104, 107, 110
International Church of the Foursquare Gospel 26, 243
International Sunday School Convention 246

Jack Armstrong—The All-American Boy 60
Jackson, Mahalia 206, 232, 271 *n*28
Jaissle, Arthur 70
James, Harry 115
James D. Vaughn Publishing Company 47, 48, 98, 99, 174, 222

General Index

Jesus Movement 2, 4
John Daniels Quartet 175, 176
John W. Peterson Music Company 193
Johnson, Floyd 31
Johnson, Jimmie 236
Johnson, Lyndon 232
Johnson, Torrey x, 9, 32, 33, 34, 36, 78, 104, 135–147, 149, 150, 152–153, 154, 155, 156, 164, 233, 236
Jones, Bob, Sr. 25, 54
Jones, Clarence 30, 31, 33, 36, 91
Jones, Howard 33
Joplin, Scott 97
The Joyful Sound 73
juke box hymns 207–208, 216

KAIM/Honolulu, Hawaii 46
Kaiser, Kurt 145
KCRC/Enid, Oklahoma 90
KDKA/Pittsburgh, Pennsylvania 1, 15–16, 20, 26, 50, 53
KEAR/San Francisco, California 257–258
Kendrick, Bervin 178
Kerr, Phil 3, 61–62, 191, 238–239, 243, 246
KFAB/Lincoln, Nebraska 91
KFBI/Salina, Kansas 89, 187, 188, 190
KFGQ/Boone, Iowa 23–24
KFI/Los Angeles, California 68, 95
KFOR/Lincoln, Nebraska 91
KFSG/Los Angeles, California 26, 93
KFUO/St. Louis, Missouri 26, 58
KGER/Long Beach, California 67, 68, 69, 72
KGGF/Coffeeville, Kansas 198
KGO/San Francisco, California 257
Kieffer, Aldine 46–47
kinescopes 256
King, B.B. 232
King, Martin Luther, Jr. 232
King's College 45, 80, 82, 84, 86, 88, 140
King's College Trumpet Trio 85
King's Karollers 153
The King's Korean Mission 86
King's Life (magazine) 87
The King's Productions 86
King's Singers 82
The Kingsmen Quartet 179
KJS/Los Angeles, California 66, 71, 77
Kleinsasser, David 95
Kline, Stanley 124, 125
KMA/Shenandoah, Iowa 91, 175
KMPC/Los Angeles, California 95
Knox, John 70
KNX/Hollwood, California 68, 69
KRDU/Dinuba, California 114
KREG/Santa Ana, California 66, 67
KRLD/Dallas, Texas 100, 101, 175
KTBI/Los Angeles, California 66, 72
KTHS/Hot Springs, Arkansas 100
KTIS/St. Paul, Minnesota 155
Kuhlman, Kathryn 214

Kunz, Al 116, 126, 127, 128–129
KVOD/Denver, Colorado 91
KVOO/Tulsa, Oklahoma 89, 90, 101, 188
KWKH/Shreveport, Louisiana 175
KYB (Know Your Bible) Club 42, 43

Lake Avenue Church 73
Lake Harbor Bible Conference 34
Lanza, Mario 207
Latham, Lance 30, 31, 33, 36, 227, 235
Laurelton Baptist Church 172
Lefevre Trio 178, 203
Let's Go Back to the Bible 152
L.I.F.E. Bible College 243
The Life of Riley 115
Light and Life Hour 90
Lillenas, Bertha Mae 239, 241
Lillenas, Haldor 227, 239–241, 245, 253
Lillenas Music Company 206, 237, 238, 240
Lindbergh, Charles 59, 99
Lister, Hovie 177–180, 182, 183, 202, 203
Lister, Mosie 9, 178, 187, 201–206
Lister Brothers Quartet 177
Little Orphan Annie 59
Loes, Harry Dixon 52, 190, 191, 227, 241–243, 245
Lombardo, Guy 118
The Lone Ranger 60
long-play (LP) records 60, 69, 100, 115–116, 174, 237
Lorenz Publishing Company 246
Los Angeles Gospel Tabernacle 249
Loveless, Robert 40–41, 42
Loveless, Wendell P. x, 3, 8, 11, 36–46, 80, 83, 189, 190, 227, 260
Lundberg, John 70
Lutheran Church Missouri Synod (LCMS) 57, 58
The Lutheran Hour 58–59, 110, 159, 161
Lutheran Laymen's League 58
Lux Radio Theater 60
Lyceum Art Conservatory 40
Lyceum movement 40
Lyles, Bill 180, 181

Ma Perkins 184
MacDougall, Bill 70
MacKenzie, Bob 215, 217–218
Madison Street Bible Church 235
Maiden Lane Church of God 214
Maier, Walter 26, 57–59, 60, 61, 62, 103, 104, 106, 109, 110, 112, 116, 159–160, 162, 163
Major Bowes and His Original Amateur Hour 60, 187
Manna Music 243
Maranatha Bible Conference 34
March of the Ages 31
Marconi, Guglielmo 17, 18
Marconi Corporation 19
Martin, Gene 198

Masters V 183
Maxwell, James Clerk 17
McCarthy, Charlie 60
McCormick Theological Seminary 247
McGranahan, James 169
McKee, Arthur 248
McNichols, Dean 96
McPherson, Aimee Semple 34, 93, 243
McSpadden, Gary 218
Mears, Henrietta 156, 157
Mecca Temple 131
Meditations in the Psalms 152
Melody-Aires (songbooks) 169, 192
Melody Masters Quartet 179, 203
Mercury Theater of the Air 60
Messiah Church 137
Midwest Bible Church 135, 138, 140, 145, 146, 149, 152
Mieir, Audrey 243-244
Mieir Choir Clinic 243
Mieir Music Foundation 243
Miles, C. Austin 177, 219
Miller, Glenn 115
Miller, Rhea 151
Miracles and Melodies 43, 152
Monaco, Gino 151
Montrose Bible Conference 169
Moody, Dwight L. 3, 7-8, 18, 24, 28, 43, 64, 105, 152, 165, 170, 248
Moody Bible Institute (MBI) x, 26, 36-43, 46, 105, 106, 118, 129, 131, 135, 136, 142, 149-150, 152, 167, 169, 190, 191, 227, 235, 242, 245, 246, 247
Moody Broadcasting Network x, 46
Moody Church 29, 32, 34, 54, 111, 131, 142-143, 154, 227, 234, 235, 242, 247
Moody Presents 43
Moody Press 169, 192
Morning Glory Club 42
Morse, Samuel F.B. 16
Morse code 17, 18, 62
Mosie Lister Publications 205, 206
Mountain Top Hour 132
Murch, James DeForest 110, 111
music charting 258
The Music Man (musical) 261
Musto, Steven 88
Mutual Broadcasting System 3, 69-70, 71-73, 79, 84, 86, 96, 103, 104-105, 109-110, 131, 152, 159, 184, 256
Myers, Lee 98
Myers, Paul 8, 62, 92-97, 103, 116
Myers, Thelma 93, 94-95

National Association of Evangelicals (NAE) 107, 108, 109, 110, 111, 138, 139, 146
National Baptist Convention 231
National Barn Dance 60
National Broadcasting Corporation (NBC) 21, 50, 53, 69, 73, 79, 96, 103-104, 105, 106, 108, 109, 112, 114, 115, 149, 151, 159, 163, 177, 220, 256, 261
National Convention of Gospel Choirs and Choruses 233
National Council of Churches 103, 112, 208
National Electric Signaling Company 18
National Quartet Convention 182
National Radio Chapel 31
National Radio Pulpit 105
National Religious Broadcasters (NRB) ix, 1, 111, 160
Nazarene Church of Alexandria 209
Nazarene Publishing Company 240
Nazarene Tabernacle of Lawrenceburg 49
NBC v. United States 115
Neilsen, James 33
Nelson, Kenny 95, 96
New England Fellowship (NEF) 106
New Gaither Vocal Band 218
Nicholson, Willie 76
Niebuhr, Reinhold 156
Noble, Edward 115
Norse Gospel Trio 89, 90, 188
Northern Baptist Seminary 138
Northwestern Schools 155-156, 163

Oak Ridge Boys 176, 177
Ockenga, Harold 106-107
Office of War Information 115
Old Fashioned Meeting 73, 256
Old Fashioned Revival Hour ix, x, 3, 9, 11, 61, 68-74, 104, 109, 117, 159, 185, 186, 189, 261
Old Fashioned Revival Hour Choir 71
Old Fashioned Revival Hour Quartet 3, 11, 62, 70-71, 168, 186
Old Time Gospel Hour 73
Oldham, Doug 213-214
Oliver, Richard J. 33
Oliver, Richard W. 33
Olsen, Erling 152
Orr, J. Edwin 156
Ortlund, Anne 71
Osbeck, Kenneth 227
Ott, Doy 179
Ozzie and Harriet 115

Pacific Garden Mission 53
Paragon Music 218
Paramount Records 231
Park Street Church 106
Pathfinders Quartet 209-211, 212, 214
Patti, Sandi 218
Paul Rader Tabernacle (Los Angeles) 70
Payne, Ernie 95, 96
Payne, Glen 101, 211
payola 185
Peale, Norman Vincent 208
Pearson, Drew 163
Peniel Mission 239
penny press 7

General Index 289

The People's Church 249, 250
Peterson, John W. x, 4, 9, 84, 89, 134, 168, 169–170, 171, 172, 187–193, 242, 245
Peterson, Marie 190
Phi Gamma 127
Phil Kerr Singers 243
Philpot, Ford 236
Pietsch, Paul 113
Pilgrim Baptist Church 230, 231, 233
The Pilgrim's Hour 67, 72, 109
Pinebrook Book-of-the-Month Club 80
Pinebrook Bookstore 80
Pinebrook Camps ix, 11, 45, 79–80, 82, 83–84, 86, 88, 121–123, 124, 127, 128, 133, 167
Pinebrook Praises 86, 87, 88
Pinebrook songbooks 11, 82, 84, 133
Placentia Bible Class 65
Placentia Presbyterian Church 64, 65
Pocket Testament League 126, 129
portable radios 60, 185
Praise Gathering for Believers (event) 218
Presley, Elvis 206, 232
Princeton Theological Seminary 145, 156
Providence Bible Institute 132
Puritans 6

Rader, Paul ix, x, 8, 26, 27–36, 54, 64, 66, 70, 73, 78, 91, 130, 132, 136, 137, 138–139, 142, 164, 190, 227, 233, 234, 235–236, 241, 242, 243, 248, 249
Radio Act of 1912 19
Radio Act of 1927 38
Radio Bible Class 67, 68, 69
Radio Chapel Service 25
Radio Rangers 31
Radio Revival Hour 69
Radio School of the Bible 42, 43
Rainbow Point 53, 55, 223
Rainbow Ranch 55
Rainbow Records 55
Rainey, Ma 231
Rangers Quartet 178, 180, 202
RCA Victor Records *see* Victor Records
The Right Start for the Day 111
Riley, William Bell 155, 156
Rimmer, Harry 53, 118, 137
Ritter, Tex 157, 194
Roberts, Oral 237, 257, 258
Robertson, Pat 88, 259
Rockwood Park Assembly of God 201
Rodeheaver, Homer x, 3, 8, 11, 27, 47, 49–56, 101–102, 151, 189, 221, 222, 250, 261
The Rodeheaver Company 51, 220, 221, 246, 249
Rodeheaver Hall-Mack Company 55, 134
Rogers, Roy 157, 194, 232, 233
The Romance of Helen Trent 59
Roosevelt, Franklin 68, 114, 115
Rosell, Mervin 12
Rowe, James 48

Ruebush, Ephraim 46–47
Ruebush Kieffer Normal School 47
Ruth, Babe 99

Sacred Harp 47
Salina Bible Hall 188
Salvation Army 33, 157
Sankey, Ira 3, 18, 165
Sarnoff, David 20
satellite television 2, 21, 259
Sawdust Trail 157–158, 193, 194, 195
Say Amen, Somebody (film) 233
Schaeffer, Verne 23
Schilling, George 117–118, 119–120, 125
School of Sacred Music x, 52, 55, 222, 245
Schuler, George 190, 227, 245–246
Schuller, Robert 259
Scofield Reference Bible 8
Scopes "Monkey Trial" 4, 6, 12
Scott, Randolph 157, 194
Scottish Common Sense Realism 7
Seattle Pacific College 90
Sebren, George 47
Second Great Awakening 7
Second Mate Bobbie *see* Bob Bowman
78 rpm records 99, 176, 237
Seymour, Samuel 88
The Shadow 60
Shantymen's Christian Association 248
shaped notes 47
Shaw, Bill 180
Shea, George Beverly x, 55, 128, 131, 135, 139, 140, 142, 143, 149–153, 154, 158, 159, 161, 164–165, 168, 193, 194
Shepherd Hour 31
Sherlock Holmes 59
Showalter Music Company 98, 99
Shut-In Hour 191
Simpson, A.B. 29, 63, 130
The Singing Brocks 224
The Singing Farm Boy 187–188, 190
Singing Time in Dixie 182
Singspiration Publishing Company 11, 152, 167–168, 169–170, 171, 172, 192, 193, 237
Skylight Records 182, 209
Slaughter, Henry 215
Smith, Alfred B. x, 3, 9, 45, 152, 165–173, 190, 191–192, 193, 243, 245
Smith, Bessie 231
Smith, Catherine 169
Smith, Daisy 248
Smith, Gypsy 81, 173
Smith, Nancy x, 171, 172, 173
Smith, Oswald 36, 53, 221, 246–251
Songs in the Night 32, 139, 140, 146, 147, 149, 152–153, 154, 163, 164
The South Meridian Sings (record album) 213
The South Meridian Sings, Vol. 2 (record album) 213

General Index

Southern California Bible College 95
Southwestern Baptist Theological Seminary 89
Speer, Ben 209, 214
Speer, Brock 99
Speer family 177, 209, 214
Spencer, Tim 243, 244
Stam, Betty 188
Stam, John 188
Stamps, Frank 98, 99, 101, 174, 175
Stamps, Virgil O. 8, 47, 97–102, 174, 175
Stamps All-Star Quartet 99, 176
Stamps-Baxter Company 98, 99–100, 222, 226, 228, 230
Stamps-Baxter School of Music 101, 174, 175, 177, 200
Stamps Quartet 3, 97, 99, 100, 101, 183, 233
Stamps Quartet Music Publishing Company 101, 183
Stanley, Charles 257
Stanphill, Gloria 200, 201
Stanphill, Ira 9, 197–201
Stanphill, Zelma 198, 199–200, 201
The Statesmen Quartet 3, 9, 177–180, 181, 182, 187, 202, 203, 204, 206, 210, 233, 237
Stebbins, George C. 165, 248
Stories of Great Christians 43
Straton, Bob 88
Straton, John Roach 152
Straw, Perry x, 82
Strickland, Bobby 178, 179, 180, 204
Studley, Ray 118, 120, 125
Sullivan, Ed 59, 115, 233
Sumner, J.D. 101, 181–183, 233
Sunday, Billy 3, 24, 25, 49, 50, 51, 52, 53–54, 55, 56, 105, 117, 118, 119, 136, 220, 235
Sunday, Nell 52, 54, 144
Sunday School Hour 68, 69
Sunny South Quartet 202, 203
Sunshine Boys 177, 181
Swaggart, Jimmy 258
Swindoll, Chuck 257

Talmadge, Herman 179
Taylor, Herbert J. 152
Taylor University 211
Teen Quest (magazine) 91
Telecasters Quartet 88
Telecommunications Act of 1996 259
televangelism 258–259
television 114, 115, 186, 256–257, 258–259
television remotes 259
Templeton, Chuck 145, 156
Tennessee Music and Printing Company 237
Tenth Presbyterian Church 26
Terry and the Pirates 60
Thomas, Lowell 129
Tom Mix 60
Toronto Bible College 247
Torrey, Reuben Archer 64, 77, 136, 247

Towner, Daniel B. 3, 169, 227, 245, 247–248
Townsend, Frances 166
Townsend, Grace 166
transcription discs *see* long-play (LP) records
Trotter, Mel 52–53
True Life Library 255
Truman, Harry 144, 161
Tunney, Gene 99
Turner, Charley 96

UHF (Ultra High Frequency) channels 257
United Evangelical Action (newspaper) 107
University of Northwestern 155
Upper Canada Bible Society 247

Vallee, Rudy 59
Vandall, N.B. 251–253
Van Kampen, Robert 148, 149
Vaughn, Charles 47
Vaughn, James D. 8, 46–49, 97
Vaughn Family Visitor (journal) 47
Vaughn Phonograph Records 47
Vaughn Quartet 47, 48, 173, 175
Vaughn Radio Quartet 177
Vaughn School of Music 203
Vaus, Jim 159
VHF (Very High Frequency) channels 257
Victor Records 42, 52, 70, 92, 99, 100, 164, 180, 181, 194, 216
Victor Talking Machine Company *see* Victor Records
Village Church 149, 150, 153
V.O. Stamps Music Publishing Company 98
V.O. Stamps Quartet 100
Vom Bruch, Harry 136
Voss, Herman 152

Walter F. Bennett Advertising Agency 161
Walton, R.A. 51
War of the Worlds 60
Wayne, John 157, 159, 194, 196, 197
WBBC/Brooklyn, NY 129, 130, 131
WBBM/Chicago, Illinois 31, 32, 35
WBT/Charlotte, North Carolina 178
WBU/Chicago, Illinois 30
WBZ/Boston, Massachusetts 106
WCFL/Chicago, Illinois 139, 140, 146, 149
WCON/Atlanta, Georgia 178, 179, 202
WCRF/Cleveland, Ohio 46
WDLM/East Moline, Illinois 43, 46
WEAF/New York, New York 21
WEAS/Atlanta, Georgia 178
Weatherford, Earl 211
Weatherford Quartet 211, 212
Webb, T. Myron 90, 91
Weigle, Charles 11, 253–255
Welles, Orson 60
Welsh, Evan 137
WENR/Chicago, Illinois 37

General Index

Wesleyan Methodist Church 150
Western Electric 37, 130
Western Springs Baptist Church 148
Westinghouse Corporation 15, 20, 21
Westminster Seminary 78, 79, 83
Westmont College 71
Wetherington, James "Big Chief" 179, 182
WFIL-TV/Philadelphia, Pennsylvania 85
WGES/Chicago, Illinois 36, 37
WGST/Atlanta, Georgia 178
Wheaton Christian Student Union 148
Wheaton College 36, 78, 136, 137, 138, 146, 148, 149, 153, 167, 168, 169, 242
Wheaton Evangelical Free Church 45
Wheaton United Gospel Tabernacle 148
Wheeler, J.E. 98
Wheeler, Palmer 99
Wheeler, Roy 99
WHEF/Kosciusko, Mississippi 174
Whitaker, Hudson "Tampa Red" 231
Whitney, Lorin 95, 96
Whittemore, Lewis B. 15–16
Whitwell, Cutler 72
WHK/Cleveland, Ohio 58
WHN/New York, New York 105, 130, 131, 152
WHT/Chicago, Illinois 30
Wild Cats Jazz Band 231
Wiley, Bill 124, 126
Wilhoit, Bert x, 245
Williams, Clara Tear 150
Willson, Meredith 261
Wilson, George 155, 163
Wilson, Ira B. 246
Wilson, Woodrow 19
Winchell, Walter 163
Winona Lake Bible Conference 45, 52, 55, 144, 224, 242
Winrod, Gerald B. 9
Winsett, R.E. 189, 230
WIP/Philadelphia, Pennsylvanis 79
Wireless Ship Act of 1910 19
Wireless Telegraph Company 17
WJBT/Chicago, Illinois 32, 35
WJDX/Jackson, Mississippi 174
WKBA/Chicago, Illinois 38
WMBI/Chicago, Illinois 26, 37–46, 135, 142, 149, 150, 152, 169, 190, 191–192, 242
WMPS/Memphis, Tennessee 180
WNAX/Yankton, South Dakota 91
WNOX/Knoxville, Tennessee 176
WOAI/San Antonio, Texas 100
WOAN/Larenceburg, Tennessee 48
WOAW/Omaha, Nebraska 24–25

WOI/Ames, Iowa 23
Woodhaven Baptist Church 120
Word of Life Fellowship ix, 45, 81, 128–135, 139, 142
Word of Life Hour 131–132, 134, 135, 191
Word of Life Melodies (songbooks) 134
Word of Life Today 134
Word of Truth 26
Word Music 55, 134
World Radio Congregation 25
World Vision 96
WOW/Omaha, Nebraska 24
WOWL/Fort Wayne, Indiana 211
WPCA-TV/Philadelphia, Pennsylvania 87, 88
WQAQ/New York, New York 152
WREC/Memphis, Tennessee 48
WRFD/Worthington, Ohio 207, 210
Wright, J. Elwin 106, 107–109, 110
WSM/Nashville, Tennessee 48–49, 100, 173, 176–177, 209
Wynn, Ed 59
Wyrtzen, Jack x, 9, 45, 81, 83–84, 116–135, 136, 139, 140, 142, 151, 164, 166, 167, 186, 191
Wyrtzen, Marge 120–123, 124, 125, 127–128, 129, 135, 167
Wyzenbeek, Andrew 29, 31

XENT 100
XERL 100

Yandell, M.L. 99
Younce, George 211, 229
Young Ambassador (magazine) 91
Young Men for Christ 126–127
Young Men's Christian Association (YMCA) 51, 118, 120,
Young People's Church of the Air (YPCA) ix, 9, 11, 61, 79, 80, 82, 83, 84–85, 86, 88, 117, 120–121, 152, 185, 186, 189, 191, 261
Your Hit Parade 60
Youth for Christ (YFC) 11, 32, 78, 87, 113, 116, 131, 135, 139–146, 153, 154–155, 156, 159, 164, 168, 169, 208, 233, 236, 238
Youth for Christ Magazine 145
Youth Haven Ranch 224
Youth on the March 85–86, 88, 256, 257
Youth on the March Fishing Clubs 86
Youth Today (magazine) 80, 127

Zamperini, Louis 159
Zondervan Company 92, 167, 170, 171, 201

Song Index

After 252–252
All Glory to Jesus 49
All My Life Long 150
All That I Want Is in Jesus 242
All the Way My Savior Leads Me 192
All Things in Jesus I Find 242
Almost Persuaded, Now to Believe 148
Alone with Thee 248, 251
Amazing Grace 49
Angels in the Sky 207
Are We Downhearted? 238
Assurance March 45
At Dawning 119
At the End of the Road 220
At the End of the Trail 237

Be Thou Exalted 172
Be Thou Near 250
Because He Lives 217
Believe on the Lord Jesus Christ 227
Beyond the Shadows 221, 250
Beyond the Sunset 222–225
The Bible Stands Like a Rock Undaunted 240
Blessed Redeemer 227–228, 242
Bound for That City 225
Boys and Girls for Jesus 45
The Breaking of the Day 249
Brighten the Corner Where You Are 55
Bringing in the Sheaves 99
Broadcasting for Jesus 239
The Broken Threads of Life 250
Brown-Eyed Texas Rose 194

Christ Is Coming Back Again 248
The Church in the Wildwood 208
Church Twice on Sunday 208
Come Just as You Are 241
Come with Your Heartache 251
Crossing the Bar 97

The Dawning of the Morning 249
Deeper and Deeper 246, 248, 250

Did You Ever Go Sailing? 225
Do Lord 85
Do You Know My Jesus? 237

Every Day with Jesus 45, 85
Everybody Ought to Love Jesus 242
Everybody Will Be Happy Over There 222

Faith Is the Victory 171
Fill All My Vision 227
The Finest of the Wheat 248, 250
For All My Sin 134
For God So Loved the World 166, 167, 168
For Me 243
Forgive Me for Forgetting God 250

Give the World a Smile 99, 100, 182
The Glory of His Presence 221, 250
Go Right Out 225
God Bless Our Boys 141
God Holds the Future in His Hands 48
God Is in the Shadows 249
God Is Waiting in the Silence 249
God Understands 221, 246, 249
God's Final Call 189
God's Gentle People 225
Going Home 213
Golden River 194
Good Night and Good Morning 53
Goodbye 46
Goodbye, World, Goodbye 206
Great Is Thy Faithfulness 164
The Greatest of These Is Love 182

Happiness Is the Lord 201
Happy Days Will Come Again 249
Have I Grieved the Holy Spirit? 249
Have You Had a Gethsemane? 213
Have You Talked to the Man Upstairs? 180
Haven of Rest 95
He Lives 220
He Owns the Cattle on a Thousand Hills 168, 190

Song Index

He Set Me Free (Brumley) 225
He Set Me Free (Lillenas) 240
He the Pearly Gates Will Open 74
He Touched Me 214
He Was Wounded for Our Transgressions 237
He Washed My Eyes with Tears (That I Might See) 201
He Will Hold Me Fast 238
He Will Not Forget 241
He Will Remember Me 222
Heaven Came Down 193
Heavenly Love 237
Heavenly Sunlight 72
Heavenly Sunshine 72, 131
Heaven's Joy Awaits 237
Heaven's Radio Station Is on the Air 225
He'll Put a Little Heaven in Your Soul 182
He's a Wonderful Savior to Me 222
He's the One I Love 253
Hiding in the Shadow of the Rock 238
His Banner Over Me Is Love 171–172
His Hand in Mine 204–206
His Hands 196
His Love Is All My Plea 249
His Name Is Wonderful 243–244
Hold the Fort 170
Holy, Holy Is What the Angels Sing 132
How Great Thou Art 186
How Long Has It Been? 206

I Am Coming Home 221
I Believe 208
I Believe in Miracles 4, 193
I Believe in the Old Time Way 182
I Can Hear Them Singing Over There 225
I Could Never Outlove the Lord 213
I Do, Don't You? 231
I Dreamed I Searched Heaven for You 49
I Have Christ in My Heart 45
I Have Never Lost the Wonder of It All 173
I Heard My Mother Call My Name in Prayer 222
I Just Want a Daddy I Can Call My Own 231
I Know a Name 240
I Know He Can Save Me Too 253
I Know Who Holds Tomorrow 201
I Love Thee, My Savior 239
I Love to Tell the Story 92
I Need the Prayer 49
I Never Loved Him Better Than Today 215
I Want to Tell the World About His Love 182
I Was There When It Happened 88
I Will Meet You by the River 225
I Will Meet You in the Morning 225
I Will Pilot Thee 97
I Will Serve Thee 214
I Will Trust 250
I Would Be Like Jesus 48
I'd Rather Have Jesus 151–152, 164

If I Could Hear My Mother Pray Again 49
If I Don't Get There 231
If I Had the Wings of An Angel 225
If We Never Meet Again 225
If You Don't Believe I'm Leaving, You Can Count the Days I'm Gone 231
If You Only Know the Lord 182
If Your Heart Keeps Right 56
I'll Fly Away 225–226
I'll Never Be Lonely 243
I'll Walk with God 207
I'm Feelin' Fine 203–204
I'm Free 214
I'm Free Again 237
I'm Singing for the Lord 251
I'm So Glad I'm a Part of the Family of God 217
In Jesus 238
In Love with the Lover of My Soul 239
In the Upper Room with Jesus 213
In Times Like These 97
Into My Heart 78
It Is Glory Just to Walk with Him 240
It Is No Secret (What God Can Do) 159, 164, 196, 207
It Is Wonderful 85
It Took a Miracle 84, 190–191, 192
It Was for You 81, 85, 88
I've Been to Calvary 207, 208–209, 212
I've Found the Way 33–34

Jesus Gives Me a Song 132
Jesus Has Lifted Me 227, 240
Jesus, Hold My Hand 225
Jesus Is Always There 241
Jesus Is Coming Again 193
Jesus Is Coming Soon 189
Jesus Led Me All the Way 192
Jesus Loves Me 118
Jesus Only 248
Jesus Saves 3, 70, 72, 73
Jesus Savior Pilot Me 97
Joy in Serving Jesus 221, 246, 249
Joy in the Camp 213
Just a Little Talk with Jesus 228–229
Just As I Am 148, 234
Just One Glimpse 253
Just One Way to the Gate 49

The King Is Coming 216, 217
King's College Victory March 45, 80

Leave Your Burden at the Place of Prayer 241
Let King Jesus Reign 249
Let Me Touch Him 237
Let's Just Praise the Lord 217
Little Old Rag Doll 194
Little Pine Log Cabin 225
The Little White Church on the Hill 220
Living Above 132

Song Index

Living for Jesus 254
The Longer I Serve Him 213
Look for Me 47
Love Found a Way 227, 242, 243
Love Leads the Way 99
Love Lifted Me 48
Lovest Thou Me More Than These? 213

Make Me a Blessing 246
Man Behind the Plow 97
The Man of Galilee 221
Mansion Over the Hilltop 198–199
Maple Leaf Rag 97
May the Good Lord Bless and Keep You 261
Melody Divine 239
The Men Will Never Wear Kimonos by and by 222
Muddy Water Blues 231
My God Can Do Anything 237
My God Won't Ever Let Me Down 183
My Heart's Desire 250
My Home, Sweet Home 253
My Hope Is in the Lord 134
My Loved Ones Are Waiting for Me 49
My Mary 194
My Prayer 101
My Sins Are Blotted Out, I Know 237
My Sins Are Gone 132, 253
My Song 192
My Wonderful Lord 240, 241

Near to the Heart of God 88
The Need of the World Is Jesus 250
No Burdens Yonder 238
No Longer Lonely 238
No One Ever Cared for Me Like Jesus 254–255
No One Understands Like Jesus 191, 192
Nothing Is Impossible 92
Now I Belong to Jesus 4, 133–134

O It Is Wonderful 142
O, What a Day! 245
Oh, How I Love Jesus 217
The Old Country Church 182
Old Man River 209
The Old Razor Strop 222
The Old Rugged Cross Made the Difference 217
One Day 166
Only Believe 30, 142
Only Believe and Live 238
Only One Life 4, 227, 237
Only Jesus 227
Onward, Christian Soldiers 85
Open Up Your Heart and Let the Sun Shine in 196
Opened for Me 237
Our Great Savior 238
Out on the Texas Plains 194

Over in Glory 239
Over the Moon 237
Over the Sunset Mountains 192
Overshadowed 245

Peace in the Valley 230, 232–233
The Peace That Jesus Gives 240
Precious Hiding Place 43, 45, 227
Precious Lord, Take My Hand 229–230, 232–233

Remember Me, I'm the One Who Loves You 194
Rescue the Perishing 99
Resting in His Love 222
A Revival Hymn 248, 249
Ring the Bells 135
Room at the Cross for You 198

Satisfied 150
Satisfied with Thee 249
Saved! 246, 248
Saved by the Blood 241
The Savior Can Solve Every Problem 248, 249
Search Me, O God 156
Service March 45
Shadows 238
Shine on Me 97
Sing and Smile and Pray 222
Singing 132
Sixteen Tons 208
Some Golden Daybreak 239–240
Somebody Cares 51
Somebody Knows 221
Something Beautiful 210, 217
Something Happened 76–77
Something That He Cannot See 245
Sometime, All Sorrow Will Be O'er 238
The Song of the Soul Set Free 246, 250
Songs in the Night 32, 138–139, 140, 146, 147, 149–150, 152–153, 154, 163, 164
Springs of Living Water 193
The Stranger of Galilee 132–133
Such a Love 238
Suppertime 200
Surely Goodness and Mercy 170–171
Surrender 248, 250
Sweet, Sweet Spirit 215
Sweeter as the Days Go by 48
The Sweetest Song I Know 225

Take an Old Cold Tater and Wait 222
Tenderly 182
Thanks to Calvary 214
That's What Jesus Means to Me 217
Then I Met the Master 206
Then Jesus Came 52–53, 246, 250
There Is a Change 237
There's Something About That Name 215, 216, 217

Song Index

These Are They 85
Thine, Lord 238
This Ole House 196–197, 208
Tight Like That 231
'Til the Storm Passes by 206
To God Be the Glory 164
Turn Your Radio on 1, 225, 226
'Twill Be Glory There for Me 225

Under the Atoning Blood 240
Until Then 196

V Is for Victory 45, 83
Victory in Jesus 222

Waiting on Thee 249
Walk Through the Valley of Peace 232
Walking and Talking with My Lord 182
We Shall See His Lovely Face 132
We Shall Shine as Stars in the Morning 143
We'll Soon Be Done with Troubles and Trials 228
What a Day That Will Be 209
What Lola Wants 208
When God Dips His Love in My Heart 228
When I Got Saved 237
When I See My Savior Hanging on Calvary 238
When the Autumn Leaves Have Turned to Gold 249
When the Saints Go Marching in 101
When We Sing Around the Throne Eternal 225
When You Pray 243
Where Dreams Come True 249
Where He Leads Me I Will Follow 127
Where No One Stands Alone 205–206
Why Should He Love Me So? 238
With Eternity's Values in View 168
The Wonder of It All 164–165
Wonderful Grace of Jesus 240, 241
Wonderful Peace 240
Wonderful Words of Life 131
Working in the Sawmill for Jesus 182

Yet There Is Room 189
You Can't Keep a Good Man Down 222
You Must Open the Door 52
Your First Day in Heaven 197
Youth for Christ 144–145
The *Youth on the March* Theme Song 85, 267n56

www.ingramcontent.com/pod-product-compliance
Lightning Source LLC
Chambersburg PA
CBHW051210300426
44116CB00006B/504